"This book is an excellent source for visitors who prefer
comfortable accommodations in the area's small communities,
as well as the off-the-beaten-track resorts and lodges…
a great book to keep handy."
—Outdoor Retailer

"… a top-notch trail guide opus. Directions to the trailhead are
explicit, the maps are simple and clear, the index is good, and
the trail descriptions are excellent, detailed beyond any other
trail guide you are likely to find."
—Sierra Club Bonanza

"Morey makes the High Sierra appealing and accessible,
combining marvelous dayhikes with comfortable lodging."
—Library Research Associates

"Good idea. Helps hikers commune with nature by day
and have comfort by night."
—Los Angeles Times

"… this book is a good read in itself."
—Sierra Heritage

"I loved the detail of the description … an excellent guide
for hiking trips."
—Sierra Club Loma Prietan

"With this book you need no longer quail before the
soaring massif of the Sierra Nevada range. It tells you
everything you need to know."
—Books of the Southwest

"… a top-notch trail guide."
—Toiyabe Trails

Cathedral Peak

Hot Showers,
Soft Beds, &
Dayhikes
in the Sierra

WALKS & STROLLS NEAR LODGINGS

Kathy Morey

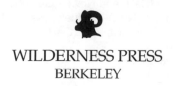

WILDERNESS PRESS
BERKELEY

FIRST EDITION October 1996
Second printing June 1998
SECOND EDITION October 2002
Second printing June 2002

Photos and maps by the author except as noted
Cover design: Larry B. Van Dyke
Book design: Margaret Copeland/Terragrafix
Fact checking: Teddy Hargrove
Editors: Tom Winnett, Kris Kaiyala, Jessica Lage
Managing editor: Jannie Dresser

Front cover photo: Merced River, Yosemite Valley (Trip 69) © 2002 by Kathy Morey
Back cover photo: Marsh Lake, (Trip 14) © 2002 by Kathy Morey

International Standard Book Number 0-89997-310-8

Manufactured in the United States of America

Published by **Wilderness Press**
　　　　　　　1200 5th Street
　　　　　　　Berkeley, CA 94710-1306
　　　　　　　(800) 443-7227; FAX **(510) 558-1696**
　　　　　　　mail@wildernesspress.com
　　　　　　　www.wildernesspress.com
　　　　　　　Contact us for a free catalog

Cataloging Data for Libraries
Morey, Kathy.
　　Hot showers, soft beds, and dayhikes in the Sierra / Kathy Morey
　　　　p. cm.
　　Includes bibliographical references (p.) and index.
　　ISBN 0-89997-310-8
　　　1. Hiking—Sierra Nevada (Calif. and Nev.)—Guidebook. 2. Tourist camps, hostels,
etc.—Sierra Nevada (Calif. and Nev.)—Guidebooks. 3. Hotels—Sierra Nevada (Calif.
and Nev.)—Guidebooks. 4. Sierra Nevada (Calif. and Nev.)—Guidebooks. 1. Title.
　　GV199.42.S55M66 2002
　　917.94'4—dc20　　　　　　96-35574

To the moms:
Paula Todd Morey Zietan
(my mother)
Florence Bergman Schwartz
(my mother-in-law)

Heads Up

Hiking in the backcountry entails unavoidable risk that every hiker assumes and must be aware of and respect. The fact that a trail is described in this book is not a representation that it will be safe for you. Trails vary greatly in difficulty and in the degree of conditioning and agility one needs to enjoy them safely. On some hikes, routes may have changed or conditions may have deteriorated since the descriptions were written. Also, trail conditions can change from day to day, owing to weather and other factors. A trail that is safe on a dry day or for a highly conditioned, agile, properly equipped hiker may be completely unsafe for someone else or unsafe under adverse weather conditions.

You can minimize your risks on the trail by being knowledgeable, prepared, and alert. There is not space in this book for a general treatise on safety in the mountains, but there are a number of good books and public courses on the subject, and you should take advantage of them to increase your knowledge. Just as important, you should always be aware of your own limitations and of conditions existing when and where you are hiking. If conditions are dangerous, or if you are not prepared to deal with them safely, choose a different hike! It's better to have wasted a drive than to be the subject of a mountain rescue.

These warnings are not intended to scare you off the trails. Millions of people have safe and enjoyable hikes every year. However, one element of the beauty, freedom, and excitement of the wilderness is the presence of risks that do not confront us at home. When you hike you assume those risks. They can be met safely, but only if you exercise your own independent judgment and common sense.

Contents

Acknowledgments

My deepest thanks go, as always, to my husband, Ed Schwartz, who has supported me both emotionally and financially as I abandoned an aerospace career for that of an author.

Still more thanks must go to the inspired, dedicated, and hardworking crew at Wilderness Press for their patience, good ideas, and creativity. I must especially recognize for this book the efforts of Jannie Dresser, Jessica Lage, Kris Kaiyala, Larry Van Dyke, Teddy Hargrove, Margaret Copeland, and editor emeritus, Tom Winnett. This book was originally Tom's idea and, as always, a great one.

—K.M.

Hot Showers, Soft Beds, & Dayhikes in the Sierra

Walker River

CHAPTER 1

Introduction

God put mosquitoes in the Sierra to remind us we are not yet in heaven.
—Scott Simons

But you can't get any closer in this life.
—Kathy Morey

Hikes from lodgings throughout California's Sierra Nevada mountain range? It's a huge subject! Geologists say the entire range is, as the crow flies, about 430 miles long and 50–80 miles wide. The range runs from southeast to northwest in eastern California and barely dips its toes into western Nevada. It's bracketed by good roads on its east and west; invaded but not crossed by some good roads in its southern half; and crossed by several good roads in its northern half. The range reaches its greatest elevation on its east side—that's where its crest is. There, the range rises very abruptly from Owens Valley at 4000 feet to its crest ranging from 11,000–14,491 feet—the last is the elevation of Mt. Whitney, the highest peak in the contiguous 48 states. Good roads climb in 2–24 miles from east-side towns and junctions to trailheads ranging from 7600–10,230 feet. On its west, the range rises very slowly from California's Central Valley, near sea level, through rolling foothills and up long, gentle, wooded slopes toward the crest. From the west, good roads wind into the southern Sierra for as much as 80 miles to high trailheads, but don't cross the crest; the high road point is a non-crest pass, Kaiser Pass at 9200 feet. Also from the west, good to adequate roads find their way across the northern Sierra for as much as 100 miles over crest passes; Yosemite National Park's Tioga Pass at 9945 feet is the highest and southernmost pass crossed by those roads.

The range is justly famed for its beauty, its good weather (for a mountain range), and its accessibility. Its hiking opportunities are simply the best in California. There are far more trails than I can find room for in this book, but the hikes you find here are some of the best.

Millions come to enjoy the Sierra Nevada every year. Some backpack, some car camp, and some stay in lodgings. This book is aimed at helping those who prefer to stay in lodgings to broaden their Sierra experience by introducing them to lodgings and trailheads they may not have known about. This book is also aimed at helping those who've never stayed in lodgings, but who've wanted to try it, to learn where to stay, where to hike, and what to expect from the lodgings as well as from the trails. The book also offers ideas for things non-hikers can do at trailheads while other members of the party hike.

I backpack, car camp, and stay in lodgings throughout the range. Take it from me, exploring mountain trails while staying in lodgings is a wonderful way to experience our glorious Sierra Nevada!

Area covered. The area this book covers is the most scenic part of the Sierra Nevada, the part that—

- ▶ lies wholly within California
- ▶ lies above 6000 feet. *Exceptions:* The great valleys of the national parks: Kings Canyon, Wawona, Yosemite Valley, and Hetch Hetchy Valley. There is also one hike off Interstate Highway 80 that starts below 6000 feet but whose destinations are above 6000 feet.
- ▶ lies east of State Routes 41, 49, and 99
- ▶ lies west of U.S. Highway 395
- ▶ lies north of a line roughly connecting Visalia on the west with Lone Pine on the east
- ▶ lies south of Interstate 80

Overview: California and the Sierra Nevada

This book divides that area into nine major regions: the Eastern Sierra and the Western Sierra within the southern Sierra, and the flanks of the highways that cross the range (State Routes 120, 108, 4, 88, 89; U.S. Highway 50; Interstate 80) in the northern Sierra. Within a region, the hikes are organized from south to north or east to west, depending on the orientation of the major roads serving the region. As you'll see on the map at the top of the next page, there's a little overlap between these regions.

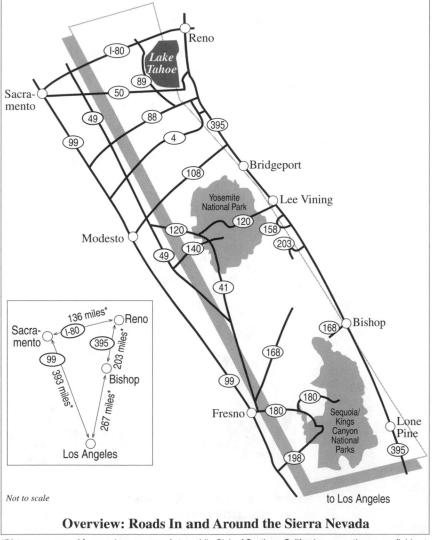

Overview: Roads In and Around the Sierra Nevada

*Distances summed from various sources: Automobile Club of Southern California maps, other maps, field notes.

Hikes included. To be included in this book, a hike must lie within the area covered (above). In addition, hikes must—

▶ be 10 miles long or less—preferably shorter. Most hikes identify interim destinations so you can adjust the hike's length to suit yourself. In a very few cases, the farthest destination identified for a hike pushes that 10-mile limit a little bit, to 10+ miles.

▶ have no more than 2600 feet of elevation gain—preferably less.

▶ have few long, very steep stretches—preferably none.

▶ go to a worthwhile final destination: a fantastic viewpoint, a beautiful lake, a thundering waterfall, or a grove of giant sequoias. Meadows, streams, and woods are okay as interim destinations.

▶ be on official, maintained trail. Brief excursions onto well-trod use trails are okay if they go to destinations you can see from the main trail. No bushwhacking.

▶ be within an hour's drive (roughly, 30 miles) of at least one lodging or one town that qualifies for this book. This criterion includes some subjective considerations: the quality of the driving experience, including road conditions; the traffic to be encountered; and the area's sensitivity to an increase in

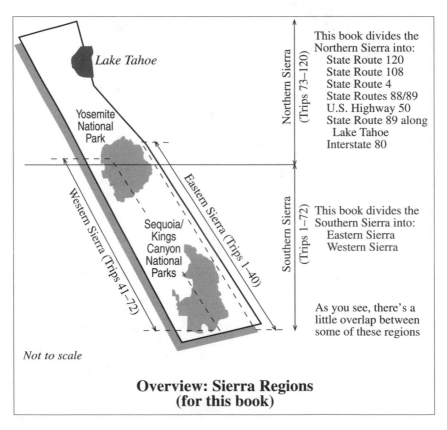

**Overview: Sierra Regions
(for this book)**

traffic. No outrageously long, difficult drives—a few come close, though. No drives that demand four-wheel drive (4WD), but 4WD may be nice to have as an option for a very few drives.

Lodgings and towns included. To be included in this book, a lodging or a town must lie within the area covered (above) or be within an hour's drive (roughly, 30 miles) of at least one hike that qualifies for this book. More on lodgings and towns in Chapter 3.

History, geology, biology, and maps. This book is big enough without my writing as much as I'd like to about the Sierra's history, geology, and biology. I've had to keep information on those subjects to a minimum. You'll find references given throughout this book to other sources of information that go into those subjects in depth. For the entire Sierra Nevada, I recommend—

▸ Farquhar, Francis P., *History of the Sierra Nevada*. Berkeley: University of California Press, 1965. A little out of date but nonetheless a valuable, very readable classic about the range's human history.

▸ Johnston, Verna R., *Sierra Nevada: The Naturalist's Companion*. Berkeley: University of California Press, 1998. An excellent and engaging natural history guide, published since 1970 and updated.

▸ Huber, N. King, *The Geologic Story of Yosemite National Park*. Yosemite National Park: Yosemite Association, 1989. With its fine illustrations and clear explanations, this booklet will help you understand not only Yosemite but most of the Sierra Nevada range. Slip it into a self-sealing gallon bag and drop it in your daypack to cushion your spine!

▸ Reid, Robert Leonard, ed., *A Treasury of the Sierra Nevada*. Berkeley: Wilderness Press, 1983. An enormously entertaining anthology of writings about the range that will leave you longing to read the originals from which these well-chosen extracts come, and to experience the places described.

▸ Browning, Peter, *Place Names of the Sierra Nevada: From Abbot to Zumwalt*. 2nd ed. Berkeley: Wilderness Press, 1991. Especially enjoyable because many of the explanations of place-names are mini-histories of the named places.

▸ *Sierra Nevada Mountains Areamap: A Gousha Travel Publication*. Hendersonville, North Carolina: Gousha Travel Publications, 1992. A driver's/vacationer's overview of the Sierra Nevada in a single slim, folding, glove-compartment-sized map. Take the distances only as guidelines. Get the latest edition.

▸ For trail and topographic maps of the Sierra Nevada, check offerings from Wilderness Press (www.wildernesspress.com or 1-800-443-7227), The Map Center (510-841-6277 or themapcenter@aol.com), and Tom Harrison Maps (415-456-7940 or tomharrisonmaps@attbi.com).

Second Edition. For this second edition I've rehiked and updated many trips but have replaced only one, the former Trip 19, Mammoth Rock. Bikes make this trail unsafe and unpleasant for hikers (I'm adamantly opposed to bikes on singletrack hiking trails). New Trip 34, the northern route to Walker Lake, replaces it.

CHAPTER 2

Hiking Hints

This book isn't intended to teach you how to hike. This book is intended to let you know where you can hike in the Sierra Nevada, what to expect when you hike there, where to stay so you're near the hikes you want to take, and how to get to the trailhead for each hike. And that, I hope, will help you decide which hikes to take.

This section contains suggestions which I hope will make your hikes safer and more enjoyable, and perhaps will better protect you and the environment.

It's up to you. No book can substitute for, or give you, five things only you can supply: physical fitness, preparedness, experience, caution, and common sense. Don't leave the trailhead without them.

Minimum equipment for easy hikes. Wear or carry these items as a minimum:

- Sunglasses
- Coach's whistle. You can blow a whistle for help longer and louder than you can shout
- Appropriate footwear. Recommended: hiking boots
- Strong sunblock applied before you set out
- Insect repellent if you are attractive to mosquitoes and deerflies
- Food. Recommended minimum for easy hikes: high-energy, concentrated-nutrition snack bars
- Water. No open source of water in the U.S. is safe to drink untreated, so fill water bottles at your lodgings. Recommended minimum: 1 pint for easy hikes, 1–2 quarts for moderate hikes, 2 quarts for strenuous hikes
- Lightweight "space blanket"—a couple of ounces of metallized mylar film usable for temporary shelter or rain protection
- Appropriate clothing so you can keep warm when the temperature drops, when it rains, or when it gets windy. Sierra weather can turn very nasty very abruptly. Be prepared with extra, appropriate clothing—especially a warm cap—when it does so. See **Hypothermia**, below.
- If you wear corrective lenses and/or require special medications, take extra lenses and carry a small supply of your medications

Minimum equipment for moderate and strenuous hikes. Start with the minimum equipment for easy hikes, above. Add—

- Extra food and water. For moderate and strenuous hikes, carry lunch and some snack bars
- Extra appropriate clothing. See **Hypothermia**, below

- ▶ Map (and compass if you can use it)
- ▶ Flashlight with extra bulb and batteries
- ▶ The means to dig a hole 6–8 inches deep in order to bury solid body wastes; tissue that you will also bury (or pack out)
- ▶ Pocket knife
- ▶ First-aid kit—backed by first-aid training
- ▶ Waterproof matches and something you can use to keep a flame going (such as a candle) *only when necessary to start a fire in order to save a life*

Whom to hike with. The standard advice is to never hike alone. But thousands of people do, including me. Recommended if you hike alone: be overprepared; be prepared to bivouac; know and respect your limits; carry and know how to navigate with map and compass; know first aid; stick to major, well-marked trails; and always leave your itinerary with a friend or relative who can be trusted to notice if you are overdue and to call the authorities. Be sure to call your friend or relative when you return safely! Finally, learn to hike by taking classes from reputable organizations and by hiking in the Sierra with others before you hit the trail alone.

Sanitation. Preferably, take care of body wastes at lodgings or at trailhead toilets. Otherwise, eliminate body wastes at least 100 feet from any body of water and any trail or potential campsite. Bury solid wastes in a hole 6–8 inches deep. Carry out toilet tissue, facial tissue, sanitary napkins, tampons, and disposable diapers rather than burying them. Those items if buried can last long enough to be exhumed by animals or by spring runoff. To carry them out, put them in a heavy-duty self-sealing bag. I use a quart-size Ziploc bag. If I'm feeling squeamish about handling an item, I'll coax it into the bag with the help of a small stick or two.

Hunting season. Hunting is legal in the Sierra's national forests, though not in national parks, typically from a little after Labor Day until some time in December (check for exact dates). Be visible during hunting season by wearing bright colors; an inexpensive cap-and-vest set in fluorescent orange or red will do the trick. Even if you are hiking in a national park, dress brightly during hunting season: arrows and bullets know no boundaries, and illegal hunting has occurred in national parks.

Other hazards. Rattlesnakes are found in the Sierra though they are rarely seen above 7000 feet. If you hear a snake rattle, stand still long enough to determine where it is, then leave in the opposite direction. Consider carrying a snake-bite kit. Most bears want to avoid you, so make some noise as you walk—talk, sing, tap rocks with your hiking stick—to warn them of your approach so they can scramble out of your way.

Sun protection. I can't overemphasize the importance of protecting your skin from the sun. Not only is skin cancer a serious, potentially fatal problem, but a sunburn will ruin at least part of your vacation—maybe even keep you off the trail for a few days (gadzooks!). Sun exposure also ages your skin. Americans are realizing that a "glorious tan" today means wrinkled, leathery skin and skin cancer tomorrow. Sun protection is especially important at higher altitudes where the amount of ultraviolet radiation (the cancer-causing rays) striking your skin is much greater than at sea level.

Short of staying indoors, your major lines of defense are clothing and sunblock. Instead of T-shirts and tank-tops, wear lightweight but opaque, long-sleeved shirts. Consider wearing long pants instead of shorts. Wear a hat with a brim sufficient to shade your face. Lightweight gloves will protect hands, which always seem to get burnt no matter how much sunblock you put on them.

For sunblock, choose the highest "sun protection factor" (SPF) number of water-resistant cream or lotion you can find from a reputable manufacturer. Spray-on products are less effective. Apply as directed to face, ears, neck, and any other areas that may be exposed. Allow 20–30 minutes for the sunblock to react with your skin to form a protective barrier. Reapply as necessary. Don't forget to use a sunblocking lip-protectant, too.

When using sunblock with insect repellent, apply the sunblock first and give it time to "bond" with your skin before applying the repellent. The only effective repellent, DEET, reduces the effectiveness of sunblock, so this is another reason to get the highest SPF sunblock you can find. Don't waste your money on products that combine sunblock and insect repellent; they're self-defeating.

And don't imagine that lots of natural skin pigmentation will protect you. The worst sunburn I ever saw was on a friend of mine who thought that because she was black, she didn't need sunblock. Personally, I use an SPF 50, water-resistant, baby-formula, unscented sunblock with titanium dioxide every day, rain or shine, indoors or out, and carry more in the car. That way, I'm set to go when the urge to hike hits.

Hypothermia. One of the leading causes of death in the mountains is hypothermia; the old-fashioned term is "death by exposure." A combination of being exhausted and getting chilled leads to an insidious downward spiral. You become more and more chilled, and the more chilled you become, the more irrational you become. As the downward spiral continues, you become so chilled and therefore so irrational that you can't go on. You lie down to rest. You fall asleep. You lapse into a coma. You die when your body's core temperature drops far enough that your vital organs can't perform their functions any more. It can happen in a matter of hours. It happens every year to unprepared hikers.

Most hypothermia cases reportedly occur at moderate temperatures as high as the 50s, not at freezing ones. Perhaps that's because we know enough to be well-prepared when the day starts out icy-cold. We get into trouble when the day starts out sunny or unsettled and then turns nasty.

The best "cure" for hypothermia is prevention: don't get hypothermic in the first place. Budget your energy; eat and drink often; rest when you need to; don't let yourself become exhausted. Know when to turn around and head home. Do your best to stay warm and reasonably dry—more on this in the next paragraph.

To stay warm, you have to help your body produce heat, and you have to conserve the heat produced. To help your body produce heat, eat high-energy foods often and drink water often. To help your body conserve the heat it produces, wear

appropriate clothing, clothing that won't squander your body heat by letting wetness and wind steal it away. You can't help but get wet when you hike; even when
it doesn't rain, you'll sweat. So it's imperative that you wear clothing made of fab-
ric that insulates when wet. Wool and most synthetics insulate when wet. Cotton
not only does not insulate when wet but greatly accelerates your heat loss by holding wetness against your body. This cooling effect, so welcome on a hot day, can
kill when the weather turns nasty. Remember: for hiking in the Sierra, cotton is
rotten. Most importantly, put on a warm cap: you lose much of your body heat
through your head. To help keep rain and wind from carrying away your body
heat, wear an outer layer of wind- and rain-proof, not just -resistant, clothing.
Most rain gear is windproof, but not all wind gear is rainproof. A poncho with a
hood will do; a rain suit (pants, jacket with hood) gives more complete protection.

It's hard to monitor yourself for hypothermia, so each member of a party should
keep an eye on the others for signs of hypothermia: stumbling; slurred speech;
uncontrollable shivering followed (later) by no shivering. If a fellow hiker seems to
be hypothermic, help the hypothermia victim to put on additional, appropriate
clothing and, if fully conscious, to eat and drink properly.* Don't be surprised if a
hypothermia victim resists help; persist, remembering that a hypothermia victim
is irrational. Above all, turn around, get back to the trailhead, and then get to your
cozy lodgings as soon as possible!

* Never give anything by mouth to a person who is not fully conscious. A fully conscious person can
tell you what day it is, who he/she is, where he/she is, and why he/she is there. Never give alcohol;
it aggravates hypothermia.

CHAPTER 3

Lodgings and Communities

"Tell the boss I've found Paradise and I won't be back till next week!"
—OVERHEARD FROM THE PHONE BOOTH AT A MOUNTAIN LODGING

This book's hikes are grouped geographically into regions of the Sierra Nevada, and each regional chapter includes descriptions of the qualified lodgings and communities in that region. Moreover, each individual hike write-up includes a list of qualified lodgings and communities within range of that hike. (See **Introduction** for criteria.)

More and more lodgings and communities, like Mammoth Lakes, have "pages" on the World Wide Web. Surf the 'Net for the latest information!

Listings are based on the latest data I have. Many lodgings operate year-round or at least have summer and winter seasons. If you enjoyed your summer vacation at a particular lodging, consider asking about a winter vacation, too!

All the lodgings in this book take reservations, unless otherwise noted. Most require a reservation deposit. Almost any lodging will take drop-ins as long as it has unreserved space.

Lodgings and communities vary widely; here is the way this book categorizes them.

Lodgings

Here's what a description of a lodging looks like; see below for definitions of these entries:

Lodging's name
Lodging's address   Lodging's phone number
Elevation (feet). Location. *Category of lodging.* Kind(s) of rooms. Other facilities (or notable lack thereof). Unusual policies if any. Pet policy. [Year] rates.

Here's how to interpret the information in that description:

Lodging's name • Lodging's address and phone number
Self-explanatory, except when lodging's name is followed by "(agency)." Absentee owners of private homes and other kinds of units in desirable vacation areas may engage agencies to represent them in renting out and maintaining the properties. When you see "(agency)," the "lodging's" name, address, and phone number are that of an agency representing rental properties in the area.

Elevation (feet)

Self-explanatory. May be important in judging the suitability of a lodging for those who have heart problems or are unused to higher altitudes.

Location

The lodging's location with respect to important local features, such as nearby communities.

Categories of lodgings for this book

True mountain lodgings ("Mountain"), which I list individually, lie within the area covered by this book, as defined in the Introduction. They are at or above 6000 feet. They are removed from the bustle of communities and from the noise of highways. They rarely have telephones, televisions, or radios. They may have some rough edges; I think rusticity is better than luxury in true mountain lodgings. Few lodgings I rate as true mountain lodgings qualify for listing in the California tour-book of the national auto-club to which I belong, for reasons I think aren't important compared to the pleasures of a rustic cabin in the Sierra. The experience of staying in true mountain lodgings isn't a House Beautiful experience. It's Mountains Beautiful, House Okay. See more in **Appendix A, Hints for Staying in Lodgings.**

Lodgings of interest ("Of Interest"), which I also list individually, are like true mountain lodgings in most respects, but they fail to meet one or two of the criteria for true mountain lodgings. Maybe they're below 6000 feet, or located in a busy little community, or situated on a noisy highway. Also, lodgings in downhill ski areas lose points, so to speak, because in summer the tangle of lift equipment lends a blighted, industrial look and feel. The ideas in **Appendix A, Hints for Staying in Lodgings** apply to many lodgings of interest.

Other lodgings ("Other") meet the **Introduction**'s criteria of proximity and comfort but don't meet most of the other criteria. Typically, they are located in busy communities below 6000 feet. They are more numerous than true mountain lodgings and lodgings of interest. They are more likely than true mountain lodgings and lodgings of interest to meet my national auto-club's criteria for tour-book listing. Nearly all "other" lodgings are in communities, so see under **Communities**, below.

Kinds of rooms

Most lodgings in this book offer electricity and electric or gas heat. Whether pets are permitted or not is the lodgings' option. Some "lodgings" listings are actually for agencies that help local vacation-home owners rent out their private homes or condominiums when the homeowners aren't using them. The kinds of rooms you'll find within lodgings in this book are—

Bed-and-breakfasts (B&Bs). Typically, a private home in which a guest rents a bedroom. The hosts, who are the homeowners, provide "maid service": they make the beds and tidy the rooms daily. A B&B room may have a private or a shared bath. Breakfast, prepared and served by the hosts, is included in the room rent.

Guests share common rooms with hosts, like a living room or a game room. A few B&Bs were once hotels and are managed more like hotels than like private homes, but their prices still include breakfast.

Cabins, "cottages," and "chalets." Typically, a small, separate house (a few are like duplexes) that has its own bath (toilet, sink, shower and/or tub). Rarely, cabins share centrally-located bath facilities; the facilities are segregated by sex. The cabin has basic furnishings (beds with linens; a place to store clothing; tables; chairs; lamps). "Cottages" is just a cozier name for cabins; "chalets" is just a fancier name for cabins. There are two kinds of cabins:

▶ *Housekeeping cabins* come equipped with kitchens and dining areas. The kitchen has a refrigerator, a stove (range/oven), and enough cookware and tableware that you can prepare and serve simple meals. No daily maid service, but occasional service can be arranged, perhaps for an extra fee.

▶ *Sleeping cabins* have no provisions for preparing and serving meals; you will be asked not to cook in your cabin. May have periodic, though not necessarily daily, maid service.

▶ *Tent-cabins.* A special kind of sleeping cabin, the tent-cabin, has a solid floor with canvas sides and roof or a solid floor and walls with canvas roof. Tent-cabins have Spartan furnishings—maybe just cots and a place to store clothing— and no bath; they share a centrally-located bath/shower; they may not have maid service; if they have electricity, they may be lit only by a single bare bulb.

Condominiums. An apartment with all necessary housekeeping facilities. A condominium is probably someone's vacation home but is available for rent when the owner isn't using it. Typically, the condominium complex is professionally managed; you won't deal with the homeowner. Condominiums are usually quite modern, and condominium complexes may offer modern amenities—such as cable television, telephones, swimming pool, exercise room, Jacuzzi, sauna—that some other kinds of lodgings lack. This can be an important consideration if the party includes young children and/or people who won't be hiking (non-hikers).

Dormitory. A very few lodgings offer dormitories: guests of one sex rent a bed in a room with several beds; the other beds are occupied by other guests of the same sex. Guests may have to provide their own bedding. Guests share bath facilities.

Hotel, lodge, and motel rooms. A multiple-room building in which a guest rents a bedroom that usually has a private bath. Most such rooms have no provisions for preparing and serving meals, and you will be asked not to cook in your room. Most have daily maid service. In lodges, the bedrooms are often on the upper floors, while the common rooms (where guests can meet and relax) are on the ground floor. In some lodges, guests of one sex share bath facilities with other guests of the same sex. Such shared bath facilities provide privacy for a guest who is showering or using the toilet. They also provide sinks, mirrors, etc. You walk through the lodge to get to your room. Hotel rooms are like lodge rooms; the difference is whether the lodging as a whole is called a lodge or a hotel. Motel rooms open to the outside, and motels seldom have common rooms.

Private homes. Self-explanatory.

Unusual policies, if any

A few lodgings have unusual policies. For example, guests at Clair Tappaan Lodge perform one housekeeping chore per day that they also eat there.

Other facilities (or lack thereof)

Many lodgings have other facilities like a store, a restaurant, boat rentals, and so on. Unless otherwise specified, rooms/cabins have electricity and any restaurant or café on the premises serves breakfast, lunch, and dinner.

Pet policy

Whether the lodging allows pets (many don't); in what kinds of rooms pets are allowed; whether there's an extra fee for pets; and what kinds of pets are allowed. If the lodging hasn't specified a pet policy, the write-up says, "No stated pet policy"; assume it's no pets. Note that pets are prohibited on all national-park trails. Recommendation: leave pets at home.

Rates

This book gives the latest rates I have for each lodging, along with the date those rates applied. You can extrapolate from those rates if necessary.

Unless otherwise specified, rates quoted are high-season summer rates and do not include any local taxes (the final price you pay typically includes a local bed tax). Spring and fall rates may be lower; winter rates, if the lodging is open in winter, may be higher; holiday rates may be higher. Many resorts require a minimum stay to make a reservation, typically 2 or 3 nights. Some resorts have very complicated rate schedules; I've tried to give representative rates for them.

Saving money. The cost of a cabin shared by several occupants can be quite reasonable on a per-occupant basis. Tent-cabins are usually the cheapest kind of cabin. You may be able to save money by choosing accommodations with a shared bath over accommodations with a private bath. Many resorts offer weekly rates or special packages that represent significant savings over paying by the night.

How to pay. Note that many mountain lodgings won't accept credit cards. You'll need cash, personal checks, or traveler's checks. Check with the lodging when you make your reservation.

Communities

A few communities, like those in the Eastern Sierra's Owens Valley, are close enough to trailheads so that lodgings in them qualify for this book on the basis of proximity. As noted above, lodgings in these communities fall into the "other" category. Most such communities are recreation-oriented and have Chambers of Commerce or Visitors Bureaus that are happy to provide potential visitors with free packets of information, including listings for lodgings. Some will even help further by referring you to lodgings (though they usually won't make the reservation for you). So rather than list their lodgings individually, I've listed the community, its Chamber of Commerce or Visitors Bureau and how to get in touch with it, and a brief word about the community's location. If a community doesn't have an appropriate chamber or bureau, then I list the lodgings individually, giving only their phone numbers.

Finally...

Be sure to read the **Appendix A, Hints for staying in lodgings.** True mountain lodgings and lodgings of interest are usually quite rustic; staying in them isn't like staying in your average big-city motel. The appendix will give you an idea of what to expect, especially if you've never stayed in rustic lodgings before.

Some lodgings simply don't appear in this book. Lodgings I never found fall into that category; I'm sorry I missed them and would be glad to learn about them. I left out lodgings you must walk or ride a horse to, like Yosemite's High Sierra Camps and Sequoia's Bearpaw Meadow Lodge. I also left out any lodgings that gave me the creeps; I can't refer you to a place I wouldn't stay in myself.

Note also that while I have visited all of the true mountain lodgings and lodgings of interest in this book except individual units run by agencies or condo complexes, I haven't stayed at all of them; more on that in **Appendix D, How I got the data.** I've also visited the communities listed in this book.

In researching this book, I did not ask for or accept free lodgings or any other "freebies"—I wasn't offered any, anyway.

CHAPTER 4

About the Hikes

What the write-ups look like
In addition to the information illustrated below, trips include embedded maps made especially for this book. Here's a sample write-up:

14. Little Lakes Valley ☼ 🍁

Place	Total Dist.	Elevation	Level	Type
Start	0	10,230	—	—
Marsh Lake *only*	2	10,420	E	O&B
Heart Lake *only*	2½	10,420	E	O&B
Long Lake *only*	4	10,540	M U	O&B
Gem Lakes	6½	10.940	S U	O&B

Permit required:

Topo(s): WP Mt. Abbot 15'; Mt. Abbot, Mt. Morgan 7½'

Where to stay:
   Mountain: Rock Creek Lakes Resort, Rock Creek Lodge, Convict Lake Resort
   Of Interest: Tom's Place, Rainbow Tarns, Sierra Gables Motel, Mono Sierra Lodge
   Other: Town of Mammoth Lakes

Highlights:

How to get to the trailhead:

At the trailhead:

On the trail:

What the write-up information means
Hike number and title. Self-explanatory. Following this are one to three icons that indicate the best season for the hike; see below for their definitions.

Best season (icons). This is a judgment call. For example, waterfalls are best in early season when runoff is high. Flowers are best in early and mid season. Fall color belongs to late season. And the previous winter's snow may keep higher elevations snowbound until late summer. The trips in this book start from just under 4200 feet to as high as 10,230 feet; at those elevations, the winters are longer than at sea level, and the other seasons are briefer and compressed into a shorter period. For

17

purposes of this book, "early" season extends roughly from late May to early July, "mid" season from early July to late August, and "late" season from late August to mid-October. These are somewhat-arbitrary divisions and vary from year to year depending on the weather. Many trips have more than one "best season." For example, a trip whose highlights include both flower displays and lakes is worth taking in early season for both the flowers and the lakes, and in mid to late season for the lakes. Some very-high-elevation hikes are best in late season because only then are they snow-free. Icons show the "best season(s)"—remember, these are Sierra seasons:

 Early season, for the flowers that typically bloom in early season

 Mid season, for the warm sunshine typical of a Sierra summer

🍁 Late season, for autumn's display of yellow-to-red leaves

Trip summary. A table that summarizes the trip's major "places," from the start to each interim destination to the final destination:

Place. "Start" is self-explanatory. Subsequent names are worthwhile interim destinations you can choose from. You can shorten most hikes to suit your energy and available time by going to an interim destination instead of the final destination. The last name is usually the final, farthest destination. There are a few hikes where you walk a significant distance to a junction or junctions where you must choose among destinations because going to all would be outside the mileage limits of this book (more than 10+ miles total). The write-up explains these cases and describes the options.

Total distance. Typically, the total miles *to and from* the place. On loop, semi-loop, and shuttle trips, the total distance may be *to* the place, because you don't go back *from* it; the trip's write-up clarifies this. The stated mileage for a place typically includes the mileage for all previously-listed destinations; if it doesn't, the write-up will clarify that.

Elevation. The elevation (in feet) at the named place. Footnotes explain where there are significant high points or low points between destinations; that can be important in budgeting your energy for a trip.

Level. An indication of the level of effort the hike to the named place requires:

E   means *easy*. The hike is 3 miles or shorter, has 500 feet or less of total elevation gain/loss between the start and the named destination, and has no long, steep stretches.

M   means *moderate*. The hike is 6 miles or less and has 1500 feet or less of elevation gain/loss between the start and the named destination.

S   means *strenuous*. The hike is over 6 miles and has more than 1500 feet of elevation gain/loss between the start and the named destination.

U   means *upside-down*. This is in addition to the E, M, or S rating. Most hikes in the Sierra require you to ascend as you walk out to your destination(s) and descend on your way back. On an upside-down trip, you *descend* as you walk out to your destination and *ascend* on your way back. That's "upside-down" compared to most Sierra hikes, and you may want to budget your energy differently for an upside-down trip—save a little for that haul back up the hill. Most upside-down trips aren't really that simple, but they all have this in common: there's a relatively significant climb on your way back.

Assigning a level is a judgment call. Contrary to what most people think, elevation gain/loss and the rate of gain/loss are more important in determining a trip's level than is distance alone. When the elevation gain/loss or gain/loss rate is high, I usually assign a trip the next-higher level. I may also assign a trip a higher level if the trail is unusually rough or hard to follow.

Type. A hike is one of four types:

▶ **O&B.** Out-and-back trip: you walk out to the destination and return the same way. Most hikes in this book are out-and-back trips.

▶ **Loop.** Loop trip: you walk out to the destination by one route and return by a different route.

▶ **Semi.** Semiloop trip: the trip has a significant loop part and a significant out-and-back part.

▶ **Shuttle.** Shuttle trip: you begin at one place and end at a different one. In this book, shuttle trips have you leave your car near the hike's *end*, then take public transportation to the hike's *start*.

Loop and semiloop trips may have interim destinations that you can treat as out-and-back trips, and that's how the hike write-up will show those interim destinations.

Permit required. Most Sierra dayhikes don't require you to have a permit, but if one is required, this will tell you where to get it. As of this writing, you need permits for dayhikes in this book only for Desolation Wilderness west of Lake Tahoe. All Desolation Wilderness hikes in this book start at trailheads that have stations where you can issue yourself a dayhiking permit.

Topos. Topographic maps ("topos") that cover the area you'll traverse. Wilderness Press (**WP**) maps are 15′ topographic maps published by Wilderness Press; they are more up-to-date and more accurate than most government-issued maps. Also listed are the United States Geological Survey (USGS) 7½′ maps that cover the area. Maps that cover specific areas, like the map series for the Federal wilderness areas (USDA/USFS maps), may also be helpful. Although this book provides its own maps, you'll want a topo to help you identify features outside the range of the book's maps and for map-and-compass navigation if necessary.

Where to stay. Each region's eligible lodgings are described in alphabetical order in the region's introductory text. Within each region, each trip write-up includes "Where to stay," a table of lodgings and communities that qualify for this book and that are within an hour's drive (about 30 miles) of the trip's trailhead; see **Chapter 1, Introduction.** As defined in detail in **Chapter 3, Lodgings and communities, Mountain** means "true mountain lodgings"; **Of interest** means "lodgings of interest"; **Other** means just that—usually nearby communities, if any.

Highlights. What makes this hike worth taking. These aren't just Sierra hikes, these are some of the *best* Sierra hikes, and each one has something special to offer you. Remember, however, that some highlights are strictly seasonal: you won't find fall color in early or mid season, or flower displays in late season.

How to get to the trailhead. Driving directions in terms of some reasonable, local reference point. For example, on the Sierra's east-west highways, the reference point is that highway's Sierra-crest pass. Where appropriate, I give directions that bracket points that drivers might otherwise miss (e.g., "You have overshot the trailhead if you get to Tuolumne Meadows while eastbound or Olmstead Point while westbound.").

At the trailhead. This book assumes that many people will be traveling in groups that include hikers and non-hikers. The book says whether there's anything at the trailhead that the party's non-hikers might enjoy if they want to wait there for their hiker friends, and if there is, what it is.

On the trail. A description of the trail you'll travel, its destinations, pleasures, high points, things to look out for, and so on. I've walked every mile of every trail that appears as a trip in this book. Destinations are given in boldface together with their *one-way* distances and elevations. To keep the size of the book down, I've left out much of the history, geology, and biology. But the introduction to each region refers you to books that more than make up for those omissions.

Maps. There's a map showing each trip in this book Most trips have their own maps. Some trips share a map with one or more other trips in the same area. If that's the case, the trip write-up will tell you where the map is. If I had to plot all or part of the trail from my field notes and sketches rather than from the USGS or WP topo, I noted "leg approximated" or "route approximated" on the map. Destinations are shown in boldface on the maps. The map legend is on the next page.

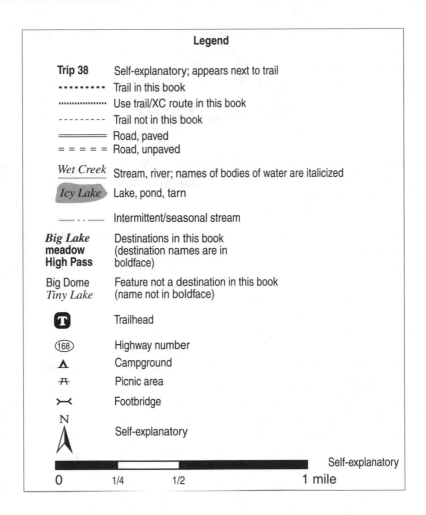

Legend

Trip 38   Self-explanatory; appears next to trail

- - - - - - -   Trail in this book

....   Use trail/XC route in this book

- - - - - -   Trail not in this book

═══════   Road, paved

= = = = =   Road, unpaved

Wet Creek   Stream, river; names of bodies of water are italicized

Icy Lake   Lake, pond, tarn

—— - - ——   Intermittent/seasonal stream

Big Lake
meadow   Destinations in this book
High Pass   (destination names are in
                boldface)

Big Dome   Feature not a destination in this book
Tiny Lake   (name not in boldface)

T   Trailhead

(168)   Highway number

Λ   Campground

⊼   Picnic area

⤨   Footbridge

N
↑   Self-explanatory

                                              Self-explanatory

0   1/4   1/2   1 mile

CHAPTER 5

Hiking Table

The following table summarizes the hikes. Here's what the table headers mean:

Trip No. and **Name** are self-explanatory, although the trip name may have been shortened to fit the table.

Type refers to the type of hike dictated by the farthest-out, final ("last") destination. On most semiloop and loop trips, the interim destinations are out-and-back (O&B) trips.

Total Distances lists the total distance to and from the first interim destination, if any, followed by the total distance to and back from the last destination. For example, "3–9" means it's 3 miles to and back from the first interim destination and 9 miles to and back from the last destination.

Levels refers to the level of difficulty for the first interim destination, if any, followed by the level for the last destination. For example, "E–S" means it's an easy hike to the first interim destination and a strenuous hike to the last destination.

Best Features has subcategories. **Lks** means that I think that a lake—or several lakes—is the hike's best feature. **Flora** means the hike features a fine, but seasonal, display of flowers. **Falls** means the hike features waterfalls—this includes what I think are notable cascades as well as classic falls like Rainbow and Yosemite. Note that for **Falls**, I'm including hikes where you enjoy excellent views of a waterfall as well as those on which you actually go to a waterfall. **View** means that the hike features one or more outstanding views; all Sierra hikes offer wonderful things to look at, but these hikes have superb, long-ranging views. **Clr** means the hike features a fine, but seasonal, fall-color display. I'd like to list more subcategories of "Best Features," but there isn't room.

Also see **Appendix C, Top Picks**, for my choices for the best hikes to take if you're seeking a particular feature, especially one not listed here, like meadows or streamside walks or interesting ruins.

NO.	NAME	TYPE	TOTAL DISTANCES	LEVELS	Lakes	Flora	Falls	View	Color
1	Chicken Spring Lake	O&B	3–9	E–S	•			•	
2	Lone Pine Lake	O&B	5½	M	•		•		•
3	Kearsarge Trail Lakes	O&B	3⅓–6⅔	M–S	•		•		
4	Big Pine Lakes	O&B	½–9½	E–S	•		•		
5	Treasure Lakes	O&B	6	S	•			•	
6	Marie Louise Lakes	O&B	4	M	•				
7	Chocolate Lakes	Semi	4½–7½	M–S	•			•	
8	Bishop Lake	O&B	4½–8⅔	M–S	•			•	
9	Sabrina Lakes	O&B	6–9⅔	S	•				
10	Lamarck Lakes	O&B	3½–7½	M–S	•				•
11	Piute Lake	O&B	6⅔–9	S	•	•	•		•
12	Francis or Dorothy Lk	O&B	5½–8½	M–S	•	•			
13	Hilton Lakes	O&B	8⅔–10	S	•				
14	Little Lakes Valley	O&B	1–6½	E–S	•	•		•	
15	Mono Pass	O&B	1–9	E–S	•			•	
16	McGee Canyon	O&B	6–10	S	•	•			•
17	Convict Lake	Semi	2	E	•				
18	Sherwin, Valentine Lks	O&B	4–9½	M–S	•				
19	Heart Lake	O&B	2	E	•			•	
20	Duck Pass	O&B	2⅔–9⅓	E–S	•			•	
21	Emerald, Skelton Lakes	Loop	1½–3¼	E–M	•				
22	Barrett, T J Lakes	O&B	1–1½	E	•				
23	Mammoth Crest	O&B	2¾–6	E–S	•		•	•	
24	Red Cones	Semi	1–7⅔	E–S	•	•		•	
25	San Joaquin Ridge	O&B	4½	M		•		•	
26	Olaine, Shadow Lakes	O&B	3–7	M–S	•		•		
27	Minaret Falls	O&B	1–3½	M			•		
28	Johnston Lake	O&B	1–5	M	•		•		
29	Rainbow, Lower Falls	O&B	2–3	E			•		
30	Fern, Yost Lakes	O&B	3–5⅔	M–S	•			•	
31	Agnew, Gem Lakes	O&B	5–7	S	•		•	•	
32	Parker Lake	O&B	3	M	•				•
33	Walker, Lwr Sard Lks	O&B	½–7	M–S	•			•	•
34	Walker Lake	O&B	4-6	M	•				•
35	Gibbs Lake	O&B	6½	S	•				•

NO.	NAME	TYPE	TOTAL DISTANCES	LEVELS	Lakes	Flora	Falls	View	Color
36	Oneida Lake	O&B	5¾–6⅔	S	•				•
37	Lundy Canyon	O&B	1⅓	E–M	•		•		•
38	Virginia Lakes	O&B	⅔–6	E–S	•			•	
39	Green, E., and W. Lakes	O&B	6–8¼	M–S	•	•		•	
40	Barney Lake	O&B	6	S	•	•		•	•
41	Soda Spring	O&B	2½	E		•	•		
42	Eagle or Mosquito Lk	O&B	7 or 7⅔	S	•		•	•	
43	Lower Monarch Lake	O&B	9	S	•			•	
44	Sequoia Loop	Loop	2–5½	E–M		🌲			
45	Panther Gap	O&B	5	M		•		•	
46	Heather Lake	Semi	8	S	•			•	
47	Tokopah Falls	O&B	3½	M			•		
48	Little Baldy	O&B	3⅓	M				•	
49	Muir Grove	O&B	3⅓	M		🌲			
50	Weaver Lake	O&B	3¾	M	•				
51	Big Baldy	O&B	4	M				•	
52	Buena Vista Peak	O&B	1⅔	E				•	
53	Redwood Mtn, Canyon	Loop	4–6	M–S		🌲			
54	Park Ridge	Loop	⅓–4¼	E–M				•	
55	Sheep Creek Cascades	O&B	2	M			•		
56	Hotel-Lewis Loop	Loop	5⅔–7	S				•	
57	Falls, Zumwalt Mdws	Semi	½–4	E–M			•		
58	Mist Falls	O&B	7⅓	S			•		
59	Dinkey Lakes	Semi	5–6½	M–S	•			•	•
60	Rancheria Falls	O&B	1⅓	E			•		
61	Twin Lakes	O&B	4–6¼	M–S	•	•		•	
62	Dutch Lake	O&B	6¼	S	•				
63	Doris, Tule Lakes	O&B	1½–3	E–M	•				
64	Lake Edison	O&B	9	S	•			•	•
65	Mariposa Grove	Semi	1⅓–5⅓	E–M		🌲			
66	Chilnualna Falls	O&B	8–8½	S			•	•	
67	Sentinel, Taft	Loop	2–4½	E–M				•	
68	Great Waterfalls	Shuttle	7¾	S			•	•	
69	Four Mile Trail	Shuttle	5⅓	M			•	•	
70	Waterfall Semiloop	Semi	1½–6	M–S			•	•	•

🌲 = Giant Sequoia

NO.	NAME	TYPE	TOTAL DISTANCES	LEVELS	BEST FEATURES				
					Lakes	Flora	Falls	View	Color
71	Lookout Point	O&B	2⅔	E		•		•	
72	Hetch Hetchy	O&B	3–4	E–M		•	•	•	
73	Bennettville, Lakes	O&B	1½–3¾	E–M	•			•	•
74	Gardisky Lake	O&B	2	M	•			•	
75	20 Lakes Basin	Loop	2½–7½	E–S	•			•	
76	Gaylor Lakes	O&B	2–4	M–S	•			•	
77	Summit, Spillway Lks	O&B	7–8½	S	•			•	
78	Dog Lake, Dome	Semi	2½–3⅔	E–M	•			•	
79	Tuolumne Meadows	Loop	4⅔	M		•		•	
80	Elizabeth Lake	O&B	4	M	•				•
81	Cathedral Lakes	O&B	6⅔	S	•			•	
82	Lower Sunrise Lake	O&B	6½	S	•	•		•	
83	May Lake	O&B	2	E	•			•	
84	North Dome	O&B	8	S				•	
85	Lukens Lake	O&B	4⅔	M	•	•			
86	Harden Lake	O&B	4	M	•				
87	Leavitt Meadow	Semi	5⅓–6	M–S	•			•	•
88	Relief Reservoir	O&B	6¼	S	•			•	•
89	Boulder Creek, Lake	O&B	4⅔–8⅔	M–S	•				•
90	Sword Lake	O&B	4¾	M	•				
91	Sherrold, Upr Kin Lks	O&B	1–3	E–M	•				
92	Noble Lake	O&B	3½–7⅔	M–S		•		•	
93	Heiser, Bull Run Lakes	O&B	4–9	M–S	•				
94	Duck Lake	Semi	3⅓	M	•				
95	Three Lakes	Loop	Negl.–4⅔	E–M	•				
96	Dardanelles, Round Lks	O&B	1–7½	E–S	•	•			
97	Lily Pad, Upr Suns Lks	O&B	3¾–4½	M	•	•			
98	Granite Lake	O&B	3½	M	•				
99	Frog, Winnemucca Lks	O&B	2–4	E–M	•	•		•	
100	Meiss, Round Lakes	O&B	2–9¾	E–S	•	•		•	
101	Woods Lake Loop	Loop	2⅔–4	M	•	•		•	
102	Emigrant Lake	O&B	7¾	S	•				
103	Lake Margaret	O&B	4⅔	M	•				
104	Granite, Hidden Lakes	O&B	2–6	E–M	•			•	
105	Shealor Lake	O&B	2½	M	•			•	

NO. NAME	TYPE	TOTAL DISTANCES	LEVELS	BEST FEATURES				
				Lakes	Flora	Falls	View	Color
106 Shriner Lake	O&B	3⅓	M	•				
107 Devils Lake	O&B	2	M	•			•	
108 Tamarack, Triangle Lks	Semi	7–9⅓	S	•			•	
109 Bloodsucker Lake	O&B	4	M	•	•			
110 Grouse, Hemlock Lakes	O&B	4⅔–6	M–S	•				
111 Twin, Island Lakes	O&B	5½–7	M–S	•			•	
112 Angora Lakes	Loop	2½–4⅓	M–S	•	•		•	
113 Grass Lake	O&B	4½	M	•				
114 Gil, Half Mn, Susie Lks	O&B	8½–10	S	•				
115 Gran, Velma, Dicks Lks	O&B	1–20	E–S	•			•	
116 Fall and Lakes	O&B	⅖–10	E–S	•		•	•	
117 Meeks Creek Lakes	O&B	8–10	S	•	•			•
118 Five Lakes Basin	O&B	4	M	•				
119 Long Lake	O&B	1⅓	E	•				
120 Loch Levn, Salmon Lks	O&B	5½–9½	M–S	•				

Leopard lilies

CHAPTER 6

The Eastern Sierra: Crest Country

Life is uncertain, so eat dessert first.

—T-SHIRT SLOGAN

The Eastern Sierra is simply the best—the most wild, the most ruggedly scenic—part of the range. In the southern part of the Eastern Sierra, from Lone Pine to Bishop, it slopes up abruptly to its crest from Owens Valley by as much as 10,000 feet in just a few miles. From the communities along U.S. Highway 395 in Owens Valley, side roads branch past mountain lodgings to some of the range's highest trailheads. What caused this, to oversimplify millions of years of geological evolution, is that as the Sierra Nevada rose, Owens Valley sank. In the northern part of the Eastern Sierra, from Toms Place to Bridgeport, the range slopes up less abruptly but just as scenically from plateaus at 6000–7000 feet. Here again, side roads branch past mountain lodgings to splendid trailheads.

People came to the Eastern Sierra for mineral riches but rarely found them. Some stayed to farm and ranch, but after Los Angeles diverted most of the area's water, the farms and ranches literally dried up. Now the area is devoted largely to recreation, and what a magnificent playground it is! Once people discover the Eastern Sierra for themselves, they return again and again.

Recommended reading

▶ Putman, Jeff and Genny Smith, eds., *Deepest Valley: Guide to Owens Valley, Its roadsides and mountain trails.* 2nd ed. Mammoth Lakes, CA: Genny Smith Books, 1995. A highly readable, entertaining, and educational overview of the southern part of the Eastern Sierra beside Owens Valley, as well as of Owens Valley itself.

▶ Semb, George and Patricia, *Day Hikes on the Pacific Crest Trail.* 1st edition. Berkeley, CA: Wilderness Press, 2000. Hikes on the 2665-mile Pacific Crest Trail that you can do in a day, with accessible entry and exit points. The book covers all of the PCT in California.

▶ Smith, Genny, ed., *Mammoth Lakes Sierra: A handbook for roadside and trail.* 6th ed. Mammoth Lakes, CA: Genny Smith Books, 1993. Like its companion

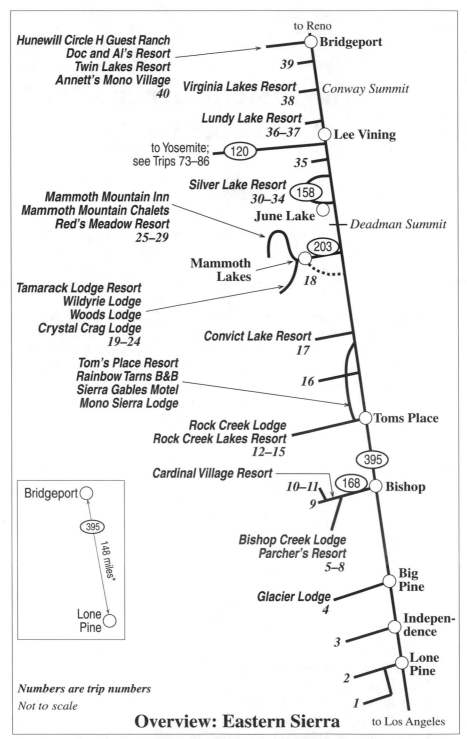

to Reno

Bridgeport

Hunewill Circle H Guest Ranch
Doc and Al's Resort
Twin Lakes Resort
Annett's Mono Village
40

39

Virginia Lakes Resort   *Conway Summit*
38

Lundy Lake Resort
36–37   **Lee Vining**

to Yosemite;   (120)
see Trips 73–86   *35*

Silver Lake Resort   (158)
30–34
June Lake

Mammoth Mountain Inn
Mammoth Mountain Chalets
Red's Meadow Resort
25–29   — *Deadman Summit*

(203)

Mammoth
Lakes
18

Tamarack Lodge Resort
Wildyrie Lodge
Woods Lodge
Crystal Crag Lodge
19–24

Convict Lake Resort
17

Tom's Place Resort
Rainbow Tarns B&B
Sierra Gables Motel   *16*
Mono Sierra Lodge

Toms Place

Rock Creek Lodge
Rock Creek Lakes Resort
12–15   (395)

Cardinal Village Resort
10–11   (168)   **Bishop**
9

Bishop Creek Lodge
Parcher's Resort
5–8   **Big**
Pine

Glacier Lodge
4   **Indepen-**
dence

3

Lone
Pine
2

1

Bridgeport ○

(395)

148 miles*

Lone
Pine ○

Numbers are trip numbers
Not to scale

Overview: Eastern Sierra   to Los Angeles

*Distances summed from various sources: Automobile Club of Southern California maps, other maps, field notes.

book above, a highly readable, entertaining, and educational overview of the northern part of the Eastern Sierra, along the high plateaus.

▶ Winnett, et. al., *Sierra South*. Berkeley, CA: Wilderness Press, 2001. A comprehensive guide to the southern Sierra backcountry. Includes mostly backpack trips, but also some dayhikes, and is a good reference for the area.

Recommended maps

In addition to those listed in the trip write-ups, your library of maps should include the following. Get the latest edition/revision you can find. They're widely available, certainly at any of the local ranger stations.

▶ United States Department of Agriculture, Forest Service (USDA/USFS), Pacific Southwest Region, *A Guide to the John Muir Wilderness and the Sequoia-Kings Canyon Wilderness*. San Francisco: U.S. Forest Service. A huge, two-sheet/three topographic map set that's too big to carry on the trail but that's a fascinating, invaluable overview of most of the southern Sierra, from east to west.

▶ USDA/USFS, *Inyo National Forest*. No topographic information, but invaluable road information.

▶ USDA/USFS, *Toiyabe National Forest, Bridgeport Ranger District*. No topographic information, but invaluable road information.

▶ *Guide to Eastern Sierra*. Los Angeles: Automobile Club of Southern California. Some topographic information by means of shaded relief; includes descriptions of camping and recreational opportunities from Lone Pine to Bridgeport and into the White Mountains.

Lodgings

Alphabetically, the true mountain lodgings and lodgings of interest in the region are—

Annett's Mono Village, Inc.   www.monovillage.com
summer: P.O. Box 455, Bridgeport, CA   (760) 932-7071
winter: P.O. Box 198, Wellington, NV 89444   (702) 465-2314

7000 feet. West of Bridgeport at head of Twin Lakes. *Mountain*. Housekeeping cabins and motel rooms. Oriented to fishing and hunting. Store (groceries, gifts, fishing supplies), coffee shop, cocktail lounge, launch ramp, boat/motor rentals, trailer/RV park, campground. No stated pet policy. 2003 rates: $50–100/cabin or room/night.

Bishop Creek Lodge
Rt. 1, South Lake Road, Bishop, CA 93514   (760) 873-4484

8375 feet. On South Lake Road west of Bishop. *Mountain*. Housekeeping cabins sleeping 1–8 persons, with outdoor barbecues and picnic tables. Café, saloon, store, complimentary continental-style breakfast, lunch and dinner available. Pets okay with extra fee: $10/day/pet. 2002 rates: varies by cabin size, $85/night/2 persons to

$205/night/8 persons; single night $15 higher. Extra person beyond maximum number specified for cabin $15/night. 7th night free on weekly stays. Same management as Parcher's Resort (below).

Cardinal Village Resort
Route 1, Box A-3, Bishop, CA 93514   (760) 873-4789

8400 feet. Off State Route 168 (east) along Bishop Creek, near community of Aspendell, west of Bishop. *Mountain.* Housekeeping cabins accommodating 1–16 persons. Restaurant, store. Stores, restaurants in Bishop. No pets. 2002 rates: $90–275/night depending on cabin and/or number of persons. $15 for rollaway.

Convict Lake Resort   convictlake.com
Route 1, Box 204, Mammoth Lakes, CA 93546   (800) 992-2260, (760) 934-3800

7600 feet. On Convict Lake just west of U.S. Highway 395, south of Mammoth Lakes. *Mountain.* Housekeeping cabins sleeping 1–10 persons plus one house sleeping 1–20 persons. Outstanding restaurant (dinner); general store; snacks, sandwiches in store; launch ramp; boat, canoe rentals; guided horseback rides. Pets okay with extra fee: 2002 rates: number of persons accommodated depends on cabin/house size, and ranges from $90–110/2 person cabins/one night; $578/weekly; and $360/holiday weekend. Larger cabins are priced from $102–235/one night; $668–1210/weekly; and $430–770/holiday weekends. Deluxe cabins that house from 8–10 people range in price from $240–320/night; $1660, weekly; and $1050/holiday weekend. Larger group houses for 15-35 people are priced at $480–695/nightly; $3750/weekly; and $2300/holiday weekends.

Crystal Crag Lodge   mammothweb.com
Box 88, Mammoth Lakes, CA 93546   (760) 934-2436

8880 feet. On Lake Mary in Lakes Basin west of Mammoth Lakes. *Mountain.* Housekeeping cabins, most with fireplaces. Boat dock with rowboats, power boats. Nearby store, café, boat rentals. Dogs okay, $8/dog/night. 2002 rates vary by cabin size, number of persons: $85/night for 1 person in studio cabin to $195/night for 8 persons in 4-bedroom/2-bath cabin. Open summer season only.

Doc and Al's Resort
85 Twin Lakes Rd., P.O. Box 266, Bridgeport, CA 93517   (760) 932-7051

7000 feet. On Robinson Creek just off Twin Lakes Road between Twin Lakes and Bridgeport. *Mountain.* Housekeeping cabins sleeping 1–10 persons; rustic cabins sleeping 1–4 persons with shared central showers and toilets; housekeeping house-trailers sleeping 1–7 persons. Coin-op laundry, RV and camping spaces, showers, firewood, volleyball, horseshoes, ping pong, bait, tackle. Restaurants, stores in Bridgeport. 2003 rates: housekeeping cabins (2 persons) $52–98/night; rustic cabins (2 persons) $42; housekeeping house trailers (2 persons) $51–61. There is a charge for each extra person and for pets.

Glacier Lodge   jewelofthesierra.com
P.O. Box 370, Big Pine, CA 93513   (760) 938-2837

7800 feet. At end of Crocker Street/Glacier Lodge Road west of Big Pine. *Mountain.* Lodge rooms, some with private baths, some with shared baths; housekeeping cabins. Restaurant, general store, RV park, showers, on-premises trout pond, overnight parking for non-guests (fee). Pets (dogs and cats only) okay in cabins only, $15 per stay per pet. All cabins are fully equipped with showers, kitchens, and basic kitchen utensils. Towels and linens are provided. There is no daily maid service. All cabins sleep 2–9 people. Rates are for double occupancy: $70/night for non-holidays, with a charge of $15 for each additional person; $75/night for holidays, with a charge of $18 for each additional person. There is a 2-night minimum.

Hunewill Circle H Guest Ranch   hunnewillranch.com
summer: P.O. Box 368, Bridgeport, CA 93517   (760) 932-7710
winter: Hunewill Ranch, 200 Hunewill Lane, Wellington, NV 89444   (702) 465-2201

6500 feet. Just west of Bridgeport. *Mountain.* Rooms in ranch house and sleeping cabins by the week. Lodging include 3 meals, horse (lodging is equestrian-oriented), ranch activities (scheduled rides, family dance night, family game night, campfire sings, skit and talent night, hayrides, coin-operated washer (bring own soap), pay phone. Stores and restaurants in Bridgeport. No pets. 2002 rates: Weekly rates range from $1070–1200 depending on the number of adults and children in your party.

Lundy Lake Resort
summer: P.O. Box 550, Lee Vining, CA 93541   no phone
winter: 9656 Craiglee St., Temple City, CA 91780   (626) 309-0415

7800 feet. At head of Lundy Lake, west of U.S. Highway 395 between Bridgeport and Lee Vining. *Mountain.* Rustic housekeeping cabins with shared public baths/showers; housekeeping cabins; housekeeping mobile homes. General store, boat rentals, trailer park, camp huts, camper and tent sites. Restaurants, stores in Lee Vining. Pets okay. 2002 rates: rustic housekeeping cabin $55–60/1–2 persons/night, housekeeping cabin $65–80/1–2 persons/night, mobile home $60–70/1–2 persons/night.

Mammoth Mountain Chalets
P.O. Box 513, Mammoth Lakes, CA 93546   (800) 327-3681, (760) 934-8518

8800 feet. On State Route 203 west of Mammoth Lakes and opposite main lodge of Mammoth Mountain Ski Area/Mountain Bike Park. *Of interest.* Housekeeping chalets accommodating 1–10 persons. Next to Mammoth Mountain Inn; across from Mammoth Mountain Ski Area/Mountain Bike Park; see them for nearby facilities. Stores, restaurants in Mammoth Lakes. 2002 summer rates range from $145–185; winter rates are $217–307, midweek; $262–347, weekend; and $332–427, holidays. There is a minimum stay of 2 nights, and 3-4 nights on holidays. A refundable security deposit of $100 is due upon arrival.

Mammoth Mountain Inn   mammothmountain.com, (800) 228-4947
P.O. Box 353, Mammoth Lakes, CA 93546   (760) 934-2581, fax (760) 934-0700

8800 feet. On State Route 203 west of Mammoth Lakes and opposite main lodge of Mammoth Mountain Ski Area/Mountain Bike Park. Operated by ski area. *Of interest.* Hotel rooms: standard rooms and deluxe suites (some with kitchens). In-room direct-dial phones, cable TV, room service in main building; licensed child-care facilities; shuttle bus; gift shop; game room; covered parking; spa; cocktail lounge; 2 restaurants; sport shop; adventure course; mountain bike park. No stated pet policy. Rates given in terms of 2- and 3-night packages that include taxes and gratuities, daily breakfast, one picnic or barbecue lunch, scenic gondola ride to summit of Mammoth Mountain, tickets for Reds Meadow Shuttle, card for local discounts. 2003 rates: $99–520; special packages available.

Mono Sierra Lodge   monosierralodge.com
Rt. 1, Box 88, Crowley Lake, CA 93546   (800) 723-5387

7000 feet. On Crowley Lake Drive west of U.S. Highway 395 between Bishop and Mammoth Lakes. *Of interest.* Housekeeping units, some with fireplaces, and motel rooms. Restaurant, store, laundromat, gas station nearby. Well-behaved pets okay, $10/night, pet deposit may be required. 2002 rates: motel room $75/2 persons/night, housekeeping units without fireplaces $80/2 persons/night, housekeeping units with fireplaces $140/4 persons/night. Extra person: motel room and housekeeping units without fireplaces $15/night; housekeeping units with fireplaces $25/night.

Parcher's Resort   bishopcreekresorts.com
Rt. 1, South Lake Rd., Bishop, CA 93514   (760) 873-4177

9290 feet. On South Lake Road west of Bishop. *Mountain.* Cabins with bathrooms, outdoor barbecues, and picnic tables; 3 types: standard housekeeping with kitchenette, sleeps 1–4; rustic housekeeping with kitchen sleeps 1–4; rustic without kitchen sleeps 1–2. Store, café (breakfast, lunch), complimentary continental-style breakfast, deli-sandwiches for sale for lunch. Generates own electricity; don't bring high-wattage appliances. Boat rentals at South Lake. Pets okay with extra fee: $10/day/pet. 2002 rates: varies by cabin size, $70–145/night. Extra person beyond maximum number specified for cabin $15/night. 7th night free on weekly stays. Same management as Bishop Creek Lodge (above). There is a 2 night minimum stay.

Rainbow Tarns Bed and Breakfast   rainbowtarns.com
Route 1, P.O. Box 1097, Crowley Lake, CA 93546   (888) 588-6269

7000 feet. Off Crowley Lake Drive on Rainbow Tarns Road, near Toms Place, between Bishop and Mammoth Lakes. *Of interest.* Bed-and-breakfast. 3 beautifully decorated guest rooms, each with private bath. Breakfast and afternoon snacks; sack lunch available for small charge. Store, restaurant at Toms Place. Smoking on decks, grounds. No pets except horses (pens provided, no extra charge for guests' horses cared for by guests). 2002 rates (2 persons): $115–140/summer and $95–120/winter.

Red's Meadow Resort   mammothweb.com, summer: (760) 934-2345
P.O. Box 395, Mammoth Lakes, CA 93546   winter: (760) 873-3928

7500 feet. At end of Devils Postpile Road, near Devils Postpile National Monument, west of Mammoth Lakes. *Mountain.* Motel rooms and housekeeping A-frame cabins. General store, café, pack station (resort is equestrian-oriented), scheduled pack trips, daily rides, and special events. Dogs okay. Reservations accepted. 2002 rates: motel room $65/night/2 persons, A-frame cabin $100/night. Extra person $10/night/motel room.

Rock Creek Lakes Resort   rockcreeklake.com
P.O. Box 727, Bishop, CA 93515   (760) 935-4311

9700 feet. West of Toms Place on U.S. Highway 395, just off Rock Creek Road. *Mountain.* Deluxe housekeeping cabins accommodate 2–8 persons depending on cabin. General store, café. No pets. 2002 rates: 1 bedroom cabin, $100/2-4 people nightly, $630 weekly; 2 bedroom cabin, $135/4–6 people nightly, $850 weekly; large 2-bedroom cabin, $163/4–7 people nightly, $1027 weekly; 2-story cabin, $250/8–12 people nightly, $1575 weekly; and two new non-smoking 2-bedroom cabins with a one-week minimum stay, $1039/4–6 people (add $165 for each additional day). There is a $8 per night fee for each additional person.

Rock Creek Lodge   rockcreeklodge.com
Route 1, Box 12, Mammoth Lakes, CA 93546   (877) 935-4170

9360 feet. West of Toms Place on U.S. Highway 395, just off Rock Creek Road. *Mountain.* Housekeeping cabins: rustic (centrally-located, common shower house) and modern (bathrooms with hot showers). General store, lodge with dining room and common room, sauna, bait and tackle facility, sporting-goods rentals. There are 3 cabin styles: rustic which sleeps up to 8 people: $85/per night double occupancy, $10 for each extra person; modern (3 night minimum), sleeps 4, $105/nightly, $15 for each extra person; A-frame large cabins, up to 15 people, $145 per night (triple occupancy, (3 night minimum), $15 each extra person; and single level large modern cabins, $145/per night (3 night minimum). Pets are allowed for a fee of $15 dollars per night per pet.

Sierra Gables Motel   sierragables.com
Star Route 1, Box 94, Crowley Lake, CA 93546   (760) 935-4319

7000 feet. On Crowley Lake Drive west of U.S. Highway 395 between Bishop and Mammoth Lakes. *Of interest.* Housekeeping units accommodating 4 or more persons. Restaurant, store, laundromat, gas station nearby. No stated pet policy. 2001 rates: studio unit $60/2 persons/night, 1-bedroom unit $70/2 persons/night. Extra person $10/night. Weekly and monthly rates available. 7th night free.

Silver Lake Resort   (760) 648-7525,
P.O. Box 116 or Rt. 3, Box 17, June Lake, CA 93529   fax (760) 648-7253

7240 feet. On State Route 158 (June Lakes Loop) next to Silver Lake and Rush Creek Trailhead. *Of interest.* Housekeeping cabins. General store, café (breakfast, lunch), RV park, boat rentals. No pets. 2002 rates: $78–215/cabin/night depending on cabin's capacity (2–8 people maximum).

Tamarack Lodge Resort   tamaracklodge.com
P.O. Box 69, Mammoth Lakes, CA 93546,   (760) 934-2442, fax (760) 934-2281

8560 feet. In Lakes Basin west of Mammoth Lakes. *Mountain*. Lodge rooms (some share a bath) and housekeeping cabins. Outstanding restaurant (breakfast, dinner); boat and canoe rentals; complete, catered wedding weekends. Stores, restaurants in Mammoth Lakes. No pets. Ten lodge rooms rent at $84–230/night; one suite which sleeps up to 4 people is $230; 29 cabins rent at $84–350 night for non-holidays and sleep anywhere from 2 to 8 people.

Tioga Pass Resort
summer: P.O. Box 7, Lee Vining, CA 93541   tiogapassresort.com
winter: P.O. Box 307, Lee Vining, CA 93541   (209) 372-4471

9600 feet. On State Route 120 east of Tioga Pass. *Of interest*. Housekeeping cabins accommodating 1–6 persons depending on unit, and sleeping-only motel units. Store, café, boat rentals. 2002 rates: summer, various-size cabins, sleep 1-6 people, $700–860, weekly; deluxe-cabin for 4 people maximum, $900; winter, private cabins, $125/night; dorm rooms, $105–115/night. Children five and under are free; up to 12 years, half-price, and over 12, full price. Contact for organized group policy information. A mid-week special is also offered.

Tom's Place Resort   tomsplaceresort.com
Rural Station, Bishop, CA 93514   (760) 935-4239

7000 feet. At junction of Crowley Lake Drive and Rock Creek Road, just off U.S. Highway 395 between Bishop and Mammoth Lakes. *Of interest*. Lodge rooms, housekeeping cabins, and dormitories. General store, post office, café, bar. Pets okay except no pets in dormitory. 2002 rates: lodge rooms $45–55/night, dormitory room $20/bunk/night, cabin $50–100/night. Weekly and monthly rates.

Tuolumne Meadows Lodge   yosemitepark.com
Yosemite Reservations, 5410 East Home Ave., Fresno, CA 93727   (559) 252-4848

8900 feet. Just off State Route 120 in Yosemite National Park west of Tioga Pass and east of Tuolumne Meadows. *Mountain*. Tent-cabins. Restaurant, store, stables, gas station, climbing school. No pets. 2002 rates: $59/night. Extra person: adult $8/night; child under 12 staying in same room as adult, $4. Rollaways and cribs available; may be additional fee.

Twin Lakes Resort   thesierraweb.com
P.O. Box 248, Bridgeport, CA 93517   (760) 932-7751

7200 feet. On Twin Lakes Road, on Twin Lakes, west of Bridgeport. *Mountain*. Housekeeping cottages. Laundromat, showers, general store, fishing tackle, boats and boat landing, trailer park. Restaurants, stores in Bridgeport. No pets. 2002 rates: $82–155/2 persons/night. Extra person $15/night.

Virginia Lakes Resort

HCR 1, Box 1065, Bridgeport, CA 93517   (760) 647-6484

9770 feet. Next to Virginia Lakes on Virginia Lakes Road, west of U.S. Highway 395 at Conway Summit between Lee Vining and Bridgeport. Housekeeping cabins; some cabins share a shower; some cabins have fireplaces; cabins accommodate 1–12 people depending on cabin. Store, café (breakfast, lunch), rowboat rentals. No gas motors on or swimming in lakes. Pets okay; $25 charge if cabins left dirty from pets. 1996 rates: $55–185/night, $303–1072/week, depending on cabin's capacity, facilities. Extra person $15/night; total number of occupants may not exceed cabin's specified maximum.

Wildyrie Resort   mammothweb.com

P.O. Box 109, Mammoth Lakes, CA 93546   (760) 934-2444

8880 feet. On Lake Mamie in Lakes Basin west of Mammoth Lakes. *Mountain.* Housekeeping cabins accommodating 1–10 persons. Boat rentals. Stores, café in Lakes Basin; stores, restaurants in Mammoth Lakes. No smoking. No pets. 2002 rates: $111–246/night depending on cabin. Extra person, rollaway, or crib, $8/night. Same management as Woods Lodge, below.

Woods Lodge   mammothweb.com

P.O. Box 108, Mammoth Lakes, CA 93546   (760) 934-2261

9010 feet. On Lake George in Lakes Basin west of Mammoth Lakes. *Mountain.* Housekeeping cabins accommodating 1–4 persons, some with fireplaces. Launch ramp, store, boat rentals. Stores, café in Lakes Basin; stores, restaurants in Mammoth Lakes. No smoking. Pets okay in some units, $8/night/pet; inquire when booking. 2002 rates: $83–251/night depending on cabin. Extra person, rollaway, or crib, $8/night; check to be sure extra person(s) will not exceed cabin maximum. Same management as Wildyrie Lodge, above.

Communities

Alphabetically, these are the communities along the Eastern Sierra that are eligible for this book—

Big Pine Chamber of Commerce

P.O. Box 23, Big Pine, CA 93513   (760) 938-2114

Big Pine straddles U.S. Highway 395 in Owens Valley north of Independence and south of Bishop. Big Pine is not only a gateway to the Sierra, it is the principal gateway to the next range to the east, the White Mountains. You can visit the White Mountains by daytripping from Big Pine; the Whites have campgrounds but no water and no lodgings. This Great Basin range is home to some of the world's oldest known living things, the ancient bristlecone pines, some of which are far older than the giant sequoias—as old as 4500 years! Lying in the rain shadow of the Sierra, the Whites are achingly dry but, in their own way, stunningly beautiful. Views of the Sierra and Owens Valley from the Whites are matchless. If you want to bag a 14,000-foot peak but don't want to tackle Mt. Whitney—permits extremely hard to get, dayhike extraordinarily punishing—consider 14,246-foot White Mountain Peak, California's third highest peak. After a long drive from Big Pine, you *start* at 11,500 feet. It's a 15-mile round trip with 2700 feet of elevation gain—strenuous but not nearly as brutal as Mt. Whitney—through a surreal landscape, all on a rough road that's closed to the public's vehicles but open to mountain bikes and hikers. See Gary Suttle's *California County Summits* (Wilderness Press, 1994) for a detailed write-up, including a topographic map. Once a year in some years, the road is open to the public as far as the University of California's Mt. Barcroft laboratory, for an open house there. That cuts 4 miles off the round trip and lets you start at (gasp) almost 12,500 feet. Call the White Mountain Research Station in Bishop for more information ((760) 873-4344).

Bishop Chamber of Commerce
690 N. Main St., Bishop, CA 93514,   (760) 873-8405

Bishop straddles U.S. Highway 395 in Owens Valley north of Big Pine and south of Mammoth Lakes. It's the largest town in Owens Valley at a little under 4000 people.

Bridgeport
Bridgeport straddles U.S. Highway 395 north of Lee Vining and south of the junction of State Route 108 with 395. Bridgeport's Chamber of Commerce is defunct for now; don't waste your time trying to call the listed number. Nearby Bodie State Historic Park, at the end of State Route 270, preserves one of the Wild West's most notorious towns in a state of "arrested decay." Lodgings:

Best Western Ruby Inn,
   (760) 932-7241
Bodie Motel, (760) 932-7020
Bridgeport Inn, (760) 932-7380
Cain House Bed and Breakfast, The,
   (760) 932-7040
Log Cabin Motel, (760) 932-7760
Redwood Motel, (760) 932-7060
Silver Maple Inn, (760) 932-7383

Victorian Hotel, (760) 932-7020—No reservations; building reportedly was once a brothel in Bodie; handled by adjacent Sportsmen's Inn
Virginia Creek Settlement,
   (760) 932-7780
Walker River Lodge, (760) 932-7021
Willow Springs Motel, (760) 932-7725

Independence
See Lone Pine Chamber of Commerce (it handles Independence, too).

Independence straddles U.S. Highway 395 in Owens Valley north of Lone Pine and south of Big Pine. Site of Eastern California Museum.

June Lake Chamber of Commerce
P.O. Box 2, June Lake, CA 93529   (760) 648-7584

June Lake lies west of U.S. Highway 395, north of Mammoth Lakes and south of Lee Vining, along State Route 158 (June Lakes Loop), which connects with 395 at two points. Be sure to enjoy a wonderfully scenic drive on the June Lakes Loop. Early season brings numerous cascades bounding down the steep slopes surrounding the community. The fall color display around the June Lakes Loop is almost unmatched in the Eastern Sierra, especially on the far side of Grant Lake, where the aspens turn a vivid red.

Lee Vining Chamber of Commerce
with Mono Lake Committee Information Center,
Highway 395 at Third Street, Lee Vining, CA 93541   (760) 647-6595

Lee Vining sits on U.S. Highway 395 between Bridgeport and June Lake, on the edge of Mono Lake. Don't miss Mono Lake. It's not in this book because it's a Great Basin, not a Sierra, feature. Its unique ecology, fascinating tufa formations, and magnificent setting are worth your time. As part of the Pacific Flyway, it hosts hundreds of thousands of migrating birds; also, most California gulls nest here, explaining a strange Eastern Sierra phenomenon: seagulls—yes, the ones that in other seasons try to steal your French fries along the Venice Beach boardwalk—in alpine lakes. Guided hikes are given during the summer; call the Mono Lake Visitor Center at (760) 647-3044. Nearby Panum Crater, off *eastbound* Highway 120, is a small lava dome with a good trail system that makes it a worthwhile stop, too; you can pick up a flyer about it at the Mono Lake Visitor Center.

Lone Pine Chamber of Commerce
P.O. Box 749, Lone Pine, CA 93545   (760) 876-4444

Lone Pine straddles U.S. Highway 395 in Owens Valley south of Independence and in the shadow of Mt. Whitney, highest peak in the contiguous 48 states.

Mammoth Lakes Visitors Bureau   (800) 367-6572,
P.O. Box 48, Dept. P, Mammoth Lakes, CA 93546 (760) 934-2712, fax (760) 934-7066

Mammoth Lakes is on State Route 203 west of U.S. Highway 395, north of Bishop and south of June Lake.

Hikes
1. Chicken Spring Lake ☼ 🍁

Place	Total Dist.	Elevation	Level	Type
Start	0	9920	—	—
Streamside stop	3	9960	E	O&B
Cottonwood Pass	8	11,200	S	O&B
Chicken Spring Lake	9	11,270	S	O&B

Permit required: None

Topo(s): Cirque Peak 7½'

Where to stay:
   Mountain, Of Interest: None
   Other: Town of Lone Pine

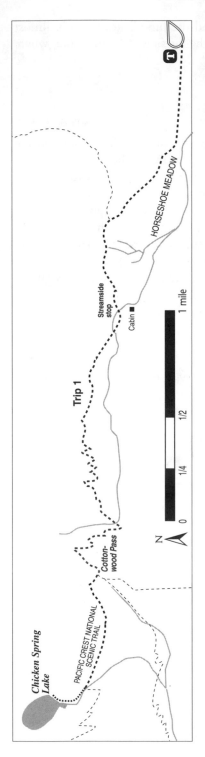

Highlights: The drive to the trailhead is very scenic—and very airy. You're in the high country from the minute you step out of your car. The well-graded trail takes you through a wonderfully varied alpine landscape up to superb views at Cottonwood Pass. Chicken Spring Lake, tucked right under Cirque Peak, is starkly beautiful.

How to get to the trailhead: From the traffic light in Lone Pine, at the intersection of Highway 395 and Whitney Portal Road, turn west on Whitney Portal Road and follow it 3½ miles to Horseshoe Meadow Road. Turn left (south) onto Horseshoe Meadow as it snakes up the mountainside to a fork at about 20 miles: ahead (left) to Horseshoe Meadow and the Kern Plateau trailheads; right to the Cottonwood Lakes Trailhead. Go left and follow the road to its end at a parking lot, ½ more mile. Water, toilets.

At the trailhead: You don't have to hike to be in the high country *here!* Non-hikers may enjoy lunch at the nearby picnic area—follow signs to it.

On the trail: Pick up the sandy trail by a large information sign to the right of the toilets and head west through an open forest of lodgepole and foxtail pines, soon entering Golden Trout Wilderness. The gradually-rising trail stays in the forest edge as you skirt broad, dusty Horseshoe Meadow and pass a use trail left to Trail and Mulkey passes. You stay on the main trail and near the west end of Horseshoe Meadow cross a couple of forks of Cottonwood Creek one after the other (they look like one crossing on the book's map). Just beyond there's a lovely, shady, **streamside stop at 1½ miles and 9960 feet**, with lots of nice rocks to sit on. Sharp-eyed hikers may spot an old log cabin to the south—go over and look, but don't disturb.

Continuing, you cross the creek once more, presently pass a small, flowery meadow, and then begin switchbacking on a moderate grade, up toward Cottonwood Pass. Views soon open up over Horseshoe Meadow, and the higher you go, the better they get. They're good excuses for taking breather stops—even though the grade is only gradual-to-moderate, the elevation is very high. You cross the creek again partway up, where there's a fine display of flowers. Just below the pass, a signed but unmapped STOCK BYPASS ROUTE branches right; you go left, staying on the main trail. You shortly reach **Cottonwood Pass at a little less than 4 miles and 11,200 feet.** The view westward, over Kern Plateau and Kern Canyon, toward one of the Sierra's most beautiful sub-ranges, the Great Western Divide, is simply sublime. There are good rocks to rest on here.

A few steps west of Cottonwood Pass you meet the Pacific Crest Trail at a three-way junction: left (south) and right (northwest) on the Pacific Crest Trail and ahead (west) to Big Whitney Meadow and Rocky Basin Lakes. You turn right on the Pacific Crest Trail and follow it for almost ⅔ mile to the rocky outlet stream of Chicken Spring Lake. Turn right and follow the outlet, which is often dry by late season, upstream a short way to reach **Chicken Spring Lake at 4½ miles and 11,270 feet.** There are picnic spots on either side of the lake, so pick one from which to savor your view of this alpine treasure and then settle down for lunch. This beautiful lake is a popular spot, so you'll probably have company.

Return the way you came.

2. Lone Pine Lake ☼ 🍁

Place	Total Dist.	Elevation	Level	Type
Start	0	8365	—	—
Lone Pine Lake	5½	10,040	M	O&B

Permit required: None to go to Lone Pine Lake, but required to go farther

Topo(s): WP Mt. Whitney 15'; Mt. Langley, Mount Whitney 7½'

Where to stay:
Mountain, Of Interest: None
Other: Town of Lone Pine, Town of Independence

Highlights: Experience the easiest and prettiest part of the famous, crowded, and brutal trail to the summit of Mt. Whitney on this delightful, moderate hike to the area's loveliest lake, Lone Pine Lake.

How to get to the trailhead: At the traffic light in Lone Pine where Highway 395 intersects Whitney Portal Road, turn west onto Whitney Portal Road and follow it into the steep canyon below Mt. Whitney for 12 miles to its end at Whitney Portal. One of the best views of Mt. Whitney's sheer, massive east face is available from the roadside, a little before you duck into the forest cover at Whitney Portal. There are a couple of tiers of parking here, and you may have to hunt for a spot. The trailhead is on the north side of the road, not the parking lot, by some information signs. Water, toilets, store.

At the trailhead: Whitney Portal may be the most famous trailhead in the Sierra: in the 1941 gangster flick *High Sierra*, the law chases crook Humphrey Bogart and moll Ida Lupino to Lone Pine, finally nailing Bogey at Whitney Portal. Non-hikers may enjoy the shady picnic area here; Lone Pine Creek tumbles down in pretty cascades nearby.

On the trail: From the information signs, climb northeast gradually to moderately under white firs and Jeffrey pines, on coarse granite sand. During the summer, especially on weekends, you may find yourself moving along in a small crowd—the trail is that popular! A few switchbacks bring you out onto the open, sagebrush-dotted northwest side of the canyon, and this traverse offers good views east over the Owens Valley and west toward Mt. Whitney. In season, there's a good show of fall color in this canyon. As you tackle more switchbacks, a dashing cascade draws your attention: it's Lone Pine Creek.

You cross a couple of streams, soon enter open-to-sparse forest cover, and reach the boundary of John Muir Wilderness a little beyond ⅔ mile. Just beyond the next switchback turn, you'll find a good resting log by the cascading, willow-lined creek, where lodgepole pines now dominate the forest. It's not long before you cross the creek, and beyond the crossing you soon reach the junction with the spur trail to Lone Pine Lake. Turn left, leaving the crowds behind, and descend ¼ mile to the edge of lovely **Lone Pine Lake at 2¾ miles and 9940 feet**. Picnic spots abound, there's a nice beach, and a cross-country walk around the lake reveals its perch to be high above the canyon you've been ascending—the views are surprising from the far side of the lake.

Retrace your steps to Whitney Portal.

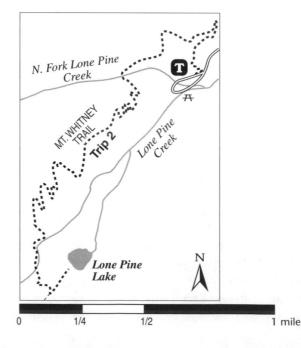

3. Kearsarge Trail Lakes ☼ 🍁

Place	Total Dist.	Elevation	Level	Type
Start	0	9200	—	
Little Pothole Lake *only*	3⅓	10,050	M	O&B
Gilbert Lake *only*	5	10,400	M	O&B
Flower Lake *only*	5⅓	10,530	M	O&B
Matlock Lake	6⅔	10,560	S U	O&B

Permit required: None

Topo(s): Kearsarge Peak 7½'

Where to stay:
Mountain, Of Interest: None
Other: Town of Lone Pine, Town of Independence

Highlights: Four lovely lakes lie along a well-graded trail that also offers fine views over Owens Valley. Each lake has its own charm—can you decide which is your favorite?—and there's a wonderful display of flowers in season.

How to get to the trailhead: From Highway 395 in the town of Independence, turn west on Market Street, which is a little south of the courthouse. Follow this road as it makes a steep, switchbacking climb for 13⅓ miles to a circular parking area that serves three trailheads. Day-use parking is by the restrooms. Toilets, water.

At the trailhead: This is a lovely area: an amphitheater of handsome peaks, graced by the cascading outlets of Robinson and Golden Trout lakes. Non-hikers may enjoy spending some time here; there's no picnic area, so bring your own picnic gear.

On the trail: Of the three trailheads here, yours is the middle one, for Kearsarge Pass, reached by heading southwest on a well-marked trail just past the restrooms. You begin a gradual-to-moderate ascent on rocky-dusty switchbacks in the scant shade of red fir, foxtail pine, and western white pine; there's a dazzling array of flowers. These are some of the longest switchback legs I've ever encountered in the Sierra; that makes for easy going. Near ⅓ mile, be sure to avoid a use trail that veers off to the right.

In ¾ mile you reach the boundary of John Muir Wilderness and pause to enjoy over-the-shoulder views back to the Owens Valley. The switchbacks grow shorter as they carry you near a tumbling creek where you'll find some cool, shady, flowery nooks. Marshy and dry sections alternate as you climb, until you find yourself overlooking **Little Pothole Lake at 1⅔ miles and 10,050 feet.** The willow-ringed lake is nice, but the real show here is the pair of beautiful cascades, one on the south, the other on the west, that are the lake's inlets. From here you have good views of University Peak to the south, Independence Peak to the east-southeast, and Kearsarge Peak to the north-northeast.

You resume your ascent, brushing up to a slopeside meadow before emerging onto a talus slope where the trail has been cleared through the talus. You top a bench, level out, and reach flower-ringed **Gilbert Lake at 2½ miles and 10,400**

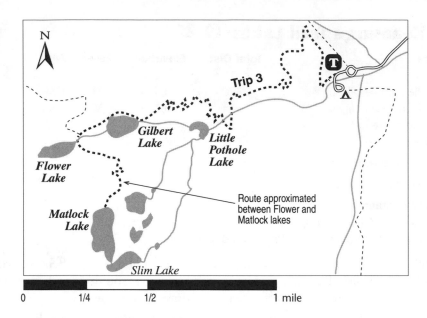

Route approximated between Flower and Matlock lakes

feet—what a beauty! You'll surely want to stop here to enjoy the view. The metal box on Gilbert's north side is a bearproof food storage locker.

Leaving Gilbert, the trail switchbacks through some huge boulders to reach a marked junction with the spur trail to Matlock Lake that's right next to the east end of **Flower Lake at 2⅔ miles and 10,530 feet**. Take a minute to follow either of a couple of use trails down to Flower's serene, cliff-backed shoreline.

Back at the Matlock-Flower junction, turn south to cross Flower Lake's outlet and begin switchbacking up the ridge that separates Matlock and its companion lakes from Flower and Gilbert lakes. Just beyond the top of the ridge, at 10,660 feet, you have a view of Matlock Lake and the unnamed, roundish lake to its east, as well as of Dragon and Kearsarge peaks to the northwest and north. You descend moderately to splendid **Matlock Lake at 3⅓ miles and 10,560 feet**, sitting in a beautiful cirque. You'll want to find a spot where you can rest, enjoy this lovely place, and have your lunch.

Return the way you came. If you went as far as Gilbert Lake, on the way back as you're descending from Gilbert, you'll enjoy stunning views eastward, clear over the tops of the Inyo Mountains and on into Nevada.

4. Big Pine Lakes 🌸 ☼ 🍁

Place	Total Dist.	Elevation	Level	Type
Start	0	7800	—	
First Falls *only*	½+	7950	E	O&B
Second Falls viewpoint *only*	3	8950	E	O&B
First Lake *only*	9	10,000	S	O&B
Second Lake	9½	10,100	S	O&B

Permit required: None

Topo(s): Split Mountain, Coyote Flat 7 ½'

Where to stay:
Mountain: Glacier Lodge
Of Interest: None
Other: Town of Big Pine

Highlights: Showy cascades and flower-blessed streamside meadows along North Fork Big Pine Creek make rewarding goals. Beyond them lie splendid alpine lakes that mirror rugged peaks like Temple Crag, whose convoluted face offers at least a score of world-class climbing routes. It's a thrilling sight even for us non-climbers!

How to get to the trailhead: From the intersection of Highway 395 and Crocker Street, turn west on Crocker Street and follow it for 11 winding miles to the trailhead, which is at the roadend and just past the spur road to Glacier Lodge. Trailhead parking is for day users only; overnight users must use the lot farther down and just off the road. If the trailhead parking is full, there's limited day-use parking along the spur road to Glacier Lodge. Toilets.

At the trailhead: Glacier Lodge is right next to the trailhead, so non-walkers can enjoy a meal at its restaurant (call ahead to be sure it's open). Of course, if you're staying there, you can just relax or try your angling luck at the lodge's trout pond or along Big Pine Creek.

On the trail: From the roadend, head west-southwest past a locked gate, on a continuation of the road you drove in on and next to rushing Big Pine Creek. The trail is marked SOUTH FORK BIG PINE TRAIL TO NORTH FORK BIG PINE TRAIL. You pass a number of summer cabins from which roads and paths sprout to your right; don't take any of them. The road soon dwindles to a sandy footpath, although near ⅓ mile you make a brief jog onto a bit of paved road. But you're soon back on the trail, climbing moderately on an open hillside. A switchback leg brings you to a bridged crossing of the creek just below the handsome cascades known as **First Falls at a little over ¼ mile and 7950 feet.**

Just beyond the bridge, you reach a junction: left (southwest) to destinations along South Fork Big Pine Creek, right along North Fork Big Pine Creek. You turn right and begin a series of very short, moderate to steep, open switchbacks next to the creek and soon have a view over the bouldery wash of South Fork Big Pine Creek. The grade eases as the shade increases, and use trails dart off to creekside.

Staying on the main trail, you meet an old road at a **T**-junction near ⅔ mile: left (south) to the South Fork, right (north) to the North Fork. You go right on the old road—the part you walk is shown as a trail rather than a road on the book's map—almost immediately crossing the creek on another bridge and reaching another junction: left (north-northwest) on the old road, right (east-southeast) and up to marked UPPER TRAIL, and hard right (southeast) and level to marked TRAIL CAMP. You can go left on the old road or right on UPPER TRAIL (which soon makes a switchback turn to go the same general direction as the old road but many feet above the old road). The confusion of roads and trails here reflects a long-gone era when there was a car campground here, Second Falls Campground on the topo.

If you take the road, your route remains level as it passes use trails that lead left to the stream; if you take the upper trail, you'll climb steeply, make a switchback turn, and then climb gradually on an open slope. Either way, the long cascades of Second Falls soon come into view ahead as you head northwest, skirting Mt. Alice to the southwest. If you're on the road, it narrows back to a trail as it passes under some cottonwoods and begins climbing; avoid a use trail left to the falls as you approach a switchback turn.

No matter which route you took, you'll have a good view of **Second Falls near 1½ miles and 8590 feet** at a junction where you rejoin UPPER TRAIL: right (east) and up to Baker Lake; right (southeast) and down to the earlier UPPER TRAIL-road junction; and left (northwest) to Big Pine Lakes. After taking in the view, you go left on the hot, open trail, switchbacking moderately up to the brink of Second Falls. The trail straightens out just above the falls and begins a gradual climb on the north side of the creek. A flower-filled meadow lines the creek, while the trail stays somewhat higher on open, sandy soil. Around 2⅓ miles, the trail alternates through patches of cool forest and squishy, flowery meadow. At 2⅔ miles you pass a spur trail (not on the map) left to signed BIG PINE CREEK WILDERNESS RANGER CAMP. This handsome, streamside stone cabin at Cienaga Mirth was once a vacation home for actor Lon Chaney. Now it's enjoying a second, and I think better, life as a backcountry summer-ranger station.

After a brief, sunstruck stretch you ascend to a lodgepole-studded granite bench. Meadow and forest alternate atop the bench here, the flower display is delightful, and the creek is never far away. You cross the stream as you near the 4-mile mark and again shortly beyond 4 miles.

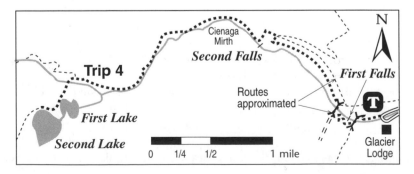

Then, with the inspiring sight of Temple Crag to the southwest, you begin a series of hot switchbacks to a junction at 4⅓ miles: right (northeast) to Black Lake, left (west) to First through Seventh lakes. You turn left, cross a tiny stream, and duck into forest cover, soon passing a use trail that goes left down to campsites on First Lake's shore. Keep going to the next switchback turn, to a viewpoint above beautiful **First Lake at 10,000 feet and 4½ miles**. The rugged peaks surrounding First and Second lakes make perfect settings for these two alpine gems.

To continue to Second Lake, stay on the main trail and ascend gradually, at 4⅔ miles passing another use trail left to campsites above First Lake. It's just a few more steps to a big erratic near which there are picnic sites overlooking splendid **Second Lake at 10,100 feet and 4¾ miles**.

After enjoying your lunch at First or Second Lake, return the way you came.

5. Treasure Lakes ☼ 🍁

Place	Total Dist.	Elevation	Level	Type
Start	0	9800	—	
Treasure Lakes	6	10,688	S	O&B

Permit required: None

Topo(s): Mt. Thompson 7½'

Where to stay:
   Mountain: Parcher's Resort, Bishop Creek Lodge, Cardinal Village Resort
   Of Interest: None
   Other: Town of Bishop

Highlights: You'll cross one flower-lined stream after another before climbing to the Treasure Lakes, the lower two of which are breathtakingly lovely. There are stunning views along the way. The lakes are so close together that I've treated them as a single destination.

Caution: As if to compensate for so much beauty, there's a stream crossing a little below the lakes that can be very dangerous in early season.

How to get to the trailhead: From the traffic-light-controlled intersection of U.S. Highway 395 and West Line Street in the town of Bishop, turn west onto West Line Street (State Route 168) and follow it up into the mountains to its junction with the marked road to South Lake. Turn left onto the South Lake road and follow it for 7 more miles, past Bishop Creek Lodge and Parcher's Resort, to its end at a day-use parking lot just above South Lake, 22.3 miles. Toilets.

At the trailhead: A magnificent panorama of granite peaks rises around South Lake; the most striking is Hurd Peak. Non-hikers will enjoy this spot and may also enjoy a visit to the marked picnic area about a mile back down the road, on rushing South Fork Bishop Creek.

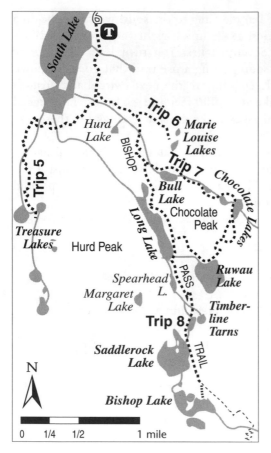

On the trail: Head south on the Bishop Pass Trail, into John Muir Wilderness and past an information sign, almost immediately crossing two tiny footbridges over a marshy, wonderfully flowery spot. In a few steps you reach a junction where a stock trail from the pack station comes in sharply from the left; note this, as you'll want to avoid the stock trail on the way back. The trail dips briefly, and use trails dart off toward the shoreline (right). You're soon climbing gradually to moderately, and the scenery over the lake is simply spectacular. You reach a marked junction with the Treasure Lakes Trail at a little over ¾ mile: right (south) to Treasure Lakes, left (southeast) to stay on the Bishop Pass Trail.

Go right for Treasure Lakes, toward four-pronged Hurd Peak, and descend gradually to a footbridge over the first of South Lake's many inlets—more than appear on the map, many seasonal. You'll be curving down and around the head of the valley in which South Lake lies and crossing several inlets. Around those inlets you'll find lovely flower gardens. But first you bob over a low ridge and make a dry southwest traverse, at times heading for a prominent crag between Mts. Gilbert and Johnson. A patch of thinning forest along this traverse allows for good views over South Lake's south bay.

The roar of a runoff stream heralds the next inlet, and you descend steeply to moderately to cross it on a footbridge. Beyond it, the next inlet is unbridged, and multiple tracks tell of hikers' searches for places to cross safely. Depending on the season, there may be one or more other streams before the last major one, which is near the west wall of the valley, where the stock crossing is obvious but you may need to hunt for a good foot crossing. Avoid a use trail that strikes north near the stock crossing.

Pick up the Treasure Lakes Trail on the west side of the stream near the stock crossing and cross an intermittent stream before beginning to climb moderately to steeply on rocky-dusty switchbacks, up the valley wall. It's not long before the forest thins and the grade eases as you reach an outstanding viewpoint: South

Southernmost Treasure Lake

Lake to the north, the rugged Inconsolable Range to the east, and Hurd Peak to the southeast.

Soon the trail begins a southward ascent over open granite slabs, toward Peak 12047. Look for ducks as well as for the trail-tread in the soil between the slabs. You curve eastward briefly to cross the Treasure Lakes' raging outlet as best you can—dangerous in early season and dicey just about any time. Climbing again, you pass some seasonal ponds and then begin a steep, switchbacking climb on a trail blasted out of the polished granite slabs of knoll 10718.

The climb soon ends, and you're at the shore of the **first Treasure Lake at just under 3 miles and 10,668 feet**. With Peak 12047 towering over it and red heather blooming along its edges, the lake is glorious—well worth the hike. You may want to climb trailless knoll 10718, just north of the lake, for a spectacular view over the entire area.

The trail continues around the lowest lake's northeast shore and reaches another alpine gem, the **second Treasure Lake at 3 miles and 10,688 feet** (after that, there's only a use trail).

You'll be reluctant to leave, but eventually you must return the way you came.

6. Marie Louise Lakes ☼ 🍁

Place	Total Dist.	Elevation	Level	Type
Start	0	9800	—	
Marie Louise Lakes	4	10,620+	M	O&B

Permit required: None

Topo(s): Mt. Thompson 7½'

Where to stay:
　　Mountain: Parcher's Resort, Bishop Creek Lodge, Cardinal Village Resort
　　Of Interest: None
　　Other: Town of Bishop

Highlights: Few people veer off the well-beaten Bishop Pass Trail to see the most tranquil lakes in the South Fork Bishop Creek drainage, the pretty pair called the Marie Louise Lakes. But you will, and you'll be glad you did.

How to get to the trailhead: Follow the driving directions of Trip 5 to South Lake.

At the trailhead: See Trip 5.

On the trail: See Trip 5's map. Follow Trip 5 to the Treasure Lakes Trail-Bishop Pass Trail junction; go left (southeast), staying on the Bishop Pass Trail.

　　Nearing 1½ miles, you reach a signed junction: ahead (right, south) to continue on the Bishop Pass Trail, left (north-northeast) to what the topo and *Place Names of the Sierra Nevada* say are the Marie Louise Lakes and the sign—which may be missing—says are the MARY LOUISE LKS.

　　You curve north-northeast, descending gradually and then steeply, into a flowery, meadowy little valley below Chocolate Peak (to the southeast). You cross the little stream at the valley's bottom and then bear southeast along the meadow's edge to begin a sometimes-steep ascent of the valley's northeast wall on a rocky trail. The grade eases a little as you zigzag up to a tiny bench that offers excellent views of the peaks to the west and of Chocolate Peak.

　　As the trail veers east-southeast into boulders, the **larger Marie Louise Lake at just under 2 miles and 10,620 feet** is only a few feet ahead, half-hidden from view by granite outcrops on your side (west) and backed by a handsome granite cliff on the far side (east). The setting seems tranquil and intimate, sheltered from the jagged peaks that tower over most lakes in this wild region. A beaten path leads to the lake's west shore, where the sense of intimacy lingers in spite of the fact that from the shoreline, you have a splendid view of Chocolate Peak, Mt. Goode, Hurd Peak, and rugged Cloudripper, at 13,525 feet the highest peak of the Inconsolable Range, one of the most dramatic subranges of the Sierra. What a spot for a picnic!

　　The two Marie Louise Lakes are quite close together—close enough to count as a single destination. You're at the larger, slightly lower lake. To visit the smaller, slightly higher lake, pick up a very rough use trail (not on the map) northeast along the larger lake's west shore and follow it as it climbs a little. Where it peters out, scramble a few feet over some talus to the south end of the **smaller Marie Louise**

Lake at 2 miles and 10,640 feet. It's pretty, too, but lacks good picnic spots; you'll want to return to the larger lake for lunch.

Return the way you came.

7. Chocolate Lakes Loop ☼ 🍁

Place	Total Dist.	Elevation	Level	Type
Start	0	9800	—	—
Bull Lake *only*	4½	10,780	M	O&B
Long Lake *only*	4½	10,753	M	O&B
Ruwau Lake *only*	6½	11,044	S	O&B
Entire semiloop	7½	11,340	S	Semi

Permit required: None

Topo(s): Mt. Thompson 7½'

Where to stay:
Mountain: Parcher's Resort, Bishop Creek Lodge, Cardinal Village Resort
Of Interest: None
Other: Town of Bishop

Highlights: This is one of the most scenic trips in this book—and the full trip is one of the most rugged and demanding. But you have lots of wonderful options. You can have a moderate out-and-back trip to splendid Long Lake or to beautiful Bull Lake—provided you head directly to Bull Lake from the Bishop Pass Trail rather than loop around the Chocolate Lakes. It's a strenuous out-and-back trip to lovely Ruwau Lake. Once you commit to going to the Chocolate Lakes, you'll be on a rugged, rocky trail that's more like a use trail and that's often choked with snow until very late season. But what wonderful scenery you'll enjoy and what an adventure you'll have as you work your way down the three Chocolate Lakes to Bull Lake and back to the Bishop Pass Trail!

How to get to the trailhead: Follow the driving directions of Trip 5 to South Lake.

At the trailhead: See Trip 5.

On the trail: See Trip 5's map. From South Lake, follow Trips 5 and 6 up the Bishop Pass Trail, going left at the Treasure Lakes Trail junction, right at the Marie Louise Lakes Trail junction.

Beyond the Marie Louise Lakes junction, a footbridge helps you cross a willow-choked meadow, and soon you're winding up short switchbacks to a fine view of Hurd Lake. You continue zigzagging up with cocoa-topped Chocolate Peak in view ahead, and at almost 2 miles reach the junction with the trail to Bull Lake: left (southeast) to Bull and Chocolate lakes, right (south) to Long Lake and Bishop Pass. The loop part of this trip starts and ends here. If your group is "mixed"— some people want to take the full trip, others want to spend the day relaxing at a beautiful spot—you'll want to find a place where some of you can hang out and all of you can meet up later on. **Bull Lake at 2¼ miles and 10,780 feet**—just ¼ mile away on the left fork—is a great choice.

On the other hand, no one will want to miss Long Lake, a little over ¼ mile more on the right fork, so go right on the Bishop Pass Trail. Islet-dotted **Long Lake at 2¼ miles and 10,753 feet** is breathtaking—a deep-blue jewel in a setting of awesome peaks. The trail rolls along beside the lake for another half-mile before reaching a junction at 2¾ miles with the trail to Ruwau Lake: left (east-northeast) to Ruwau, Chocolate, and—yes—Bull lakes; right (south) to Bishop Lake (Trip 8) and Bishop Pass.

Go left on the narrow track to Ruwau Lake, climbing very steeply for about ⅓ mile, to a bench overlooking Margaret Lake to the west. Catch your breath and continue climbing moderately to rocky, sparkling **Ruwau Lake at 3¼ miles and 11,044 feet**. Trace Ruwau's north shore to an unmarked, unmapped junction where an angler's trail forks right along the shore and your trail begins a sometimes-steep, sometimes-rocky, sometimes-hard-to-follow ascent on the left fork.

The trail breaks its climb by dipping across a rocky chute that trends south to Ruwau, then climbs again to the Ruwau-Chocolate lakes saddle at 4 miles. The saddle is the high point of this trip, an 11,340-foot perch where it seems as if you're so close to 13,525-foot Cloudripper, the highest peak of the Inconsolable Range— a subrange of the Sierra—that you could reach out and touch it. Any questions about why it's called "Cloudripper"? …I didn't think so.

Below you to the northeast lies the highest and largest Chocolate Lake, and the steep chute you must descend is often filled with snow until late season. If that's the case when you're here, I recommend that you retrace your steps from here. If the chute is snow-free, the route is still rough, more like an angler's route than a maintained trail. The topo shows two routes, one to the west, clinging to the side of Chocolate Peak, another to the east that's largely under talus.

The west route is the better choice, so carefully pick your way down it. The highest Chocolate Lake is surrounded by talus, and the trail makes a rocky, loose, up-and-down angler's route along its western edge. In descending along the Chocolate Lakes, you'll see many confusing use trails, but the standard route follows the highest lake's west shore, the middle lake's east shore, and the lowest lake's west shore.

With that in mind, squish through a marsh and cross the stream that connects the highest and middle lakes. Scramble along the middle lake's pretty east shore, then descend a little to cross the stream between the middle and lowest lakes just below the stream's cascade from the middle lake. Climb up and over an outcrop, cross a patch of scree, and descend the meadow that stretches along the lowest lake's west side. Near the north end of the lowest lake, you'll meet a use trail leading to the lake's east side. Continue north here to begin a long, steep, rocky, often damp, northwest-trending descent to Bull Lake, 200 feet below, along the stream that connects the lakes.

Just before you reach Bull Lake, you cross the stream and curve northwest around Bull Lake's lovely north shore. The sight of Chocolate Peak—it should be "Chocolate Sundae Peak"—reflected in Bull Lake is unforgettable. Use trails lead to campsites here and there, so keep a sharp eye out for the main trail—which is finally starting to look like a real main trail again.

Reluctantly leaving behind Bull Lake and the most adventurous part of this trip, you make a short, steep, loose descent, then rise slightly to meet the Bishop Pass Trail, 5½ miles from your start at South Lake and 1½ miles from the saddle.

Turn right (north) onto the Bishop Pass Trail and retrace your steps to the parking lot at South Lake.

8. Bishop Lake ☼ 🍁

Place	Total Dist.	Elevation	Level	Type
Start	0	9800	—	
Long Lake *only*	4½	10,753	M	O&B
Timberline Tarns *only*	7⅓	11,080	S	O&B
Saddlerock Lake *only*	8	11,128	S	O&B
Bishop Lake	8⅔	11,240	S	O&B

Permit required: None

Topo(s): Mt. Thompson, North Palisade 7½'

Where to stay:
   Mountain: Parcher's Resort, Bishop Creek Lodge, Cardinal Village Resort
   Of Interest: None
   Other: Town of Bishop

Highlights: Like Trip 7, this is one of the most scenic trips in this book; unlike Trip 7, it's leisurely, with only gradual-to-moderate climbs. You wander up a magnificent chain of lakes—one of the most beautiful Sierra chains accessible by dayhiking—in a setting of spectacular peaks. Twelve-thousand-foot peaks are so common in this region that most of them aren't even named!

How to get to the trailhead: Follow the driving directions of Trip 5 to South Lake.

At the trailhead: See Trip 5.

On the trail: See Trip 5's map. From South Lake, follow Trips 5, 6, and 7 up the Bishop Pass Trail, going left at the Treasure Lakes Trail junction, right at the Marie Louise Lakes Trail junction, right at the Bull Lake junction, and right at the Ruwau Lake junction.

Beyond the Ruwau Lake junction, you continue above Long Lake and, nearing 3 miles from your start, descend a little to cross one of its inlets—this one happens to be the outlet of Ruwau Lake. There's a sublime over-the-shoulder view of Long Lake and Chocolate Peak from here. Now you begin a steady, gradual-to-moderate climb, passing well above Spearhead Lake, which is quickly turning to meadow. Switchbacks above Spearhead also offer excellent views of Long Lake.

At the top of the climb, you descend a little, cross an outlet stream, pass the westernmost of the pretty **Timberline Tarns at 3⅔ miles and 11,080** feet, and then climb along the lovely cascades that connect Saddlerock Lake above with the Timberline Tarns. You cross the stream to reach austerely beautiful **Saddlerock Lake near 4 miles and at 11,128 feet**; its rocky setting is softened only a little by alpine flowers and by the sparse pines on its northwest shore.

As you continue climbing past Saddlerock, look over to the bench that forms its northwest shore for a glimpse of small Ledge Lake. Soon you pass a seasonal tarn, noted on the topo as a marsh, and then pass a meadow with snow-survey markers. At an unmarked junction near the snow-survey markers, a well-trod use trail veers right (south) to a rise above multi-lobed Bishop Lake, the highest and starkest large lake in the drainage of South Fork Bishop Creek.

Follow that use trail right and a short distance up to the top of the rise, where you find a good perch above **Bishop Lake at 4⅓ miles and 11,240 feet,** and also some storm-stunted whitebark pines that offer a little shelter from the fierce winds that may sweep across the lake. Stop here and savor the awe-inspiring view. Ahead to the south is the headwall of this glacier-carved cirque you've been ascending. To the west is 13,085-foot Mt. Goode; looking eastward from Mt. Goode, Peaks 12,916, 12,689, and 12,286; to the south-southeast, Bishop Pass; to the southeast, 13,893-foot Mt. Agassiz; and to the east, the southeast end of the Inconsolable Range with 13,265-foot Aperture Peak at its end.

Here, the thin, cold air sears the throat and the lungs. Even after the hottest of days, nighttime temperatures drop to freezing, and people camped at Bishop Lake may wake to find ice in their water bottles. All seems stark and lifeless at first, but observant hikers will spy not only their own kind but scurrying rodents, dwarf willows, and some of the loveliest Sierra wildflowers, like Davidson's penstemon and Coville's columbine.

When you can tear yourself away from this alpine splendor, retrace your steps.

9. Sabrina Lakes ☼ 🍁

Place	Total Dist.	Elevation	Level	Type
Start	0	9060	—	—
Blue Lake *only*	6	10,380	S	O&B
Donkey Lake *only*	8½	10,580	S	O&B
Emerald Lakes *only*	8+	10,460	S	O&B
Dingleberry Lake	9⅔	10,489	S	O&B

Permit required: None

Topo(s): Mt. Darwin, Mt. Thompson 7½'

Where to stay:
    Mountain: Parcher's Resort, Bishop Creek Lodge, Cardinal Village Resort
    Of Interest: None
    Other: Town of Bishop

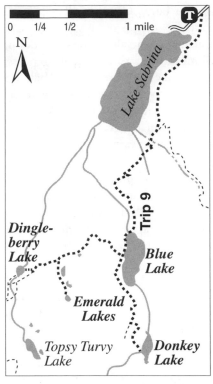

Highlights: Lovely Lake Sabrina makes an inviting start to this wonderful but demanding hike—there's a long climb from Sabrina to your first stop at spectacular Blue Lake. When you see Blue Lake and then the higher lake(s), you'll know the climb was worth it.

How to get to the trailhead: From the traffic-light-controlled intersection of U.S. Highway 395 and West Line Street in the town of Bishop, turn west onto West Line Street (State Route 168) and follow it up into the mountains past the turnoff to South Lake. Stay on Highway 168 (ahead, right) here and continue past the turnoff to North Lake to *day-use* parking just beyond that turnoff at Lake Sabrina, 22.1 miles.

At the trailhead: Lake Sabrina boasts a splendid, peak-ringed setting where non-hikers may enjoy soaking in the sunshine and scenery.

On the trail: Find the trailhead on the left side of the road as you face Lake Sabrina's dam, just below that dam. Head south on a trail as wide as an old road, passing wilderness signs as you go. You soon switchback up and level out overlooking the pine- and aspen-ringed lake, up whose southwest headwall you'll hike to get to this trip's destinations. But for now, you enjoy an easy stroll, climbing very gradually, along Sabrina's rocky, flowery shore.

Nearing a mile, you begin climbing more steeply and presently reach the junction with the trail to George Lake: left (northeast) to George Lake, right (south) to Blue Lake. Go right here, ducking into aspens and crossing George Lake's seasonally roaring outlet. Now you zigzag up a lodgepole-pine-clad slope, and at the next stream crossing (seasonal), you have a great view north over Sabrina toward the White Mountains. The switchbacks carry you up and generally northwest across a ridge overlooking Lake Sabrina and offering sweeping views.

At last you curve south-southeast into a forested draw and follow the trail up short switchbacks to top out by some picturesque tarns above **Blue Lake at 3 miles and 10,380 feet**, spectacularly set beneath Thompson Ridge and the Sierra crest—a sight guaranteed to take your breath away. Hikers throng around Blue Lake—no wonder! But you're going on to more-peaceful shores, and following the trail you wander over granite slabs lining Blue Lake's west shore—the route is marked by lines of rocks. Near 3¼ miles, you descend a little to a junction with the trails to Donkey Lake (left, south) and Emerald and Dingleberry lakes (right, northwest). From Blue Lake you can go to either Donkey Lake *or* to Emerald and Dingleberry

lakes but not to all within the mileage limits of this book. Going to all is certainly possible for sturdy hikers who get an early start.

To go to Donkey Lake. Go left for Donkey Lake, strolling along the duff trail in
the company of numerous flowers, through still meadows, past fine old lodgepoles,
and over rocky outcrops. A little beyond 3¾ miles you come abreast of the Baboon
Lakes' outlet stream and reach a faint junction that may be unmarked: left (east-
southeast) on a rocky trail down toward the stream and to Donkey Lake; right
(south-southwest) on a rocky track toward the Baboon Lakes. (The trail to the
Baboon Lakes, which still appears on some maps, shortly vanishes, and the route
requires boulder-scrambling skills.)

Go left again for Donkey Lake, crossing the stream and picking up the increasingly faint trail on the other side. Bear right (south-southeast) on the other side of
the stream, past a campsite, and wind up a little knoll. With the help of ducks, you
head south-southeast, past a little tarn on your right, and come out on the rocks
above pretty **Donkey Lake's west shore at 4¼ miles and 10,580 feet**. You've earned
the pleasure of having your lunch here!

Retrace your steps from here.

To go to Emerald and Dingleberry lakes. At the junction on Blue Lake's west
shore, go right to Emerald and Dingleberry lakes, bobbing up and down through
lodgepoles and then zigzagging across a slope where the trail has been blasted out
of the granite. There's a fabulous view of Piute Crags from this slope. You pass a
pretty tarn that's an outlier of the Emerald Lakes and then, curving toward the
Sierra crest, meet a spur trail at 3¾ miles—the Emerald-Dingleberry junction—
left (south) to the Emerald Lakes, right (southwest) to Dingleberry.

Go left on the spur trail, across a meadow that may be very muddy, and follow
a well-beaten path generally southward with the help of ducks, past the meadow-
ringed ponds and lakelets that make up lower Emerald Lakes, to an overlook of
upper Emerald Lake. Veer right to descend to the grassy shore of **upper Emerald
Lake a little over 4 miles and at 10,460 feet**. The lake is cupped in a little cirque
under Peak 11,800 (to the south). Around these little lakes, the shorelines blend
into the meadows, and the lakes' waters simply ripple away into stands of tall,
emerald-green grasses. It's an unexpectedly intimate setting for this rugged region,
and the contrast heightens the lakes' beauty.

To go to Dingleberry Lake, return to the Emerald-Dingleberry junction and turn
left (southwest) to Dingleberry. You pass a tarn that's like a giant's bathtub as you
climb gradually, curving around a little valley. At the ridge nose just beyond, you're
treated to great views of the Owens Valley and the White Mountains. Now you hike
over granite slabs to find yourself high above the south end of delightful
Dingleberry Lake. Pick a use trail and descend to the shore, where there are good
rocks to lounge on. **Dingleberry Lake is at a little over 4¾ miles and 10,489 feet**—
including the ⅔ mile to and from upper Emerald Lake. Don't plan on picking dingleberries for lunch; the lake was named, says *Place Names of the Sierra Nevada*, for
"dingleberries" on the fannies of the sheep that once grazed in this area.

Return the way you came.

10. Grass and Lamarck Lakes ☼ 🍁

Place	Total Dist.	Elevation	Level	Type
Start*	0	9260/9362	—	—
Grass Lake *only*	3½	9860	M U	O&B
Lower Lamarck Lake	6¼	10,662	S	O&B
Upper Lamarck Lake	7½	10,918	S	O&B

Permit required: None

Topo(s): Mt. Thompson, Mt. Darwin 7½'

Where to stay:
   Mountain: Parcher's Resort, Bishop Creek Lodge, Cardinal Village Resort
   Of Interest: None
   Other: Town of Bishop

Highlights: Few high-Sierra trips offer both the sheltered feel of little Grass Lake and the open, wild feel of the Lamarck Lakes. Surprisingly few people head for this lovely area; most hikers are bound for the next drainage north, toward Piute Pass (Trip 11). Fine scenery on the way adds to your enjoyment of this trip; aspens along the trail provide good fall color.

How to get to the trailhead: From the traffic-light-controlled intersection of U.S. Highway 395 and West Line Street (State Route 168) in the town of Bishop, turn west and follow State Route 168 up into the mountains past the turnoff to South Lake to the turnoff to North Lake, just before Lake Sabrina. Turn right onto the North Lake road and follow this narrow, sometimes-unpaved road on an airy traverse of the ridge separating North Lake and Lake Sabrina. You turn into the pretty valley that holds little North Lake, pass the lake on your right, and a little beyond it, turn right on the marked spur to the pack station and to parking. Pass the pack station's entrance and continue to one of two parking lots for hikers, 19.7 miles.

The official trailhead is ½ mile farther up the road, at the upper end of North Lake Campground, but you can't park there, although you can let passengers and equipment off there. So, for all practical purposes, your trip starts here, at the parking lots. Toilet at the parking lots, toilets and water in the campground.

At the trailhead: East of the parking lot, meadowy little North Lake is a delightful spot, though it's hardly more than a puddle compared to lakes like South Lake and Lake Sabrina. Look for a picnic site on its north shore, not its marshy south shore. On its way to fill North Lake, Grass Lake's noisy outlet makes a showy cascade down the southwest side of this valley. Flowers throughout the valley delight the eye; in season, the marshy area near the pack station may be a sheet of wild blue iris. The many aspens make this area a fall-color treat.

On the trail: Mileages for this trip assume that you start at the parking lot and that you make the ½-mile, 100-foot loss/gain, out-and-back visit to Grass Lake.

* 9260 feet at the parking lot (where this trip starts); 9362 at the trailhead in the campground (where you can't park but can drop off some of your party and gear).

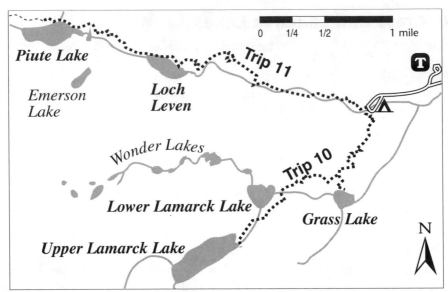

From the parking lot, walk back on the spur road past the pack station, and turn right on the North Lake Road. Follow the road to the campground and take either branch of the campground road—the right branch is slightly shorter—to a parking spot for some walk-in sites at ½ mile at the upper end of the campground, where the road is blocked so that cars can't continue. Continue on the blocked-off road a few more feet to the marked trailhead: left (south) to Grass and Lamarck lakes, right (west) to Loch Leven, Piute Lake, and Piute Pass.

Go left through a delightful mix of forest and flowers. You cross three little wooden footbridges (not shown on the book's map), pass a use trail on the left, and shortly begin a long series of moderate switchbacks. From this ascent, the orange-tinted rock of rugged Piute Crags makes splendid backdrop to the green shimmer of aspen leaves along the trail. You slant up a boulder-strewn slope and then briefly level out on a delightful, lodgepole-shaded bench. You soon resume the switchbacks, and at 1½ miles you reach the Grass Lake-Lamarck Lakes junction: left (south) to Grass Lake, right (northwest) to the Lamarck Lakes.

Go left to Grass Lake, at first proceeding levelly across a lodgepole- and boulder-studded moraine at about 9960 feet. Then, as you begin a rocky descent of about 100 feet, a broad meadow comes into view. Soon you're at meadowed **Grass Lake at 1¾ miles and 9860 feet**—no need to ask where it gets its name—which is cupped by forested slopes. An obvious saddle to the south will make you wonder, *What's over there?* (You'll get an answer on the next leg.) Rocks and logs around Grass's edges provide good spots from which to savor this pretty setting, 1¾ miles from your start. Return to the Grass-Lamarck junction when you're ready.

Back at the Grass-Lamarck junction—2 miles into the trip now—you turn right (northwest) to the Lamarck Lakes. You soon resume your switchbacking ascent and get an answer to your earlier question when, briefly, you have a view over the saddle south of Grass to the beautiful glaciers and peaks of distant Thompson Ridge, on the far side of Lake Sabrina. You leave the forest behind and switchback across open slopes pungent with sagebrush, enjoying wonderful views of the North Fork Bishop Creek drainage east to the White Mountains. The views from unforested stretches of the trail are increasingly expansive as you rise. Having passed a pond just below the trail on your right, you reach beautiful **Lower Lamarck Lake at just over 3 miles and 10,662 feet**, slightly off-trail to your right. It lies under the stern gaze of Peaks 12153 and 12691, cradled in granite and outlined by stunted lodgepoles and whitebarks. You'll find some nice picnic rocks around its edge.

Reluctantly leaving Lower Lamarck Lake, you dip across its outlet just below a lovely pool, round an outcrop, and begin walking up a narrow valley. The sandy trail crosses the valley and traverses rocky slopes, where a wonderful view of Lower Lamarck Lake and its dashing inlet stream opens up on your right. You pass a use trail down to the lake's shore and instead begin switchbacking steeply up the east side of the inlet-outlet stream's gully, curving southwest with the gully. You cross the stream about halfway up and continue the loose ascent on the gully's west side until you reach a beautiful, stream-threaded meadow below Upper Lamarck Lake. Here you may see a sign pointing out the cross-country route that goes south over trailless Lamarck Col and into Darwin Canyon—a route that's only for the highly experienced and well-prepared backpacker!

Turn west-southwest on the main trail, cross the outlet stream once more just below the lake, and emerge at the **Upper Lamarck Lake at 3¾ miles and 10,918 feet**. The lake is big by high Sierra standards, a long sheet of brilliant blue water that seems to end abruptly at a steep moraine. On the crest, slightly to the left of the far end of the lake, you'll see Mt. Lamarck; Lamarck Col is a little left of it; Peak 12153 towers to the right. Picnic spots are few at this rockbound beauty, so after feasting your eyes here, you may want to take your lunch back to Lower Lamarck Lake for that picnic.

Return the way you came.

11. Loch Leven and Piute Lake ☼ ❦

Place	Total Dist.	Elevation	Level	Type
Start*	0	9260/9362	–	–
Loch Leven *only*	6⅔	10,743	S	O&B
Piute Lake	8⅔–9+	10,958	S	O&B

Permit required: None

Topo(s): Mt. Thompson, Mt. Darwin 7½'

Where to stay:
   Mountain: Parcher's Resort, Bishop Creek Lodge, Cardinal Village Resort
   Of Interest: None
   Other: Town of Bishop

* 9260 feet at the parking lot (where this trip starts); 9362 at the trailhead in the campground (where you can't park but can drop off some of your party and gear).

Highlights: The walk up North Fork Bishop Creek toward Piute Pass ranks as one of the most scenic in the Sierra. The first leg is famous for its summer flower gardens and fall color; the third leg takes you along a string of glorious ponds and lakes. Marking the abrupt altitude change on the second leg, the creek splashes out of a pool below Loch Leven and over 300 feet down a narrow slot in the rocks—a cool sight for a hot climb. This is a very popular as well as a spectacular trail.

How to get to the trailhead: Follow the driving instructions of Trip 10.

At the trailhead: See Trip 10.

On the trail: See Trip 10's map. As detailed in Trip 10, start from the parking lot and walk back on the spur road, pass the pack station, turn right on the main road, and follow it into the upper campground past its blocked-off end and to the Grass/Lamarck-Loch Leven/Piute junction.

Go right (west) toward Piute Pass on a rocky, very dusty trail favored by equestrians. Moderate forest cover is interspersed with openings that offer lush, brilliantly colored wildflowers. The trail gradually swings nearer the creek, where the flower display gets even better, and you have occasional glimpses of orange-y Piute Crags and of Mt. Emerson. Around 1¼ miles, you cross the creek twice—may be difficult in early season. Beyond here, open spots begin to offer wonderful over-the-shoulder views down-canyon—good excuses to pause and catch your breath. Nearing 2 miles, the forest cover dwindles to scattered whitebark pines on the scree and talus slopes below Piute Crags and Mt. Emerson; this leg can get very hot on a warm day. The trail ascends in lazy, dusty switchbacks, and the roar of water signals you to look for the cascade below Loch Leven.

At 2¾ miles you begin winding moderately to steeply up stone "stairs" through granite outcrops on a reconstructed segment of the trail. Back on the older trail, you turn west past a pond below Loch Leven, climb a little more, and emerge a little above **Loch Leven at 3⅓ miles and 10,743 feet**—the prettiest lake in this chain, I think. The trail descends to Loch Leven's shore, where you have an exhilarating view west over the lake toward Piute Pass. The trail then follows the rocky shore, where there are plenty of little picnic spots under the whitebark pines. As if to defy the high altitude and the long, bitter winters, abundant wildflowers carpet the shoreline and shelter among the boulders here.

Continuing, you wander through beautiful meadows and up past several more picturesque ponds and lakelets, each different, yet all brightened by the same sturdy alpine wildflowers. You pass a probably-defunct stock fence as the now-sandy, now-rocky trail ascends gradually. Be sure to pause often to enjoy views up and down this spectacular canyon.

You reach windswept **Piute Lake at 4⅓ miles and 10,958 feet**, the largest in this chain. There's a snow-survey cabin on the south side of its outlet—don't disturb it. Follow the trail along the north side of this beautiful lake as far as a multibranched inlet stream at 4½ miles. Beyond here, the trail climbs again, and you'll find numerous perches from which you can enjoy lunch as you take in the incredible panorama up toward the crest and down toward Owens Valley. It doesn't look it from here, but 11,423-foot Piute Pass lies almost 1½ miles farther on, nearly 6 miles from your start, so this is a great place to stop.

Retrace your steps to the trailhead.

12. Francis and Dorothy Lakes ☼ 🍁

Place	Total Dist.	Elevation	Level	Type
Start	0	9695	—	—
Francis Lake *only*	5½	10,860	M	O&B
Dorothy Lake *only*	6	10,500	M	O&B
Both lakes	8½	10,860	S	O&B

Permit required: None

Topo(s): Mt. Morgan 7½'

Where to stay:
   Mountain: Rock Creek Lakes Resort, Rock Creek Lodge, Convict Lake Resort
   Of Interest: Tom's Place, Rainbow Tarns, Sierra Gables Motel, Mono Sierra Lodge
   Other: Town of Mammoth Lakes

Highlights: You may wonder what you've got yourself into on the first part of this journey, which is up and across the top of a large, dry, sandy moraine. Good, because that makes beautiful, meadow-blessed Francis and Dorothy lakes all the more fun to discover. Francis's setting is more rugged, Dorothy's more flowery and tranquil; both are delightful.

How to get to the trailhead: From U.S. Highway 395, turn west on Rock Creek Road at Tom's Place and cross Crowley Lake Drive. Follow the road through a dry pinyon-pine forest and past several turnoffs into campgrounds, past the turnoff to Rock Creek Lodge, as far as the turnoff left to Rock Creek Lake and Rock Creek Lake Campground, which is just past the first turnoff right to Rock Creek Lakes Resort. Turn left as if for Rock Creek Lake Campground and follow the spur road past picnic areas and into the campground parking lot. The trailhead is actually in the campground; look for parking spaces marked for day use rather than for camping, on the east side of the spur road, opposite a cinderblock restroom, about 9.2 miles from 395. Some spaces are reserved for those camping here, so be sure *you* pick a day-use space. Toilets, water; store and cafe at nearby Rock Creek Lakes Resort.

At the trailhead: Rock Creek Lake is a lovely spot, perfect for relaxing. Aspens throughout this valley lend dramatic colors in fall. You'll find picnic tables here along the shoreline; little strolls around the sandy lakeshore are sure to please (it's possible to loop all the way around the lake if the water isn't too high).

On the trail: At the TAMARACK TRAILHEAD sign, curve right at the sign (left goes into a campsite) and begin a steady, moderate-to-steep climb under sparse lodgepole cover on a rocky-sandy trail, east-northeast up a gully on the moraine east of Rock Creek Lake. This initial climb can be hot on a sunny day. In ¼ mile you reach a **T**-junction with an old road (shown as a trail on the book's map); turn left (north) here and follow the old road up, heading generally east and enjoying views toward Mono Pass (south) and over Rock Creek Lake. From here to the turnoff to Kenneth Lake, your hiking route overlaps the Sand Canyon Mountain Bike Trail.

A little beyond ½ mile, the grade eases in the welcome shade of a clump of lodgepoles, and you have fine over-the-shoulder views of Mt. Huntington, Mt. Stanford, and Rock Creek Lake. Still on the old road, you ramble through dry forest, climbing gradually, to a junction at nearly 1 mile: left (northeast) to Wheeler Crest, right (east) to Kenneth, Dorothy, and Francis lakes.

Go right to Kenneth Lake, shortly entering the John Muir Wilderness, crossing a low ridge, and skirting a meadow. Work your way up a shallow draw to a sandy, lupine-dotted saddle, from which you have magnificent views of Mt. Morgan, Broken Finger Peak, and Wheeler Ridge. Descending, you cross another meadow, wander over another low ridge, this one pleated with little gullies, and reach another junction at 1⅔ miles: right (south) to Francis Lake, left (ahead, east) to Kenneth, Dorothy, and Tamarack lakes. We'll call this the Francis-Kenneth junction.

To go to Francis Lake, at the Francis-Kenneth junction, take the right fork and begin climbing steeply. The grade soon eases, and you begin a gradual-to-moderate traverse of this slope, from which you can look down on Kenneth Lake. After crossing a seasonal trickle, you reach the willow-choked outlet of Francis Lake, along which you ascend moderately to steeply, with the help of a few switchbacks. Whitebarks replace the lodgepoles as you climb, and midway you swing west of the outlet. The trail levels off as it swings back toward the outlet, and there are

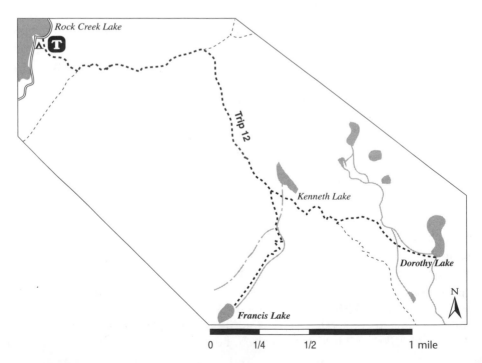

wonderful flower gardens along the stream here. You continue along the outlet to the north shore of sparkling **Francis Lake at 2¾ miles and 10,860 feet**. The gentle meadow immediately around this pretty lake contrasts wonderfully with the surrounding rugged slopes that are outliers of Mt. Morgan and Broken Finger Peak. There's a fine lunch-rock on the other side of the outlet. Retrace your steps when you're ready to leave.

To go to Dorothy Lake, at the Francis-Kenneth junction, take the left fork over one more ridgelet and descend to pretty Kenneth Lake, which by late season in a dry year may be little more than "Kenneth Puddle" and which may even dry up completely late in a very dry year. But there's a fine wildflower display here, deep in the meadow that Kenneth's shrinkage has left behind. After crossing a seasonal inlet, you ascend another ridge moderately to steeply, enjoying good views from open spots. At 2¼ miles from your start, *not* including a jaunt to Francis Lake, you reach another junction: left (east) to Dorothy Lake, right (southeast) to the Tamarack Lakes (beyond the mileage limits of this book). Go left to Dorothy, soon spotting a broad, flower-strewn meadow along a bright stream below to your left. Descending from the ridge to the meadow, you walk through the meadow, hopping over streamlets, toward Broken Finger Peak. You arrive at the south end of lovely **Dorothy Lake at 3 miles and 10,500 feet**, where the inlet and outlet streams are only a few steps apart. In late season, the display of gentians in Dorothy Lake's meadow is dazzling. The topo shows a maintained trail looping around Dorothy's east side and back to an old road that (says the topo) connects with the old road you hiked between the **T**-junction at ¼ mile and the junction where the foot trail turned off to Kenneth, Dorothy, and Francis lakes. As far as I could tell, that trail does not exist. Instead, a faint angler's path loops right around Dorothy Lake, and you'll find some nice picnic spots here and along that path.

When you're ready, retrace your steps to the trailhead.

13. Hilton Lakes ☼ ❦

Place	Total Dist.	Elevation	Level	Type
Start	0	9860	–	–
Hilton Lake 3* *only*	8⅔	10,300	S U	O&B
Hilton Lake 4*	10	10,353	S U	O&B
Hilton Lake 2* *only*	10	9852	S U	O&B
Davis Lk. (Hilton Lk. 1)* *only*	10+	9808	S U	O&B

Permit required: None

Topo(s): Mt. Morgan, Mt. Abbot, Convict Lake 7½'

* First, you must top a ridge on a saddle at 10,380 feet—higher than any of the lakes—before descending to the junction where you select which lake(s) to see. Second, it's not within the mileage limits of this book to see all four lakes, so you need to choose. Within this book's range you can see Hilton Lakes 3 and 4, *or* Hilton Lake 2, *or* Davis Lake; see **Highlights** for some criteria. All four lakes are within the range of sturdy hikers who get an early start.

Where to stay:
　　Mountain: Rock Creek Lakes Resort, Rock
　　　　Creek Lodge, Convict Lake Resort
　　Of Interest: Tom's Place, Rainbow Tarns,
　　　　Sierra Gables Motel, Mono Sierra Lodge
　　Other: Town of Mammoth Lakes

Highlights: After a long, long traverse and a climb over the ridge between Rock and Hilton creeks, this trail leads to a junction where you'll have to choose which lake(s) to see. To the south and higher are Hilton Lakes 3 and 4, which will appeal to lovers of open, alpine lakes; both are within the range of this book. To the north and lower are Hilton Lake 2 and Davis Lake, which will appeal to those who prefer their lakes densely fringed by forest. You'll have to choose further between going to Hilton Lake 2, the prettier, or Davis Lake, which has tiny beaches. But you can't lose, whichever way you go.

Hilton Creek Lakes

How to get to the trailhead: As for Trip 12, from U.S. Highway 395 turn west on Rock Creek Road at Tom's Place, cross Crowley Lake Drive, and follow the road past Rock Creek Lake to a parking area on the right side of the road, 9.3 miles from 395. The Hilton Lakes trailhead is about 400 feet back down the road from here. No facilities; toilets and water in Rock Creek Lake Campground; store and cafe at nearby Rock Creek Lakes Resort.

At the trailhead: Nearby Rock Creek Lake offers picnic spots and great scenery. See Trip 12.

On the trail: You immediately begin a gradual-to-moderate climb north-northeast, first through a lodgepole-aspen forest, then on exposed slopes that boast an amazing array of flowers in season. A switchback turn affords excellent views over Rock Creek Lake and the peaks south, around Little Lakes Valley, and tantalizing glimpses into the basin west of Wheeler Ridge, where Trip 12 goes. Nearing ½ mile, you cross a seasonal channel, and at ⅔ mile cross a stream and reach the John Muir Wilderness boundary. You ford a few more creeks and dry channels and note that a junction shown on the 7½' topo, with a steep trail down to Pine Grove Campground, no longer exists. As this long, very gradually descending traverse continues, you start to wonder if you'll wind up back at Tom's Place.

But a little past 1⅔ miles, the trail curves northwest, dips across a forested gully, and then swings up the next ridge, through shrubby aspens. A little past 2 miles, you reach a junction whose left fork has been intentionally blocked off; you go right (northwest) and enjoy glimpses of Peaks 11950 and 11962 upslope on your left.

You curve through an open, sandy forest of lodgepoles and skirt a large meadow that's fringed with aspen and invaded by lodgepoles, then curve generally west around the bases of Peaks 11950 and 11962. Around 2⅔ miles, the grade increases, and you slog uphill on the wide, sandy trail to top out on a saddle at 10,380 feet—higher than any of the lakes—north of Peak 11962, where you glimpse the Sierra crest through breaks in the forest. Heading west toward Peak 12508, you cross an area covered by the sun-bleached trunks of trees felled by an avalanche in the early 1980s. The re-established trail dodges through this giant-sized game of pick-up sticks and descends on gradual-to-moderate switchbacks to a pocket meadow and then a trail junction at 4 miles: left (southwest) to Hilton Lakes 3 and 4; right (north) to Hilton Lake 2 and Davis Lake.

To Hilton Lakes 3 and 4. From the junction at 4 miles, go left to cross a seasonal stream, pass a small meadow, and begin a series of unrelenting switchbacks up, leveling out at fabulous views northward over Hilton Lake 2, Davis Lake, and across Long Valley to Glass Ridge. You cross the stream connecting Lakes 3 and 2; Hilton Lake 3 is visible upstream. The main trail is rather faint around here. Leave it and briefly follow a use trail upstream to the lake's edge, where you find a breathtaking alpine scene: flower-ringed **Hilton Lake 3 at 4⅓ miles and 10,300 feet**, with a dramatic backdrop of Mts. Huntington and Stanford.

Now return to the main trail, which crosses the stream and curves southwest along the lake's northwest shore—contrary to what the 7½′ topo says, there's no trail branching left to the next-higher set of lakes. The trail then veers west across a low ridge from which you have a fine view of the dashing cascades of Hilton Lake 5's outlet. You descend to cross the outlet in a meadow, bob over another ridgelet, and reach **Hilton Lake 4 at almost 5 miles and 10,353 feet.** This lake is another glorious alpine sight, and the stunning peak on the lake's far side is Mt. Huntington. When you can tear yourself away, retrace your steps.

To Hilton Lake 2 or Davis Lake. From the junction at 4 miles, go right, generally northwest, soon crossing a boggy area in moderate-to-dense lodgepole forest. You make a gradual-to-moderate descent, then angle across a lightly wooded slope and soon spot Hilton Lake 2 below. You reach an unmarked **Y**-junction a little more than ½ mile beyond the junction at 4 miles, 4½ miles total from your start: left (north-northwest) to Hilton Lake 2; right (north) to Davis Lake.

To Hilton Lake 2. Going left at the unmarked **Y**-junction, you descend gradually, curve around a knoll, and, as you approach Hilton Lake 2's outlet stream, meet a use trail and hook abruptly left on it. A log jam backs up the outlet a little below the lake and creates a lush, very wet meadow. You reach stunning, forested, cliff-backed **Hilton Lake 2 at 5 miles and 9852 feet.** Retrace your steps from here.

To Davis Lake. After going right at the unmarked **Y**-junction, you meet a second **Y**-junction, this one unmarked and unmapped, in just a few steps. Go right (northeast) to Davis Lake, through dense, spindly lodgepoles and stepping over a streamlet where there's a long, grassy meadow to your right. You pass more grassy meadows on your left as the trail curves toward Davis Lake, soon visible through the trees. Continuing, you shortly find use trails darting west to tiny, sandy coves at pretty **Davis Lake at just over 5 miles and 9808 feet.** Pick a use trail to the shore, where you can soak your toes in water that's warm for the Sierra and enjoy a picnic. Retrace your steps from here.

14. Little Lakes Valley ☼ ❦

Place	Total Dist.	Elevation	Level	Type
Start	0	10,230	—	—
Viewpt by Mono-Morgan jct *only*	1	10,460	E	O&B
Marsh Lake *only*	2	10,420	E	O&B
Heart Lake *only*	2½	10,420	E	O&B
Long Lake, south end *only*	4	10,540	M	O&B
Gem Lake, highest	6½	10,940	S	O&B

Permit required: None

Topo(s): WP Mt. Abbot 15'; Mt. Morgan, Mt. Abbot 7½'

Where to stay:
    Mountain: Rock Creek Lakes Resort, Rock Creek Lodge, Convict Lake Resort
    Of Interest: Tom's Place, Rainbow Tarns, Sierra Gables Motel, Mono Sierra Lodge
    Other: Town of Mammoth Lakes

Highlights: What can you say about a trail that starts at the Sierra's highest trail-head and, climbing gradually for the most part, carries you past spectacular flower gardens and one pretty lake after another, all in a valley ringed by some of the range's loveliest peaks? You'd say, "Let's go see it!"

How to get to the trailhead: As for Trip 12, from U.S. Highway 395, turn west on Rock Creek Road at Tom's Place, cross Crowley Lake Drive, and follow the road past the Hilton Lakes trailhead. The road gets quite narrow beyond Rock Creek Lake. Follow it to its end at Mosquito Flat, 10.7 miles from 395. There's plenty of parking for this trailhead—extremely popular in spite of the fact that Mosquito Flat comes by its name honestly. Toilets.

At the trailhead: This is a very beautiful trailhead, situated along an exceptionally scenic stretch of Rock Creek. Look for picnic tables in the pines across the creek (bridged); they're for a one-night campground *only* for backpackers starting a trip from Mosquito Flat the next day—a properly-issued permit is necessary to establish your right to occupy a site. Even non-hikers, if ambulatory, should follow this trip to the viewpoint near the junction of Morgan and Mono pass trails—read "On the trail" below to learn about the pleasures of that brief stretch.

On the trail: Roughly paralleling Rock Creek on the creek's west side, the broad, sandy trail is nearly level at first, soon enters John Muir Wilderness, and begins climbing moderately through a dazzling flower garden that's perhaps the best in the Eastern Sierra in season. A little short of ½ mile you reach a **Y**-junction: left (south) to Little Lakes Valley and Morgan Pass; right (southwest) to Mono Pass— the southern of two Mono Passes in the Eastern Sierra. Be sure to top the little rise you've been climbing to find a spectacular **viewpoint at ½ mile and 10,460 feet:** of Mack Lake, below to your left (east) and beyond it of Mt. Morgan; of hulking, bare Mt. Starr to the west; and of the glorious semicircle of peaks at the head of Little Lakes Valley to the south, including Mts. Mills, Abbot, and Dade, and Bear Creek Spire.

From the **Y**-junction, go left to Little Lakes Valley, descending across a noisy, flower-lined inlet and leveling out near the grassy south end of Mack Lake at nearly ⅔ mile. The trail rises and falls gradually as you stroll past broad-meadowed **Marsh Lake at 1 mile at 10,420 feet**, then sparkling **Heart Lake near 1¼ miles and 10,420 feet**—there are good lunch rocks here. Heart Lake has multiple inlets; you boulder-hop one, cross another on a footbridge (the footbridge isn't shown on the book's map). At the south end of Heart Lake, a use trail veers left toward Heart's east shore, but you stick to the main trail, which rises a little along another of Heart's inlets, up a tiny, narrow, meadowed valley, topping out above handsome Box Lake. From this viewpoint, you can see two more little lakes east of Box. They belong to a cluster of lakelets, the Hidden Lakes, that are almost completely surrounded by very wet meadows. You descend to the south end of Box Lake at a little over 1½ miles.

After a gentle-to-moderate ascent along the stream connecting Box and Long lakes, you cross that stream—may be difficult in early season—a little beyond 1¾

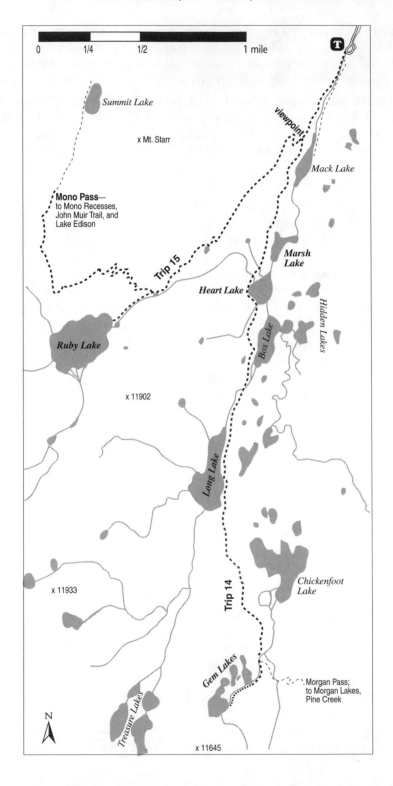

Marsh Lake

miles and soon reach splendid Long Lake, perhaps the most beautiful lake in this chain. Across the lake rise peaks whose rocks form bands of black and white. You traverse Long Lake's east shore below a low cliff; at the grassy south end of **Long Lake at just over 2 miles and 10,540 feet**, you'll find some good lunch rocks.

Now you make a gradual ascent to a junction at a little beyond 2⅔ miles with a spur trail (not on the map) that goes left (northeast) to Chickenfoot Lake, a total out-and-back excursion of about ¼ mile if you'd like to scamper over to see it. The wide main trail goes right (south) here, dipping across a culvert. This trail was once a road to the tungsten mines in the next drainage south, Pine Creek, via Morgan Pass, and along this next stretch you may see a few rusting remnants of mining vehicles. Nowadays, there's a far better road to the mines, which are currently inactive, right up Pine Creek.

The road/trail curves left (east) toward Morgan Pass and crosses a rock-filled stream. You can plainly see the old road climbing steeply to Morgan Pass, which has a nice view of the Gem Lakes. But you haven't come this far just to *look* at the Gem Lakes. You want to *go* there. Just across a rocky streambed at nearly 3 miles, you reach an unsigned and rather obscure junction: left (east) to Morgan Pass; right (south) to the three lovely Gem Lakes. (If you start climbing toward Morgan Pass, you've overshot this junction.) Turn right to Gem Lakes, reaching the shore of the easternmost Gem Lake at 3 miles—truly a gem. Angler's trails lead you on an up-and-down route to the next two lakes. You reach the **third and highest Gem Lake at almost 3¼ miles and 10,940 feet**, nestled below Peak 11645. Any of these lakes makes a great lunch stop.

You won't want to leave, but when you must, retrace your steps to the trailhead.

15. Mono Pass ☼ 🍁

Place	Total Dist.	Elevation	Level	Type
Start	0	10,230	—	—
Viewpt by Mono-Morgan jct *only*	1	10,460	E	O&B
Ruby Lake *only*	4½	11,121	S	O&B
Mono Pass	9	12,060	S	O&B

Permit required: None

Topo(s): WP Mt. Abbot 15′; Mt. Morgan, Mt. Abbot 7½′

Where to stay:
   Mountain: Rock Creek Lakes Resort, Rock Creek Lodge, Convict Lake Resort
   Of Interest: Tom's Place, Rainbow Tarns, Sierra Gables Motel, Mono Sierra Lodge
   Other: Town of Mammoth Lakes

Highlights: After enjoying the flowers and the excellent views on the first leg of this trip, you climb steeply to a spur to high Ruby Lake, then to lofty Mono Pass. It's a demanding but very rewarding trip. At 12,060 feet, Mono Pass is the highest point reached by any hike in this book!

How to get to the trailhead: See Trip 14.

At the trailhead: See Trip 14.

On the trail: See Trip 14's map. Follow Trip 14 up the Mono-Morgan pass trail to the **Y**-junction near ½ mile. After having visited the spectacular **viewpoint at ½ mile and 10,460 feet**, go right (southwest) to the southern Mono Pass, climbing moderately to steeply and soon meeting a junction with a spur trail (not shown on the book's map) from the pack station. Turn left (southwest) here and continue climbing, passing a beautiful little tarn near 1½ miles and enjoying the view of the white granite walls and peaks to the south.

At almost 2 miles you reach a junction with the spur to Ruby Lake, by a lovely pond on Ruby's outlet. Go left (southwest) on the spur trail, passing an obvious campsite, crossing a meadow, and climbing a little along the outlet. You reach **Ruby Lake at 2¼ miles and 11,121 feet**. It's ringed by whitebarks and almost completely surrounded by beautiful, light-colored granite cliffs. Ruby Lake is a real treat if you love alpine lakes, and makes a nice spot for lunch.

Retrace your steps to the main trail, having now put 2½ miles on your boots, and turn left (west) toward Mono Pass. You switchback steeply up Mt. Starr's slope, high above Ruby Lake, before breaking your climb with a traverse around Mt. Starr's south ridge. There are breathtaking views over Little Lakes Valley from this part of the trail, and they make good excuses for needed rest stops.

Now you resume your climb through wonderfully empty alpine country toward the pass, which you soon spy far ahead: a notch filled with sky, bitten out of the light-gray granite of the Sierra Crest. You work your way up a sandy draw, through tumbled rocks and over a tiny moraine, to arrive—gasp, wheeze—at **Mono Pass at 4½ miles and 12,060 feet**. The scene is stark: acres of shattered granite, unrelieved by vegetation (unless you look very closely to find tough alpine plants sheltering here and there), set against the extraordinarily deep-blue sky characteristic of this elevation. Just west of the pass you'll have a view of little Summit Lake, a turquoise oval set in cream-colored rocks. Other than that, the pass itself has few views; the best views are from the traverse you made below the pass. Pull up a rock, take out your lunch, and savor the triumph of having bagged Mono Pass.

But at last you must retrace your steps to the trailhead.

16. Grass Lake ☼ ❦

Place	Total Dist.	Elevation	Level	Type
Start	0	8136	—	—
Meadow *only*	6	9055	M	O&B
Grass Lake	10+	9826	S	O&B

Permit required: None

Topo(s): Convict Lake 7½'

Where to stay:
   Mountain: Rock Creek Lakes Resort, Rock Creek Lodge, Convict Lake Resort
   Of Interest: Tom's Place, Rainbow Tarns, Sierra Gables Motel, Mono Sierra Lodge
   Other: Town of Mammoth Lakes

Highlights: In season, one of the Eastern Sierra's finest flower gardens blooms along and above McGee Creek on the first leg of this hike. Beyond, an idyllic meadow beckons you; farther on and high above the canyon, you find meadowed Grass Lake. Colorful layers of metamorphosed rock make the McGee Canyon's walls a delight to the eye, and the aspen-lined creek is an explosion of fall color in season.

How to get to the trailhead: From U.S. Highway 395, turn southwest onto signed McGee Canyon Road. You have overshot this turnoff if you get to the Mammoth Lakes junction with State Route 203 while northbound or Toms Place while southbound. You shortly cross Crowley Lake Drive and continue southwest deeper into the canyon. You pass a campground turnoff and the pack station, and continue to the parking loop at the roadend, 3.2 miles, east of the old trailhead shown on the topo. Toilets.

At the trailhead: From the trailhead parking loop, use trails lead to the stream and to picnic tables near it in the fluttering shade of aspens. The view from the parking loop of McGee Canyon's colorful walls and peaks is marvelous.

On the trail: An old road that once served a now-vanished campground runs nearer the stream and its sheltering aspens, but your official trail leaves from the upper end of the parking loop, near its end on the right as you face into the canyon. You begin a gradual southwest ascent up a treeless, sandy moraine covered with low, colorful, fragrant high-desert shrubs.

The lack of trees allows spectacular views of McGee Canyon's walls: layers, sometimes swirled, of brick-reds, a range of browns, grays from light to charcoal, and, in the right light, tints of lavender and green. These are some of the most beautiful canyon walls in the Sierra. They're made largely of metamorphosed ancient seafloor that once overlay the gray granite for which the Sierra is better known. The forces that thrust the granite up also pushed the seafloor layers up and aside, crushed them, tilted them, twisted them, and left them to be stripped away by erosion, exposing the granite. Because the metamorphic layers once formed a "roof" over the buried granite but now consist of scattered remains left "pendant" in the great bodies of granite, the remnants are referred to as "roof pendants." Roof pendants can be huge, making up entire mountains, like "Red and Gold Mountain," site of the Mammoth Consolidated Gold Mine near Mammoth Lakes (see Trip 20), and entire subranges, like the Tioga Crest between Lee Vining and Yosemite (see the section on Highway 120). Dissolved minerals are especially likely to precipitate out of solution and be deposited at the junctions of roof pendants and granite, called "contact zones." Many Sierra mines were located on or near such contact zones.

You'll be delighted to find that your route, which looks desert-like from a distance, often intersects seeps, springs, and tributary streams that nourish wonderful flower gardens. As you continue, Mt. Baldwin and its handsome outliers come into view. You traverse a thicket of stunted aspens, cross multiple streams, and look upslope, to your right, for several pretty cascades, including a long, prominent one named Horsetail Falls. Curving south, you traverse a ledge offering nice views up and down canyon and finally, around 2½ miles, cross McGee Creek—difficult in early season. The crossing is confusing because of compet-

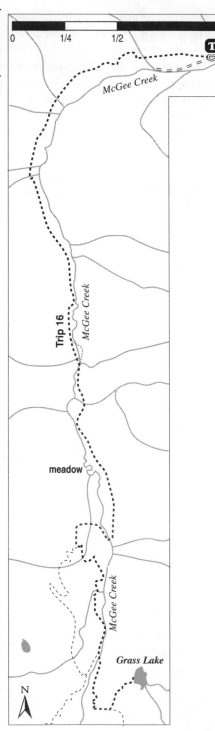

ing use trails, but your goal is to pick up the trail on the east side of the creek and continue upstream.

Gray cliffs define the canyon's west wall as you reach a beautiful **meadow near 3 miles and 9055 feet**, where the stream slows down to form sandy-bottomed pools as it meanders amid willows and grasses. Use trails lead down to the meadow, and you'll be tempted to stop here, especially if you're an angler.

Back on the main trail, you traverse a boulder field as the canyon narrows, forcing you to cross the creek again—also difficult in early season—at an outcrop. You curve north around the outcrop and then ascend gradually through moderate forest cover, to a fork at 3⅔ miles: left (east, then south) for foot traffic, right (south) for stock. You go left here, soon crossing a tributary creek, then regaining the main creek, to a junction near 4½ miles: left (south) to Grass and Steelhead lakes, right (southwest) to McGee Pass.

Go left, cross the creek, and begin a steep climb on lodgepole-shaded switchbacks, enjoying great views down-canyon as well as toward the peaks to the west. The grade eases as you approach a junction near 5 miles: left (northeast) to Grass Lake, right (east) to Steelhead Lake. Go left and reach pretty **Grass Lake at a whisker past 5 miles and 9826 feet**, fed at its south end by the long, cascading outlet of Steelhead Lake and seemingly set right underneath Mt. Stanford (to the east-southeast). Its meadowy shore offers some nice picnic spots.

Retrace your steps to the trailhead.

17. Convict Lake 🌸 ☼ 🍁

Place	Total Dist.	Elevation	Level	Type
Start	0	7620	—	—
Entire trip	3	7660	E	Semi

Permit required: None

Topo(s): Convict Lake 7½'

Where to stay:
  Mountain: Rock Creek Lakes Resort, Rock Creek Lodge, Convict Lake Resort
  Of Interest: Tom's Place, Rainbow Tarns, Sierra Gables Motel, Mono Sierra Lodge
  Other: Town of Mammoth Lakes

Highlights: Like adjacent McGee Canyon, the canyon cradling Convict Lake is a marvelous layer-cake of metamorphic rock. Aspens and cottonwoods along Convict Creek and Convict Lake glow with color in the fall. To shorten the hike by nearly 2 miles, start from one of the parking lots on Convict Lake's east or southeast shore and avoid the out-and-back from the hiker's parking lot. This makes the trip a loop.

How to get to the trailhead: From U.S. Highway 395 nearly abreast of Mammoth Airport, turn south-southwest on signed Convict Lake Road. You have overshot this

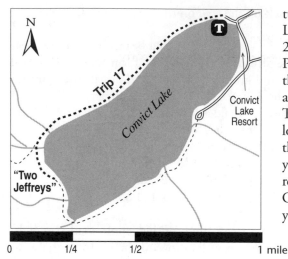

turnoff if you get to the Mammoth Lakes junction with State Route 203 while northbound or Toms Place while southbound. Follow this road uphill across a moraine, almost to Convict Lake Resort. The trailhead and its big parking lot are *not* at the roadend; rather, they're on a short, signed spur to your right as you approach the resort, 2 miles. If you cross Convict Creek just below Convict Lake, you've overshot the turnoff. Toilets. Store, gourmet restaurant (dinner; lunch in summer only), boat rentals at adjacent Convict Lake Resort.

At the trailhead: Non-hikers will probably prefer a visit to Convict Lake's southeast shore, where they'll find picnic sites with fine views of this beautiful lake. To get there, continue on Convict Lake Road past the trailhead-spur road, past the resort, and around the lake's southeast side to numerous parking spots. Or they can rent a boat or canoe and enjoy the fine fishing and paddling here.

On the trail: First, a little history. The striking peak whose vertical face overlooks Convict Lake on the lake's south side is Mt. Morrison. At this lake in 1871 a posse shot it out with and then captured six of twenty-nine convicts who'd escaped from a Carson City prison—hence "Convict Lake." Posse member Robert Morrison died in the shootout—hence "Mt. Morrison" in his memory.

Second, a little walking. You can't see Convict Lake from this trailhead, so, from the trailhead sign, head southwest up a sandy, sagebrush-dotted moraine, topping out at ¼ mile at a wonderful overlook of the lake. Mt. Morrison is obvious, ahead; to your right is Laurel Mountain; to your left are the reddish slopes of Mt. McGee. Descending moderately to steeply on this sandy trail—the route is confusing because of use trails back toward the resort—you level out at a signed junction welcoming you to the backcountry, well above the shore a little past ⅓ mile. You continue southwest on a shadeless, sandy-dusty trail that bobs up and down some 20 to 40 feet above the water. Steep use trails lead down to the water, where you'll spot many a hopeful angler.

As you continue, look for a pair of particularly tall Jeffrey pines at the lake's head. I think of them as "Two Jeffreys," and they make an easy-to-spot landmark for the pleasant stretch of lakeshore around the multistranded inlet. At 1 mile, you reach a junction: left (south) on a well-tramped trail to "Two Jeffreys" and around the lake; right (ahead) to lakes beyond the scope of this book (the nearest, Mildred Lake, is a steep, rugged 4¼ miles more). Pause here to study the wonderfully twisted, colorful rock layers to the west. You reach another junction almost immediately: hikers and anglers go left, stock users go right. You soon find yourself at "**Two Jeffreys" at a little over 1 mile and 7620 feet.** This is a great spot to rest and take in the sparkling lake. Sometimes boaters pull up on this pretty shore, so you may have company.

Near 1¼ miles, you reach the long boardwalk that spans most of the stony distributaries of Convict Creek, some of which may be dry by late season. The boardwalk, smelling of creosote where the sun warms it, threads its way between tall willows and cottonwoods before ending near 1⅓ miles. Almost immediately you cross the last distributary on a log bridge.

The trail resumes in aspens as it begins to curve around the lake's southwest end and comes to a "stairway" that helps you ascend to a traverse of the steep southern shoreline. At first the track is rocky through moisture-loving plants and trees. Numerous steep anglers' trails dash down to the water as the trail turns to sandy-dusty on a sunstruck chaparral slope before reaching the day-use/picnic area and the parkin loop on the lake's south shore at 2 miles.

An easy way to continue is to climb up to the parking loop and walk along the road past toilets and water on your right and a rough launching ramp on your left. Just past the loop, pick up a roadside walkway with a wooden fence on its lake side. Where the fence ends, turn left down a dirt track that makes one switchback on its short, steep way to the water. Past the switchback and about halfway down, you pick up a trail on your right in order to continue this shoreline traverse, now through snowberry, sage, tobacco brush, and wild rose. It may be a little overgrown, but at least you're off the road.

Convict Lake and "Two Jeffreys"

Soon you intersect a paved trail coming down from the road. There's a bench and another restroom uphill on your right, but you turn left to continue your traverse past the occasional bench and under the welcome shade of cottonwoods. Thickets of wild rose here offer colorful seasonal treats: intensely fragrant, pink, single flowers in early season; lipstick-red seed pods called "hips" in mid- to late-season; and small red leaves in the fall.

As you begin to curve around the east end of the lake, you reach an area with informational displays about the area's geology and history as well as great views across the lake. The trail shortly angles up to meet the road at another set of informational displays. After studying them, cross the bridged outlet and stick to the road's west shoulder as you pass a memorial to Clay Cutter, who died here in February 1990 while trying to save others in a tragedy that took seven lives.*

You pick up a sidewalk as you pass the official boat dock, boat rental shack, and launching ramp. Just beyond the ramp you find the sandy-dusty trail around the lake's northeast side. Ignore a steep use trail on your right and continue around the lake to close the loop part of this hike at the signed junction with the trail back to the parking lot at almost 2⅔ miles.

Retrace your steps from here, enjoying views east toward the White Mountains as you top the moraine again.

18. Sherwin and Valentine Lakes 🌿 ☼ 🍁

Place	Total Dist.	Elevation	Level	Type
Start	0	7840	—	—
Largest Sherwin lakes *only*	4+	8680	M	O&B
Valentine Lake	9½	9700	S	O&B

Permit required: None

Topo(s): Bloody Mountain 7½'

Where to stay:
> **Mountain:** Convict Lake Resort, Tamarack Lodge, Wildyrie Lodge, Woods Lodge, Crystal Crag Lodge, Rock Creek Lodge, Rock Creek Lakes Resort
> **Of Interest:** Sierra Gables Motel, Mono Sierra Lodge, Rainbow Tarns, Tom's Place, Mammoth Mountain Inn, Mammoth Mountain Chalets
> **Other:** Town of Mammoth Lakes, Town of June Lake

Highlights: Besides being one of the earlier trails to open in the Mammoth Lakes area, this trail offers wonderful views over the town and Long Valley as you ascend

---

* From a *Mammoth Times* summary by Scott Weldon of 1990 news events: "Four residents of Camp O'Neal, a private group home for troubled teens, fall through the ice [at Convict Lake] during a day outing [in February]. Three of them—Ryan Diaz, David Sellers, and Ryan McCandless—perish before rescuers can pull them out of the water. Two camp counselors, Dave Myers and Randy Porter, and two other rescuers, Vidar Anderson and Clay Cutter, die trying to rescue the boys."

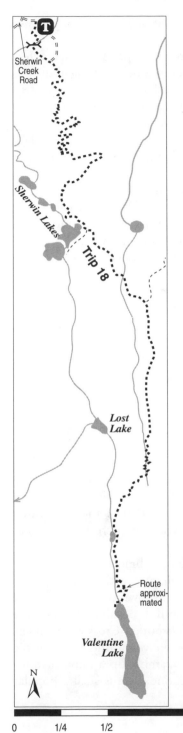

Sherwin
Creek
Road

Sherwin Lakes

Trip 18

Lost
Lake

Route
approxi-
mated

Valentine
Lake

N

0   1/4   1/2   1 mile

the Sherwin Creek moraine to the pretty Sherwin Lakes, sky-blue surprises in their chaparral setting. Beyond, larger Valentine Lake offers more-typical Sierra beauty in a setting of rugged peaks.

How to get to the trailhead: The trailhead is off mostly-dirt Sherwin Creek Road, which skirts the foot of the Sierra from a well-marked junction with U.S. Highway 395 a short distance south of the Mammoth Lakes junction (at State Route 203) to a junction with Old Mammoth Road in the town of Mammoth Lakes. From Highway 395, turn off on signed Sherwin Creek Road. You have overshot this turnoff if you get to the Mammoth Lakes junction while northbound or the Convict Lake junction while southbound. Follow Sherwin Creek Road past Sherwin Creek Campground to a signed left turn to the Sherwin Creek Trailhead and the motocross course, 4.1 miles. Turn left here and continue 0.3 mile to a spur road signed for Sherwin Lakes and Voorhis Viking Camp. Turn left again, 0.1 mile to a parking area at the trailhead, 4.5 miles total. Toilets.

At the trailhead: There's nothing here for non-hikers, who will prefer to be at their lodgings or to enjoy the amenities of Mammoth Lakes, where there are plenty of shops and restaurants, and more recreational opportunities than you can shake a stick at.

On the trail: The trail heads generally south past the restroom, under sparse Jeffrey pines. You dip across aspen-lined Sherwin Creek on a footbridge and enter moderate forest cover, passing a sign reminding you that while this is not yet official wilderness, it is backcountry and should be treated as wilderness.

The trail curves east, passing a spur left (north-northeast) to some buildings—part of private Voorhis Viking Camp. You continue ahead (right), soon working your way gradually up a moraine and curving around the head of a gully. Beyond here, you begin a series of long, lazy, sandy switchbacks that carry you farther up the moraine. Views open up over the dry meadows south of town, the town itself, and the volcanic knolls north of it, and to the distant White Mountains to the northeast. This trail is worth taking just for these views!

At 1¾ miles you top out, traverse the moraine through chaparral and sparse forest, and spot one or two of the smaller Sherwin Lakes well below the trail to your right (west). Curving around a knob, you suddenly find yourself just a few steps away from the northernmost bay on a shallow but lovely lake, one of the two **largest Sherwin Lakes at just over 2 miles and 8680 feet**. In early season, these two lakes may overflow their short connecting stream and become one. If the lake isn't so high that it's lapping at the trail, you'll find nice picnicking at this bay, just over 2 miles from your start.

Reluctantly turning away from this pretty scene, you follow the trail through boulders to a signed junction at 2¼ miles: left (southeast) to Valentine Lake, right (west) on a short spur trail to upper Sherwin Lakes. The sign is fastened to a large tree, into whose bark it almost blends. I think the best spot from which to enjoy Sherwin Lakes is the bay you stopped at earlier, so I recommend you go left here for Valentine Lake.

You walk generally east through sparse forest, dip across a sandy flat dotted with blue lupine and immense Western junipers, cross an aspen-lined channel, traverse another flat, and at 2¾ miles curve south past a sign on a big juniper that says VALENTINE LAKE. It's a short way to a now blocked-off junction with a very faint trail that leads to a YMCA camp off Sherwin Creek Road. When returning, if you notice this junction, turn left to return via Sherwin Lakes rather than take the trail to the YMCA camp—not nearly as scenic and requiring a long, dusty trudge on roads to get back to your car.

Nearing 3 miles, you enter John Muir Wilderness and begin working your way up a little valley that's now open and sandy, now densely forested, here filled with fluttering green aspen leaves, there marshy and provided with logs laid to form a "corduroy" tread in the mud. You emerge to views of the steep east faces of unnamed crags on the Sierra Crest and to the invigorating sound of a cascading creek. At 3½ miles you cross this tributary creek and soon catch over-the-shoulder glimpses of Lost Lake below. Presently you cross yet another seasonal trickle.

Around 4 miles you pass a shallow lakelet bordered by Labrador tea and fragrant red heather and at 9460 feet begin to switchback, playing tag with the creek, staying on its east side instead of crossing to its west side as shown on the topo. Near the top of the climb, you reach the north end of beautiful, peakbound **Valentine Lake at 4¾ miles and 9700 feet**, on the east side of its outlet. Cross the boulder-and-log-choked outlet to the west side of the lake, where you'll find pretty picnic spots as well as some overused campsites. You can scramble up a knoll here for panoramic views north and south. No wonder Valentine Lake is such a popular destination for dayhikers!

Return the way you came.

19. Heart Lake 🌸 ☼ 🍁

Place	Total Dist.	Elevation	Level	Type
Start	0	9120	–	–
Heart Lake	2	9610	E	

Permit required: None

Topo(s): Bloody Mountain 7½'

Where to stay:
> **Mountain:** Convict Lake Resort, Tamarack Lodge, Wildyrie Lodge, Woods Lodge, Crystal Crag Lodge, Rock Creek Lodge, Rock Creek Lakes Resort
> **Of Interest:** Sierra Gables Motel, Mono Sierra Lodge, Rainbow Tarns, Tom's Place, Mammoth Mountain Inn, Mammoth Mountain Chalets
> **Other:** Town of Mammoth Lakes, Town of June Lake

Highlights: The route to charming Heart Lake crosses slopes that support an amazing array of flowers in season, and the view from the knoll west of Heart Lake is breathtaking. A drawback for walkers is the lake's popularity with equestrians, but the trip is still worth the trouble. A bonus is that the ruins of the Mammoth Consolidated Gold Mine are right at this trailhead; it's a popular detour, though not part of this trip's write-up.

How to get to the trailhead: These directions start at the intersection of State Route 203 (Main Street), Minaret Road, and Lake Mary Road in the town of Mammoth Lakes. The intersection, which I'll call the Main-Minaret-Mary junction, is the second traffic light as you drive west from U.S. Highway 395 on State Route 203. Go straight (southwest) on the Lake Mary Road, climbing away from the town toward the Lakes Basin. At the first set of lakes, Twin Lakes, there's a pullout, an information sign, and a view across the lakes toward 300-foot Twin Falls. Leaving Twin Lakes behind, you pass a couple of junctions on your right; go left at both. Climbing, you pass the Mammoth Lakes Pack Station on your right and soon reach a **Y**-junction: right to Lakes Mamie and George and Horseshoe Lake; left to Lake Mary and Coldwater Canyon.

Go left to skirt beautiful Lake Mary on your right, Pine City Campground on your left. You shortly reach a turnoff left to Coldwater Campground; turn left here and follow the road through the campground to a large parking area beyond the camp-ground's upper end, 5.0–5.2 miles from the Main-Minaret-Mary junction, depending on where you park. This parking area serves three trailheads that are 0.1 mile apart: Heart Lake (this trip), Duck Pass (Trip 20), and Emerald Lake (Trip 21). The Heart Lake Trailhead along with Mammoth Consolidated Gold Mine is on the east side of the parking area. Toilets, water.

At the trailhead: Non-hikers may prefer to stay down by Lake Mary; it's always a treat to picnic along its lovely shore. Those up for a little stroll will enjoy a leisurely exploration of the ruins of the Mammoth Consolidated Gold Mine.

On the trail: From the stone monument marking the entrance to Mammoth Consolidated Gold Mine at the parking lot, follow the trail east-northeast under a wooden archway and across Mammoth Creek. The area is webbed with use trails, many made by visitors to the mine as they scramble around in search of more ruins. You'll need to keep your eyes peeled in order to stay on the main trail.

In the first few steps you pass an information sign—inexpensive brochures for a self-guided tour of the mine are sometimes available here—cross two equestrian trails, and at a **Y**-junction take the right fork east past an old pumphouse. In a few more steps you reach another **Y**-junction and go right (east-northeast) again, past a spur trail that comes in from the left, from the mine, to join your trail.

You continue ahead, climbing, to meet yet another trail from the mine. At this junction, turn right (east) onto that trail, emerging onto a slope sparsely shaded by lodgepoles. This leg is steep and rocky but compensates by offering views of "Red and Gold Mountain" to the north (Peak 3132T on

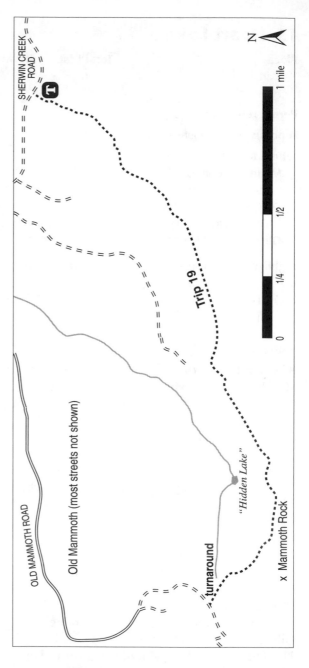

the topo—this is how the point is labeled on the 7½′ topo; the numerics are the elevation in meters; I don't know what the "T" stands for) and of Mammoth Crest to the south. The creek's roar below reminds you that water is nearby, in spite of the dryness of this rocky slope, which sports a wonderful variety of flowers in season—the golden disks of mule ears are especially striking.

At a switchback turn between ¼ and ⅓ mile, a use trail darts southeast toward the creek as the main trail jogs north, then east, continuing a steady, moderate-to-steep climb. The trail itself is unpleasantly deep in horse droppings and dust, but the ever-expanding views make up for that. A northwestward leg offers great views that include Crystal Crag to the south.

Around ½ mile, multiple use trails make the area confusing, so if in doubt, follow the horse droppings. The grade eases as you begin an eastward leg, and more than once, the trail splits into multiple tracks, most of which presently rejoin. Near ⅔ mile you meet a use trail joining the main trail from the left; you continue ahead.

At a fork near 1 mile, the trail splits into two routes, upper and lower, to the lake; only one appears on this book's map. You can take either, as they rejoin, but if you take the upper fork, ignore a use trail going uphill to the left, just before the forks rejoin. Use trails diverge as you approach Heart Lake, and you're at **Heart Lake's edge at 1 mile and 9610 feet**. There are pleasant picnic sites at this little lake. A use trail makes a short, steepish climb up the knoll west of Heart Lake, and from the knoll's summit there are outstanding views down-canyon; across the Lakes Basin to Crystal Crag; to the great, bare hulk of Mammoth Mountain; to Mammoth Crest; and beyond it to a glimpse of the distant Ritter Range.

Retrace your steps from here.

20. Duck Pass ☼ 🍁

Place	Total Dist.	Elevation	Level	Type
Start	0	9120	—	—
Arrowhead Lake *only*	2⅔	9678	E U	O&B
Skelton Lake	4⅔	9915	M	O&B
Barney Lake	6⅓	10,203	S	O&B
Duck Pass	9⅓+	10,797	S	O&B

Permit required: None

Topo(s): Bloody Mountain 7½'

Where to stay:
   Mountain: Convict Lake Resort, Tamarack Lodge, Wildyrie Lodge, Woods Lodge, Crystal Crag Lodge
   Of Interest: Sierra Gables Motel, Mono Sierra Lodge, Mammoth Mountain Inn, Mammoth Mountain Chalets
   Other: Town of Mammoth Lakes, Town of June Lake

Highlights: Winding up Mammoth Creek past several lovely lakes to knockout views at Duck Pass, you'll see why the beautiful Duck Pass Trail is one of the most popular hikes in the Mammoth Lakes area.

How to get to the trailhead: Follow the driving directions of Trip 19 from the Main-Minaret-Mary junction to the Duck Pass Trailhead by the big parking area at the end of the road. Toilets, water.

At the trailhead: See Trip 19.

On the trail: See Trip 19's map. Head generally southeast past an information sign, soon crossing an unmapped streamlet to enter John Muir Wilderness at a junction: left (north) to Mammoth Consolidated Mine and Heart Lake, right (southeast) to Duck Pass. Under moderate lodgepole-red fir cover, your Duck Pass Trail climbs gradually to moderately before beginning a series of lazy switchbacks that offer over-the-shoulder views of Mammoth Mountain and Lake Mary where the trees permit.

At 1 mile you reach an inconspicuously-marked junction at 9776: left (southeast) to Arrowhead Lake, right (south) to Duck Pass. Go left to your first lake, nearly 100 feet and ⅓ mile below, its sparkling waters barely visible from this junction. **Arrowhead Lake at 1⅓ miles and 9678 feet** lies in a steep canyon. The spur trail takes you near its cascading inlet, which supports a lovely flower garden in season. Return to the Duck Pass Trail from here, now with 1⅔ miles on your boots, and turn left to continue to Duck Pass.

You climb through lightly-wooded granite outcrops and then between a pictur-esque tarn on your right (may be dry late in a dry year) and one of the outlets—this one not on the topo—linking Arrowhead and Skelton lakes on your left. An unmarked but well-traveled trail branching right (west) past the tarn at what the book's map calls the *Emerald-Skelton junction* connects this Mammoth Creek drainage with that of Coldwater Creek; see Trip 21. A little farther on, use trails branching left lead to camping and picnic sites along Skelton Lake, as yet unseen from the Duck Pass Trail. Scamper off on one that's ⅙ mile from the Emerald-Skelton junction and that leads out to a peninsula, to find a sublime spot at beautiful **Skelton Lake at about 2⅓ miles and 9915 feet.** From here you have wonderful views across the lake to "Red and Gold Mountain," the huge roof pendant between Mammoth and Sherwin creeks; of the jagged ridge that connects Red and Gold Mountain to the Sierra Crest; and of the crest itself. Skelton Lake is my pick for the prettiest lake in this drainage.

Until late season, and after a heavy winter, the Duck Pass Trail may be under snow beyond Skelton Lake. If conditions permit you to continue, you soon make a brief traverse above Skelton's west shore—few picnic spots here but idyllic views—and then you climb moderately through more outcrops. Passing through a rocky slot, you cross streamlets at the base of an alpine meadow with a splintered, isolated peak ahead to the southeast and pass richly varied flower gardens.

You top a rise overlooking desolate Barney Lake; lodgepoles on its northwest shore shelter camping and picnicking spots. Descend to cross its outlet and begin a longish traverse of **Barney Lake's east shore at a little over 3 miles and 10,203 feet,** with tiny Red Lake to the northeast. A scree slope plunges to Barney's west shore, and there may be seasonal ponds east of the trail. Peak 3592T rises to the east-northeast, beyond a granite knoll.

The final, sometimes steep, winding ascent to Duck Pass brings spectacular views northwest as you pass pocket gardens of alpine flowers. At unmarked **Duck Pass at 4⅔ miles and 10,797 feet,** you traverse briefly southeast through boulders for a few more steps to discover a spectacular overlook of huge Duck Lake and its companion to its east, Pika Lake. Pika Lake would be a good-sized lake anywhere else, but it's a piker compared to Duck Lake. Far beyond you'll see the peaks of the Silver Divide. Find a picnic spot here; take in the view and soak in the sunshine as you enjoy your lunch. Most of you will be happy to stop here, but a few energetic hikers may want to follow an obvious spur trail down to Duck's and Pika's open shores (the main trail stays well above Duck's shore almost to Duck's outlet).

Retrace your steps from here.

21. Emerald and Skelton Lakes ☼ ❦

Place	Total Dist.	Elevation	Level	Type
Start	0	9120	—	
Emerald Lake *only*	1½	9482	E	O&B
Entire loop	3¼	—	M	Loop

Permit required: None

Topo(s): Bloody Mountain 7½'

Where to stay:

  Mountain: Convict Lake Resort, Tamarack Lodge, Wildyrie Lodge, Woods Lodge, Crystal Crag Lodge

  Of Interest: Sierra Gables Motel, Mono Sierra Lodge, Mammoth Mountain Inn, Mammoth Mountain Chalets

  Other: Town of Mammoth Lakes, Town of June Lake

Highlights: A flower- and meadow-blessed walk along Coldwater Creek leads to charming Emerald Lake, from which you enjoy an exciting climb to beautiful Skelton Lake and a downhill stroll with an optional detour to Arrowhead Lake.

How to get to the trailhead: Follow the driving directions of Trip 19 from the Main-Minaret-Mary junction to the Emerald Lake Trailhead at the south corner of the big parking area at the end of the road. The Duck Pass Trailhead (Trip 20), where you will come out, is just a short stroll to the east. Toilets, water.

At the trailhead: See Trip 19.

On the trail: See Trip 19's map. You can do this loop in reverse, but the route connecting Emerald and Skelton lakes is much easier to find and follow from the Emerald Lake Trail. The trailhead is marked but the trail's start is indistinct, smeared over the landscape by its many happy users. Just keep the toilet building on your left as you let yourself be funneled moderately up and then into the narrow little canyon of Coldwater Creek, where you meet a spur road (not on the map) going off to your left to a water tank. A sign identifies the equestrian route as the main trail rather than the creekside trail described in the trip. You can take either. The creekside route is easier for first-time visitors. Those going *only* to Emerald Lake can use the two routes to turn their hike into a semi-loop.

The trail nearly levels out along the shady creek except where it must climb over obstacles like tree roots exposed by runoff—this streambank erodes readily. Bright yellow blossoms of monkeyflower and mountain helenium color the banks here and there as you ascend very gradually to the point where a tributary, Emerald Lake's outlet (not on the topo), elbows in from the east.

Don't cross the tributary; instead, follow the trail along its northern bank, entering John Muir Wilderness at an unmarked point. Here, the tributary forms a long, sandy-bottomed pool of that wonderful green tint peculiar to mid-mountain streams, as it flows slowly between banks covered with long, satiny meadow grass.

In early season, the water here may be so high as to cover the trail; in that case, just trace the stream's edge.

Soon you leave the stream and begin a moderate ascent up a sandy slope, meeting the official route coming from your left. Together you turn right and continue ascending past granite boulders to level out at **Emerald Lake at ¾ mile and 9482 feet**. The handsome, nameless crag towering over the lake is locally called "Blue Crag." What a lovely spot this is—stop here for a snack at least.

Continuing along Emerald Lake's north shore, you shortly reach a junction: left (southeast) to Skelton Lake, right (south) to Gentian and Sky meadows. Go left toward Skelton Lake and begin a moderate-to-steep climb above a seasonal tributary of Emerald Lake, through moderate-to-open forest. You presently veer east, away from the tributary, to climb steeply up a ridge that's been on your left. Near the top of the climb, you pass a seasonal pond on your left and head for a large gray outcrop. Curve around the outcrop to climb along its east face through a very rocky, narrow gully. The trail grows very steep and rough as it nears the head of the gully, where its small switchbacks have been nearly obliterated by people cutting across them. With so much loose rock and soil, the trail seems more like a use trail here. The trail seems to split three ways at the head of the gully; the middle fork is its real continuation. A few steps after you exit from the head of the gully, look to your right for the top of the outcrop you've been climbing along; from there you'll find excellent views: Red and Gold Mountain, Lake Mary, Mammoth Mountain, Crystal Crag and the Mammoth Crest, and beyond, Banner Peak and Mt. Ritter. *If you are coming from Skelton Lake*, be aware that in this area, even though the obvious route goes out to the viewpoint I've just described, the route connecting with Emerald Lake drops into the rough, narrow gully on your right.

There are many confusing use trails in this area. Pick the track that puts the very top of the outcrop as well as Blue Crag on your right and a wooded swale with seasonal tarns on your left. The track soon dips into the swale and presently approaches a particularly large tarn or two—one huge tarn if the water is high, sometimes just a dry tarn-bed late in the season. An obvious track leads around the right side of the tarn(s) but soon peters out; the better route lies along the left side of the tarn(s). Taking the left route, you squish along the tarns as best you can to meet the Duck Pass Trail at just over 1½ miles at what the book's map calls the Emerald-Skelton junction. Turn right onto the Duck Pass Trail, toward Duck Pass, and shortly find use trails branching left to camping and picnic sites along Skelton Lake, as yet unseen from the Duck Pass Trail. As recommended in Trip 20, scamper off on one of them to find a sublime spot along beautiful **Skelton Lake at 1¾ miles and 9915 feet**.

To return to the parking lot, retrace your steps from Skelton Lake to the Duck Pass Trail and turn right (northwest), reversing the directions of Trip 20 between Skelton Lake and the parking lot. From the Emerald-Skelton junction, it's ½ mile to the junction with the spur trail to Arrowhead Lake and a ⅔-mile detour (turn right) and a nearly-100-foot descent/ascent to visit attractive Arrowhead Lake (see Trip 20).

Back on the Duck Pass Trail, turn right to continue to the Duck Pass Trailhead at 3¼ miles, from which you'll close this loop by returning to your car. A use trail behind the toilets connects the trailheads, but I find it easier to walk through the parking lot.

22. Barrett and T J Lakes ☼ ❦

Place	Total Dist.	Elevation	Level	Type
Start	0	9055	—	—
Barrett Lake *only*	1	9284	E*	O&B
T J Lake	1½	9284	E U	O&B

Permit required: None

Topo(s): WP Devils Postpile 15'; Crystal Crag 7½'

Where to stay:

Mountain: Convict Lake Resort, Tamarack Lodge, Wildyrie Lodge, Woods Lodge, Crystal Crag Lodge

Of Interest: Sierra Gables Motel, Mono Sierra Lodge, Mammoth Mountain Inn, Mammoth Mountain Chalets

Other: Town of Mammoth Lakes, Town of June Lake

Highlights: Two pretty lakes lie along this short and occasionally steep hike, and the scenery around this area is simply delightful.

How to get to the trailhead: Follow the driving directions of Trip 19 from the Main-Minaret-Mary junction. At the Coldwater Campground junction, bear right to stay on Lake Mary Road. You pass Lake Mary and reach a store and marina, beyond which there is a junction with a spur road to the left, signed for Lake George. Turn left onto this road, pass the Lake Mary Campground, cross a small bridge over the stream linking Lakes Mary and Mamie, and reach a **T**-junction. Turn right here, onto the spur road to Lake George, and follow it uphill to the lake, where you'll find a parking lot at 4.7 miles and two trailheads, one to Barrett and T J lakes, the other to Crystal Lake and Mammoth Crest. Avoid the service road on your right that leads up to Woods Lodge if you're not staying there. Beyond the parking area, on the other side from Woods Lodge, you'll find a campground (don't park in it), restrooms, and your trailhead for this trip. Toilets, water.

At the trailhead: This is one of the most appealing trailheads in this book for the non-hiker. The scenery—tranquil Lake George mirroring Crystal Crag and the Mammoth Crest—is stunning, and just off the very easy first part of the trail, lakeside picnic tables shaded by handsome pines welcome you.

On the trail: The broad, sandy trail passes in front of the restrooms, heading south on a level grade through moderate-to-open lodgepole forest. Lake George lies a lit-

---

* Steep section between George and Barrett Lake; a little boulder-scrambling may be required.

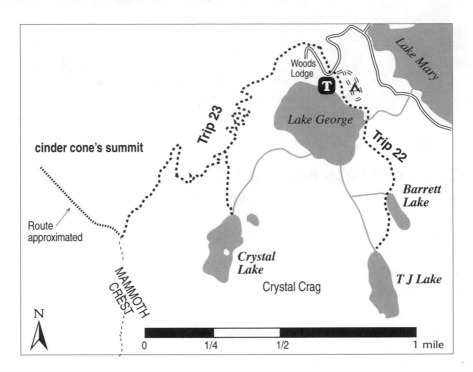

tle below you; majestic Crystal Crag and the Mammoth Crest soar above the other shore. Picnic tables dot the shoreline here. You presently cross the lake's outlet on a footbridge and curve southwest past a charming summer cabin; avoid a use trail left here—it leads only to the cabin.

A little past the cabin, you reach a fork: the main trail jogs left (south-south-east), while a use trail continues ahead (right) along the lakeshore. Follow the main trail left and ascend moderately to steeply on an open slope, paralleling one of Lake George's inlets (not on the map). Rocks at one point may require a little bouldering skill. Near the top of the ascent, you walk on shallow "terraces" made by the roots of a stout lodgepole. The grade eases, you cross the little stream, and then you briefly resume climbing. You puff up over another root-terrace to a junction a little short of ½ mile: right (south) to T J Lake, left (southeast) to Lake Mary. Go right to reach peaceful, wooded, little **Barrett Lake at ½ mile and 9284 feet**, from whose northwest shore you have a view of Red and Gold Mountain and the Mammoth Crest.

Cruise along Barrett's shoreline, until, about halfway along it, the trail veers right over a low ridge and to a junction at a little less than ⅔ mile: left (south-southeast) to Emerald Lake, right (southwest) to T J Lake. Go right here, almost immediately reaching an apparent junction where a prominent use trail branches right. Go left to keep on the main trail, on which you top out at ⅔ mile on the 9350-foot ridge overlooking dramatic T J Lake. From here, the trail descends steeply toward the lakeshore, veering right toward the outlet partway down. There are good spots just off the trail, before the outlet, to rest and enjoy **T J Lake at ¾ mile and 9284 feet** (yes, T J and Barrett lakes are at the same altitude). Lichen-streaked granite cliffs bound the northwest shore; Crystal Crag and the Mammoth Crest seem to leap into the sky above you. Although the topo shows the trail continuing beyond the outlet, the trail in fact ends at the outlet.

Retrace your steps from T J Lake.

23. Crystal Lake and Crest ☼ 🍁

Place	Total Dist.	Elevation	Level	Type
Start	0	9055	—	—
Crystal Lake *only*	2¾	9613	E	O&B
Cinder cone's summit	6	10,480	S	O&B

Permit required: None

Topo(s): WP Devils Postpile 15'; Crystal Crag 7½'

Where to stay:
    Mountain: Convict Lake Resort, Tamarack Lodge, Wildyrie Lodge, Woods Lodge, Crystal Crag Lodge
    Of Interest: Sierra Gables Motel, Mono Sierra Lodge, Mammoth Mountain Inn, Mammoth Mountain Chalets
    Other: Town of Mammoth Lakes, Town of June Lake

Highlights: This is an extremely scenic hike: one wonderful view after another; a gem of a little alpine lake; and at the top a volcanic landscape of colorful cinders and a cinder cone, reminiscent of Haleakala on Maui.

How to get to the trailhead: Follow the driving directions of Trip 22 west on Main Street, then up the Lake Mary Road, to Lake George's parking lot. The Crystal Lake Trailhead is on the side of the parking lot opposite the restrooms and the Barrett-T J trailhead and near the service road to Woods Lodge.

At the trailhead: See Trip 22.

On the trail: See Trip 22's map. The topo is wrong about the first part of this trail: it passes around and above, not through, the cabins of Woods Lodge. You head north-northwest, up long, gradual-to-moderate switchbacks and through a moderate forest of species typical of this area: lodgepole, western white pine, hemlock, and red fir. The sandy-dusty trail carries you behind Woods Lodge and through a scattering of dry-slope flowers. Beyond the lodge, the trail bursts out of the forest to a beautiful overlook of Lakes George and Mary and beyond them of Red and Gold Mountain. Views like this accompany you up the trail as you ascend the slope above Lake George, just getting better—forest cover permitting. In season, Crystal Lake's outlet splashes down the slope ahead in delightful cascades.

At last you turn away from the slope and back into the forest, where just shy of 1¼ miles you reach a junction: left (south) to Crystal Lake, right (southwest) to the

Mammoth Crest. It's a slightly-over-½-mile out-and-back detour to Crystal Lake with a 131-foot elevation loss/gain—and well worth the trouble! Turning left, you cross a saddle (9744 feet) and then make a moderate-to-steep descent to the lake's outlet stream. Turn right along a beaten track paralleling the outlet to reach **Crystal Lake at a little under 1½ miles and 9613 feet.** This jewel of a lake is tucked right under Crystal Crag and the Mammoth Crest in a wonderfully picturesque, tranquil, alpine setting. Near its mouth and along its outlet stream you'll find an eye-catching array of wildflowers.

Back at the junction with the main trail, with 1⅔ miles now on your boots, you turn left to continue up to the Mammoth Crest. The trail corkscrews moderately-to-steeply away from the junction. As the grade eases, you reach an airy perch with fabulous views: peaks in southern Yosemite; San Joaquin Ridge; Mammoth Mountain; McCloud Lake, Horseshoe Lake, Twin Lakes, and Lakes Mamie, Mary, and George in this lakes basin; Panorama Dome; the town of Mammoth Lakes; beyond, Bald Mountain, Glass Ridge, the White Mountains; across the lakes basin, Red and Gold Mountain and the Sherwin Range; Blue Crag; and Crystal Crag. Views that are variations on that theme continue to develop as you climb; the forest dwindles to a few stunted whitebark pines. The slope soon turns to volcanic material—pumice and cinders—and the trail is loose and dusty.

A little past 2½ miles a sign announces John Muir Wilderness at a huge, dark red boulder—possibly a lava bomb. The true boundary is actually a little farther on, at the crest. You cross over a ridge and descend a little among brick-red lava rocks. To the west there's a red cinder cone with a long, gentle, south slope and, facing you, an abrupt east slope up which a plain-to-see use trail winds. At an unmarked **Y** junction just beyond the ridge, the main trail goes left (southwest) to Deer Lakes and an obvious use trail goes right (west) to the cinder cone.

Go right here, curving around the top of the Mammoth Crest's cliffs, enjoying thrilling views and an amazing display: colorful volcanic rocks contrasting with the severe, light-gray granites more typical of the Sierra. The going gets steep to very steep as you veer away from the clifftop to ascend the cone on a series of tiny, tight switchbacks. The view from the **cinder cone's summit at nearly 3 miles and 10,480 feet** is spectacular, including the Minarets, Mt. Ritter, Banner Peak, and many of the features you saw earlier from the "airy perch." The volcanic rubble here offers a fine array of colors: reds, ochres, blacks, grays, soft oranges, dusty lavenders, golden browns. This is as close to being in Maui's famous Haleakala Crater as you can get in the Eastern Sierra. Take a lunch stop here so you can enjoy your remarkable surroundings at leisure.

Return the way you came.

24. McCloud Lake and Red Cones ☼ ❦

Place	Total Dist.	Elevation	Level	Type
Start	0	8990	—	
McCloud Lake *only*	1	9285	E	O&B
Entire semiloop	7⅔	9350	S U	Semi

Permit required: None

Topo(s): WP Devils Postpile 15'; Crystal Crag 7½'

Where to stay:

Mountain: Convict Lake Resort, Tamarack Lodge, Wildyrie Lodge, Woods Lodge, Crystal Crag Lodge

Of Interest: Sierra Gables Motel, Mono Sierra Lodge, Mammoth Mountain Inn, Mammoth Mountain Chalets

Other: Town of Mammoth Lakes, Town of June Lake

Highlights: Pretty McCloud Lake is easy to get to and a favorite family destination. The adventure continues over highly varied terrain with a visit to a pair of beautiful meadows and a pair of brick-red cinder cones, one of which you'll have the option of climbing for knockout views.

How to get to the trailhead: Follow the driving directions of Trips 19 and 22 from the Main-Minaret-Mary junction, staying on Lake Mary Road past Lakes Mary and Mamie—don't turn off to Lake George—to the large parking area at the road-end next to pale blue Horseshoe Lake. Toilets, water.

At the trailhead: See Trip 18.

On the trail: First, a little background. Carbon dioxide gas seeping up through the soil in measurable amounts around this trailhead is apparently responsible for the dead trees around here; it's suffocating the trees' roots. This seepage comes in small amounts that are harmless if you're in the open air; its source is magma moving deep underground. However, hanging around here or using the restroom may be unsafe: when concentrated, as in a side building, the odorless, invisible gas could suffocate you.

Second, the hike. The trailhead is right by the cinderblock restroom building and is marked by an information sign. Head west up the broad, sandy trail on a gradual-to-moderate grade, soon leaving the dead trees behind and entering a healthy forest of lodgepole, red fir, and mountain hemlock. Multiple tracks may seem confusing, but keep going generally west, then southwest, and you'll find yourself at **McCloud Lake at ½ mile and 9285 feet.** It's a breathtakingly lovely sight on a still, bright morning, when the magnificent, light-gray cliffs of the Mammoth Crest are reflected in the lake's sky-blue waters. Several picnic spots dot the shoreline, and you'll probably see people splashing in the water.

Leaving this pretty spot, you'll almost immediately reach a **Y**-junction overlooking the lake: left (west-southwest) to the south side of Mammoth Pass and to the Red Cones, right (northwest) to the north side of Mammoth Pass and to Reds

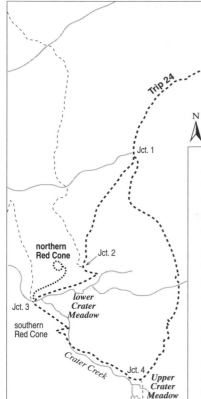

Meadow in the Devils Postpile area. You go left, skirting McCloud Lake and then climbing a little to the very broad, heavily forested saddle that's Mammoth Pass—sorry, no views here at the high point of this hike at 9350 feet. You presently begin a gradual-to-moderate descent, and at 1⅔ miles, you reach a junction near a noisy spring, where you begin the loop part of this trip: right (south) to the Red Cones, left (south-southeast) to Upper Crater Meadow. Call this *Junction 1*; "junction" is abbreviated "Jct." on the book's map. Go right here, shortly crossing a stream and descending moderately to steeply to glimpses of the brick-red cinders of the Red Cones.

At 2¼ miles, there's another junction, *Junction 2*: left (east) to continue this hike, right (west) to Reds Meadow. Go left on a sandy slope, presently skirting below the Red Cones.

Several obvious use trails scamper up the northern Red Cone's steep slopes. I recommend the use trail nearest the next junction, *Junction 3*, at a little over 3 miles. From the **summit of the northern Red Cone at about 3½ miles and 9000 feet** (the route you take affects the distance), you have a not-to-be-missed, 360° view over the drainage of the Middle Fork San Joaquin River: the back of Mammoth Mountain and Mammoth Crest; San Joaquin Ridge; the Middle Fork's canyon, including Devils Postpile National Monument; the Ritter Range (the Minarets, Mt. Ritter, Banner Peak); and south to the peaks around Fish Valley. Return to Junction 3 when you've taken in the view, having made a let's-call-it 1-mile out-and-back trek to the cone's summit.

Back at Junction 3, with let's-call-it 4 miles on your boots, it's left (southeast) to Upper Crater Meadow, right (northwest) to Reds Meadow. Go left to make a moderate to steep ascent of a sandy gully that's home to a fork of Crater Creek, crossing the saddle between the northern and southern Red Cones. The grade eases as you approach another junction, *Junction 4*, in flowery, squishy **Upper Crater Meadow at 4¾ miles and 8890 feet**: hard left (northwest) back the way you came;

middle (easy left, north) to Horseshoe Lake; and right (south) on the Pacific Crest Trail/John Muir Trail to Mt. Whitney.

Take the middle fork for Horseshoe Lake, beginning a pleasant but unremarkable leg of this trip by climbing over a broad, gentle, forested ridge whose summit at 9150 feet is the high point of this leg. You cross another fork of Crater Creek at 5¼ miles before climbing yet another gentle, forested ridge and then descending to close the loop part of this trip at 6 miles at Junction 1.

From here, turn right (north) and retrace your steps to Horseshoe Lake, 1⅔ miles more, for a total of 7⅔ miles.

25. San Joaquin Ridge ☼ 🍁

Place	Total Dist.	Elevation	Level	Type
Start	0	9175	—	
Deadman Peak	4½	10,255	M	O&B

Permit required: None

Topo(s): WP Devils Postpile 15'; Mammoth Mountain 7½'

Where to stay:

  Mountain: Convict Lake Resort, Tamarack Lodge, Wildyrie Lodge, Woods Lodge, Crystal Crag Lodge

  Of Interest: Sierra Gables Motel, Red's Meadow Resort, Mono Sierra Lodge, Mammoth Mountain Inn, Mammoth Mountain Chalets

  Other: Town of Mammoth Lakes, Town of June Lake

Highlights: A 4WD road, very rough and sometimes very steep, climbs pumice-covered San Joaquin Ridge and offers astonishing views and seasonal flower displays. Minaret Vista, almost next to your trailhead, offers views nearly as expansive together with aids to help you identify many of the spectacular peaks around you.

How to get to the trailhead: From the Main-Minaret-Mary junction described in Trip 19, turn right onto Minaret Road (now State Route 203). Follow it uphill to Mammoth Mountain Ski Area/Bike Park—in the summer, Bike Park, in the winter, Ski Area.

There may be a road-control point here; if asked, explain that you are going only to Minaret Vista. From about Memorial Day to Labor Day, this road is closed between 7:30 A.M. and 5:30 P.M. to private vehicles, from Minaret Summit to its end at Red's Meadow. It's an extremely narrow and winding, though scenic, road that leads over the Sierra Crest and down into the area around Devils Postpile National Monument. When the road is closed, you must take a shuttle bus (fee) down to/up from the trailheads in the Devils Postpile Area. To avoid the closure, plan to start any hike off this road before 7:30 A.M. or after 5:30 P.M.

Assuming you're allowed to drive your own car as far as Minaret Summit, you'll find an entrance station and a road closure there, along with a paved spur road that goes right. Take that spur road to its end at a paved parking loop, 6 miles from the Main-Minaret-Mary junction, passing a blocked-off 4WD road that branches right. Note this road: it's your trail. If the parking loop at the roadend is full, you'll find a couple of informal, unpaved parking areas back here. Park on the loop or back around the dirt road to start your hike. Toilets.

At the trailhead: Just beyond the parking loop's far end is a vista point, Minaret Vista. The views over the canyon of the Middle Fork San Joaquin River from

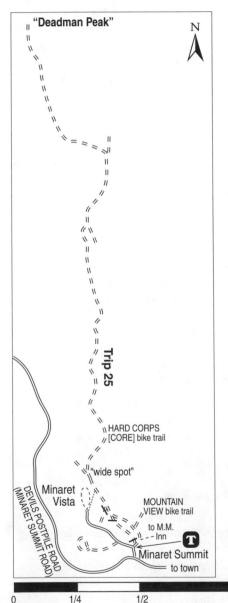

Minaret Vista are breathtaking, and you'll find viewing tubes with bases scribed to help you spot named peaks as well as a mounted metal silhouette of the peaks, labeled so you can identify them. There's also a rough little "nature trail" around the vista. This is one of the finest road-accessible viewpoints in the entire Sierra. And for the more-adventurous non-hiker, there's the scenic gondola ride (fee) from Mammoth Mountain Lodge, back down the road at the ski/bike area, to the summit of 11,053-foot Mammoth Mountain for a windy but unbeatable panoramic view. Visitors to this summit will also find, in season, world-class ski and snowboard runs; thrilling mountain-bike trails, including the infamous Kamikaze Downhill; and hiking trails leading to the Lakes Basin, to Reds Meadow, and back to the lodge.

On the trail: Be sure to pause at Minaret Vista as described in **At the trail-head**. After having taken in the view, backtrack downhill to the 4WD road you noticed on your way to the parking loop. Optionally, you can make your way downhill from Minaret Vista to the 4WD road on a use trail east of the toilets.

Turn left (north) onto the road, which cuts across coarse, light-colored pumice —volcanic rock so light it floats on water—spewed from one of the lava domes east of San Joaquin Ridge. At a fork with a closed-off road, go left, passing a foot trail to Mammoth Mountain Inn. The road you're on is open to 4WD vehicles and mountain bikes (marked MOUNTAIN VIEW and HARD CORPS trails—the latter is later on spelled HARD CORE). Multiple tracks diverge and converge where vehicles have passed each other and tried to avoid the rougher spots, but the well-traveled main road—your route—is obvious. MOUNTAIN VIEW bike route soon branches right; you continue left (ahead) on HARD CORPS. At a little over ⅓ mile, a road comes from your left and you continue ahead—right—on the main road, steeply ascending a broad knoll whose pumice-flat top offers stupendous views westward. From here on, the flower display on these open pumice flats just gets better and better. A little beyond 1¼ mile, where a road comes in from the south on your right, your road curves left and ascends very steeply for a while. You top out on a nearly level grade around 1½ miles and pass a snow-depth marker on your right. Near 1¾ miles, you reach a **Y**-junction where you take the left fork—signed HARD CORE—toward a knob to the northwest. You make another steep climb, earning superb views to the east and west.

Approaching 2 miles, you see your final goal, a summit with a tuft of trees like a wisp of hair on a baby's head. This is Peak 10,255, locally called "Deadman Peak," as it's above officially named Deadman Pass, which takes its name from Deadman Creek, which in turn is named for "the headless body of a man" found near the creek in 1868, according to *Place Names of the Sierra Nevada*. The canyon of the Middle Fork San Joaquin River yawns at your feet; distant red-brown patches of dead trees are largely from the lightning-caused 1992 Rainbow Fire. The Ritter Range fills the western skyline, and there's a sweeping view over the rugged lava terrain between San Joaquin Ridge and Long Valley to the east. These views get better and better as you slog your way to **Deadman Peak at nearly 2¼ miles and 10,255 feet**, where the trees turn out to be shrub-sized, the views 360°, and the panoramas awe-inspiring.

Linger to enjoy this spectacle, then retrace your steps to your car.

26. Olaine and Shadow Lakes ☼ ❦

Place	Total Dist.	Elevation	Level	Type
Start	0	8335	—	—
Olaine Lake *only*	3	8038	M U	O&B
Shadow Lake	6–7	8737	S U	O&B

Permit required: None

Topo(s): WP Devils Postpile 15'; Mammoth Mtn, Mt. Ritter 7½'

Where to stay:
> **Mountain:** Convict Lake Resort, Tamarack Lodge, Wildyrie Lodge, Woods Lodge, Crystal Crag Lodge, Red's Meadow Resort
> **Of Interest:** Sierra Gables Motel, Mono Sierra Lodge, Mammoth Mountain Inn, Mammoth Mountain Chalets
> **Other:** Town of Mammoth Lakes, Town of June Lake

Highlights: Grassy Olaine Lake is a little gem set off by the handsome cliffs that here bound the Middle Fork San Joaquin River. Shadow Lake is a famous beauty spot with wonderful picnic sites, at the foot of the magnificent Ritter Range; you won't want to leave it.

How to get to the trailhead: See Trip 25 for directions to Mammoth Mountain Ski Area/Bike Park. During the summer months, you can take the shuttle bus (fee) from Mammoth Mountain Ski Area/Bike Park down the Devils Postpile Road to the hairpin from which the spur road to the pack station takes off, as described in the next paragraph; walk the last 0.25 mile on that road.

Before 7:30 A.M. and after 5:30 P.M. in the summer months, and any time off-season as long as the Devils Postpile Road is open, you can drive your car to the trailhead. Follow the driving directions of Trip 25 over Minaret Summit (don't turn off to Minaret Vista). Continue down the narrow, winding, one-lane road 8.2 miles to a hairpin turn where a signed spur road goes off to the right. Turn onto the spur road and follow it past the Agnew Meadows Pack Station to either of two parking lots at 8.4–8.5 miles from the Main-Minaret-Mary junction. The trailhead is on the south side of the first of the two lots. Toilet.

At the trailhead: Non-hikers will prefer to explore Devils Postpile or the nature trail at Sotcher Lake, farther down the Devils Postpile Road.

On the trail: Look for a Pacific Crest Trail marker on a double-trunked lodgepole on the south side of the first parking lot. The well-beaten trail leaves from here, southbound, where a creek gurgles into the meadow on your left. You cross a couple of arms of the little creek, bob over a low ridge, and skirt part of extensive Agnew Meadows on your right. Colorful San Joaquin Ridge rises steeply to the north, and you cross the creek again as you leave the meadow behind and follow the lodgepole-shaded, nearly level trail as it threads its way between rocky knobs. You pass an unsigned track coming in on the right and continue ahead to a junction at nearly ⅔ mile: left (southeast) to Reds Meadow on the Pacific Crest Trail, right (northwest) on the River Trail for Olaine and Shadow lakes.

Go right, gradually descending an open, scrubby trail along rocky bluffs, until, a little after 1 mile, you reach flats flanking the river and reenter forest cover. Now the going is level again, and you soon reach the southeast end of charming **Olaine Lake at 1½ miles and 8038 feet,** reed-fringed and water-lily-dotted, set among lodgepoles and aspens, cupped by rocky bluffs. Picnic spots are scarce but worth looking for. Continuing beyond Olaine Lake, you reach a **Y**-junction just beyond 1¾ miles: left (west) to Shadow Lake, right (northwest) to continue on the River Trail. You turn left, cross a sandy flat and avoid use trails branching to the river, and then curve through aspens to a handsome footbridge across the Middle Fork San Joaquin. Once across the river, you begin a series of rocky but gentle switch-backs up the open slopes below Shadow Lake. Views open up as you climb; there's a particularly stunning view to the southeast of Mammoth Mountain framed by the river canyon's walls.

The trail turns southwest into Shadow Creek's canyon, where fine cascades plunge down its rocky throat. Near the top of the climb, the trail eases alongside Shadow Creek in thickets of alder and willow. As you cross one final ledge of rock, exquisite **Shadow Lake at 3 miles and 8737 feet** comes into view. Peaks of the Ritter Range tower over the west end of the lake, and Volcanic Ridge rises on the lake's south side. There are a number of excellent picnic spots along the lake's north side, just off the trail—especially some rocky outcrops extending into the water about halfway around the lake. You find yourself at the lake's west end, at its inlet, at 3½ miles, if you haven't already pulled off to occupy a prime picnic site.

Retrace your steps to the parking lot.

Olaine Lake

27. Minaret Falls ☼ 🍁

Place	Total Dist.	Elevation	Level	Type
Start	0	7559	—	—
Devils Postpile semiloop *only*	1	7775	M	Semi
Minaret Falls	3½	7610	M	O&B

Permit required: None

Topo(s): WP Devils Postpile 15′; Mammoth Mountain, Crystal Crag 7½′

Where to stay:
Mountain: Convict Lake Resort, Tamarack Lodge, Wildyrie Lodge, Woods Lodge, Crystal
    Crag Lodge, Red's Meadow Resort
Of Interest: Sierra Gables Motel, Mono Sierra Lodge, Mammoth Mountain Inn,
    Mammoth Mountain Chalets
Other: Town of Mammoth Lakes, Town of June Lake

Highlights: Devils Postpile National Monument hosts the eponymous columnar-basalt formation in a beautiful setting that would be worth a visit even without the Devils Postpile. Just outside the monument, you'll find Minaret Falls, not a classical waterfall at all but at peak runoff a thrilling spectacle of wild cascades. In spring, Minaret Falls is easy to spot from viewpoints on the upper Devils Postpile road, and you may even hear its roar that far away!

How to get to the trailhead: During the summer months, you can take the shuttle bus (fee) from Mammoth Mountain Ski Area/Bike Park almost to this trail-head.

Before 7:30 A.M. and after 5:30 P.M. in the summer months, and any time off-season as long as the Devils Postpile Road is open, you can drive your car to the trailhead. Follow the driving directions of Trip 25 to Minaret Summit and then continue on the Devils Postpile Road as described in the driving directions of Trip 26. Negotiate the hairpin turn, passing the spur road to Agnew Meadows, 12.3 miles from the Main-Minaret-Mary junction to the turnoff to Devils Postpile National Monument. Turn right here and follow this access road 0.3 mile more to a large parking area that's often very crowded by midday in the summer. Toilets, water, National Park Service ranger station.

At the trailhead: The Devils Postpile area is a great spot for non-hikers: very scenic, with picnic tables, and with the nearby Middle Fork San Joaquin River to fish in. Non-walkers should consider the out-and-back, ½-mile-plus jaunt to the base of the Devils Postpile (don't tackle the steep semiloop).

On the trail: To find the trailhead, walk over to the ranger station to pick up your Devils Postpile brochure; the trail is just beyond the front of the ranger station, a broad gravel path heading south-southeast across a meadow with a fine display of flowers in season. Beyond the meadow, the trail climbs moderately to level out overlooking the river as it meanders lazily through a broad meadow. In less than ¼ mile you reach a junction with a spur trail to the Pacific Crest and John Muir trails: left (ahead) to Devils Postpile, right to cross the river to Minaret Falls and

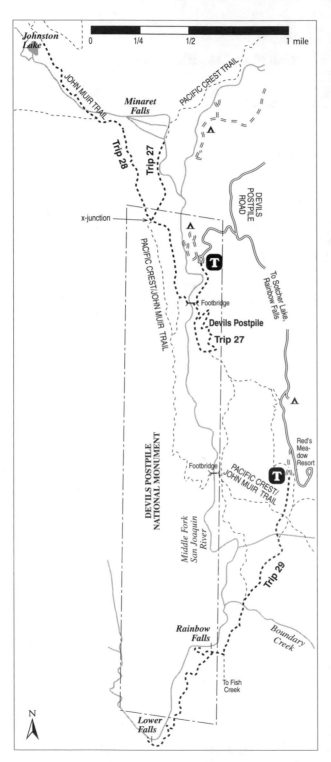

Johnston Lake via the John Muir and Pacific Crest trails. For now, you're headed to Devils Postpile, so go left (ahead) to your first glimpse of the Postpile at ¼ mile and a junction with a side trail that loops over the top of the Postpile. The side trail is quite steep, though spectacular; if you're disinclined to tackle it, just continue ahead a few steps to enjoy a wonderful view of the tall, angular columns of the Devils Postpile at ¼+ mile and 7595 feet. Many still stand, but even more lie spilled at the Postpile's base, broken and shattered.

An interpretive sign at the formation's base explains this phenomenon. According to Mary Hill's *Geology of the Sierra Nevada*, the Postpile is a remnant of a 600,000-year-old lava flow. Here, liquid rock pooled deep, and conditions during the mass's cooling were quite uniform. A cooling mass shrinks, and a uniformly cooling mass like the Postpile flow tends to crack apart "more or less all at once" from top to bottom into unusually regular polyhedrals, yielding three- to eight-sided columns. As every honeybee knows, six-sided structures are the most efficient, and six-sided columns predominate here (sources quoted say from 44.5% to 55% of the Postpile's columns). At what is now the top of the formation, glaciers have planed off and exposed the columns, leaving a now-small, shiny "pavement" of polygons that looks remarkably like a tiled floor.

To loop over the formation, turn left at the junction with the side trail and climb very steeply to reach the Postpile's top at 7775 feet in a little over ⅓ mile from the start. Sunlight glints off the polished "tiles" of the Postpile's top, and you realize that there's an amazingly steep drop to the river from here. You continue by turning away from the "tiles" and following the now-steeply-descending trail as it zigzags past columns tilted onto their sides and down into trees burnt by the lightning-caused 1992 Rainbow Fire. At ¾ mile you reach a junction: left (southeast) to Rainbow Falls, right (west) to close the loop. Turn right to soon pass the interpretive sign at the Postpile's base and **close the loop around Devils Postpile at a little over 1 mile**.

In a few more steps you're back at the junction with the spur to the Pacific Crest and John Muir trails. Mileages given from now on assume you've taken the 1+-mile semiloop around Devils Postpile. Continuing toward Minaret Falls, you soon turn left and cross a handsome footbridge over the roiling Middle Fork San Joaquin. The main trail, with you on it, turns right on the west side of the bridge. At 1¼ miles you reach a junction: left (south) to King Creek, Fern Lake, and Clover Meadow; right toward the Pacific Crest and John Muir trails. Go right here.

You reach an **X**-junction a little shy of 1¾ miles, where heavy usage may have made the junction quite confusing. Let's look at this junction as if you were facing north (you're actually facing west-northwest as you approach the junction, but face north for this exercise). You've just come up the lower right arm of the **X**. On the lower left arm, the Pacific Crest and John Muir trails, joined as usual, head southward toward Mexico and Mt. Whitney, respectively. Ahead, northward, the Pacific Crest and John Muir trails diverge: the upper left arm of the **X** is the John Muir Trail heading north-northwest for Johnston and Shadow lakes, the upper right arm of the **X** is the Pacific Crest Trail heading northeast for Minaret Falls and the canyon of the Middle Fork San Joaquin. Take the upper right arm of the **X**, the Pacific Crest Trail, here a dusty track across pumice. You soon leave the monument and descend to cross an unnamed creek (can be difficult at high water) near its junction with Minaret Creek. In early season, it's not long before you hear the roar of Minaret Falls ahead. Minaret Falls diminishes considerably by midsummer, but at runoff's peak, you soon reach the south side of a very wide, boulder-choked creekbed. It's Minaret Creek, broad and shallow as it comes to rest below the beautiful series of cascades called **Minaret Falls at 2¼ miles and 7610 feet**. Individually, no cascade is particularly spectacular, but all together…! Gaze up to enjoy the sight of the water leaping free of the rock shelves at the top of the falls. If the water isn't too high, you may want to scramble out into the boulders for a more panoramic view. The falls are very wide, and it's hard to take them all in from any one viewpoint.

You won't want to leave Minaret Falls, but retrace your steps when you must.

28. Johnston Lake 🌸

Place	Total Dist.	Elevation	Level	Type
Start	0	7559	—	—
Devils Postpile semiloop *only*	1	7775	M	Semi
Johnston Lake	5	8100	M	O&B

Permit required: None

Topo(s): WP Devils Postpile 15'; Mammoth Mtn, Crystal Crag 7½'

Where to stay:

  Mountain: Convict Lake Resort, Tamarack Lodge, Wildyrie Lodge, Woods Lodge, Crystal Crag Lodge, Red's Meadow Resort

  Of Interest: Sierra Gables Motel, Mono Sierra Lodge, Mammoth Mountain Inn, Mammoth Mountain Chalets

  Other: Town of Mammoth Lakes, Town of June Lake

Highlights: Take in the Devils Postpile before heading off toward pretty Johnston Lake, which is surrounded by a deep meadow full of low bilberry shrubs whose leaves turn fiery red in the fall.

How to get to the trailhead: Follow the driving directions of Trip 27 to parking at Devils Postpile National Monument. Toilets, water, National Park Service ranger station.

At the trailhead: See Trip 27.

On the trail: See Trip 27's map. Follow Trip 27 on its semiloop around Devils Postpile if you haven't already done so. Mileages given below include that semiloop.

Then continue as described in Trip 27 across the footbridge to the **X**-junction a little before 1¾ miles and—picturing the **X**-junction as if you were facing north—take the upper left arm of the **X**, heading north-northwest to Johnston and Shadow lakes on the John Muir Trail. The dusty trail is deep in pumice sand as it rises through a moderate-to-dense cover of fir and lodgepole. You shortly walk out of Devils Postpile National Monument and, as you near 2⅓ miles, follow the trail as it swings near the edge of a bluff where you enjoy views southeast to the Mammoth Crest area, scarred by the lightning-caused 1992 Rainbow Fire; east to Mammoth Mountain; and north along San Joaquin Ridge.

At 2½ miles you meet Minaret Creek, running deep in a rocky channel below the trail, and veer west near its south bank. Use trails branch off to the creek, but your main trail curves slightly away from it. In a few more steps you're at a junction: left (west) to Lost Dog Lake, right (northwest) on the John Muir Trail to Johnston Lake. Go right, passing through an unused drift fence. Curve right toward the creek, cross a meadow, and ford the creek at a spot that suits you around 2⅔ miles—ignore a use trail leading upstream on the south side of the creek. Don't worry, there's no need to leap across a rocky channel: the creek flows between low, sandy banks here.

Now on the north bank, the nearly-level trail heads away from the creek before curving generally northwest to offer occasional views of the Minarets through breaks in the forest cover. Soon you glimpse big Johnston Meadow and little **Johnston Lake at just over 3 miles and 8100 feet**, and use trails dart left off to the lakeshore. Pick your use trail, find your lakeside picnic spot, and enjoy! In the fall, the vibrant red of the dwarf bilberry leaves here is dazzling.

Retrace your steps to the parking lot.

29. Rainbow and Lower Falls ☼ 🍁

Place	Total distance	Elevation	Level	Type
Start	0	7610	—	—
First viewpt, Rainbow Falls *only*	2	7400	E U	O&B
Lower Falls	3	7220	M U	O&B

Permit required: None

Topo(s): WP Devils Postpile 15'; Crystal Crag 7½'

Where to stay:

  Mountain: Convict Lake Resort, Tamarack Lodge, Wildyrie Lodge, Woods Lodge, Crystal Crag Lodge, Red's Meadow Resort

  Of Interest: Sierra Gables Motel, Mono Sierra Lodge, Mammoth Mountain Inn, Mammoth Mountain Chalets

  Other: Town of Mammoth Lakes, Town of June Lake

Highlights: It's an easy hike to see Rainbow Falls, justly regarded as the most classically beautiful waterfall in the Sierra outside Yosemite. If that hike is not long enough for you, extend your stroll south to pretty little Lower Falls.

How to get to the trailhead: During the summer months, you can take the shuttle bus (fee) from Mammoth Mountain Ski Area/Bike Park almost to this trailhead.

Before 7:30 A.M. and after 5:30 P.M. in the summer months, and any time off-season as long as the Devils Postpile Road is open, you can drive your car to the trailhead, which is very near the end of the road that leads over Minaret Summit past a turnoff to Devils Postpile National Monument and down to Reds Meadow Resort. Follow the driving directions of Trips 25–27 from the Main-Minaret-Mary junction over Minaret Summit and past the turnoff to Devils Postpile. Continue almost to the road's end, to a **Y** at 13.6 miles: left (up) to Reds Meadow Resort, right on an unimpressive dirt road. Take the right fork into a large dirt parking lot, about 13.7 miles from the Main-Minaret-Mary junction. The trailhead is on the south side of the parking lot. Toilet.

At the trailhead: This isn't an attractive trailhead, and non-hikers will probably be happier at Devils Postpile or Sotcher Lake, where there are pretty views to enjoy as you relax under the majestic trees. A visit to quaint, nearby Red's Meadow Resort, with its store and café, is also possible.

On the trail: Head south on a very broad, dusty-sandy trail under moderate forest cover. The forest soon becomes patchy and includes a number of burnt trees, victims of the August 1992 Rainbow Fire, a lightning-caused blaze. For now, the thinned forest cover permits these sandy flats to support a wonderful, seasonal display of lupine. Numerous use trails dart off here and there in this heavily used area, but your main trail is easily distinguished by its considerable width. You step across an intersecting trail—the John Muir/Pacific Crest Trail—and soon pass a trail that comes in from the left. Approaching the boundary of Devils Postpile National Monument, you pass a trail that comes in from the right and then cross Boundary Creek. Soon you reach a fork: ahead (south) to Fish Creek, right (west) to Rainbow Falls. Go right.

At the Devils Postpile boundary, the trail forks; the left fork is the horse trail, the right is the foot trail. You can see the Middle Fork San Joaquin River to your right and hear Rainbow Falls thundering just downstream. Turn right here to marked **FIRST VIEWPOINT at 1 mile and 7400 feet**, a dramatic overlook a little above the top of Rainbow Falls—for lack of space, the book's map just shows "*Rainbow Falls*" for this area and its viewpoints. You descend a little to SECOND VIEWPOINT, where you get another splendid eyeful of the 101-foot sheer waterfall. Look for a trail branching left here; it's the trail to Lower Falls. You'll probably also spot a hitching rail just off to the left of your trail; horses aren't permitted at the edge of the falls.

Continuing along the brink of the falls for now, the trail angles sharply right to the top of an extremely steep "staircase." Not everyone will want to descend this part of the trail, which takes you to the base of the falls—better to wait back at Second Viewpoint if climbs as steep as this aren't on your menu. At the bottom of the descent at about 7250 feet, the rocks are perpetually wet with the dense mist from Rainbow Falls, which makes the rocks dangerous to scramble on. You're downstream of and a little lower than the base of Rainbow Falls. The view of the falls from here is awe-inspiring, and you will have to scream in order to make your expressions of admiration heard over the perpetual roar of the water.

To continue to Lower Falls, retrace your steps to the junction near Second Viewpoint and pick up the trail to Lower Falls. The dusty trails rolls generally southward on increasingly sunstruck terrain. Near its end, the trail drops steeply to the river (on your right), passing a junction with a prominent but unmapped use trail. The trail hooks right to big rocks at the top of little **Lower Falls at 1½ miles and 7224 feet**, which is by far the less high of the two falls. The big pool at Lower Falls' base often hosts an angler, and you'll find some pleasant picnic rocks.

Retrace your steps from here.

30. Fern and Yost Lakes 🌸 ☼

Place	Total distance	Elevation	Level	Type
Start	0	7300	—	—
Fern Lake *only*	3	8890	M	O&B
Yost Lake *only*	4⅔	9090	M	O&B
Both lakes	5⅔	9090	S	O&B

Permit required: None

Topo(s): June Lake, Mammoth Mtn. 7½'

Where to stay:

    Mountain: Convict Lake Resort, Tamarack Lodge, Wildyrie Lodge, Woods Lodge, Crystal Crag Lodge

    Of Interest: Sierra Gables Motel, Mono Sierra Lodge, Mammoth Mountain Inn, Mammoth Mountain Chalets, Silver Lake Resort

    Other: Town of Mammoth Lakes, Town of June Lake

Highlights: A steep trail offering lovely views over the June Lake area leads to two wonderful lakes. See one, see the other, or (best of all) see both lakes!

How to get to the trailhead: The trailhead is just off State Route 158, the June Lakes Loop, which meets U.S. Highway 395 at two points 5.6 miles apart, between the turnoff to Mammoth Lakes (State Route 203) and Lee Vining. This trailhead is much closer to the south junction, so let's assume you turn southwest, toward the Sierra, there. Follow State Route 158 over Oh! Ridge. *Oh! Ridge? Odd name, wonder why?* you think, until you top the ridge and take in the breathtaking spectacle of June Lake backed by rugged, snow-dashed peaks. *Oh!* you think, *that's why!* Drive through charming June Lake village and then past June Mountain Ski Area's base. Between 5.2 and 5.3 miles from the south junction of 395 and 158, you spot an obscurely marked trailhead turnoff on the left. Turn here and go about 100 yards on a dirt road to a parking area.

At the trail-head: Non-hikers will probably be much happier sunning themselves on the pretty beach at the north end of June Lake. Take the Oh! Ridge turnoff down through the campground to the beach. Non-hikers may also enjoy exploring quaint June Lake village.

On the trail: The trailhead is at the south end of the parking lot, past a row of large boulders. You pass an interpretive display and begin a moderate climb, avoiding use trails and enjoying the sight of Carson Peak's rugged face when the forest cover permits. Views over Silver Lake and of Reversed Peak open up as you climb. Reversed Peak is named for Reversed Creek, which connects Gull Lake (between June and Silver lakes) with Rush Creek and Silver Lake. The creek is named for the direction of its flow: the unusual shape of the valley between Reversed and Carson peaks, in which Gull lies, makes the creek flow briefly *toward*, rather than away from, the Sierra Crest, so its flow is *reversed* from normal, which would be *away from* the Crest.

The trail makes a switchback turn a little before ½ mile and begins to climb more steeply. You hear rushing Fern Creek before you see it, as views toward fantastically shaped Mono Craters open up between Reversed Peak and June Mountain. Just beyond 1 mile and just before the cascades called Fern Creek Falls, you reach a fork, the Fern-Yost fork: left (east) to Yost Lake, right (south) to Fern Lake. If you must choose between them, Fern Lake is the more spectacular, and most people head for it, leaving quiet Yost Lake a more desirable choice for those seeking to escape the crowds.

To Fern Lake. Go right to Fern Lake, climbing very steeply on a rocky, twisting trail. At 1½ miles you top out 300 feet north of Fern Lake's shore, where you'll find plenty of good picnic spots from which to enjoy the spectacular scenery. **Fern Lake at 1½+ miles and 8890 feet** sits in a steep-sided cup formed by rugged outliers of Carson Peak and San Joaquin Ridge. San Joaquin Mountain dominates views to the south, and the lake itself is exquisite. Retrace your steps to the Fern-Yost fork, enjoying excellent views of June and Gull lakes and of Mono Craters on the way back.

To Yost Lake. At the fork at 1+ mile from the parking lot, go right (east) for Yost Lake if you've come from Fern Lake (now with 2 miles on your boots), or left if you've come from the parking lot. You cross Fern Creek Falls (may be difficult in early season). Fern Creek Falls isn't much to look at from here but is seasonally showy from vantage points near Silver Lake and on the Rush Creek Trail (Trip 31). Now you climb eastward, moderately to steeply, on open slopes offering fine views of the June Lake area. Abruptly veering through a densely forested gully, you leave the views behind and climb steadily within hearing of Yost Creek. You curve generally south, paralleling the creek for a time, before climbing gradually to a junction at nearly 3¼ miles: left (southeast) to Yost Meadow, right (south) to Yost Lake.

Go right to Yost Lake, topping a low ridge before descending a little to **Yost Lake at a little over 3⅓ miles and 9090 feet**, a pretty spot guarded by an outlier of San Joaquin Ridge. A small open area along Yost Lake's west shore offers a few picnic sites, and you'll want to stay for a while.

But eventually you must retrace your steps to the parking lot.

Yes, we got no trails. This is the first hike in the June Lake area, so I want to tell you about a couple of mistakes on the USFS *Ansel Adams Wilderness* map and on some June-Lake-area handouts based on it.

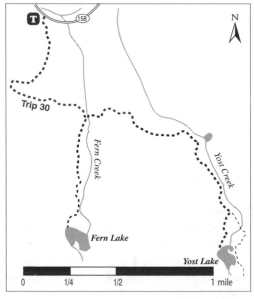

One, the "trail" to the top of Reversed Peak doesn't exist. You can follow some 4WD roads for a little way, then scramble up a steep, rough use trail a bit farther, but eventually, if you're peak-bound, you'll be bushwhacking through tick-laden shrubbery. The use trail leads to the ponds south of Reversed Peak; they're not worth your trouble.

Two, I'm told that much of the trail shown between Yost Lake and Obsidian Dome, via Glass Creek Meadow, has disappeared. I know from experience that it disappears after you get to Glass Creek Meadow from Obsidian Dome.

31. Agnew and Gem Lakes ☼ ❦

Place	Total distance	Elevation	Level	Type
Start	0	7240	—	—
Agnew Lake *only*	5	8520	S	O&B
Gem Lake overlook	7	9100	S	O&B

Permit required: None

Topo(s): Koip Peak 7½'

Where to stay:

Mountain: Convict Lake Resort, Tamarack Lodge, Wildyrie Lodge, Woods Lodge, Crystal Crag Lodge

Of Interest: Sierra Gables Motel, Mammoth Mountain Inn, Mammoth Mountain Chalets, Silver Lake Resort

Other: Town of Mammoth Lakes, Town of June Lake, Town of Lee Vining

Highlights: The view-filled ascent of the Rush Creek Trail is a treat in itself, and your strenuous climb is amply rewarded by your visit to lovely Agnew and splendid Gem lakes. The route passes near or offers good views of several beautiful waterfalls in season. Get an early start, as the trail is mostly shadeless and can be very hot.

How to get to the trailhead: Follow the driving directions of Trip 30 through June Lake village and past the ski area, but continue on State Route 158 past the Fern-Yost trailhead turnoff. As the highway curves north past Silver Lake Resort to the west and Silver Lake to the east, look for a marked trailhead turnoff beyond the resort and just past a campground and trailer park, on the west. Turn west to parking, 7.2 miles from 395. Toilet; may be seasonal USFS ranger station here.

At the trailhead: See Trip 30.

On the trail: Straight ahead from the trailhead sign, in season, you'll see the showy waterfall Alger Creek forms as it thunders down to swell Silver Lake. Almost immediately you reach a **T**-junction: left (south) to Rush Creek, right (north) to Parker Bench and Parker Lake (to which, in Trip 32, you'll get by a different, easier route). Go left, crossing one unmapped dirt road and then picking up the next briefly as the trail jogs west to cross Alger Creek on a footbridge (this stretch of dirt road is shown as part of the trail on the book's map). The trail jogs south again,

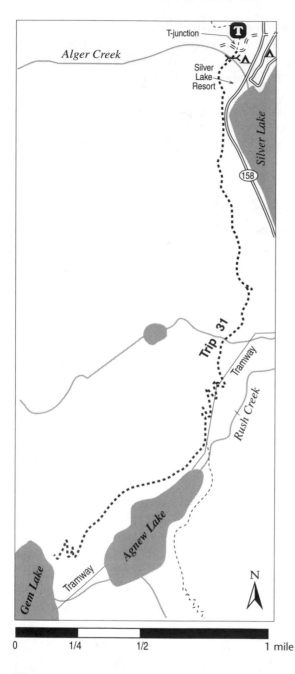

and you ford a placid creek-branch before curving behind the trailer park and cabins of Silver Lake Resort. The view of Carson Peak's convoluted north face over Silver Lake is stunning.

You climb moderately and in ¾ mile enter Ansel Adams Wilderness abreast of Silver Lake's inlet, a bright stream that meanders through a deep meadow. The upper runs of June Mountain Ski Area are visible ahead. Seasonally, you'll spy the long cascade of Fern Creek Falls tucked into a deep crevice on June Mountain's west flank. In just a few more steps, you curve around an outcrop and into Rush Creek's steep canyon, where an unnamed, seasonal waterfall on a tributary of Rush Creek dashes down the cliffs very high up on your right. Cross the tributary; from here to Agnew Lake, snowbanks stuck in the throat of this narrow canyon can be very difficult to cross safely in early season.

At 1⅔ miles you reach the tracks of the defunct tramway that helped move supplies between the Southern California Edison powerhouse below and the dammed Agnew and Gem lakes ahead—this is a hydroelectric project. You cross the tracks, switchback up, sometimes on concrete stairs, traverse a section that's blasted out of the rock, cross the tracks again, and switchback up again. Then, rounding an outcrop, you emerge above **Agnew Lake and its dam at 2½ miles and 8520 feet**, where use trails lead off to the dam and its buildings as well as to some picnic spots. Gem Lake's dam and the tramway tracks leading to it are visible across pretty Agnew Lake to the southwest, and you're right below 10,909-foot Carson Peak. Spurning the trails to the dam, you stick to the main trail, switchbacking up and climbing moderately to steeply, high above the lake. Near the head of Agnew Lake, you switchback steeply up on a rocky track, crossing a huge, rusty pipe. Take lots of breather stops to enjoy the fine over-the-shoulder views down-canyon.

At last you cross a low saddle and find yourself just below a scrub-dotted knob (to your left) of shattered, rusty rock, above big, beautiful **Gem Lake and its dam at nearly 3½ miles and 9100 feet**. This knob has many scenic, if windy, picnic spots overlooking Gem Lake, Donohue Pass, and the grand peaks of the Sierra Crest, beyond which lies the southern backcountry of Yosemite National Park. In *Mammoth Lakes Sierra*, Genny Smith and Bettie Willard call this spot, "Hat Ridge, where the wind blows hats off"—very apt. It's an easy scramble up the knob, where you find yourself a perch, enjoy your lunch, and soak in the spectacular scenery, which includes great views back to Agnew Lake.

You won't want to leave, but retrace your steps to your car when you must.

32. Parker Lake ☼ 🍁

Place	Total distance	Elevation	Level	Type
Start	0	7680	—	—
Parker Lake	3+	8318	M	O&B

Permit required: None

Topo(s): Koip Peak 7½'

Where to stay:

    Mountain: Convict Lake Resort, Tamarack Lodge, Wildyrie Lodge, Woods Lodge, Crystal Crag Lodge

    Of Interest: Sierra Gables Motel, Mammoth Mountain Inn, Mammoth Mountain Chalets, Silver Lake Resort

    Other: Town of Mammoth Lakes, Town of June Lake, Town of Lee Vining

Highlights: I don't which is more charming, pretty Parker Lake or the idyllic forest and meadow just below it. At least half the charm is that, in spite of my telling you this, they will come as surprises, for you must first ascend a sandy, sunblasted, unpromising moraine to reach them.

How to get to the trailhead: It's easier to approach Parker Lake and neighboring Walker Lake (Trips 33 and 34) from the *northern* junction of U.S. Highway 395 and State Route 158 (the June Lakes Loop). You have overshot this junction if you get to the junction with State Route 120 *westbound* to Yosemite as you are driving north or the junction with 120 *eastbound* to Benton as you are driving south. Turn west, toward the Sierra, at the northern junction and follow State Route 158 1.4 miles to a modestly-marked turnoff onto dirt roads to Parker and Walker lakes.

(There are actually 3 turnoffs here within 0.1 mile; you can take any of them. By the end of summer, they may look like one, huge, dusty turnoff.) Turn right here and follow the road 0.5 mile more to another junction: left to Parker Lake, right to Walker Lake. Turn left and follow the road generally west toward the Parker Lake trailhead, 3.7 miles from 395. At a fork with the road to Parker Creek, go left for Parker Lake. At a fork near the end, take the right branch to the trailhead. After a heavy winter, the road may wash out in the area of this fork. In that case, park off the road where you can and walk to the trailhead—it's not far.

At the trailhead: See Trip 30.

On the trail: From the information sign at the trailhead, climb moderately southwest, up a hot, scrub-dotted slope of the moraine left behind by Parker Creek's glacier. In less than ¼ mile you enter Ansel Adams Wilderness and continue to climb, sometimes steeply. Well below the trail and to your right, Parker Creek makes a noisy descent through aspens—it's a sign of treats to come. The trail's grade eases as it crosses flats dominated by sagebrush and bitterbrush, although you encounter a couple of short, steep hauls over wrinkles in the moraine. After a mile, the trail curves near the stream at last and becomes nearly level, while the terrain turns from harsh desert to appealing forest and meadow, with Parker Creek winding lazily between grassy banks. Aspens growing near the streambanks provide wonderful color in the fall.

Soon after passing a junction with a trail descending from Parker Bench and coming in on your left, you emerge on the southeast side of the forested outlet at lovely Parker Lake at just over 1½ miles and 8318 feet; Parker and Kuna peaks and Mt. Wood tower over the lake. You can see the upper part of the narrow valley down which the lake's inlet flows, and in season there's a large waterfall high in that valley. There are good picnic sites here around the outlet. This trip officially ends here, though you may want to make your way a little farther around Parker's shores. I don't recommend bashing your way all around the lake, because the use trails eventually vanish, and you'll find yourself bushwhacking through tick-laden scrub.

Retrace your steps when you must, enjoying views of Mono Lake on your descent.

33. Walker and Sardine Lakes 🌿 ☼ 🍁

Place	Total distance	Elevation	Level	Type
Start	0	8420	—	—
Walker Lake *only*	⅓	7935	M U	O&B
Lower Sardine Lake	7+	9888	S	O&B

Permit required: None

Topo(s): Koip Peak 7½'

Where to stay:

    Mountain: Convict Lake Resort, Tamarack Lodge, Wildyrie Lodge, Woods Lodge, Crystal Crag Lodge

    Of Interest: Sierra Gables Motel, Mammoth Mountain Inn, Mammoth Mountain Chalets, Silver Lake Resort

    Other: Town of Mammoth Lakes, Town of June Lake, Town of Lee Vining

Highlights: From the lush meadows and aspens of beautiful Walker Lake to the barren rocks and wild peaks around Lower Sardine Lake, this is a journey of wonderful contrasts. The stand of aspens around the head of Walker Lake is exceptionally lovely in the fall.

How to get to the trailhead: You may need a high-clearance vehicle for this drive. Follow the driving directions of Trip 32 to the turnoff at 1.4 miles from the northern 395-158 junction. There are two trailheads for Walker Lake, and you're headed for the more southerly of the two, *not* the one along Walker Creek in Bloody Canyon (Trip 34). Follow the road for Parker and Walker lakes for 0.5 mile to another junction, where you turn right toward Walker Lake on an obvious main dirt road. Follow this main road, taking the right fork at all junctions except for the one that goes through a ranch's fence—there, go left—for 0.9 mile more to a marked turnoff for Walker Lake. Follow this road west into the mountains, ignoring side roads, to trailhead parking at 2.7 more miles, 4.9 miles from 395. Toilet and four walk-in campsites/picnic sites with tables and fireplaces.

At the trailhead: See Trip 30, or enjoy a picnic at one of the trailhead sites.

On the trail: The topo is quite inaccurate concerning this trailhead and the first part of this trail. The trailhead used to be at the end of the road extending up what's marked "Sawmill Canyon." Recently, the road has been extended another 0.5–0.6 mile to a new, higher trailhead. There is no 4WD road extending from the next canyon south (from point 7678T) and northwest over the moraine to Walker Lake. There's a switchback as the foot trail descends to Walker Lake.

The sandy trail heads up a short, steep slope, soon topping out at about 8500 feet under an immense mountain mahogany at an overlook of long, beautiful Walker Lake. The docks, boats, and cabins at the northeast end of the lake are private property—no trespassing—but you're not headed that way. Instead, the trail heads moderately to steeply down the moraine toward the lake, making one long switchback and bypassing a breathtakingly steep, loose use trail that darts off on your right, straight down to the lake's edge. Staying on the main trail (left), you shortly reach a junction: left (west) to Sardine Lakes and Mono Pass, right (northwest) to Walker Lake. Go right to Walker Lake, even though you're headed for Lower Sardine Lake, in order to enjoy the wonderful aspen grove at Walker Lake's west end. In a few more steps you nearly reach the shore of **Walker Lake at ¼ mile and 7935 feet**, where use trails branch left and right. From the shoreline, a few steps away, there are wonderful views north-northwest across the lake and west toward Mono Pass (the northern one on the boundary of Yosemite National Park in Trip 77, not the one out of Mosquito Flat visited on Trip 15). In the fall, currents raft masses of golden aspen leaves ashore here.

Take the main Mono Pass Trail—marked TRAIL—northwest here, crossing Walker Lake's inlet at a little under ⅔ mile. On the other side you parallel the inlet briefly before curving through a lovely meadow beneath the aspens to a trail junction: left (west) to Sardine Lakes and Mono Pass, right (northeast) to continue around Walker Lake's shore. To continue to Lower Sardine Lake, turn left at this junction to enter Ansel Adams Wilderness at ¾ mile, where the trail crosses a slab of dark rock. Ahead to the southwest, Peak 11092T is so rugged and imposing that it's impossible that it's unnamed. On the northwest, rust-colored outliers of Mt. Gibbs pierce the blue sky. The trail curves southwest, back toward the inlet stream and through dense forest, before beginning a steep, switchbacking climb on the north side of the stream. A couple of open switchback turns offer good over-the-shoulder views of Walker Lake and far beyond it to Mono Lake. The grade eases where the trail crosses a bench within this narrow, northeast-angling canyon, infamous Bloody Canyon, named, according to Peter Browning's *Place Names of the Sierra Nevada*, for blood spattered from cuts on the legs of mules and horses, cuts made by the sharp rocks along this once-dreaded trail.

At a little over 1½ miles, you cross the flower-decked creek while on a bench. Look west-northwest near here for a showy cascade from a hanging valley and for a pretty cascade on Walker Creek itself. The trail soon grows very steep again until, at a little over 2¼ miles, you cross an aspen-covered bench opposite the hanging valley you noted earlier. You swing west-southwest across the bench, below a headwall, to cross the stream at 2½ miles and climb again toward a lodgepole-covered outcrop to the northwest. Next, you switchback up the southeast side of that outcrop, with the creek cascading down the headwall to your left. At 3 miles you gain the next bench, which is dotted with stunted trees and

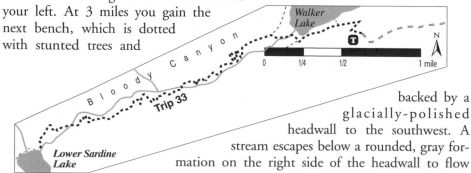

backed by a glacially-polished headwall to the southwest. A stream escapes below a rounded, gray formation on the right side of the headwall to flow down an aspen-lined channel which you soon curve west to cross. You resume ascending steeply, now across a scree slope, before curving through a slot on the west side of the gray formation to gain the next bench. You veer south below a cliff as you climb moderately and twice cross a fork of Lower Sardine Lake's outlet at 3½ miles. The main outlet stream flows in a deep, rocky channel on your left here.

You reach the northeast shore of clear **Lower Sardine Lake at just over 3½ miles and 9888 feet**, which fills a barren, rocky cirque north-northeast of Peak 11619T. From here there are fabulous views of Mono Lake to the northeast, Mt. Gibbs to the northwest, and Mt. Lewis to the south-southeast. A broad swath of willows northwest of the lake marks the course of an inlet from Mt. Gibbs's southeast slopes. Find a rocky perch on the low knolls around the lake; linger and have lunch.

Return, reluctantly, the way you came.

34. Walker Lake ☼ 🍁

Place	Total distance	Elevation	Level	Type
Start	0	7400	—	—
Walker Lake (northeast end)	4	7942	MS	O&B
Walker Lake (head)	6	7942	MS	O&B

Permit required: None

Topo(s): Mount Dana, Koip Peak 7½'

Where to stay:
   Mountain: Convict Lake Resort, Tamarack Lodge, Wildyrie Lodge, Woods Lodge, Crystal Crag Lodge
   Of Interest: Sierra Gables Motel, Mammoth Mountain Inn, Mammoth Mountain Chalets, Silver Lake Resort
   Other: Town of Mammoth Lakes, Town of June Lake, Town of Lee Vining

Highlights: There are two trails to the eastern Sierra's lovely Walker Lake. Trip 33 documents the southern one that reaches all the way to the Sardine Lakes. The northern trail, described here, is one of the last to be closed by snow in winter and often the first to open in spring for several reasons: its altitude is low altitude for the Mammoth-June area; it's largely open and sunstruck terrain; and for most of the way to the lake, the trail is a dirt road closed to public vehicles. Even when snow cloaks the slopes above 8500 feet, this route may be open.

How to get to the trailhead: Follow the directions for Trips 32 and 33 but don't turn at signed spur to Walker Lake. Instead, continue on the main road north toward Walker Lake past turnoffs to a couple of Los Angeles Department of Water and Power (LADWP) ponds on the left. The unseen second pond has an impressive roadside cascade. After passing that cascade, turn left (southwest) into the mouth of Bloody Canyon at the next dirt road with a LADWP "No Camping" sign. You parallel Walker Creek and an impressive aspen grove for another half mile to a semicircular parking area on the left (south) side of the road. Park here.

At the trailhead: Non-hikers will be happier exploring the quaint town of June Lake.

On the trail: Start walking generally southwest up the road. At about 100 there is a gate that bars most—but not all—cars. There is a private enclave at Walker Lake's outlet, and people going there have keys to this gate and can (and do) drive beyond the gate.

Hemmed in by chaparral-covered moraines, the sandy road rises gently past aspens as views open gradually ahead of (right to left) Mt. Gibbs, Mt. Lewis, and Parker Peak. At a Y junction between ½ and ⅔ mile, stay on the main road as it hooks right up a moderate grade. Go right again almost immediately to stay on the main road at the next Y junction. Near the top of this short climb you have good views ahead to Mt. Dana and east to Mono Lake, low Panum Crater, and the north end of the otherworldly Mono Craters.

The road curves southwest again as it dips into patchy forest and then levels out, briefly meeting the creek. Around 1 mile, the forest gives way to a long meadow splashed with blue iris in spring, tinted vivid green in summer, and brushed with muted gold in fall. The now-gravelly road skirts the meadow's north edge for most of the next mile, treating you to excellent views of historic Bloody Canyon up to Mono Pass on Yosemite's border, the saddle between Mts. Gibbs and Lewis, and part of a major trade route across the Sierra used by Native Americans and pioneers.

Just beyond the meadow's southwest end a large sign points to the LI'L WALKER LAKE TRAIL on the right. Another sign forbids you to go farther on the road, as the enclave is ahead. Turn right onto the broad, sandy trail in the shade of fragrant Jeffrey pines. On this trail you presently top a low rise and find yourself paralleling a fence with a hiker's pass-through at 2 miles. The lake's sparkling blue water is visible leftward through the pines, and you can toddle down to the shore (7935′) to end your hike.

To continue, pick up the trail on the other side of the fence; the needle-covered path is very faint here. Occasional views of the lake across its deeply meadowed shoreline are sure to inspire *oohs* and *aahs*. Use trails angle toward the lake as you pass an enormous juniper, but the main trail continues ahead, roughly tracing the lakeshore.

The trail ducks into a strip of lakeside aspens and reaches one of Walker Lake's several inlets. Step across on logs and into the huge aspen grove at the lake's head—a spectacular sight in its autumn glory! The trail may be very faint under fallen leaves as it begins to curve deeper into Bloody Canyon, and you shortly jump another streamlet. The trail presently arrives at a signed junction with the trail over Mono Pass and from Walker Lake's south side. At about 3 miles, this junction makes a good turnaround point. Retrace your steps to your car.

35. Gibbs Lake ☼ 🍁

Place	**Total distance**	**Elevation**	**Level**	**Type**
Start	0	7927	—
Gibbs Lake	6½	9530	S	O&B

Permit required: None

Topo(s): Mount Dana 7½'

Where to stay:
  Mountain: Lundy Lake Resort, Tuolumne Meadows Lodge
  Of Interest: Silver Lake Resort, Tioga Pass Resort
  Other: Town of June Lake, Town of Mammoth Lakes, Town of Lee Vining

Highlights: Lovely Gibbs Lake, set in a deep canyon below 12,000- and 13,000-foot peaks, is ample reward for the stiff hike required to reach it.

How to get to the trailhead: You'll need a high-clearance vehicle for the road to the trailhead and a high-clearance, 4WD vehicle to get all the way to the trailhead parking. The turnoff to the Gibbs Lake trailhead is on U.S. Highway 395 3.1 miles north of the *northern* junction of 395 and State Route 158 (the June Lakes Loop) and 1.2 miles south of the junction of 395 and *westbound* State Route 120 (the Tioga Road), seemingly in a crease in the east face of prominent Williams Butte. Look for a low, hard-to-spot marker that says HORSE MEADOWS, by a dirt road on the west side of Highway 395. Turn west and follow this dirt road, Horse Meadows Road, west and up to pretty Lower Horse Meadow, avoiding any turnoffs. Beyond Lower Horse Meadow, the road may become impassable to ordinary passenger vehicles, which should park off the road as best they can here. You're close

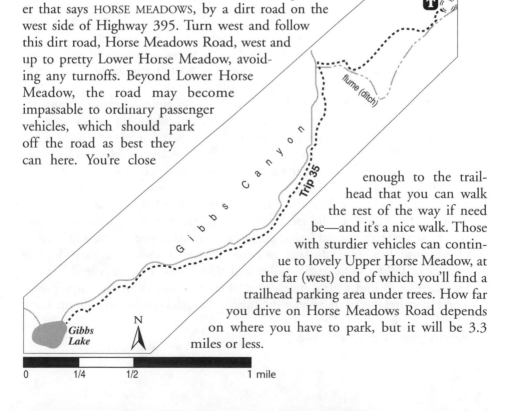

enough to the trailhead that you can walk the rest of the way if need be—and it's a nice walk. Those with sturdier vehicles can continue to lovely Upper Horse Meadow, at the far (west) end of which you'll find a trailhead parking area under trees. How far you drive on Horse Meadows Road depends on where you have to park, but it will be 3.3 miles or less.

0   1/4   1/2   1 mile

Mt. Gibbs

At the trailhead: This is not a good trailhead for non-hikers, who will be happier exploring Lee Vining (cafés, shops, Mono Lake Information Center) or enjoying the wonderful Mono Lake Visitor Center (about 2 miles north of Lee Vining; exhibits, bookstore, interpretive trails, and fabulous views of Mono Lake).

On the trail: Mileages given below are from the trailhead parking area. The trail—really a dusty road that's gated off, but is shown on the book's map as a trail—leaves from the right side of a trailhead information sign, where you should sign in. Squeeze between the fence and gate and start up the trail-road, climbing steeply to very steeply. It's impossible to imagine a car's getting up this road unless there was a winch at the top of the grade! Forest cover permitting, you'll enjoy fine over-the-shoulder views to Mono Lake at your many—*gasp!*—rest stops.

Around ¾ mile the road levels out briefly near some lovely cascades on Gibbs Creek; this is a fine spot for a snack. Beyond, the road climbs again before leveling out near the ruins of a flume. You cross the flume on the pipe the water once flowed through and curve left as the road ends to the right. Now on a footpath, you climb to a ridge above the creek. Moving off the ridge, you trudge up a dry washed lined with stunted aspens. At nearly 1⅔ miles you level out on a dry but flower-dotted shoulder above the creek, from which Mounts Gibbs and Dana are ahead to the west-southwest—quite a sight. Soon you dip into forest cover, more or less paralleling, Gibbs Creek.

At 2½ miles you enter Ansel Adams Wilderness near Gibbs Creek. Here, you enjoy the sight of the beautiful creek meandering between grassy banks made colorful by currant, fragrant red heather, and Labrador tea. The ascent is gradual to moderate until, just before the lake, you make a brief, moderate-to-steep climb to the outlet of **Gibbs Lake at 3¼ miles and 9530 feet**. Use trails lead left and right; take one to find a great lunch spot where you can enjoy this superb little lake and its matchless setting under the rugged, colorful outliers of Mounts Dana and Gibbs.

Retrace your steps to your car.

36. May Lundy Mine, Oneida Lake ☼ 🍁

Place	Total distance	Elevation	Level	Type
Start	0	7803	—	—
Blue Lake *only*	5¾	9460	S	O&B
May Lundy Mine ruins *only*	6+	9500	S	O&B
Oneida Lake	6⅔	9656	S	O&B

Permit required: None

Topo(s): Lundy, Mount Dana 7½'

Where to stay:
Mountain: Lundy Lake Resort, Tuolumne Meadows Lodge
Of Interest: Silver Lake Resort, Tioga Pass Resort
Other: Town of June Lake, Town of Mammoth Lakes, Town of Lee Vining

Highlights: A stiff but view-filled climb leads to a hanging valley aptly named Lake Canyon, where you find not only a chain of lovely lakes but the ruins of one of the Eastern Sierra's more famous mines, the May Lundy Mine.

How to get to the trailhead: North of the town of Lee Vining and south of Conway Summit on U.S. Highway 395, you'll find the westbound turnoff to Lundy Lake at the point where northbound travelers are beginning their ascent to Conway Summit and opposite the eastbound turnoff onto State Route 167 to Hawthorne, Nevada. Turn west to Lundy Lake; the fall color display along the creek that drains it, Mill Creek, is one of the best in the Eastern Sierra. Continue up the road for 3.5 miles, passing a creekside campground, to a poorly-marked turnoff left onto a dirt road. Turn left here and go 0.3 mile farther to a large, dirt parking area at 3.8 miles. Your trailhead is on the south side of Lundy Lake's dam by a locked gate.

At the trailhead: This is not a good trailhead for non-hikers unless they want to spend the day fishing in Lundy Lake. Otherwise, they'll be happier enjoying Lee Vining and Mono Lake (see Trip 35).

On the trail: Get an early start, for the first leg of this trip can be very hot. Circumvent the gate on the dam's south side and follow a rocky-dusty road west along the lake's south shore. The road forks almost immediately; go left to begin a moderate to steep climb of this sunstruck south wall of Lundy Canyon. The meadow at the lake's west end and Lundy Lake Resort come into view as you rise, and the uphill side of the road becomes defined by low, rocky outcrops. Both sides of the road presently become hemmed in by willows, and ice may linger on the road in large patches after a sub-freezing night. Around ¾ mile you pass an old road (not shown on the book's map) covered by rockfall, seeming to have come up from the head of Lundy Lake; avoid it. Instead, continue your ascent, crossing a pair of small streams, one in a culvert, and negotiating some marshy stretches. Pause to enjoy the fine views north and west into Lundy Canyon, where the next trip takes you.

At a little beyond 1⅓ miles you enter forest cover as your road veers generally south into the hanging valley called Lake Canyon, from which South Fork Mill

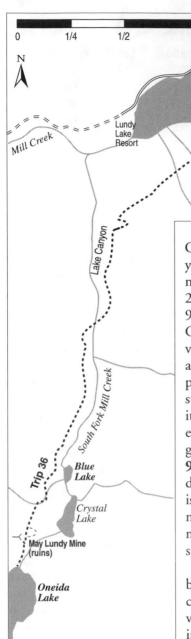

Creek cascades in a handsome waterfall. Ahead, you glimpse the striking Doré Cliffs, named for the nineteenth-century artist. The climb eases around 2 miles with views of Gilcrest Peak to the east, Peak 9148T to the west. You cross South Fork Mill Creek where it runs under the road through a culvert, then curve southeast through willow thickets at the base of a talus slope—check out the glacial polish on the rocks on your right! After a short, steep climb you're above and west of the creek and its lovely meadow, passing through patches of forest and soon coming abreast and a little west of grassy **Blue Lake at a little over 2¾ miles and 9460 feet**. Ahead, a semicircle of handsome peaks defines the head of the cirque, and the Tioga Crest is on your right (west). As you approach a low, northeast-trending ridgelet, the road forks at 3 miles: left (south) to Crystal Lake on an unmapped spur, right (south-southwest) to Oneida Lake.

Go right along the base of the ridgelet, then begin climbing moderately toward the head of the cirque. As you pass the ridgelet, you have a good view east to the head of Crystal Lake and the mining ruins south of it—collapsing buildings, toppling telegraph poles. Approaching the stream connecting Oneida and Crystal lakes, you notice debris in the rocky channel. Ahead, perched on a tailings heap, are **May Lundy Mine ruins at just over 3 miles and 9500 feet**; the tracks of its tramway are especially striking. Beginning with the discovery of ore in 1879, the May Lundy Mine yielded about $2 million in gold, and its tailings were reworked as late as 1937, says

Genny Smith in *Mammoth Lakes Sierra*. You cross the stream and veer left onto the tailings heap for another look down on the ruined mine buildings, where boilers, engines, cables, and timbers lie strewn across the meadow south of Crystal Lake. The wind seems to carry echoes of the steam whistles, clanging machinery, and cursing miners that must have made this a lively, noisy place.

Back on the trail, you cross the tramway tracks just before they head over ruined trestles into thin air. Picking up the road on the other side, you wind through more debris before making a short climb to an unmapped junction: left (south-south-east) on a use trail, right (south, ahead) on the main trail. Go right to another unmapped junction where you see the blue expanse of Oneida Lake ahead. At this junction, the right fork (southwest) curves around to a ruined stone building, while the left fork (south) descends a rocky footpath past a sign marking Hoover Wilderness to Oneida Lake's pretty north shore, passing a crumbling dam on Oneida's outlet. There's a maze of use trails here; just pick your way down to the lakeshore and find a perch where you can enjoy your lunch in the splendidly rugged setting of **Oneida Lake at 3⅓ miles and 9656 feet**.

Return the way you came.

Oneida Lake

37. Lundy Canyon 🌿 ☼ 🍁

Place	Total distance	Elevation	Level	Type
Start	0	8200	—	—
Base of first big cascade *only*	1⅓	8200	E	O&B
Base of canyon's headwall	5	8800	M	O&B

Permit required: None

Topo(s): Dunderberg Peak 7½'

Where to stay:
   Mountain: Lundy Lake Resort, Tuolumne Meadows Lodge
   Of Interest: Silver Lake Resort, Tioga Pass Resort
   Other: Town of June Lake, Town of Mammoth Lakes, Town of Lee Vining

Highlights: Beautiful Lundy Canyon is full of waterfalls in springtime, thanks mainly to Mill Creek, which runs down-canyon over a series of benches. Near the canyon's head you'll find the stairstep cascades called Lundy Falls on upper Mill Creek, which connects Lake Helen at 10,107 feet in 20 Lakes Basin (Trip 75) with upper Lundy Canyon at 8600 feet—1500+ feet of splash and spray! Nameless white ribbons, tributaries of Mill Creek, streak the canyon's high walls. Even the shortest hike here will reward you with waterfall views. And if the waterfalls are low by autumn, you won't notice because you'll be swept away by one of the Eastern Sierra's best fall-color displays.

How to get to the trailhead: You'll need a high-clearance vehicle. Follow the driving directions of Trip 36 but don't turn off to Lundy Lake's dam. Instead, continue ahead to and through Lundy Lake Resort at 5.1 miles from U.S. Highway 395, beyond

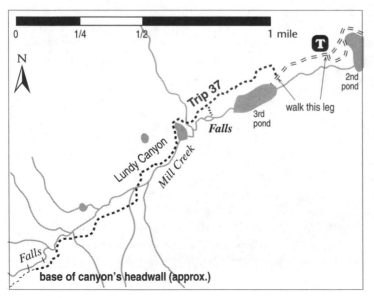

which the road is unpaved and rough. You pass a couple of charming ponds and a large, whimsically painted rock. Continue another 1.4 miles to a trailhead parking loop, 6.5 miles. The trailhead is near the upper end of the loop, on its north side. At the trailhead there is a very rough spur road that continues a little farther; you may take passengers up that road to drop them off, but you must park back here. Toilet, picnic tables.

At the trailhead: Besides Lundy Lake, three pretty beaver ponds along this road invite you to linger. The ponds are cradled in the canyon's colorful walls and graced by aspens—outstanding fall color. As you drive in, you pass the first of these ponds (off the book's map). The second pond is a few steps away from the trailhead parking lot. The third is at the end of the very rough spur road that continues a little farther from the trailhead parking lot. Find a place for your sand chair where the aspens permit, pull out that bestseller, relax, and enjoy!

On the trail: From the trailhead, walk up that very rough spur road between aspens until, a little shy of ¼ mile, you meet an obvious, marked trail on your right where the spur road curves left to that third beaver pond. Veer right onto the trail, which becomes open, rocky, and steep. You soon reach a rocky shoulder where you can see Lundy Canyon's first big cascade ahead; a big waterfall far ahead (part of Lundy Falls); and, over your shoulder, back to Lundy Lake. There are few places on the trail from which you can see Lundy Falls well; the better views are from here and from the road on the way into Lundy Canyon.

You descend a little to enter Hoover Wilderness just before ⅔ mile, bottoming out at a junction with a use trail branching left to the base of this showiest of the falls on lower Mill Creek. Stroll over to the base of this **first big cascade at ⅔ mile and 8200 feet** (labeled "*Falls*" on the book's map); if it's a hot day, you'll enjoy the falls' cooling spray. Back on the main trail, you climb to cross multiple channels of Mill Creek above the falls; the flowers here are splendid. You skirt a lovely little pond, cross another stream, and note that high on the north-northwest wall of the canyon there's a long waterfall beneath some unnamed crags. Ahead, there's another dashing cascade; you cross Mill Creek again below this cascade and parallel, then cross, a seasonal, usually-dry streambed. The aspen forest here is particularly delightful in the fall.

Veering southeast, you pass the ruins of a log cabin at 1¼ miles and emerge at an area of avalanche-downed trees. Look for cascades ahead and, seasonally, from the canyon walls on either side. You meet the creek again as you re-enter forest and pass a pond. At a junction where a use trail comes in from the left, you continue ahead (southwest) to cross an open, flowery slope as you climb gradually to moderately. This is another great spot from which to look for cascades from the canyon walls as well as ahead in the canyon proper. At the next junction with another use trail, go left, and at a little over 2 miles, climb steeply on a rocky trail through mountain hemlock to the next bench in this canyon. The waterfall between this bench and the one below it is one of the prettiest in the canyon. You ascend the bench beside a steep meadow golden with butterweed in season, then cross a scree slope before you begin switchbacking steeply up a talus slope from whose lower part you glimpse Lundy Falls dropping through a steep slot in the canyon's headwall.

Continuing beyond here requires ascending the unbelievably steep, loose, twisting, exposed trail between Lundy Canyon and Lake Helen in 20 Lakes Basin; that difficult route, briefly described in Trip 75, is not a trip in this book. Exactly where you turn around is up to you. We'll say it's here, at the **base of the canyon's headwall at about 2½ miles and 8800 feet**.

Pause at your turnaround point to take in this magnificent canyon scene; then retrace your steps to your car.

38. Virginia Lakes ☼ ❧

Place	Total distance	Elevation	Level	Type
Start	0	9860	—	—
Blue Lake *only*	⅔+	9886	E	O&B
Cooney Lake *only*	2½	10,246	M	O&B
Frog Lakes *only*	2¾+	10,370	M	O&B
Unnamed pass/viewpoint	6+	11,120+	S	O&B

Permit required: None

Topo(s): Dunderberg Peak 7½'

Where to stay:
Mountain: Virginia Lakes Resort, Lundy Lake Resort, Tuolumne Meadows Lodge, Hunewill Circle H Guest Ranch, Doc and Al's Resort, Twin Lakes Resort, Annett's Mono Village
Of Interest: Silver Lake Resort, Tioga Pass Resort
Other: Town of Lee Vining, Town of June Lake, Town of Bridgeport

Highlights: You wander up a wonderfully scenic chain of lakes to a high viewpoint from which you can look down on breathtaking backcountry scenery on the boundary of northern Yosemite National Park. The drive up offers wonderful fall color.

How to get to the trailhead: The road to Virginia Lakes strikes west from Conway Summit, which, at 8138 feet, is the highest point on U.S. Highway 395 and is between Lee Vining and Bridgeport. Turn left (west) onto the Virginia Lakes Road and follow it past side roads, one of which leads to Virginia Lakes Resort, to a large parking area at the roadend, 6.2 miles. Toilets, water.

At the trailhead: This is a beautiful trailhead, right next to the larger, upper Virginia Lake and tucked under colorful peaks like Black Mountain and Dunderberg Peak. It's also near Virginia Lakes Resort, where there are a small café and a store as well as lodgings. Non-hikers will find plenty to enjoy here.

On the trail: Head west from an information sign at the trailhead, which is next to the restroom, crossing an open slope and ignoring use trails left to the shore of upper Virginia Lake. You marvel at the colors on the slopes around you; these peaks, part of a subrange sometimes called the Dunderberg Range, are "carved" from a roof pendant (see Trip 16). You curve north around a patch of forest, meeting a stock trail that comes in on the right (east). Continue ahead here, curving west, passing a couple of ponds, and entering Hoover Wilderness around ⅓ mile.

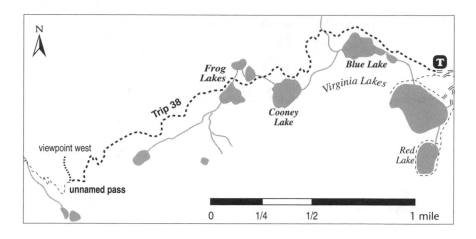

The trail begins to trace the shoreline of pretty **Blue Lake at a little over ⅓ mile and 9886 feet**. The lake's inlet cascades dramatically down the steep slope between Cooney and Blue lakes. You can't camp here, but you'll find picnic spots along the lakeshore. Paralleling Blue Lake but leaving its shoreline behind, you begin climbing moderately to steeply on a rocky-dusty trail, ascending the slope northwest of the lake. In spite of its apparent barrenness, the slope supports quite a flower display, especially near the top of the climb. At ¾ mile you cross unseen, higher Moat Lake's outlet stream, then curve south through a flowery hillside meadow before entering forest cover. At 1 mile, you pass a tiny old cabin that's remarkably well preserved. You brush past another hillside meadow as you curve northwest, then south over a rocky, open slope. Beautifully peak-rimmed **Cooney Lake at almost 1¼ miles and 10,246 feet** soon comes into view, and there are picnic perches in the rocks overlooking it.

A steep switchback carries you above Cooney Lake to a pretty bench where you cross Cooney's inlet stream and reach the lowest of the **Frog Lakes at a little over 1⅓ miles and 10,370 feet**. The three delightful little Frog Lakes nestle together on this bench all at almost the same elevation, and a stop at one is almost irresistible. Continuing, you splash across the stream linking two of the Frog Lakes and soon leave the lakes behind. You follow the trail up a series of rocky, increasingly barren little benches, passing above an unnamed pond. You make a final, steep, rocky attack on the crest that's plainly ahead, to stand atop this **unnamed pass at just over 3 miles and at 11,120 feet**. The view east, back over the Virginia Lakes, is simply astounding. But the view west is obscured by the terrain, so trek some 400 yards northwest over barren, shattered, metamorphic rock to an outcrop with awe-inspiring views northwest to Summit Lake, far below on the eastern edge of northern Yosemite; to the Sierra Crest just west of Summit Lake; and, around the corner to the northeast, the Hoover Lakes. The rock colors here are amazing—gray, gray-green, brown, rust, cream, and very-nearly-blue—and the rocks are splashed with lichens in brilliant rusts and chartreuses. Tiny alpine flowers find shelter among these broken stones.

Few hikes this short offer as much as this one does, and you get to enjoy much of it again as you retrace your steps to the parking lot.

39. Green, East, and West Lakes ☼ ❦

Place	Total distance	Elevation	Level	Type
Start	0	7900	—	—
Green Lake *only*	6	8945	M	O&B
East Lake *only*	8¼	9458	S	O&B
West Lake *only*	9⅓	9870	S	O&B

Permit required: None

Topo(s): Dunderberg Peak 7½'

Where to stay:

Mountain: Virginia Lakes Resort, Doc and Al's Resort, Hunewill Circle H Guest Ranch, Twin Lakes Resort, Annett's Mono Village

Of Interest: None

Other: Town of Lee Vining, Town of Bridgeport

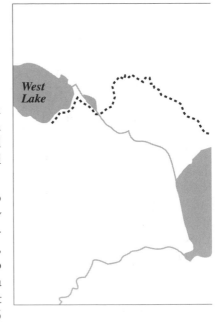

Highlights: Trailside flower gardens brighten your stroll to some gorgeous lakes, Green Lake and East Lake, or to West Lake. You'll have to choose between East and West, and it's not easy!

How to get to the trailhead: The turnoff to Green Creek Trailhead from U.S. Highway 395 is just north of State Route 270, the eastbound road to Bodie State Historical Park, and south of Bridgeport. Turn west onto marked Green Creek Road and follow it to a junction with the Summit Meadows Road at 1 mile; go left here. Continue another 2.5 miles to a junction with a spur road southbound to Virginia Lakes; go right here. Continue another 5.2 miles, veering right to a parking loop at the trailhead (left takes you to the Green Creek Campground), 8.7 miles from 395. Toilet, water.

At the trailhead: Non-hikers will probably prefer to see Bodie State Historical Park, which protects the remains of the notorious gold-mining town of Bodie. Or they may enjoy visiting quaint and pretty Bridgeport.

On the trail: You head southwest away from the marked trailhead on a dusty trail through a patchy-to-moderate Jeffrey pine forest, bobbing along high above Green Creek and crossing a creeklet beyond ¼ mile. At clearings you glimpse Kavanaugh Ridge to the south, Epidote Peak ahead to the southwest. In a little over ½ mile,

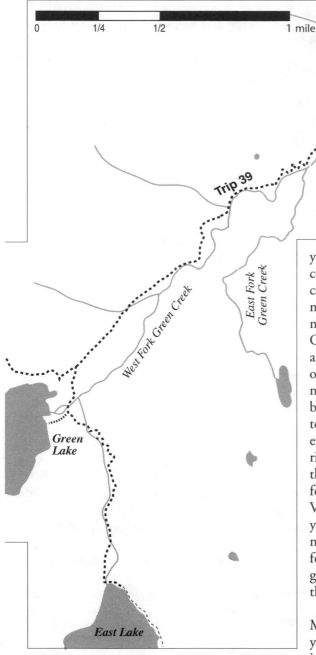

you descend to meet the road coming in on the left, from the campground, and at ⅔ mile you meet Green Creek on your left, near the former trailhead. Continuing southwest, ignore an unmapped, gated spur road on your right at a little over ¾ mile and shortly ford a creek, beyond which the trail dwindles to a footpath. You ascend moderately to steeply to an open ridgetop, then descend, meeting the creek at nearly 1¼ miles as it foams along over cascades. Veering away from the creek, you begin switchbacking on a moderate grade up a lightly forested slope, then ascend gradually to moderately above the cascading creek.

You cross a stream from Monument Ridge high above you to the northwest and reaching a marker for Hoover Wilderness at a little over 1½ miles. Beginning in this area, you enjoy wonderful flower displays along the trail, particularly in a marshy section around 1⅔–1¾ miles. Around 2¼ miles, you cross a dry wash and begin a moderate ascent southwest of an open ridge beneath Dunderberg, Epidote, and Gabbro peaks. At 2⅔

East Lake

miles you reach a junction: left (south) to Green and East lakes; right (west) to West Lake.

To Green and East lakes: Go left here, dipping to ford Green Lake's outlet at a little over 2¾ miles. On the other side, use trails branch southwest; take one to **Green Lake at nearly 3 miles and 8945 feet**. Green Lake is exceptionally scenic; its flower- and forest-lined shores are backed by pretty Glines Canyon, which lies below Virginia Pass across the lake. You'll want to stop for a snack here.

Returning to the main trail to East Lake, you turn southeast to ford East Lake's outlet for the first time, between two dashing cascades. You soon resume climbing, generally south, on small switchbacks through one dazzling patch of flowers after another. You cross the outlet again at 3½ miles, continue climbing on switchbacks, skirt a forested meadow, and cross two strands of the outlet one after another just below East Lake. You reach the shore above big, beautiful **East Lake at a little over 4 miles and 9458 feet**. Gabbro, Page, and Epidote peaks rise above East Lake's west shore. Find yourself a picnic spot and enjoy this splendid place at leisure.

Retrace your steps to your car.

To West Lake: From the junction with the trail to Green and East lakes, go right on a moderate to steep and dry, open, dusty trail through tobacco brush, junipers, and mule ears. Ahead you'll spot cascades on West Lake's outlet. In a little less than half a mile from the junction, you begin working your way through a seasonally spectacular hillside meadow, crossing a little stream as you brush past larkspur, sweet cicely, willow, lupine, stickseed, mariposa lily, and purple-flowered wild onion.

Beyond the meadow the trail climbs steeply through a patchy forest of lodgepole, occasionally skirting a meadow, and rises into a subalpine world of stunted trees, shattered rock, and wide-ranging views. Crossing seasonal trickles, the track curves around a switchback leg with heart-stopping views of Green Lake below. At a little over 1⅓ miles from the junction the trail tops out at 9880 feet near a spartan campsite off-trail to the east.

From here you descend quickly to a pond below West Lake to a good picnic site under stunted lodgepoles. Crossing the outlet on a low dam, you begin zigzagging up the now-faint trail high above the pond until the route drops abruptly to the shore of dramatic West Lake, which sits beneath the jagged peaks of Monument Ridge, 1⅔ miles from the junction and at 9870 feet. This is a good place to stop;

from here there's little more than a rough angler's path leading across steep slopes high above the water.

Return the way you came, perhaps diverting to Green Lake to rest on the way back.

40. Barney Lake ☼ 🍁

Place	Total distance	Elevation	Level	Type
Start	0	7090	—	—
Barney Lake	6*	8300	S	O&B

Permit required: None

Topo(s): Buckeye Ridge 7½'

Where to stay:
Mountain: Virginia Lakes Resort, Doc and Al's Resort, Hunewill Circle H Guest Ranch, Twin Lakes Resort, Annett's Mono Village
Of Interest: None
Other: Town of Lee Vining, Town of Bridgeport

Highlights: A leisurely and lengthy walk through woods and flower-blessed meadows, followed by a short, scenic climb, leads to beautiful Barney Lake. The route can be sunny and very hot so take plenty of water.

How to get to the trailhead: The road to the trailhead, Twin Lakes Road, branches west off U.S. Highway 395 on the northern edge of Bridgeport. Turn west onto signed Twin Lakes Road and follow it past three of the four Bridgeport area resorts and past the beautiful Twin Lakes, right into the fourth resort, Annett's Mono Village, at the head of upper Twin Lake, 13.5 miles from 395. There is limited, free public parking near the launching ramp; it's poorly marked, so ask where you should park—the person in the kiosk at the campground entrance can help you. Toilet, water, café, store.

At the trailhead: With a café, a store, boat and tackle rentals, and a beautiful location, Annett's Mono Village has lots to offer non-hikers. Or non-hikers may prefer to explore quaint little Bridgeport.

On the trail: From the parking lot near the launching ramp, walk southwest between the signed boat house/workshop, entrance kiosk, and ice house (it's easier to see this on the ground than to describe it in words). A sign on a telephone pole next to the ice house points the way to Barney Lake, as do several other signs you'll see as you follow dirt roads through the campground, generally west toward a meadow below a quartet of handsome little peaks. In less than ¼ mile you walk around the road closure at the campground's west end and continue on the road,

* Trailhead signs declare it is 3.8 miles to Barney Lake, but I stand by my own measurements of nearly 3 miles.

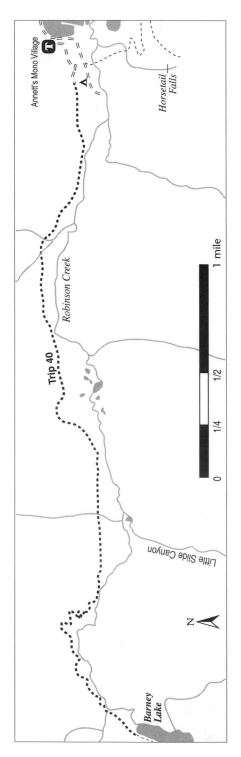

skirting the meadow (on your left) and avoiding a use trail going left into the meadow. A little short of Robinson Creek, your Barney Lake Trail bears right (northwest) off the road, and you follow it. Robinson Creek bubbles along on your left as you stroll through moderate-to-dense forest here.

You pass granite outcrops on your right before beginning a gradual climb to a wilderness information display at ⅔ mile. Beyond, the trail climbs gradually to moderately as it curves around a flowery meadow and crosses a small stream. At nearly 1¼ miles emerge at a broad valley whose floor is a huge, flowery meadow in season. The meadow sits in a beautiful amphitheater of peaks, including Robinson, Victoria, and Hunewill peaks. Ignore use trails branching left to Robinson Creek and head generally west-southwest toward the farther peaks through some amazing flower gardens. This stretch can be very hot and dusty, but the scenery makes up for that.

You pass through a couple of stands of spindly aspens before reaching the wilderness boundary at a little over 2 miles, near which you have a magnificent view southward to the raw peaks around Little Slide Canyon. Approaching 2⅓ miles, you leave the meadow for the damp banks of Robinson Creek, then veer away to begin climbing gradually on switchbacks; the climb offers beautiful over-the-shoulder views of the valley you've just traversed. Crossing several streams as you go, you continue up the long switchbacks, enjoying splendid flower gardens here and there. At 2⅔ miles you leave the flower gardens briefly as you make a short, hot climb up a low, light-colored cliff before veering back to a shadier streambank, where the grade eases back to gradual. You cross the stream, catching a view of one of the Twin Lakes. It's not long before you reach the sandy northeast shore of big, beautiful **Barney Lake at nearly 3 miles and 8300 feet**. The lake's other shores are bounded by picturesque cliffs and peaks, including Cirque Mountain, Kettle Peak, and, especially, cleft Crown Point. This beach makes a lovely, relaxing stop.

Retrace your steps; the descent from Barney Lake to the huge meadow is wonderfully scenic.

Crown Point

Nevada Fall (top) and Vernal Fall in Yosemite National Park

CHAPTER 7

Western Sierra: National Parks Country

The Western Sierra is simply the hugest part of the range—huge trees, huge valleys, huge waterfalls. Here is the part of the range deemed most worthy of protection as national parks: Sequoia, Kings Canyon, and Yosemite. Here, too, are the world's largest trees, the giant sequoias. Here are immense, glacier-sculpted valleys of breathtaking splendor: Kings Canyon, Yosemite—yes, the wonderful Yosemite Valley!—and Hetch Hetchy. Here are great waterfalls: Yosemite—one of the world's highest—Nevada, Vernal, Bridalveil, Tueeulala, and Wapama. Tucked in among all these immense wonders are smaller marvels: little jewels of lakes, gems of meadows, tumbling cascades, and lesser "yosemites" (as John Muir called glacier-sculpted valleys that weren't *the* Yosemite Valley). Main roads as well as side roads lead to these special places, and delightful lodgings beckon you to stay a while.

People came to the Western Sierra in the 19th Century to seek gold; California's gold country lies in the foothills of the Western Sierra. Now, in the 20th Century and beyond, people come to seek the lasting "gold" that lies farther east and higher in the range: the grand vistas, the many opportunities for outdoor recreation, and the renewing experience of being in the presence of so much beauty.

Sequoia and Kings Canyon National Parks

The Western Sierra hikes in this book begin in Sequoia National Park's Mineral King district, a high, beautiful valley reached by a long, difficult drive—and worth the trouble. The next hikes are those off the General's Highway, which runs through Sequoia National Park's Giant Forest district north through Sequoia National Forest and into Kings Canyon National Park's Grant Grove district. Finally, our focus dips down into the immense valley known as Kings Canyon—less famous but far deeper than Yosemite Valley to the north.

Between the parks

Between Kings Canyon and Yosemite National parks lies a region of wooded peaks and lakes the largest of which were created as part of a hydroelectric project, the Big Creek Project. Several fine hikes sample this area, the easternmost part of which, beyond Kaiser Pass, is perhaps the most remote region explored in this book.

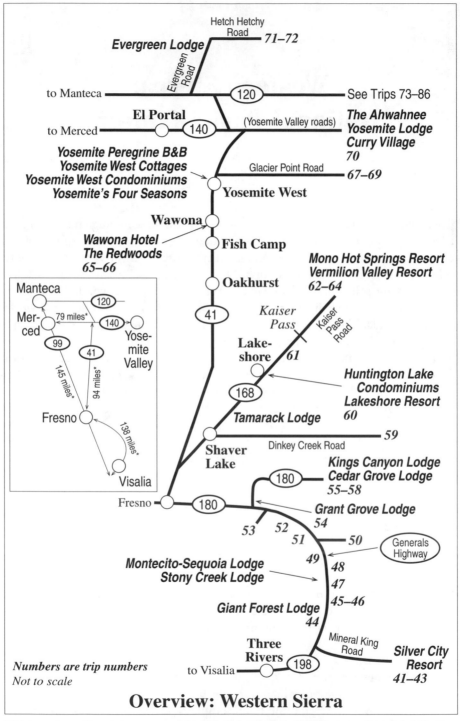

Overview: Western Sierra

*Distances summed from various sources: Automobile Club of Southern California maps, other maps, field notes.

Merced River

Yosemite National Park

Beginning with Yosemite's southernmost district, the Wawona district, the hikes sample deep valleys and the high ridges separating them. Wawona is the home of Yosemite's best giant-sequoia grove. The next hikes are in the park's stunning Glacier Point Road district high above Yosemite Valley. Finally, there's a hike that originates in Yosemite Valley itself but that zips out of the Valley as fast as it can. Early in the morning and late in the evening, Yosemite Valley is sublimely beautiful. But at midday, the Valley is hot, dusty, crowded, and noisy. The best way to enjoy Yosemite Valley then is to go somewhere else! Continuing north, the hikes take you to Yosemite's lovely Hetch Hetchy district. (For another, completely different Yosemite district, see the hikes from State Route 120 in the next chapter.)

Recommended reading

▶ Dilsaver, Lary M., and William Tweed. *Challenge of the Big Trees: A Resource History of Sequoia and Kings Canyon National Parks.* Three Rivers, California: Sequoia Natural History Association, 1990. The authors have created a well-written page-turner of these parks' histories and of the current issues surrounding their management and development. Dr. Tweed has been on the parks' staff for a number of years.

▶ Krist, John, *50 Best Short Hikes in Yosemite and Sequoia/Kings Canyon.* Berkeley: Wilderness Press, 1993. Concise descriptions of park history support a selection of hikes that are rated with children in mind. Well-written; easy-to-use maps. A somewhat different selection of hikes from those presented herein (Krist and I have different tastes in hikes). Especially useful for those traveling with children.

▶ Schaffer, Jeffrey P., *High Sierra Hiking Guide: Yosemite: The Valley and Surrounding Uplands.* 5th ed. Berkeley: Wilderness Press, 2002. Invaluable pocket hiking guide with detailed trail descriptions.

▶ —, *Yosemite National Park: A Natural-History Guide to Yosemite and Its Trails.* 4th ed. Berkeley: Wilderness Press, 1999. A well-written yet scholarly description of Yosemite's natural and human history as well as an exhaustive inventory of its trails. The outstanding *Yosemite National Park and Vicinity* map from Wilderness Press is this book's "pocket" map (see below).

▶ Semb, George and Patricia, *Day Hikes on the Pacific Crest Trail.* 1st ed. Berkeley, CA: Wilderness Press, 2000. Hikes on the 2665-mile Pacific Crest Trail that you can do in a day, with accessible entry and exit points. The book covers all of the PCT in California.

▶ *Sequoia and Kings Canyon National Parks.* Los Angeles: Automobile Club of Southern California, 1993. A concise booklet summarizing major features and opportunities for hiking, camping, and lodging in the parks. Good gray-scale maps.

▶ White, Michael C., *Snowshoe Trails of Yosemite.* 1st ed. Berkeley, CA: Wilderness Press, 1999. For winter wanderings in the Yosemite area.

▶ Winnett, et. al., *Sierra South.* Berkeley, CA: Wilderness Press, 2001. See recommended reading for Chapter 6.

▶ Winnett, Thomas, et. al., *Sierra North.* 8th ed. Berkeley, CA: Wilderness Press, 2002. A comprehensive guide to the northern Sierra backcountry. Includes mostly backpack trips, but also some dayhikes, and is a good reference for the area. Companion guide to *Sierra South.*

Recommended maps

In addition to those listed in the trip write-ups, your library of maps should include the following. Get the latest edition/revision you can find.

▶ USDA/USFS, *Sequoia National Forest; Sierra National Forest; Stanislaus National Forest;* No topographic information, but invaluable road information.

▶ USDA/USFS, Pacific Southwest Region, *A Guide to the John Muir Wilderness and the Sequoia-Kings Canyon Wilderness.* San Francisco: U.S. Forest Service.

▶ *Guide to Yosemite National Park. Los Angeles: Automobile Club of Southern California.* Some topographic information by means of shaded relief, plus concise descriptions of history, recreational opportunities, etc.

▶ *Yosemite National Park and Vicinity, Calif.* Berkeley: Wilderness Press, 1999. Also available as pocket map to Jeffrey Schaffer's *Yosemite National Park: A Natural-History Guide to Yosemite and Its Trails,* above. A superb overview of the park and the region around it; detailed park information on the back. Topographic. Scale too small for navigation when dayhiking, but great for driving and for identifying distant features when hiking. For hiking, prefer the WP 15′ and USGS 7½′ topos.

▶ *Yosemite High Country Trail Map*. Shaded-relief on plastic. Tom Harrison Maps, 2002.

▶ *Sequoia & Kings Canyon National Parks Recreation Map*. Shaded-relief on plastic. Tom Harrison Maps, 2001.

Lodgings

Alphabetically, the true mountain lodgings and lodgings of interest in the region are—

Ahwahnee, The   yosemitepark.com
Yosemite Reservations, 5410 East Home Ave.   webportal.com/ahwahnee
Fresno, CA 93727   (559) 252-4848

4000 feet. In Yosemite Valley. *Of interest*. Hotel rooms, cottages, "parlors." Outstanding restaurant, gift shops, cocktail lounge, swimming pool, tour desk. Stores, restaurants, bakery, deli, ice-cream parlor, pizza parlor, equipment rentals (e.g., bicycles), banking services, bookstore, museum in nearby Yosemite Village. No pets. 2003 rates: $348–359/night. Extra person: adult $22/night; child under 12 staying in same room as adult, free. Rollaways and cribs available; may be additional fee.

Cedar Grove Lodge
Kings Canyon Park Services, P.O. Box 909,   rescentre.com
Kings Canyon National Park, CA 93633   (559) 565-0100

4640 feet. Off State Route 180 in Cedar Grove Village on Kings River in Kings Canyon National Park's Cedar Grove district down in Kings Canyon proper. *Of interest*. Motel units. Market, gift shop, snack bar, service station, showers, laundromat. No pets. 2002 rates: $99–110/night. For extra people, a crib, or rollaway bed, there is a $12 charge for each.

Curry Village   yosemitepark.com
Yosemite Reservations, 5410 East Home Ave., Fresno, CA 93727   (559) 252-4848

4000 feet. In Yosemite Valley. *Of interest*. Standard rooms, sleeping cabins with bath, sleeping cabins without bath, sleeping tent-cabins without bath; latter two types share centrally-located bath, shower facilities. Cafeteria, fast-food service, stores (camping, mountain equipment), climbing school, swimming pool, equipment rentals (rafts, bicycles), tour desk. Stores, restaurants, bakery, deli, ice-cream parlor, pizza parlor, rentals, banking services, bookstore, museum in nearby Yosemite Village. No pets. 2003 rates: standard room $112/night, cabin with bath $92/night, cabin without bath $77/night, canvas tent-cabin $59/night. Extra person: adult $9.25–10.75/night depending on unit type; child under 12 staying in same room as adult, free except $4/night in tent-cabin. Rollaways and cribs available; may be additional fee.

Evergreen Lodge   evergreenlodge.com
33160 Evergreen Road, Groveland, CA 95321   (209) 379-2606 (voice and fax)

4300 feet. On the road to Hetch Hetchy. *Of interest*. Sleeping cabins. Includes continental breakfast. Restaurant (lunch, nightly barbecue), bar, deli, general store, mountain bike rentals. Tennis courts, swimming pool, horseback riding at nearby Camp Mather. No pets. 2002 rates: double cabin, $89/night; family cabin $109/night; large family cabin $124/night.

Grant Grove Cabins
Grant Grove Village, Highway 180
Kings Canyon National Park, CA 93633   (866) K CANYON

6600 feet. Off State Route 180 in Grant Grove Village in Kings Canyon National Park's Grant Grove district. Mountain Rustic cabins without baths, without electricity; cabins with electricity, baths. Rustic cabins (without baths) share centrally located bathhouses. Restaurant, store, visitor center (sells books and maps). Guest in rustic cabins may wish to bring sleeping bags. No pets. 2002 rates: rustic cabin $55–60; cabins with bath, $105–112.

Huntington Lake Condominium Vacation Rentals (agency)   shaverlake.com
c.o. Rancheria Enterprises, P.O. Box 157, Lakeshore, CA 93634   (800) 879-8989

7000 feet. Next to Huntington Lake just past the end of State Route 168 (west). *Mountain*. Various 2-, 3-, and 4-bedroom condominiums; amenities, maximum number of renters, etc., depends on each condo's owner; please be sure when you book that the condo you rent fits your needs. Bring your own towels. No pets. 1995 rates: 2-bedroom unit $145/night and up, 3-bedroom unit $220/night and up, 4-bedroom unit $275/night and up. Discounts for 5- and 7-night rentals. Off-season rates differ.

John Muir Lodge
Grant Grove Village, Highway 180   sequoia-kingscanyon.com/lodging.html
Kings Canyon National Park, CA 93633   (866) K CANYON

6600 feet. Off State Route 180 in Grant Grove Village in Kings Canyon National Park's Grant Grove district. Restaurant, store, visitor center (sells books and maps). The new John Muir Lodge offers 30 modern rooms, including 6 deluxe suites. 2002 double-occupancy rates: spring, $99–189; in-season, $140–240; rates exclude holiday periods; children under 12 stay free with adults. No stated pet policy.

Kings Canyon Lodge
P.O. Box 820, Kings Canyon National Park, CA 93633   (559) 335-2405

3740 feet. On State Route 180 east of Grant Grove and west of Cedar Grove districts of Kings Canyon National Park. *Of interest*. Restored 1930s hunting lodge offering cabins with fireplaces; family-owned and -operated. Restaurant, bar. Stores in Cedar Grove, Grant Grove. No pets. 2002 rates: $69–159/night.

Lakeshore Resort   lakeshoreresort.com
P.O. Box 197, Lakeshore, CA 93634   (559) 893-3193, fax (559) 893-2193

7000 feet. Next to Huntington Lake just past the end of State Route 168 (west) *Mountain*. Sleeping and housekeeping cabins accommodating 1–6 persons depending on cabin. Saloon with giant-screen TV; restaurant, general store, antique shop; lodge hall for special events, RV park, laundry facility. Cleaning/loss deposit on housekeeping cabins, $50. Dogs okay, $15/day; no large dogs or cats. 2002 rates: $88–135, depending on cabin and number of people; children 7 years or older are $10 extra per night; $20 fee for twin-size rollaway; $3 per day for extra vehicles (2 vehicles allowed per cabin). Stays of 3 nights or more earn a 10% discount (except during holidays). Two-night minimum on weekends; 3 nights on long holidays. No refunds or cancellations.

Mono Hot Springs Resort   monohotsprings.com
summer: General Delivery, Mono Hot Springs, CA 93642   (559) 325-1710
winter: P.O. Box 215, Lakeshore, CA 93634   (559) 325-1710

6500 feet. Off Kaiser Pass Road east of Kaiser Pass between Florence Lake and Lake Edison. *Mountain*. "Modern" housekeeping cabins, rustic housekeeping cabins, rustic sleeping cabins; some cabins share centrally-located bathhouse; rustic housekeeping cabins do not have electricity; linens are not furnished for housekeeping cabins. Store, restaurant, hot mineral baths and showers (fee), massage (fee). Adjacent campground. Electricity is generated by resort and is turned off between 10 P.M. and 6 A.M. Pets are $4 per night. 2002 rates: housekeeping cabins range from $45–85, depending on number of people and specific cabin. All except the rustic cabin ($45/night) have indoor plumbing, electricity, and hot water. The rustic cabin has some furnishings, a fire pit outside, and water faucet (with hot water) and flush toilet outside. Bedding is extra for the stone cabins and rustic cabins.

Montecito-Sequoia Lodge   mslodge.com; info@mslodge.com
Sequoia National Forest   (800) 227-9900
800 Generals Highway Box 858   (800) 843-8677
Kings Canyon National Park, CA 93633   fax (650) 967-0540

7500 feet. Off General's Highway (State Route 198) in Sequoia National Forest between Kings Canyon and Sequoia national parks. *Mountain*. Lodge rooms with baths (no maid service) and rustic cabins that share centrally located bathhouse; room rates include dinner and breakfast. Buffet restaurant, hospitality snack bar, cocktail bar, private lake with many water-oriented sports available, tennis, volleyball, spa, horseshoe pit, guided hikes, ping pong, heated pool, cross-country ski and snowboard rentals in winter, climbing wall, children's programs, mountain biking, campfires. 2000 rates for summer season are $473–897/per person/per night, $412–842, for youths 5–16/per person/per night; rates for fall/spring overnight packages are $79–99/per person/per night; $39–59 for youths 4-12; and rates for winter are $109–159/per person/per night; $59–79/per person/per night.

Redwoods, The   redwoodsinnyosemite.com
P.O. Box 2085, Wawona Station, CA 95389   (209) 375-6666, fax (209) 375-6400

4000 feet. On Chilnualna Falls Road off State Route 41 in Wawona district of Yosemite National Park. *Of interest.* Housekeeping vacation homes of 1–4 bedrooms, many with fireplaces and barbecues, accommodating 1–10 persons. Nearby stores, museum, gas station, restaurant, golf course, stables. Dishwashing liquid, condiments, and paper towels not provided; maid service (no dishwashing) available, $10/bedroom. Pets are $10 extra. 2002 rates: $87/1–2 persons/night to $617/1–10 persons/night; holidays slightly higher. Extra person: $15–25, depending on unit.

Silver City Mountain Resort   silvercityresort.com
summer: P.O. Box 56, Three Rivers, CA 93271   (559) 561-3223
winter: 2570 Rodman Dr., Los Osos, CA 93402   (805) 528-2730, fax (805) 528-8039

6040 feet. On Mineral King Road in southern Sequoia National Park, west of Mineral King. *Mountain.* Housekeeping cabins—"rustic" and 3 "luxury chalets"— and rustic sleeping cabins. Some cabins share centrally-located bath facilities; 4 housekeeping cabins and the 3 luxury chalets have private showers and/or toilets. Linens provided for double beds; bring sleeping bags for twin beds, ice chests with ice for housekeeping cabins without refrigerators. Store, restaurant (3 meals Thursday–Monday, snacks Tuesday–Wednesday). Propane and/or kerosene lamps for light, woodstoves and wood for heat). No smoking. No pets. 2002 rates: $70–150 for rustic housekeeping and sleeping cabins (bring your own linens); $200–250/night for chalets for first 3 days, $175–225/night thereafter, 2-night minimum stay.

Stony Creek Lodge   sequoiakingscanyon.com
Kings Canyon Park Services, P.O. Box 909,   (559) 565-3909
Kings Canyon National Park, CA 93633   (559) 335-5500

6300 feet. On General's Highway (State Route 198) in Sequoia National Forest between Sequoia and Kings Canyon national parks. *Of interest.* Motel units. Restaurant, market, gift shop, showers, laundromat. No pets. 2002 rates: $137.50/night.

Tamarack Lodge
P.O. Box 175, Lakeshore, CA 93634   (559) 893-3244

7000 feet. Just off State Route 168 between Shaver and Huntington lakes. *Mountain.* Studio units with kitchens and baths, most with fireplaces; extra beds available. Stores, restaurants in Shaver Lake and Lakeshore. Pets okay if you call first. 2002 rates (2 persons): $75–125/night, $400–800/week (7 nights). 4 people maximum; $15/person/night for each extra person.

Vermilion Valley Resort

P.O. Box 258
Lakeshore, CA 93634

edisonlake.com
(559) 259-4000 (seasonal),
(559) 855-6558 (office)

7600 feet. Near end of Kaiser Pass Road, east of Kaiser Pass, on Lake Edison. *Mountain.* Motel rooms, some with kitchenettes; tent-cabins. General store, restaurant, marina, boat rentals, ferry service, ferry tours, guided fishing trips, sporting goods sales and rentals, showers, USFS interpretive tours of lake in cooperation with resort. No stated pet policy. 2002 rates: $75/night/2 persons/no kitchen/weeknight and $80/weekend; $85/night/2 persons/with kitchen/weeknight and $90/weekend. Tent cabins are $40-45/night.

Wawona Hotel

Yosemite Reservations, 5410 East Home Ave., Fresno, CA 93727

yosemitepark.com
(559) 252-4848

4000 feet. On State Route 41 in Wawona district of Yosemite National Park. *Of interest.* Hotel rooms with and without bath; rooms without bath share centrally-located bathroom, showers. Very good restaurant, swimming pool, golf course (9 holes), stables, tennis, store, gas station, museum. No pets. 2002 rates: room with bath $168/night, room without bath $113/night. Extra person: adult $16.40/night; child under 12 staying in same room as adult, free. Rollaways and cribs available; may be additional fee. In the off season, rates are lower. Tent cabins are $40–45/night.

Wuksachi Village

P.O. Box 89
Sequoia National Park, CA 93262

visitsequoia.com/html/wuksachi.html
(888) 252-5757 or (559) 253-2199

6800 feet, 6 miles north of Giant Forest and 2 miles north of Lodgepole on General's Highway in Sequoia National Park. Open year-round. Wuksachi Lodge is full-service hotel with 102 guest rooms (standard, deluxe, and superior), gift shop, and full-service restaurant. 2002 double-occupancy rates: value season: $86–123; peak season: $150–219; holidays may be higher; rollaways, cribs, and additional occupants, $10/night. No stated pet policy.

Yosemite Lodge

Yosemite Reservations, 5410 East Home Ave., Fresno, CA 93727

yosemitepark.com
(559) 252-4848

4000 feet. In Yosemite Valley. *Of interest.* Lodge rooms: deluxe, standard rooms, rooms without bath; sleeping cabins: with bath, without bath; units without bath share centrally-located bath, shower facilities. 3 restaurants, cocktail lounge, swimming pool, bicycle rentals, gift shop, tour desk. Stores, restaurants, bakery, deli, ice-cream parlor, pizza parlor, equipment rentals (e.g., bicycles), banking services, bookstore, gas station, museum in nearby Yosemite Village. No pets. 2002 rates: $143/night/in season; $118–122/night/off season; extra person, $11.50; child $10–12; standard room, $112. Rollaways and cribs available.

Yosemite Peregrine Bed and Breakfast, The   yosemiteperegrine.com
7509 Henness Circle   (800) 396-3639, (209) 372-8517,
Yosemite West, CA 95389   fax (209) 372-4241

6000 feet. In Yosemite West, west of State Route 41 (Wawona Road), near the Chinquapin junction between Yosemite Valley and Wawona. *Mountain*. Bed-and-breakfast. 5 beautifully-decorated guest rooms each with private bath and fireplace; no smoking; full home-cooked breakfast or picnic breakfast to go. Nearest stores, restaurants in Yosemite Valley and Wawona. No pets. 2003 rates (1 or 2 persons): $110–200/night, depending on room. No extra persons.

Yosemite West Condominiums
5410 E. Home Ave., Fresno, CA 93727   (888) 296-7364

6000 feet. In Yosemite West, west of State Route 41 (Wawona Road), near the Chinquapin junction between Yosemite Valley and Wawona. *Mountain*. Housekeeping condominiums (studio and loft) accommodating 1–6 persons. Nearest stores, restaurants in Yosemite Valley and Wawona. No pets. 2002 rates: studio (1–2 persons) $95–115/night; loft (1–2 persons) $110–125/night. Extra person: adult $10/night. Stays of 1 week or more discounted 20%.

Yosemite West Cottages/Yosemite West Lodging, Inc. (agency)
P.O. Box 36, Yosemite National Park, CA 95389,   (559) 642-2211
or P.O. Box 507, Bass Lake, CA 93604   weekdays 9 a.m. to 5 p.m.

6000 feet. In Yosemite West, west of State Route 41 (Wawona Road), near the Chinquapin junction between Yosemite Valley and Wawona. *Mountain*. Housekeeping duplex and condominium units, townhomes, cottages, vacation homes, mountain homes; depending on unit, accommodates 1–8 people. Nearest stores, restaurants in Yosemite Valley and Wawona. No unregistered guests, no motorhomes/campers, no sleeping bags. No pets. 2002 rates: $155–345/night depending on kind and size of cabin; rooms in condos, $85–185, with kitchen.

Yosemite's Four Seasons (agency)
7519 Henness Circle,   (800) 669-9300, (209) 372-9000,
Yosemite National Park, CA 95389   fax (209) 372-8800

6000 feet. In Yosemite West, west of State Route 41 (Wawona Road), near the Chinquapin junction between Yosemite Valley and Wawona. *Mountain*. Housekeeping rooms, studios, homes, apartments. Amenities vary by unit. Nearest stores, restaurants in Yosemite Valley and Wawona. Pets okay in one older home only; $250 security/damage deposit required. Security/damage deposit required. 2002 rates range from $88–600 per night, depending on size and type of accommodation, number of people, and length and season of stay.

Communities

Alphabetically, these are the communities along the Western Sierra that are eligible for this book—

El Portal
See Mariposa County Chamber of Commerce

El Portal is mostly a string of motels on State Route 140 west of Yosemite National Park's Yosemite Valley district.

Fish Camp
See Southern Yosemite Visitors Bureau. See also Mariposa County Chamber of Commerce

Fish Camp straddles State Route 41 south of and just outside Yosemite National Park's Wawona district.

Mariposa County Chamber of Commerce
Yosemite/Mariposa County Chamber of Commerce,   (800) 208-2434,
P.O. Box 425, Mariposa, CA 95338   (559) 966-2456

Communities in Mariposa County west and south of Yosemite National Park eligible for this book: Fish Camp, Yosemite West (lodgings listed separately as "mountain," above), El Portal.

Oakhurst
See Southern Yosemite Visitors Bureau

Oakhurst straddles State Route 41 south of Yosemite National Park's Wawona district.

Shaver Lake Chamber of Commerce
P.O. Box 58, Shaver Lake, CA 93664   (559) 841-3350

Town straddling State Route 168 (west), on Shaver Lake, east of Fresno.

Southern Yosemite Visitors Bureau
49074 Civic Circle, Oakhurst, CA 93644   (559) 683-4636, fax (559) 683-0784

Community this bureau represents that's eligible for this book: Oakhurst.

Three Rivers
No Chamber of Commerce or Visitors Bureau, so lodgings are listed below. Small community strung out along State Route 198 and along Kaweah River just outside Sequoia National Park's Ash Mountain entrance station and just within range of Sequoia's Giant Forest district (but not of Mineral King or Grant Grove). National-parks-provided information:

Buckeye Tree Lodge, (559) 561-5900
Gateway Lodge, (559) 561-4133
Sequoia Village, (559) 561-3652
River Inn, (559) 561-4367
Three Rivers Motel, (559) 561-4413
Sierra Lodge, (800) 367-8879
Sequoia Motel, (559) 561-4453
Lake Elowin Resort, (559) 561-3460
Kaweah Park Resort, (559) 561-4424
Best Western Holiday Lodge, (559) 561-4119
Lazy J Ranch Motel, (559) 561-4449

Hikes
41. Soda Spring ☼ 🍁

Place	Total distance	Elevation	Level	Type
Start	0	7820	—	—
Soda spring	2½+	8040	E	O&B

Permit required: None

Topo(s): WP Mineral King 15'; Mineral King 7½'; Sequoia Natural History Association, "Mineral King"

Where to stay:
   Mountain: Silver City Mountain Resort
   Of Interest: None
   Other: None

Highlights: This easy stroll to a spring offers wonderful views up and down Mineral King Valley. Getting to the spring isn't the real goal; enjoying the views is.

How to get to the trailhead: From the junction of State Route 198 and Mineral King Road in the community of Three Rivers, it's 21.1 slow, twisting, painful miles (1½ hours) on narrow, partly paved Mineral King Road to get to Silver City Mountain Resort, the only lodgings within range of Mineral King. Don't even *think* about trying to daytrip to Mineral King from Three Rivers! From Silver City, continue east on Mineral King Road, perhaps stopping at Cold Springs Ranger Station at 2.5 miles to get the latest trail information. Continue east and then south, passing the parking lot for the trail to Timber Gap, Monarch Lakes, and Sawtooth Pass at 3.3 miles, to a fork: left (south) on a spur road to the Mineral King Pack Station, right (southwest) to the parking lot for the trail to Eagle and Mosquito lakes. Your trailhead for all practical purposes is as near this fork as possible; you can't park along the pack-station spur. You'll find turnouts along the road just before the fork and along the road to the Eagle-Mosquito parking lot; if

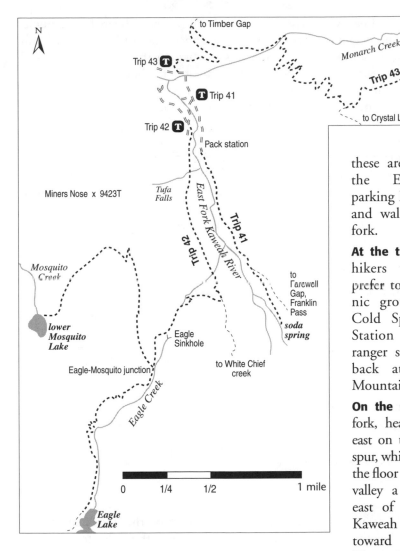

N

to Timber Gap

lower
Monarch
Lake

Monarch Creek

Trip 43 **T**

Trip 43

Trip 41 **T** Trip 41

to Crystal Lake

Trip 42 **T**

Pack station

Miners Nose x 9423T

*Tufa
Falls*

East Fork Kaweah River

Trip 42

Trip 41

*Mosquito
Creek*

to
Farewell
Gap,
Franklin
Pass

*lower
Mosquito
Lake*

Eagle
Sinkhole

*soda
spring*

Eagle-Mosquito junction

to White Chief
creek

Eagle Creek

0   1/4   1/2   1 mile

*Eagle
Lake*

these are full, park in the Eagle-Mosquito parking lot at 3.5 miles and walk back to the fork.

At the trailhead: Non-hikers will probably prefer to be at the picnic ground near the Cold Springs Ranger Station and at the ranger station itself or back at Silver City Mountain Resort.

On the trail: From the fork, head south-southeast on the pack-station spur, which runs right up the floor of Mineral King valley a short distance east of the East Fork Kaweah River and toward Farewell Gap. There is a handsome flower display alongside the road in spite of the road's deep dust and sand. You shortly pass the pack station entrance, reach the roadend at ¼ mile, and pick up the footpath. The open, rolling, sometimes-rocky track offers excellent views up Mineral King valley. Look west across the river for the noisy cascades of Tufa Falls. The river here is hardly more than a big creek as it slips through the broad, flowery meadow below, to your right. Mineral King, a name dreamed up by a 19th-century promoter of mining here, was Mineral Bust: no deposits of any real commercial value were ever found here. Ron Felzer's *High Sierra Hiking Guide: Mineral King* briefly tells the story, amusing to us but probably frustrating to heartbreaking for those who lived it.

A little beyond ¾ mile you cross the distributaries of Crystal Creek. Look up to your left here to see Crystal Creek's seasonally spectacular cascades, far more striking than Tufa Falls. In a few more steps you reach a fork where the main trail hooks left (southeast) and begins to climb the valley's east wall toward Farewell Gap and Franklin Pass, while a row of boulders blocks the branch that you can see ahead (right, south-southeast). The boulders may be suitable for blocking vehicles that dare to stray this far, but they are no barrier to the hiker.

You continue ahead on the right fork, through the boulders, following a some-times-faint trail—probably once a road—and climb a little to pass a lone red fir and enter a flower-splashed meadow. Nearing 1¼ miles, you rise gradually just before descending a little to a rusty-looking spring—the **soda spring at slightly over 1¼ miles and 8040 feet**—next to a little fork of the river, across which there's a low, flowery bluff. Find a dry spot around here where you can pause to enjoy a snack and take in the beautiful view back down Mineral King valley.

Great views accompany you as you retrace your steps.

42. Eagle or Lower Mosquito Lake ☼ 🍁

Place	Total distance	Elevation	Level	Type
Start	0	7830	—	—
Eagle Lake *only*	7⅔	10,010	S	O&B
Mosquito Lake *only*	7	9060	S U	O&B

Permit required: None

Topo(s): WP Mineral King 15'; Mineral King 7½'; Sequoia Natural History Association, "Mineral King"

Where to stay:
   Mountain: Silver City Mountain Resort
   Of Interest: None
   Other: None

Highlights: This stiff hike to one of two lovely lakes high on the ridge that bounds Mineral King valley on the south offers superb views over the valley to the Great Western Divide, the glorious subrange that bounds the valley on the north and east. Splendid Eagle Lake is an alpine jewel; pretty lower Mosquito Lake is a well-forested mid-altitude gem. Flower gardens brighten your climb, and a curious feature called Eagle Sinkhole is sure to leave you puzzled.

How to get to the trailhead: Follow the driving directions of Trip 41 to the road fork: left (south) on a spur road to the Mineral King Pack Station, right (south-west) to the parking lot for the trail to Eagle and Mosquito lakes. Bear right and park in the Eagle-Mosquito parking lot at 3.5 miles; the trailhead is at the far (southwest) end of the lot, from which there are nice views up-valley.

At the trailhead: See Trip 41.

On the trail: See Trip 41's map. Pause to read the trailhead information sign and then head southwest on the trail, ignoring a use trail that almost immediately darts right and up to a private cabin—don't disturb Mineral King's cabins. The rocky-dusty, gradually climbing trail is well-forested uphill but is broad enough and lightly-forested enough downhill that it can be quite hot at midday. You pass another cabin and at ¼ mile cross a footbridge over the stream below Tufa Falls (hidden from view here). A little beyond ⅓ mile, an unmapped use trail descends steeply to the river on your left, but you stay on the main trail.

Around ¾ mile, you begin to enjoy excellent views of the long, showy cascades on Crystal Creek eastward across the valley and of Farewell Gap far ahead to the southeast. You shortly dip into a cool nook and ford a creek; emerging, you see the cascades of Franklin Creek ahead across the valley. The climb becomes steep as you reach a junction a little beyond 1 mile: left (south-southwest) to White Chief creek, right (west-northwest) to Eagle and Mosquito lakes. You go right, beginning a steep, switchbacking climb in patchy forest. Around 1½ miles you switchback through a wet and wonderfully flowery hillside meadow, leveling out briefly near the top of the meadow to enjoy over-the-shoulder views up the Crystal Creek drainage to Mineral Peak, Glacier Pass, and Empire Mountain.

You climb steeply again as you leave the meadow behind, veering away from the valley views to level out in moderate forest. The creekbed adjacent to your trail is strangely dry, just a channel of shattered metamorphic rock—*Where's the water?* you'll wonder. One mystery is solved and another posed when, just shy of 2 miles, you dip slightly to pass Eagle Sinkhole, where bubbling Eagle Creek simply disappears into a funnel of broken rock. Maybe it reappears as the spring that nourishes the hillside meadow you traversed earlier—maybe not: some experts say that's not Eagle Creek's water. About all *you* can do is to shake your head and continue, now roughly paralleling the little creek. You reach a junction, the Eagle-Mosquito junction, a little beyond 2 miles: left (south) to Eagle Lake, right (west) to Mosquito Lake. Choose one; going to both is about 10½ miles, which is beyond this book's mileage limits but within the range of sturdy hikers who get an early start.

To go to Eagle Lake, bear left at the Eagle-Mosquito junction, at first walking more or less near the creek on a level track. It's not long before you resume climbing on a worn old trail up tiny, rocky, steep switchbacks. Pause often to enjoy the superb views over your shoulder to the Great Western Divide again, where Sawtooth Peak is now plainly visible. You level off briefly at a meadowed bench, then begin climbing up the head of the bench through talus. The going gets very rough at times; you may need your hands for balance, and in places the trail is just a slot blasted through huge slabs of granite. At the head of this bench, Eagle Creek slips down a steep granite wall; rest stops amid the sunstruck talus let you savor views of the peaks and streams on the Divide.

At the top of this climb, the trail levels out on another meadowy bench, at the end of which it begins a gradual climb up the next series of tiny benches. The trail is faint in places; keep your eyes peeled. You climb southward through granite boulders to a point abreast of a little dam on your left that raises Eagle Lake's level slightly. Several of Mineral King's lakes have been dammed as part of a hydroelectric project dating from the early 20th century; they're still maintained by Southern California Edison. From Eagle Lake's dam you have your first good view of lightly-forested, beautiful but overused **Eagle Lake at a little less than 4 miles and 10,010 feet**. Another few steps bring you to a junction with a use trail that climbs uphill on your right to an outhouse, while the main trail continues around the lake on your left. The lake's real size—it fills this little cirque—is camouflaged by a peninsula and some rocky islets. Numerous picnic spots dot the lakeshore; pick one from which to enjoy this wonderful scenery.

Retrace your steps to the Eagle-Mosquito junction and then to your car.

To go to Lower Mosquito Lake, turn right at the Eagle-Mosquito junction. You cross a patch of damp woods before beginning a hot ascent up a dry, meadowed slope. The loose, dusty trail levels out before descending to cross some rockslides; there are fine views across the valley to the Great Western Divide here. Now you begin a long ascent, traversing the slopes south of Miners Nose in forest. You top the ridge at a saddle at 9360 feet a little south of Miners Nose at almost 3 miles, then begin a moderate-to-steep descent to pretty **lower Mosquito Lake at almost 3½ miles and 9060 feet.** In mid-season the lake's forest- and meadow-lined shores may be a-whine with mosquitoes; in late season, they may be abuzz with dragonflies. Shattered white cliffs rise across the lake, making a dramatic backdrop. Find a perch here from which to enjoy this charming spot.

Retrace your steps to the Eagle-Mosquito junction and then to your car.

43. Lower Monarch Lake ☼ 🍁

Place	Total distance	Elevation	Level	Type
Start	0	7820	—	—
Lower Monarch Lake	9+	10,380	S	O&B

Permit required: None

Topo(s): WP Mineral King 15'; Mineral King 7½'; Sequoia Natural History Association, "Mineral King"

Where to stay:
　　Mountain: Silver City Mountain Resort
　　Of Interest: None
　　Other: None

Highlights: A long ascent leads through glorious flower gardens and past numerous viewpoints to beautiful lower Monarch Lake in a breathtaking cirque right under Sawtooth Peak. Get an early start: the first leg of the hike, to the ford of Monarch Creek, is steep, shadeless, and very hot by midday.

How to get to the trailhead: Follow the driving directions of Trip 41 to Silver City and continue east on Mineral King Road to the parking lot for the trail to Timber

Gap, Monarch Lakes, and Sawtooth Pass at 3.3 miles. There is parking on either side of the road; the trail leaves from the lot on the north side of the road. Toilet.

At the trailhead: See Trip 41.

On the trail: See Trip 41's map. Check out the trailhead information sign before heading northwest on the rocky-dusty trail on a grade that's gradual at first but soon grows steep, through a landscape stripped for now of its chaparral cover by the lightning-caused August 1994 Empire Fire. Just beyond ⅔ mile you reach a junction with the trail to Timber Gap: left (north-northeast) to Timber Gap, right (southeast) to Monarch and Crystal lakes. There's a great view of Mineral King valley from here, which includes your car in the parking lot below. As often happens in a fire's wake, there's a fine display of annual flowers until the chaparral grows back. The trail presently curves into the drainage of Monarch Creek and climbs steeply to moderately again, beetling high above Monarch Creek, on whose opposite bank you see a spring burst forth in a pretty cascade at 1⅓ miles. The trail is hot, steep, loose, and airy here, so watch your footing. A little farther on, you reach another junction: left (northwest) on an old trail that's now out of use; right (southeast) to Sawtooth Pass.

Turning right, you traverse a small meadow, ford Monarch Creek at nearly 1½ miles, and find yourself in the welcome shade of a fir grove. Leaving the fire-scarred region behind, you enjoy patches of forest alternating with fine displays of wildflowers as you traverse a slope with good views of the valley and begin a long ascent that has you winding up seemingly endless, gradually graded switchbacks. At 2¾ miles a use trail darts left at a switchback turn where you go right to stay on the main trail. The raw slope of Empire Mountain rises to the north as you continue your climb. At a little over 3 miles you round a ridgelet and get a fine view of White Chief canyon and Eagle Creek's drainage across the way (see Trip 42), and of Vandever Mountain at the head of Farewell Canyon.

In the shade of sparse foxtail pines, you reach another junction at nearly 3½ miles: left (northwest) to Monarch Lakes, right (east) to Crystal Lake. Go left and negotiate one more switchback before swinging back over the ridgelet to overlook Monarch Creek. Ahead you see the steep alpine meadows lining Monarch Creek's beautiful cascades as they pour out of lower Monarch Lake. Even more exciting, you have a glimpse northwest clear over Timber Gap to the high ridge that includes Alta Peak. Closer at hand, you see Empire Mountain, Glacier Pass, aptly-named Sawtooth Peak, and Sawtooth Pass. Westward views extend all the way to the bleached foothills around the Central Valley. You can also see your trail cutting across rocky slopes of reddish metamorphic rock.

Aiming at Sawtooth Peak, you resume your hike on the gradual, rocky trailbed, slowly curving into the cirque that holds lower Monarch Lake. Snowmelt trickles across the trail, supporting a handsome flower display in spite of the porous, thin soil. The fantastic cockscomb of Mineral Peak comes into view, and you cross a pair of briskly-flowing outlet streams before ascending to an overlook of lower Monarch Lake. Across the sparkling lake, the stream connecting it to upper

Monarch Lake spills steeply down high granite slabs in splendid cascades. Descend slightly to the shore of **lower Monarch Lake at a little over 4½ miles and 10,380 feet**. Find a nice rock along this lovely shoreline and have your picnic. There's a dilapidated pit toilet in the rocks above and northwest of the lake.

Retrace your steps to the trailhead, enjoying tremendous views as you go.

Upper Monarch Lake. Hikers with Class-2 experience who want to see upper Monarch Lake (not part of this trip) will find a number of airy routes to that high, delightfully barren, dammed lake. A route from the north side of the lower lake, its start mostly hidden in the willows, offers a followable track with fine views back down to the lower lake. The obvious route that starts as a deep rut near the cascading stream that connects the lakes quickly leads out onto steep, water-slick slabs—not recommended.

Lower Monarch Lake

44. Giant Forest Sequoia Loop 🌲 ☼ 🍁

Place	Total distance	Elevation	Level	Type
Start	0	6920	—	—
Congress Trail loop *only*	2+	7040	E	Loop
Entire loop	5½+	7350	M	Loop

Permit required: None

Topo(s): WP Triple Divide Peak 15'; Giant Forest, Lodgepole 7½'; Sequoia Natural History Association "Giant Forest"

Where to stay:
   Mountain: Montecito-Sequoia Lodge, Grant Grove Cabins, John Muir Lodge
   Of Interest: Wuksachi Lodge, Stony Creek Lodge
   Other: Town of Three Rivers

Highlights: This hike begins and ends near the world's most famous giant sequoia tree, the General Sherman Tree, and visits many other giant sequoias in an area that attract thousands of visitors. But this hike also includes time away from the throngs, time in quiet nooks where you can be alone—well, almost—among the great, cinnamon-barked trees that are the largest living things on Earth. The hike uses two famous trails, the Congress Trail and the Trail of the Sequoias. You can cut it short by hiking only the busier Congress Trail.

How to get to the trailhead: From Giant Forest Museum, the point of reference for hikes in Sequoia National Park, drive 2.1 miles north on the Generals Highway to the turnoff for the General Sherman Tree. Turn east to the General Sherman Tree and continue 0.1 mile to the parking lot, which is often choked with cars by mid-morning—it's a good idea to get an early start on this hike! Toilets, water.

At the trailhead: Benches under the giant sequoias, along with amenities like toilets and drinking fountains, make this a pleasant as well as a beautiful place to linger. Non-hikers may also enjoy exploring Giant Forest Museum with its shops, gallery, restaurants, and short walking trails.

On the trail: From the parking lot, follow signs along a paved trail to the General Sherman Tree, past a section of a giant sequoia tree set up to demonstrate the great age to which these trees live and how they record the events of their lives in their growth patterns; according to a sign, this one sprouted in 261 B.C. At ⅒ mile you reach the General Sherman Tree, fenced to keep people off the most vulnerable parts of its shallow root system. Mature giant sequoias have no taproots and depend instead upon a huge network of relatively shallow roots that may be damaged when the soil around them is compacted too much, as by years of human trampling. Walk around the tree, which is believed to be the most massive living thing on Earth. It's estimated to be 2300–2700 years old and is still growing vigorously.

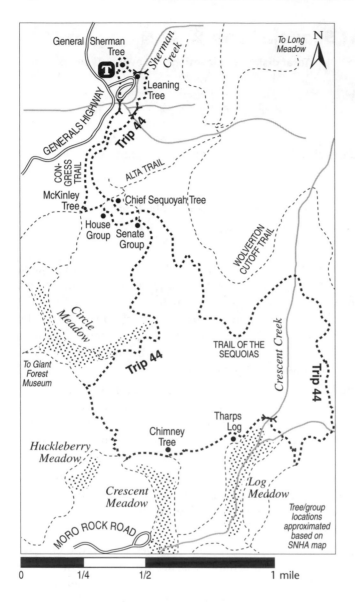

On the far side of the General Sherman Tree, you meet the signed Congress Trail, which takes its name from a couple of dense clumps of giant sequoias along it, the House Group and the Senate Group. The Congress Trail is a short loop trail oriented roughly north-south and thus with east and west "sides." Bear left (east-south-east) at this junction, onto the east side of the Congress Trail, and toward the parking-lot access road, which you skirt but do not cross. You shortly curve left toward the Leaning Tree, a tilting giant sequoia growing out of a gully that you cross on a footbridge. The paved trail is covered with a light scattering of forest debris, and in spite of the crowds, shade and silence prevail. A little past ⅓ mile, a burned but still-standing giant sequoia forms a huge, black, abstract spire. You cross another footbridge beside a mossy spring and under a fallen giant sequoia that's been slightly hollowed out for your passage—but even short people will need to duck. At ½ mile you reach a junction that's not on the map: left (south) for the full Congress Trail, right (west) to cut the Congress Trail short by picking up the west side of its loop and heading back to the parking lot. You go left, continuing on the east side of the Congress Trail and climbing gradually, noticing the interesting forms taken by giant sequoias that have survived fires and passing an especially massive, fire-scarred giant with a manzanita bush growing near its truncated top.

You reach another junction a little beyond ¾ mile: left (south) on the Trail of the Sequoias, right (southwest) to remain on the Congress Trail. Those confining their hike to the Congress Trail go right here; see the paragraph below beginning, "You reach a junction with the paved Congress Trail…." Hikers wanting to enjoy the entire trip go left on the Trail of the Sequoias, passing the huge Chief Sequoyah ·Tree and shortly reaching another, unmapped junction: left (southeast) to continue on the Trail of the Sequoias, right (south and down) to return to the Congress Trail, in case you've changed your mind.

Go left here, toward Tharp's Log—still some distance away—and leave the crowds behind. You're far from the highway now, and the special silence of a giant sequoia grove is almost palpable—a fluid you drift through. You climb gradually to moderately on a duff trail, observing that a giant-sequoia grove is far from being a pure stand of giant sequoias. In fact, although you're still within the Giant Forest Grove, you've left the giant sequoias behind for now. Many other species occur within the giant-sequoia groves, like white firs, sugar pines, Jeffrey pines, and a variety of wildflowers. Near 1⅔ miles you reach the hike's high point on a dry shoulder dotted with granite boulders. You cross a small saddle before beginning a moderate descent through a dense white-fir forest, rejoining the giant sequoias some 150 feet down as the terrain grows damper.

At 2 miles you cross a stream above an immense sequoia, then walk through the shattered trunk of an even larger, but fallen, one. Pause often to look around you, for here the giant sequoias grow by ones to fews in quiet niches tucked into steep slopes, and in the company of firs and ferns. You step across a trickle at 2¼ miles, then ford a couple of unmapped, alder-choked creeklets at 2⅔ miles. Nearing 3 miles, you meet another junction: left (southwest) on the Trail of the Sequoias, right (north) to Tharp's Log. Go right for Tharp's Log and curl steeply down a slope to a T-junction on the edge of lovely Log Meadow: left (south) to the High Sierra Trail, right (north) to Tharp's Log. Go right for Tharp's Log, fording a stream at 3 miles and crossing another on a footbridge shortly thereafter. You continue around the meadow, staying in its forest edge, finally descending at almost 3¼ miles to the hollowed-out giant sequoia log that served Hale Tharp as a summer home while his cattle grazed the meadow, from 1861 to 1890. Benches allow you to rest here while you study the unique cabin and enjoy the view across Log Meadow.

The cabin has distinct "door" and "root" ends; leaving Tharp's Log and Log Meadow, you take the trail from the "root" end instead of the one near the "door" end, going northwest on a moderate climb, then descending on steps cut into a fallen tree. You pass the fragile shell of the Chimney Tree at 3½ miles and meet a junction here and another junction in ⅛ mile; go right at both junctions (left leads to Crescent Meadow). There are crowds here: Crescent Meadow is easily accessible and very popular. Speaking of junctions, there are so many of them in this heavily used area—more than the book's map can show—that you may think you're in a junction grove, not a giant sequoia grove. You're trying to work your way back to the General Sherman Tree, and the trail signs point back to features you want to aim for: the General Sherman Tree, the Congress Trail, the Senate Group, the House Group, and so on.

At nearly 3⅔ miles you reach a **Y**-junction: left (west) to Huckleberry Meadow, right (northwest) to the General Sherman Tree. Go right to climb over a small ridge in the quiet forest, on the far side of which you reach another **Y**-junction at 4 miles: left (ahead, northwest) to Giant Forest Museum, right (east-northeast) to the Congress Trail. Go right, descending steeply, and soon reach yet another **Y**-junction: left (northwest) to the Alta Trail, right (northeast) to the Senate Group and the Congress Trail. Go right toward the east lobe of Circle Meadow, which you can see ahead. The trail climbs steeply over a rocky outcrop in order to avoid the meadow, then skirts the meadow circuitously, undulating. Ford a meadow-feeding streamlet at 4½ miles, and nearing 5 miles curve through an exceptionally fine stand of mature giant sequoias, the Senate Group.

You reach a junction with the paved Congress Trail by the Senate Group: left (ahead, west) to the House Group along the west side of the Congress Trail, right (north) to the east side of the Congress Trail—the side you've already traveled. Go left and pass the House Group of giant sequoias. Just beyond 5 miles, you meet a spur trail right to the east side of the Congress Trail. Go left, staying on the west side. Almost immediately there's another junction: ahead (left, southwest) on the Alta Trail, right (northwest) on the Congress Trail. Go right here and right again at each of the next two junctions, the second one of which is with a spur to a "picture point of the McKinley Tree." You curve around the McKinley Tree and go north-northeast, traversing high above the noisy highway.

At last you begin a moderate to gradual descent, passing through a cut in another toppled giant. At a little over 5⅓ miles you reach another junction: ahead (left, north) to the General Sherman Tree, right (southeast) on a use trail (not shown on the map) to make a shortcut across the Congress Trail. Go left, continuing to descend. With the parking lot now in view, you cross a stream on a footbridge and climb a little to the lot, closing your loop at just over 5½ miles.

45. Panther Gap 🌾 ☼ 🍁

Place	Total distance	Elevation	Level	Type
Start	0	7340	–	–
Panther Gap	5+	8520	M	O&B

Permit required: None

Topo(s): WP Triple Divide Peak 15′; Lodgepole 7½′; Sequoia Natural History Association "Lodgepole/Wolverton"

Where to stay:
  Mountain: Montecito-Sequoia Lodge, Grant Grove Cabins, John Muir Lodge
  Of Interest: Wuksachi Lodge, Stony Creek Lodge
  Other: Town of Three Rivers

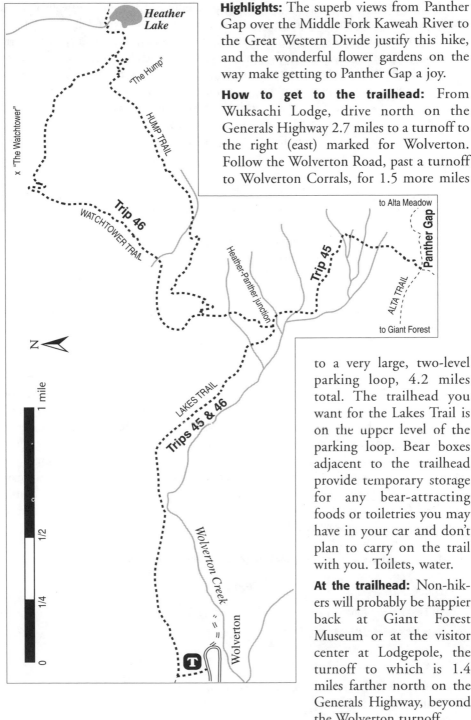

Highlights: The superb views from Panther Gap over the Middle Fork Kaweah River to the Great Western Divide justify this hike, and the wonderful flower gardens on the way make getting to Panther Gap a joy.

How to get to the trailhead: From Wuksachi Lodge, drive north on the Generals Highway 2.7 miles to a turnoff to the right (east) marked for Wolverton. Follow the Wolverton Road, past a turnoff to Wolverton Corrals, for 1.5 more miles to a very large, two-level parking loop, 4.2 miles total. The trailhead you want for the Lakes Trail is on the upper level of the parking loop. Bear boxes adjacent to the trailhead provide temporary storage for any bear-attracting foods or toiletries you may have in your car and don't plan to carry on the trail with you. Toilets, water.

At the trailhead: Non-hikers will probably be happier back at Giant Forest Museum or at the visitor center at Lodgepole, the turnoff to which is 1.4 miles farther north on the Generals Highway, beyond the Wolverton turnoff.

On the trail: Climb concrete steps leading generally north from the well-marked trailhead and from the upper leg of the parking lot. You ascend moderately to steeply on the dusty duff Lakes Trail through a moderate to dense fir forest, shortly passing a dusty stock trail coming in from the left and then a spur going left to Lodgepole. At both of these junctions you go right, staying on the Lakes Trail. As the grade eases, you pass yet another junction, this one on your right, with a now-closed track back to the Wolverton parking lot; stay on the Lakes Trail (left). Three junctions in the first ⅒ mile! The trail gradually works its way up and then along a forested ridge, where breaks in the forest offer glimpses of peaks and granite domes to the north. At ¾ mile you traverse above musical little Wolverton Creek, then descend to the meadow along the creek for a welcome and flowery break from the dense forest. At 1 mile the trail hooks right (southeast), and dry openings in the forest provide an abundant flower display. The grade steepens around 1½ miles, and you soon ford a stream.

At 1⅔ miles you reach a junction that I'll call the *Heather-Panther junction*: left (north) to continue on the Lakes Trail to Heather Lake and its sister lakes, right (east-southeast) to Panther Gap and Mehrten Meadow. For this hike, you go right for Panther Gap. The trail to Panther Gap ascends gradually to moderately through hillside meadows and across creeklets and springs—more than maps can show—and from one glorious flower garden through a patch of dense forest to the next garden. At 2⅓ miles you cross the final stream and meadow; ahead, blue sky appears over the rim of a ridge.

You climb moderate to steep switchbacks toward that sliver of sky; the last switchback is very steep. Near the top, you meet the Alta Trail high above the Middle Fork Kaweah River. Use trails lead away from this junction to viewpoints. I suggest you go left on the Alta Trail very briefly, till it breaks out on the ridgetop at **Panther Gap at a little over 2½ miles and 8520 feet**. Pick a use trail leading south toward any open spot, from which the view will surely be sublime: across the Middle Fork Kaweah River, the granite domes of Castle Rocks; to the southeast and east, the jagged, light-colored peaks of the Great Western Divide, notably Empire Mountain, Sawtooth Peak, Needham Mountain, and, to the east around Kaweah Gap, Mt. Stewart and Eagle Scout Peak.

You'll turn away from this breathtaking spectacle with regret but be cheered by the flower gardens as you retrace your steps.

46. Heather Lake ☼ 🍁

Place	Total distance	Elevation	Level	Type
Start	0	7340	—	—
Heather Lake	8	9260	S	Semi

Permit required: None

Topo(s): WP Triple Divide Peak 15'; Lodgepole 7½'; Sequoia Natural History Association "Lodgepole/Wolverton"

Where to stay:
   Mountain: Montecito-Sequoia Lodge, Grant Grove Cabins, John Muir Lodge
   Of Interest: Wuksachi Lodge, Stony Creek Lodge
   Other: Town of Three Rivers

Highlights: Dramatic views over beautiful Tokopah Valley and a visit to pretty Heather Lake are your rewards on this hike.

Acrophobics beware! One branch of the loop, the Watchtower Trail, has a final leg that's extremely exposed above Tokopah Valley as it approaches Heather Lake—great views, but a potential 2000-foot fall down a steep granite cliff from a narrow, rocky trail. People with even mild cases of acrophobia will be better off taking the other branch, the steeper but less exposed Hump Trail, both ways, turning the trip into an out-and-back instead a semiloop. You get a great view of Tokopah Valley from the less-airy Hump Trail above Heather Lake. The branches are about equidistant, but the Hump Trail climbs higher (9500 feet, well above Heather Lake).

How to get to the trailhead: Follow the driving directions of Trip 45.

At the trailhead: See Trip 45.

On the trail: See Trip 45's map. Follow Trip 45 as far as the Heather-Panther junction at 1⅔ miles, where you go left (north) for Heather Lake. Climb moderately to steeply away from the junction, re-crossing the stream, and reaching another junction at 2 miles: left on the more-gradual Watchtower Trail with its vertiginous last leg; right on the much steeper but much-less-exposed Hump Trail. Both trend generally north at this point. Just to cover all the bases, I'll write this up as a semiloop: out to Heather Lake on the Watchtower Trail, back to the Heather-Panther junction on the Hump Trail. But remember: anyone with the slightest degree of acrophobia should take the Hump Trail both ways. I'm only mildly acrophobic, but on the Watchtower Trail I was seized with the worst attack of acrophobia I've ever had.

Going left on the Watchtower Trail, you find the grade easing considerably as you once more traverse a ridge. At a little over 2⅓ miles you cross a multistranded stream that nourishes a steep hillside meadow. As you approach the granite monolith called The Watchtower, which bulges away from Tokopah Valley's south wall, the trail's downslope side grows steeper. Open spots permit views westward to granite domes and beyond them to Central Valley smog, and you can hear the noise of the Generals Highway here. You begin a series of moderate-to-steep switchbacks on decomposed granite sand, reaching an airy overlook of Tokopah Falls at 3¼ miles. There's a fork here; go right on the main trail (left is a use trail to more airy overlooks). You shortly pass behind The Watchtower, whose summit stands free of the valley walls here. More switchbacks carry you higher, and you begin a narrow, exposed leg on an exposed track blasted out of the cliff face. The track's downslope edge sits on an extremely steep drop down long granite slabs that sweep far, far down into Tokopah Valley. There are views over the valley and of Silver Peak and the Silliman Crest beyond.

The airy stretch ends a little before the next junction at 4 miles, where the Watchtower and Hump trails rejoin in a sparse lodgepole forest. You descend very slightly to pass a couple of junctions where use trails go left to the Heather Lake pit toilet. Staying on the main trail, you pass overlooks above Heather Lake before descending a little more to cross **Heather Lake's outlet at a little over 4 miles and 9260 feet** and then find a nice picnic spot on Heather's east shore. This rock-bound lake is mighty pretty in its forested, granite cirque, which is a hanging valley high above Tokopah Valley.

Retrace your steps to the last junction of the Watchtower and Hump trails, now with almost 4⅓ miles on your boots. Go left (west-northwest) on the Hump Trail, ascending steep, sandy switchbacks to a 9500-foot saddle just south of The Hump, a high point west of Heather Lake. There are fine over-the-shoulder views of Tokopah Valley as you make this climb. From this saddle at 4½ miles, you begin a very steep descent on loose terrain, eventually coming alongside a pretty, meadowed creek. At 5⅓ miles you cross the creek in a beautiful meadow, then resume your descent in moderate forest, till the grade eases and you pass through another lovely little meadow at a little over 5¾ miles. A few more steep switchbacks bring you to the lower junction of the Hump and Watchtower trails at nearly 6 miles.

A much more moderate descent brings you to the Heather-Panther junction at almost 6⅓ miles. Turn right here to retrace your steps to the Wolverton parking area at a little under 8 miles.

47. Tokopah Falls 🌸 ☀

Place	Total distance	Elevation	Level	Type
Start	0	6740	–	–
Tokopah Falls viewpoint	3½	7360	M	O&B

Permit required: None

Topo(s): WP Triple Divide Peak 15'; Lodgepole 7½'; Sequoia Natural History Association "Lodgepole/Wolverton"

Where to stay:
Mountain: Montecito-Sequoia Lodge, Grant Grove Cabins, John Muir Lodge
Of Interest: Wuksachi Lodge, Stony Creek Lodge
Other: Town of Three Rivers

Highlights: Beautiful Tokopah Valley is a perfect example of a small-"y" "yosemite," as John Muir called them: steep-sided, granite-walled, glacier-carved valleys that aren't *the* Yosemite Valley. At Tokopah Valley's head, the long, showy cascades called Tokopah Falls crash down the granite slabs.

How to get to the trailhead: From Giant Forest Museum, drive north on the Generals Highway for 4.4 miles to a turnoff to the east to Lodgepole Visitor Center. There are also other visitor facilities at Lodgepole, like a gas station, a snack bar, and an ice-cream parlor. But continue for another 0.6 mile beyond the visitor center parking, through the Lodgepole Campground entrance station—you may need to check in here—to trailhead parking in a lot near the trailhead and a bridge over the Marble Fork Kaweah River, 5 miles. Toilets and water in the campground.

At the trailhead: Non-hikers may enjoy a stop at the visitor center and a chance to explore the facilities around it, or they may prefer to be at Giant Forest Museum; see Trip 44.

On the trail: The Tokopah Valley trailhead is on the north side of the bridge. From there, the trail heads generally east, gradually ascending along the young Marble Fork Kaweah River, here splashing along over picturesque slabs and around granite boulders. The trail is very wide, worn, and dusty, and there are many use trails descending to the riverbank. You generally parallel the river, though from time to

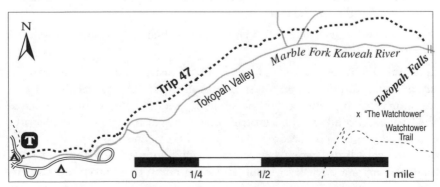

time you veer away from it briefly, and the patchy forest provides some shade on hot days. Nearing ⅔ mile, you can see a 1600-foot monolith aptly named "The Watchtower" standing out from Tokopah Valley's sheer granite south wall (see Trip 46 for a closer look at The Watchtower). A little beyond 1 mile you cross three stream channels—only two are on the map—in quick succession, on footbridges, enjoying the flower gardens the streams support.

Lovely Tokopah Falls is in view by now, and the trail ascends moderately on a rocky track blasted through huge chunks of fallen rock. The trail ends at **a viewpoint of Tokopah Falls at 1¾ miles and 7360 feet**: some enormous, flat-topped boulders offering picnic spots as well as excellent views of the cascades and the sheer granite cliffs down which they leap. It's dangerous to approach any closer to the falls. In the fall, if you're very lucky, you may see a soon-to-hibernate bear gorging on the harsh fruit of the many bitter-cherry bushes along the last leg of this trip.

Return the way you came.

48. Little Baldy ☼ ❦

Place	Total distance	Elevation	Level	Type
Start	0	7340	—	—
Little Baldy's summit	3⅓	8044	M	O&B

Permit required: None

Topo(s): Giant Forest, Muir Grove 7½'

Where to stay:
   Mountain: Montecito-Sequoia Lodge, Grant Grove Cabins, John Muir Lodge
   Of Interest: Wuksachi Lodge, Stony Creek Lodge
   Other: Town of Three Rivers

Highlights: Three hikes along the Generals Highway take you to summits with outstanding views, and of them, Little Baldy offers the best views east into the backcountry of Sequoia and Kings Canyon national parks.

How to get to the trailhead: From Giant Forest Museum, drive 11 miles north on the Generals Highway, to Little Baldy Saddle. There is parking on both sides of the road; the trailhead is on the east side.

At the trailhead: Non-hikers will prefer to be at their lodgings or at Grant Grove or Lodgepole visitor center.

On the trail: From the marked trailhead on the east side of the road, start up the dusty duff trail through dense forest, climbing moderately to steeply at first. The grade soon eases to gradual as you negotiate a series of long, leisurely switchbacks; at the first and second switchback turns, make the entire turn—don't veer off onto use trails. The forest soon becomes patchy, and the open spots support a wide variety of flowers. A little beyond 1 mile, you reach a forested ridgetop on which you dip a little, enjoy a brief, level stroll, and then climb briefly to a more-open area

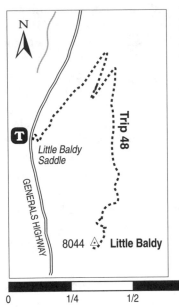

N

Little Baldy
Saddle

Trip 48

GENERALS HIGHWAY

8044 ⚠ Little Baldy

T

0   1/4   1/2   1 mile

where you discover fine views southeast to Castle Rocks and Sawtooth Peak. You pass some granite outcrops and slabs, then make a moderate drop to the saddle below Little Baldy's summit.

The final ascent is moderate to steep and sometimes rocky. Near the top, the trail seems to peter out. That's no problem: just meander a few steps more to the old brass benchmark hammered into the broad, bare summit. There used to be a lookout here at **Little Baldy's summit at 1⅔ miles and 8044 feet**, and it's obvious why. There are spectacular views in all directions: Castle Rocks; the Great Western Divide, including Sawtooth and Eagle Scout peaks; Kaweah Peaks Ridge, including Black Kaweah, Red Kaweah, and Mt. Kaweah; Alta Peak; upper Tokopah Valley (Trip 47); Silliman Crest; Buck Rock; and Shell Mountain in the Jennie Lakes Wilderness (Trip 50).

Retrace your steps when you must—you won't be in any hurry to leave.

49. Muir Grove 🌿 ☼ 🍁

Place	Total distance	Elevation	Level	Type
Start	0	6720	—	—
Muir Grove	3⅓	6860	M	O&B

Permit required: None

Topo(s): Muir Grove 7½'

Where to stay:
Mountain: Montecito-Sequoia Lodge, Grant Grove Cabins, John Muir Lodge
Of Interest: Wuksachi Lodge, Stony Creek Lodge
Other: Town of Three Rivers

Highlights: A pretty hike out of Dorst Campground leads to a secluded grove of giant sequoias, the Muir Grove. In late season, when the campground is closed, you may have the grove all to yourself.

How to get to the trailhead: From Wuksachi Lodge, drive 12.7 miles north on the Generals Highway to the entrance to Dorst Campground. Turn south into Dorst Campground and stop if necessary to get permission at the campground entrance station. Follow signs to the Dorst Amphitheater parking, curving left on the main road where a spur curves right into the group campground and then going left where a spur goes right to sites 193–218. Park in the Dorst Amphitheater parking, almost 0.7 mile more (13.4 miles). Shortly before the amphitheater parking, you'll

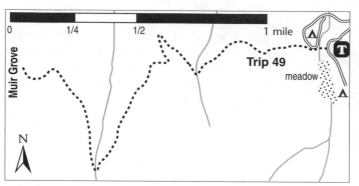

pass the trailhead, so from the parking lot, walk back to the trailhead, which is on the west side of the road. Toilets and water in campground (when open).

If Dorst Campground is closed, park as best you can near its entrance without blocking its gates; there's a fairly large turnout on the opposite side of the highway from the entrance. Walk downhill through the campground, curving left on the main road where a spur curves right into the group campground, to the trailhead on the west side of the road, ⅔ mile.

At the trailhead: Similar to Trip 48.

On the trail: Note that the topo is wrong about this trailhead: the topo shows the trail starting from the group-campground loop, but the trail actually starts from the next road east and brushes right by the lower end of the group-campground loop. Go west on the beaten path, which almost immediately dips to cross a flower-lined tributary of Dorst Creek on a footbridge. On the other side, the trail rises steeply to a **Y**-junction with a use trail to the group campground, the road loop for which you can see just a few feet away to the right (north). Go left (southwest) for Muir Grove.

The forest becomes denser as you descend gradually to moderately along a meadow sporting a fine wildflower display. You presently find yourself high above the steep little valley through which unseen Dorst Creek flows generally westward. Your gradual descent continues high above the creek until, at nearly ¾ mile, you reach an apparent junction with a use trail that veers right; you go left (southeast), making a switchback turn up a ridge. Gaining the forested ridgetop, you may want to veer right to its open, rock-strewn nose, dominated by a single huge Jeffrey pine. From the nose, you notice the blunt crowns of Muir Grove's giant sequoias on the next ridge west. The next ridge seems very close but is farther away than you think, because the two ridges are separated by a sizable north-south gully holding a tributary of Dorst Creek.

After returning to the main trail, you make a mostly-gradual descent through dry forest, at one point climbing over loose slabs on a steep slope—poor footing here. The vegetation grows increasingly lush as you curve into the steep, narrow, damp head of the gully. At 1⅓ miles you ford the densely-meadowed tributary and begin a gradual climb up the east side of the next ridge. You pass through beautiful thickets of red osier dogwood, catching glimpses ahead and uphill of huge reddish-brown trunks. At 1⅔ miles you reach a small saddle that has a fine stand of about a dozen giant sequoias just below it to the west. Giant sequoias are scattered through the forest as far as you can see—which isn't very far, as the forest is pretty dense. This is **Muir Grove at 1⅔ miles and 6860 feet** (at the saddle). Explore the area with care, following numerous use trails—the main trail peters out a little west of the saddle. Fallen logs near the saddle make nice picnic seats.

Retrace your steps to the trailhead.

50. Weaver Lake 🌸 ☼ 🍁

Place	Total distance	Elevation	Level	Type
Start	0	7880	—	—
Weaver Lake	3¾	8707	M	O&B

Permit required: None

Topo(s): Muir Grove 7½'; USDA/USFS Monarch Wilderness & Jennie Lakes Wilderness

Where to stay:
   Mountain: Montecito-Sequoia Lodge, Grant Grove Cabins, John Muir Lodge
   Of Interest: Wuksachi Lodge, Stony Creek Lodge
   Other: Town of Three Rivers

Highlights: Few wilderness lakes are readily accessible from the Generals Highway, but charming Weaver Lake, tucked under Shell Mountain, more than makes up in its quality for that lack of quantity. It's a shorter hike than you may think from looking at the topo: a new, unmapped but official trail that begins a little north of Fox Meadow saves you a lot of hiking as compared to starting at the mapped Big Meadows Trailhead.

How to get to the trailhead: This trailhead isn't on the topo; you'll need a high-clearance vehicle to get to it. From the junction of State Route 180 and the turnoff to Grant Grove visitor center—the reference point for hikes in the Grant Grove area of Kings Canyon National Park and adjacent Sequoia National Forest—drive 1.5 miles south to The Wye (where State Route 180 meets the Generals Highway). Go south on the Generals Highway 6.8 more miles to the turnoff east onto Big Meadows Road, 8.3 miles from Grant Grove Visitor Center. Follow this beautiful road generally east past the marked Big Meadows Trailhead and past primitive Big Meadows Campground on the south side of the road. Beyond here, the road becomes quite narrow and crosses a bridge over Big Meadows Creek. Take the first right turn after the bridge, onto a dirt road that quickly climbs away from Big Meadows Road. Following this dirt road, you find two junctions; go left at the first junction, right at the next. These junctions are so close together that they may look like one big three-way junction. Your goal is on the topo even if the trailhead isn't: the roadend at about 7880 feet, just east of Fox Creek and north of Fox Meadow. There's a wide turnaround at the roadend; park here, 1.4 miles from Big Meadows Road and 15.2 miles from Grant Grove Visitor Center. The informally marked trailhead is at the south end of the turnaround.

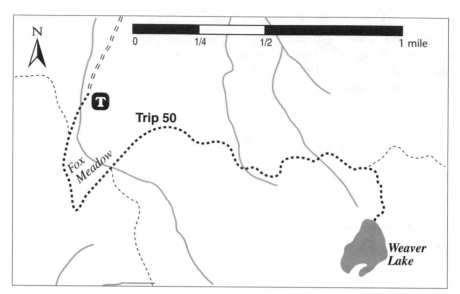

At the trailhead: Non-hikers will prefer to be at their lodgings or to explore Grant Grove Village.

On the trail: The trail heads generally south, almost immediately veering right to ford the red-fir-lined creek that drains Fox Meadow at a wonderfully flowery spot. Curving south again, the trail makes a gradual-to-moderate ascent roughly paralleling the creek and meeting the main trail coming up from the Big Meadows Trailhead a little shy of ¼ mile: left (south-southeast) to Jennie Lakes Wilderness, right (north) back to Big Meadows Trailhead. Note this obscure junction for your return, as it could be easy to miss. Turn left on the sandy-dusty main trail, ascending through dense forest past Fox Meadow. A moderate ascent brings you to a saddle, where the trail curves northeast without having crossed over the saddle. As you ascend moderately, breaks in the forest offer glimpses of Fox Meadow far below.

You reach a junction just before crossing the creek that feeds Fox Meadow: ahead (left, northeast) to Weaver Lake, right (southeast) to Jennie Lake. Go left to Weaver Lake, fording the creek and climbing rather steeply onto a ridge where, at ¾ mile, you enter Jennie Lakes Wilderness. The open forest here permits views west and north as you curve generally east along the ridge through patchy, then moderate, forest. A little beyond 1 mile you wind across a lovely meadow with a tiny stream as you continue your generally eastward way, climbing gradually to moderately. At 1½ miles you cross a seasonal stream, and just past 1⅔ miles you reach another junction: left (northeast) to Rowell Meadow, right (east, then south) to Weaver Lake. Go right here, ascending gradually to beautiful, sparkling **Weaver Lake at a little over 1¾ miles and 8707 feet**. The lakeshore is alternately meadow and rocky outcrops; the setting under slabby, gray Shell Mountain is delightful. You'll find plenty of picnic spots here on the rocks amid the red heather, rosy spiraea, and shooting stars.

It's not easy to leave this lovely spot, but retrace your steps when you must.

51. Big Baldy ☼ 🍁

Place	Total distance	Elevation	Level	Type
Start	0	7560	–	–
Big Baldy's summit	4	8209	M	O&B

Permit required: None

Topo(s): General Grant Grove 7½'

Where to stay:
   Mountain: Montecito-Sequoia Lodge, Grant Grove Cabins, John Muir Lodge
   Of Interest: Wuksachi Lodge, Stony Creek Lodge
   Other: Town of Three Rivers

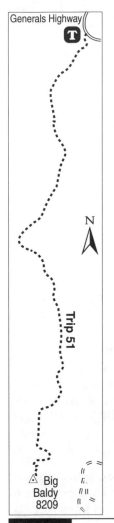

Highlights: A beautifully woodsy hike leads to fine views from the top of Big Baldy peak. Of the three superb view hikes off the Generals Highway, Big Baldy has the best views westward.

How to get to the trailhead: From the junction of State Route 180 and the turnoff to Grant Grove visitor center, drive to The Wye and pick up the Generals Highway southbound to a small turnout near the apex of a near-hairpin curve, on the south side of the road and marked for Big Baldy. Park here, 8.2 miles from Grant Grove. The trailhead is right next to the turnout.

At the trailhead: See Trip 49.

On the trail: The trail heads generally south and southwest on a duff surface, through moderate fir-forest cover. Ignore a use trail that shortly darts off to the left, where you'll see red diamonds on the trees—wintertime snowmobile-route markers. In ⅒ mile you step into Kings Canyon National Park at a marked boundary and begin a moderate-to-steep climb on the northwest side of a forested ridge. Views to the west and northwest are excellent where breaks in the foliage permit, and the flower display is amazing for an area as well-forested as this one is. As you cross an open, rocky area, pause to note that downhill to your right is Redwood Canyon and beyond it Redwood Mountain, Trip 53, home of perhaps the world's largest giant sequoia grove. The tops of most of the pine and fir trees you can see have a marked taper; the more-rounded crowns of the giant sequoias stand out in that crowd, rather like giant broccoli tops amidst asparagus spears.

   The grade eases and the trail settles down for a rolling ridgetop traverse, often but not always along the ridgeline. Soon you're back in moderate-to-dense forest broken by flowery patches. At the next forest opening, the rocky summit of

Big Baldy is plainly visible ahead to the south, thanks to a slight eastward curve in the ridgeline. The next forested stretch is followed by a rocky, airy traverse above Redwood Canyon. Now it's time for the final climb on a winding, rocky, moderately-graded trail. At **Big Baldy's summit at 2 miles and 8209 feet**, views are superb in every direction, although nearby ridges cut off *long* views to the east and south. You can see Shell Mountain (Trip 50) to the east and the peaks of the Monarch Divide to the northeast, along with Buck Rock, which really has a hawk-nosed profile from here. To the west, beyond Redwood Canyon, the wrinkled, pale, heat-seared foothills bear dark patches of trees as well as what seem to be black scars of brushfires—mute testimony to the fiery, dry Central Valley summers and to human presence. The contorted hills seem reminders of immense tectonic forces, caught as these foothills are between the upthrusting Sierran granite and the crushing, grinding collision of the Pacific and North American plates—a collision that constantly shudders through California, shattering and reshaping it.

Retrace your steps to your car.

52. Buena Vista Peak 🌿 ☼ 🍁

Place	Total distance	Elevation	Level	Type
Start	0	7360	—	—
Buena Vista Peak's summit	1⅔	7605	E	O&B

Permit required: None

Topo(s): General Grant Grove 7½'

Where to stay:
　　Mountain: Montecito-Sequoia Lodge, Grant Grove Cabins, John Muir Lodge
　　Of Interest: Wuksachi Lodge, Stony Creek Lodge
　　Other: Town of Three Rivers

Highlights: Of the three view hikes off the Generals Highway, the pretty stroll to Buena Vista Peak is the easiest—though it's by no means trivial—and offers surprisingly good views for such a short walk.

How to get to the trailhead: From the unction of State Route 180 and the turnoff to Grant Grove visitor center, drive back to The Wye and take the Generals Highway southwest, past the wonderful Kings Canyon Overlook on the north side (be sure to stop here and take in the view) and just around the next curve in the road to a wide, dusty turnout on the west side of the highway. Park here, 4.7 miles, by the trailhead.

At the trailhead: See Trip 49.

On the trail: You head west-northwest away from the parking area, at first through open forest where granite slabs and boulders line the trail. The climb is moderate to steep on a dusty trail that shortly curves south and levels out amid immense, glacier-deposited boulders—"erratics"—then toddles gradually along the east side of a

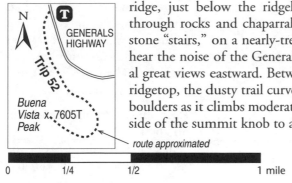

N

GENERALS
HIGHWAY

Trip 52

Buena
Vista x 7605T
Peak

route approximated

0   1/4   1/2   1 mile

ridge, just below the ridgeline. The trail presently winds through rocks and chaparral, then over slabs and up crude stone "stairs," on a nearly-treeless slope from which you can hear the noise of the Generals Highway and enjoy occasional great views eastward. Between ⅔ and ¾ miles, nearing the ridgetop, the dusty trail curves west, then northwest through boulders as it climbs moderately to steeply, traversing the east side of the summit knob to a tiny saddle.

From here, you make a very short ascent on some trailless slabs toward two stunted Jeffrey pines on the still-higher knob that is **Buena Vista Peak's open summit at a little over ¾ mile and 7605 feet**. This is indeed *una buena vista*! To the southeast is Big Baldy (Trip 51); to the southwest, Redwood Mountain and Redwood Canyon (Trip 53); to the north, the Monarch Divide; to the northeast, Buck Rock; to the east-southeast, the Silliman Crest. From this summit more than from the other view trips off the Generals Highway (Trips 48 and 51) you can appreciate how much of this country is glacially-polished granite domes—less spectacular than Yosemite's but still remarkable. Plan to spend some time here, walking around the broad summit and enjoying the different views.

At last you must retrace your steps to your car.

53. Redwood Mountain 🌸 ☼ 🍁

Place	Total distance	Elevation	Level	Type
Start	0	6220	—	
Redwood Mountain high point	4	6960	M	O&B
Entire loop	6	5520	S U	Loop

Permit required: None

Topo(s): General Grant Grove 7½'

Where to stay:
Mountain: Montecito-Sequoia Lodge, Grant Grove Cabins, John Muir Lodge
Of Interest: Wuksachi Lodge, Stony Creek Lodge
Other: Town of Three Rivers

Highlights: The grove of giant sequoias that covers Redwood Mountain and fills Redwood Canyon is probably the largest in the world. Oddly, and fortunately, it's little-visited because it lies at the end of a rough dirt road, has no amenities, and is outside both parks' main visitor areas. Most casual visitors to the giant sequoias are down south in the other huge grove, easily-accessible Giant Forest in Sequoia National Park (see Trip 44). Come to Redwood Mountain Grove to enjoy its

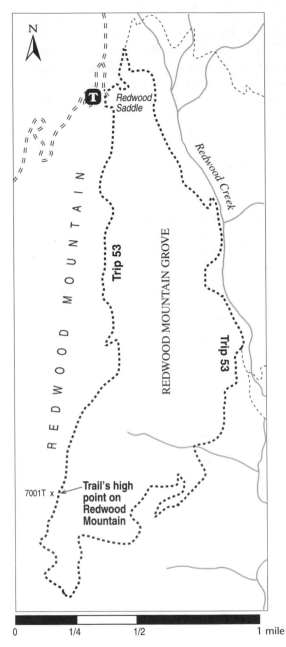

magnificent trees, hushed remoteness, and awe-inspiring beauty as you climb Redwood Mountain and return through Redwood Canyon via a "nursery" of baby sequoias.

How to get to the trail-head: You'll need a high-clearance vehicle for this drive. From the junction of State Route 180 and the turnoff to Grant Grove visitor center, drive back to The Wye and head 5 miles southwest on the Generals Highway to a well-marked turnoff northward for Hume Lake at Quail Flat. There's an ill-marked turnoff southeastward here, for Redwood Mountain Grove; that's your turnoff. Follow this rough, winding dirt road for 1.9 more miles to a **Y**-junction near a structure; go left 0.1 mile more to parking on Redwood Saddle at a well-marked trailhead in the dense shade of numerous giant sequoias, 7 miles.

At the trailhead: Non-hikers who've wished they could just relax in the beauty of the giant sequoias will appreciate this quiet area, so unlike the bustling sequoia groves to the south. There are no amenities, so bring lunch and water as well as a sand chair and current book, or binoculars and birding guides. Other non-hikers may prefer to be at their lodgings or to explore Grant Grove Village.

On the trail: As you face the trailhead information sign, you'll notice two trails leaving the parking area, the one on your left descending (it's your return trail) and the one on your right ascending. Take the ascending trail and head generally southwest on a wiggly track, climbing moderately to steeply through giant sequoias, sugar pines, red firs, and white firs. You are truly Gulliver in Brobdingnag! The silence is broken only by a few birds and by the *plop!* of falling cones. You ascend Redwood Mountain by stages: a steep haul up, then a longer, more-gradual stretch on which to enjoy these beautiful trees. On the drier sections you meet incense cedars, black oaks, and willows, too. At 1 mile you pass the Burnt Grove with its many standing but burnt trees. Beyond, you zigzag up to an opening from which you have views eastward and where the forest is briefly dominated by live oaks and ponderosas, with a fragrant understory of kit-kit-dizze. Below, in Redwood Canyon, you can see dozens—maybe hundreds—of giant-sequoia crowns. You reach the trail's **high point on Redwood Mountain at almost 2 miles and 6960 feet**, just below the knob that is its actual summit. Take in the view of Redwood Canyon here before continuing (or before retracing your steps, if you're doing the shorter, optional out-and-back).

Those continuing to Redwood Canyon begin a moderate descent that switches over to the west side of the long ridge that is Redwood Mountain, through moist woods full of giant trees. The trail suddenly veers back to the drier east slope, bringing an abrupt change in vegetation: bye-bye, giant sequoias—for now; hello, incense cedars, black and live oaks, and kit-kit-dizze and other chaparral species. You begin a long descent down Redwood Mountain's east slope, where the forest remains dry and the giant sequoias absent until, around 3½ miles, you cross a creeklet and near 3⅔ miles spot a couple of giant sequoias just downslope of the trail. In a few more steps you reach a stand of very young sequoias, most less than 5 feet high, some barely 1 foot high—*bonsai*-sized by giant sequoia standards. They are the beneficiaries of the Park Service's new policy of conducting controlled burns, which clear the forest floor for seedlings, produce the mineral soil that sequoia seedlings require, and allow hen's-egg-sized and -shaped sequoia cones to open so their oatmeal-flake-sized seeds can disperse. At this stage, giant sequoias have the slender, tapering shape more typical of conifers rather than the blunt-crowned shape of mature giant sequoias—the product of hundreds, even thousands, of years of growth.

At 4 miles and nearly 5520 feet you are definitely down in Redwood Canyon, and you reach a junction: right (southeast) to the Hart Tree, left (northwest) to the parking lot. Go left after admiring a very handsome group of giant sequoias at the junction. The canyon floor is lush with low-altitude growth: dogwood, rose, ginger, raspberry, blackberry, strawberry, selfheal. You pass young incense cedars and firs as you begin a gradual-to-moderate climb up Redwood Canyon paralleling Redwood Creek. Nearing 4⅔ miles you leave the creek behind and switchback once up Redwood Canyon's west slope. You continue uphill, presently walking through the shattered trunk of a huge, fallen sequoia. The state of this trunk demonstrates one reason the timber industry hasn't stripped the mountains of their giant sequoias: giant sequoia wood is weak and brittle, making it commercially unprofitable. You soon climb up and around another fallen monster, reaching a junction guarded by a particularly huge sequoia at 5½ miles: right (north) to the Hart Tree, left (south) to the parking lot at Redwood Saddle.

You go left, switchbacking up to the parking lot, passing many fine, mature giant sequoias, and closing your unforgettable loop at 6 miles. There are more trails to see here, like the loop that includes the Hart Tree and that is described in John Krist's excellent *50 Best Hikes in Yosemite and Sequoia/Kings Canyon*. And south of both loops, a trail extends miles farther down Redwood Canyon. But that's for another day. Now it's time to head for a hot meal at your lodgings—you've earned dessert!

54. Park Ridge Loop 🐾 ☼ 🍁

Place	Total distance	Elevation	Level	Type
Start	0	7420	—	—
Panoramic Point *only*	⅓	7520	E	O&B
Entire loop	4¼+	7761	M	Loop

Type: Loop with optional, shorter out-and-back

Topo(s): General Grant Grove, Hume 7½'; Sequoia Natural History Association "Grant Grove"

Where to stay:
   Mountain: Montecito-Sequoia Lodge, Grant Grove Cabins, John Muir Lodge
   Of Interest: Wuksachi Lodge, Stony Creek Lodge
   Other: Town of Three Rivers

Highlights: The Park Ridge Loop is an outstanding trail for its views and is my favorite Grant Grove hike. The entire loop is really a double loop—sort of a lumpy figure-8.

How to get to the trailhead: From the junction of State Route 180 and the turnoff to Grant Grove visitor center, continue east on the road that separates the visitor center from Grant Grove Village's restaurant, lodge check-in, and gift shop, away from 180. You curve left past the first set of Grant Grove Cabins, then bear right at a marked **Y**-junction onto Panoramic Point Road. Follow this narrow road, paved until near its end, passing lovely Summit Meadow and, on the right, a gated-off dirt road that will be part of your trail, as you bump into a parking area in a fir grove. Park here, 2.4 miles. Toilet, picnic tables.

At the trailhead: Non-hikers should seriously consider the short out-and-back to Panoramic Point, a must-see viewpoint; they may also enjoy a picnic at the tables near the parking lot. Otherwise, non-hikers will probably prefer to be at their lodgings or at Grant Grove visitor center.

On the trail: The marked trailhead is on the east side of the parking area, from which you switchback up a moderate grade on a paved trail to a spectacular viewpoint with benches and interpretive signs. This is **Panoramic Point at ⅙ mile and 7520 feet**, a worthwhile destination in itself. The breathtaking view eastward

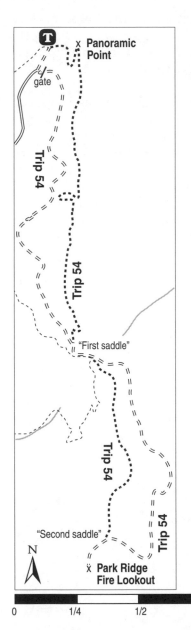

x **Panoramic Point**

gate

Trip 54

Trip 54

"First saddle"

Trip 54

"Second saddle"

Trip 54

N

x̌ **Park Ridge Fire Lookout**

0   1/4   1/2   1 mile

sweeps from Mt. McGee on the north to Eagle Scout Peak in the south, and the interpretive signs help you identify many features in between as well as nearer. You'll want to linger here.

If you're continuing on the loop, as opposed to returning to the parking lot, pick up a gradually-graded dirt path where the paved trail ends. Numerous use trails dart left to airy viewpoints, and you may want to explore a few of them. But for the most part, you stick to the main trail, which stays high on the ridge and slightly back from its edge, undulating over low knobs. Having savored eastward views, you enter moderate, viewless forest cover before crossing the ridgeline to enjoy some views west at an open spot. But soon you're back in the forest, gradually to moderately ascending a dusty duff trail through a variety of flowering shrubs and plants.

A little beyond 1 mile you reach the hike's high point—not much to see here, thanks to the forest. After a moderate descent, you meet the park's fire road at a poorly-marked junction on a long saddle at a little less than 1½ miles. Let's call this "the first saddle." From the first saddle, you can cut the loop short by turning right (northwest) on the fire road and returning to Panoramic Point Road (see the last leg of this hike, below, at "Continue on the road, ..."). To continue, turn left (south-southeast) on the fire road. The next trail junction is very hard to spot from the first saddle, so stay on the fire road for now and plan to pick up the trail again on your return from Park Ridge Fire Lookout, which is your next destination.

The fire road, lined with handsome firs, climbs gradually as you pass an area logged many, many years ago, then dips to pass around the head of a pretty meadow. You resume your gradual ascent and at a little over 2 miles approach a small saddle where the road veers southwest and a footpath comes in sharply from the right (north-northeast). Let's call this "the second saddle." Note the footpath; it's part of your return route and is unmarked except for red metal tags pounded into the occasional tree trunk. Staying on the road for now, you head southwest toward the building, antennas, and power and telephone lines you can see ahead; they're at the lookout. You reach **Park Ridge Fire Lookout at 2¼ miles and 7540 feet**, where there are nice views westward. There are no public facilities here except for a rickety picnic table. The lookout tower is someone's home, so be sure to ask permission before you ascend the tower for even better views, though the chances are you'll be invited up even before you ask.

Retrace your steps to the second saddle, now with 2⅓ miles on your boots, and go left (north-northeast) on the footpath you noted earlier. You ascend steeply through sparse forest to a little summit where the sometimes-indistinct trail continues on the west side of the ridge (left as you face away from the lookout tower). You undulate moderately on this steep west slope, fairly near and occasionally crossing over the ridgeline. At an area of slabs, where the trail is very faint, you continue ahead a short distance to find the trail again. You descend to the first saddle at just over 3 miles and reach a junction from which the fire road is visible about 25 feet away to the right. The junction's own trail markers are so low that they're all but invisible from the fire road. To the left (west), a spur leads to a junction with the Manzanita and Azalea trails. With the fire road in sight, you turn right to meet the road and then turn left (northwest) onto the road. You shortly pass the poorly-marked trail junction where you reached the first saddle coming from Panoramic Point.

Continue on the road, gradually ascending through a pleasant but viewless forest. At 3½ miles, an open stretch offers fine views westward over Grant Grove. Eventually you re-enter forest and at a little over 3⅔ miles curve along a delightfully flowery meadow. You presently begin a gradual descent, passing above Summit Meadow, and reach a gate at just over 4 miles. Beyond the gate you meet Panoramic Point Road, on which you drove up. Turn right (northeast) onto the road for a brief uphill stretch to close the loop at the parking lot, just over 4¼ miles.

55. Sheep Creek Cascades 🌸 ☼ 🍁

Place	Total distance	Elevation	Level	Type
Start	0	4680	—	—
Bridge over cascades	2+	5200	M	O&B

Permit required: None

Topo(s): Cedar Grove 7½'; Sequoia Natural History Association "Cedar Grove"

Where to stay:
   Mountain: Grant Grove Cabins, John Muir Lodge*
   Of Interest: Cedar Grove Lodge, Kings Canyon Lodge
   Other: None

---

* It's 29 long, winding miles from Grant Grove Village to Cedar Grove Village, so while Grant Grove Cabins and Lodge are the only eligible *mountain* lodgings, they are not the most desirable in terms of proximity. Kings Canyon Lodge and Cedar Grove Village are much nearer.

Highlights: Views northward from the higher part of this trip are followed by a visit to the beautiful little cascades on Sheep Creek. Get an early start; the ascent can be quite hot.

How to get to the trailhead: Leave your car parked at Cedar Grove Lodge—the reference point for Cedar Grove drives—and walk to the start of this trip. I've factored that small distance into this trip. Toilets, water, store, coffee shop at Cedar Grove Village.

At the trailhead: Non-hikers will enjoy relaxing along the river—the South Fork Kings River—that runs right by Cedar Grove Village; they may also enjoy exploring the village.

On the trail: From Cedar Grove Lodge, head generally south toward State Route 180, crossing the bridge over the Kings River. Just about 100 yards past the bridge, you'll notice a rock-bordered path that veers left from the left side of the road, just where there's a pedestrian crossing from Sentinel Campground; this is the point marked on the book's map with the trailhead symbol. This path leads quickly to the highway, just opposite the Don Cecil Trailhead; carefully cross the highway to the official, signed trailhead. The entire walk from Cedar Grove Lodge to this point is barely ⅓ mile. The trail begins with a generally southeast-trending segment under the shade of live oaks, incense cedars, sugar pines, white firs, ponderosa pines, and black oaks; Cedar Grove's black oaks lend a wonderful splash of color in the fall. Now curving southwest, you pass a nice view of the overlook that you get to on the Hotel Creek Trail (Trip 57). At ½ mile you step across a road and pick up the trail on the other side.

Now you begin a moderate-to-steep climb along Kings Canyon's south wall. A little before 1 mile you enjoy great views of the nearby north wall of Kings Canyon, including North Mountain, and above and beyond them of the beautiful Monarch Divide. At 1 mile you reach the hike's high point, where the forest cover opens to treat you to another, similar northward view. Descending a little into a moist, shady nook, you reach a pretty **bridge over Sheep Creek at just over 1 mile and just under 5200 feet,** where, just upstream, idyllic little cascades slip over granite slabs under the cool, green shade of alders. You may be tempted to splash in the water, but a sign warns NO SWIMMING/DOMESTIC WATER SUPPLY (Sheep Creek supplies Cedar Grove's water). Lovers of shady retreats will want to linger here for their snack, while those who fancy views will want to go back to that last great viewpoint.

Retrace your steps when you must.

56. Cedar Grove Overlook 🌿 ☼ 🍁

Place	Total distance	Elevation	Level	Type
Start	0	4680	—	—
Overlook *only*	5⅔	6086	S	O&B
Entire loop	7	6220	S	Loop

Permit required: None

Topo(s): Cedar Grove 7½'; Sequoia Natural History Association, "Cedar Grove"

Where to stay:
Mountain: Grant Grove Cabins, John Muir Lodge*
Of Interest: Cedar Grove Lodge, Kings Canyon Lodge
Other: None

Highlights: The spectacular views up, down, and over Kings Canyon from Cedar Grove Overlook are the rewards for this hike, and there are other splendid viewpoints along the way. Get an early start: the ascent above Hotel Creek is mostly exposed and can be very hot.

How to get to the trailhead: Leave your car parked at Cedar Grove Lodge and walk to this trailhead. I've factored that small distance—⅕ mile—into this trip.

At the trailhead: See Trip 55.

On the trail: From Cedar Grove Lodge, walk to the access road that brought you into the lodge's parking lot and turn right (north), away from State Route 180. A sign here says ←RANGER STATION/ ←CAMPGROUND, pointing left; you go the other way. At ⅙ mile you reach a junction with the pack-station road, where you turn right (east) toward the pack station and almost immediately find the trailhead on your left (north) at ⅕ mile. There are two trails here: the one on your left, coming in from the west, is a trail you can eventually close this loop on (but it's not the best choice); the other on your right, heading east, is the start of the Hotel Creek Trail.

After pausing to read the trailhead information sign, you take the righthand trail and head uphill on the hot, sandy Hotel Creek Trail. Soon you begin a series of switchbacks that carry you upward, high above Hotel Creek's west bank. From early switchbacks you have views of the Sheep Creek drainage to the south, across Kings Canyon (Trip 55). As you climb higher, you gain inspiring views of the high peaks to the east. Most of the signs of civilization, except for the road noise, soon disappear, hidden by the valley floor's substantial forest. At nearly 2½ miles on the nose of a ponderosa-clad ridge, you reach a junction with a spur trail to Cedar Grove Overlook: left (west) to the overlook, right (north) to Lewis Creek. There are glimpses of the Monarch Divide to the north and northwest from here. Go left to the overlook, dipping across a saddle before ascending a little to spectacular **Cedar**

---

* It's 29 long, winding miles from Grant Grove Village to Cedar Grove Village, so while Grant Grove Cabins and Lodge are the only eligible *mountain* lodgings, they are not the most desirable in terms of proximity. Kings Canyon Lodge and Cedar Grove Village are much nearer.

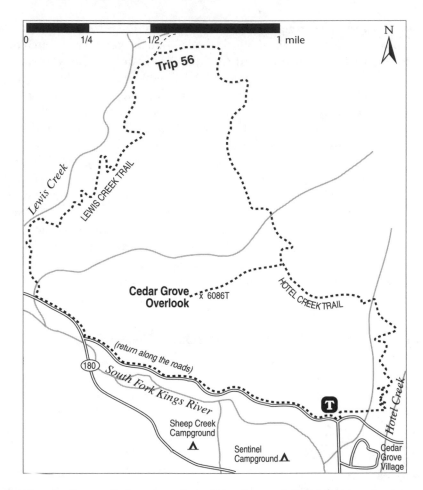

Grove Overlook at a little more than 2¾ miles and 6086 feet: to the west, deep in Kings Canyon, the South Fork Kings River rolls toward its confluence with the Middle Fork; below, Cedar Grove Village; across, Lookout Peak; to the east, Buck Peak and Glacier Monument; to the north, Lewis Creek's canyon and the Monarch Divide; Stag Dome to the northwest; Comb Spur to the northeast.

Retrace your steps to the Hotel Creek Trail junction, now with a little less than 3¼ miles on your boots. At the junction, those taking the out-and-back trip turn right and return to Cedar Grove Village, while those continuing on the loop turn hard left toward Lewis Creek. Continuing on the loop, you begin a north-northwest descent through a scorched, open forest. You cross an unnamed creek with a pleasant flower garden before angling gradually northwest up the next ridge. As you stroll over this ridge, which is the hike's high point, you have fine views of the Monarch Divide. Beyond, the dusty trail descends, curving westward almost toward Stag Dome, on a fire-scarred slope. You meet the Lewis Creek Trail at almost 4½ miles: left (southwest) to return to Cedar Grove Village, right (northeast) toward Frypan Meadow.

Turn left here and begin zigzagging down a series of longish, moderate-to-gradual switchbacks on a dusty trail with little shade, though there's a nice patch of forest—a good snack stop—just beyond the junction. Shortly before you reach the road back to Cedar Grove Village, you reach a junction by a ditch: left (east) to close the loop on a use trail not shown on the book's map, right (ahead, south) to the Lewis Creek Trailhead on State Route 180. I recommend you go right to the Lewis Creek Trailhead and close the loop by walking on the shoulders of the roads; the exposed, hot, dusty, loose, undulating use trail is used primarily to move stock between the Hotel Creek and Lewis Creek trailheads. Taking that advice, you reach the Lewis Creek Trailhead in a few more steps and turn left (east) along the shoulder of the highway, facing traffic. The road soon forks: right to stay on State Route 180's shoulder, left to take a much-more-pleasant secondary road back to Cedar Grove Village and the pack station. Follow the left fork's shoulder under incense cedars, closing your loop at the spur road that leads right to Cedar Grove Lodge at almost 6¾ miles. From here, turn right and retrace your steps to the lodge's parking lot for a total of almost 7 adventurous miles.

57. Falls and Zumwalt Meadows 🌿 ☼ 🍁

Place	Total distance	Elevation	Level	Type
Start	0	4860	—	—
Roaring River Falls *only*	½	5000	E	O&B
Entire semiloop	4+	5010	M	Semi

Permit required: None

Topo(s): The Sphinx 7½'; Sequoia Natural History Association "Cedar Grove"

Where to stay:
   Mountain: Grant Grove Cabins, John Muir Lodge*
   Of Interest: Cedar Grove Lodge, Kings Canyon Lodge
   Other: None

Highlights: Deep in Kings Canyon, Roaring River crashes down through a slot in the steep south wall, giving visitors a chance to see its last few cascades—Roaring River Falls—before it joins the South Fork Kings River. Up-canyon, you'll find idyllic Zumwalt Meadows, with the placid river meandering by.

How to get to the trailhead: From Cedar Grove Village, return 0.2 mile to State Route 180 and turn left (east) toward Roads End (Cedar Grove Roadend). Continue to marked parking for Roaring River Falls at 3 miles. Park here.

---

* It's 29 long, winding miles from Grant Grove Village to Cedar Grove Village, so while Grant Grove Cabins and Lodge are the only eligible *mountain* lodgings, they are not the most desirable in terms of proximity. Kings Canyon Lodge and Cedar Grove Village are much nearer.

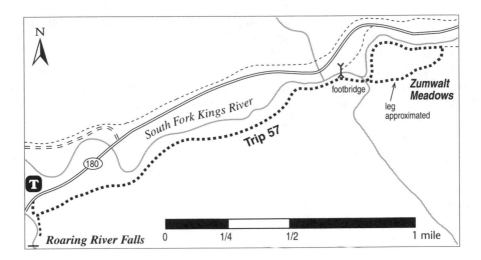

At the trailhead: Even non-hikers will want to make the easy jaunt to Roaring River Falls. Otherwise, there is little for them here; they'll prefer being back at Cedar Grove Village.

On the trail: Head south on a paved trail, bypassing for now a trail that takes off left for Zumwalt Meadows, and ascend to a large viewing area for **Roaring River Falls at less than ¼ mile and 5000 feet**. Most of the upper cascades are hidden by the deep, convoluted slot through which Roaring River drops, but the lowest cascades make a fine display as they thunder through huge boulders. The cascades are short on height, but in early season they make up for that in volume: their roar is deafening, and you may be drenched by their chilly spray.

Reluctantly turning away from the spectacle, you retrace your steps to the Zumwalt Meadows junction you passed earlier, now at about ⅓ mile. Turn right (east) here and follow it under incense cedar and live oak as it swings disconcertingly near the highway, then mercifully away, climbing over a moraine. The floor of Kings Canyon is full of nested moraines, left by successively smaller glaciers. Beyond the moraine, you briefly meet the river, then skirt a half-meadowed, half-forested area damp enough to support an understory of bracken and horsetail. The river is always within hearing if not within sight as you wend your way through waist-high bracken and under black oaks and pines. At 1⅓ miles you puff your way over the next moraine and meet the Zumwalt Meadows trail at a bridge at almost 1⅔ miles. At this junction, a trail goes left over the bridge to Zumwalt Meadows' own parking lot, while the trail to the meadows goes ahead (right); you can make a short semiloop around Zumwalt Meadows from that parking lot. But you're more adventurous, so, without crossing the bridge, you continue ahead, over an unnamed creek, to meet the loop trail around **Zumwalt Meadows at 1⅔ miles and 4880 feet**. The right branch keeps to the forest edge, while the left heads for the beautiful meadow, which lies entirely on the south side of the river. Arbitrarily, you take the right branch for now, passing huge glacial erratics and climbing over a rockfall opposite imposing North Dome. Willows and box elders block most of the meadow view from here but add fall color.

At a little over 2 miles you reach a junction: left (north) to continue around Zumwalt Meadows, right (east) to Road's End (Cedar Grove Roadend). Turn left here to curve around Zumwalt Meadows' north end and head generally west, now in forest, now at the meadow's edge, where the placid South Fork Kings River curls picturesquely between its sandy banks. Birders will want to pull out their guides and binoculars and spend some time here. Too soon, you close the loop part of this trip and head back for Roaring River Falls. At the junction by the footbridge, now at a little over 2½ miles, you again avoid crossing the bridge and instead continue ahead (west), retracing your steps to Roaring River Falls's parking lot, just over 4 miles.

58. Mist Falls 🌸

Place	Total distance	Elevation	Level	Type
Start	0	5040	—	—
Mist Falls	7⅓	5800	S	O&B

Permit required: None

Topo(s): The Sphinx 7½'; Sequoia Natural History Association "Cedar Grove"

Where to stay:
   Mountain: Grant Grove Cabins, John Muir Lodge*
   Of Interest: Cedar Grove Lodge, Kings Canyon Lodge
   Other: None

Highlights: Lovely Mist Falls is a favorite destination for visitors to Kings Canyon. Its volume diminishes considerably over the season, but it remains a charming spot to visit. On the way, you enjoy beautiful views of the South Fork Kings River, and there are spectacular over-the-shoulder views toward the curious formation called The Sphinx on Kings Canyon's south wall.

How to get to the trailhead: From Cedar Grove Village, return 0.2 mile to State Route 180. Turn left (east) toward Road's End (Cedar Grove Roadend), 5.8 miles. Park at the large roadend loop; the trailhead is near the north end of the loop. Toilets, water, summer ranger station.

At the trailhead: Non-hikers will prefer to be back at Cedar Grove Village, enjoying its riverside location.

On the trail: Three trails leave from this trailhead: on the far left, a footpath heads west down the valley floor; on the left, the steep Copper Creek Trail claws its way

---

* It's 29 long, winding miles from Grant Grove Village to Cedar Grove Village, so while Grant Grove Cabins and Lodge are the only eligible *mountain* lodgings, they are not the most desirable in terms of proximity. Kings Canyon Lodge and Cedar Grove Village are much nearer.

up Kings Canyon's north wall; and on the right your trail, the Paradise Valley Trail, heads generally east. Take the Paradise Valley Trail, passing the information sign and the ranger station, enjoying the woodsy fragrance of the forest. You cross two streams as you pass the site of long-gone Kanawyers (kah-NOY-ers) Camp. The trail is sandy, sometimes shady and sometimes exposed and hot. You twine down into a damp area thick with horsetails and bracken ferns, curving north along the west side of the South Fork Kings River, here flowing north to south away from Paradise Valley. At 1½ miles you reach a junction: left (northeast) to Mist Falls and Paradise Valley, right (southeast) over a handsome footbridge to Bubbs Creek and Junction Meadow. You're going left, but before you do, you may want to walk out onto that bridge to enjoy the river scene from it.

Back on the Paradise Valley Trail, you ascend a rocky ramp and then bob along, paralleling the river, sometimes climbing over or through rockfalls. Near 2⅔ miles, you reach a pleasant area of lunch-worthy rocks overlooking some beautiful pools and cascades. Beyond, you ascend granite slabs still bearing patches of polish, the work of long-gone glaciers. Check the opposite canyon wall occasionally for the seasonally showy cascades of Glacier Creek. Pause often to look back over your shoulder at the strange "horns" of The Sphinx, high on the opposite side of Kings Canyon. At 3½ miles you reach a marked overlook of beautiful Mist Falls, where, in season, the spray rising into the narrow, shady canyon explains the falls' name. Use trails lead off to the base of the falls here, and many people brave the slippery scramble to get closer to the crashing water. Rocks near the base make fine picnic spots if they're far enough from the falls that you won't get soaked. Or you can head farther up the Paradise Valley Trail until you're opposite the **top of Mist Falls at 3⅔ miles and 5800 feet**, for a different view.

Retrace your steps to your car, enjoying more of those wonderful views of The Sphinx on your way.

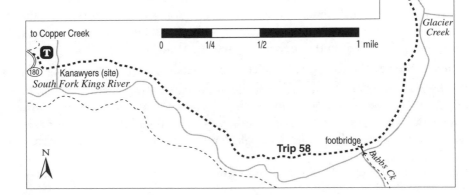

59. Dinkey Lakes ☼ ❦

Place	Total distance	Elevation	Level	Type
Start	0	8620	—	—
First Dinkey Lake *only*	5+	9239	M	O&B
Mystery Lake *only*	3	8963	M	O&B
Entire semiloop	6½+	9380	S	Semi

Permit required: None

Topo(s): Dogtooth Peak 7½'*; USDA/USFS Dinkey Lakes Wilderness

Where to stay
  Mountain: None
  Of Interest: None
  Other: Town of Shaver Lake

Highlights: Dinkey Lakes Wilderness is spectacularly beautiful—lakes, meadows, peaks—but the drive to it is hair-raising. Nevertheless, you'll agree that the Dinkey Lakes are worth the trouble.

How to get to the trailhead: Look on this drive as an adventure. A sturdy, stable, high-clearance vehicle is essential; 4WD is desirable, even if only as a security blanket. This is a very long drive, taking just over an hour one way, and is extremely rough near the end. It would have disqualified a less-attractive hike. From the town of Shaver Lake, which straddles State Route 168 between Clovis and Huntington Lake, turn east off 168 and onto Dinkey Creek Road. Follow two-lane, paved Dinkey Creek Road 9.2 miles to a junction with paved Rock Creek Road. Turn left onto scenic, one-lane Rock Creek Road (Forest Road 9S09) and follow it 6 more miles as it gets progressively narrower and rougher, to a T-junction with Forest Road 9S10. Go right onto partly-paved Forest Road 9S10 and bounce along to the first major junction at 4.7 more miles, where you make a hard right onto unmarked Forest Road 9S62 to begin the last and worst 2.2 miles. You ascend potholes—sorry, you ascend the road—to a shoulder from which you make a heart-in-mouth descent that passes a couple of forks to the right. Go left, staying on the "main" road, at each fork; they lead to/from an OHV trailhead. Beyond them, you jounce fairly levelly through a sandy-floored forest to a large trailhead-parking area. Park here, 22.1 nerve-racking miles from Highway 168 and not far from the spot labeled on the topo as "Limestone Campsite."

At the trailhead: Non-hikers will prefer to explore the pretty town of Shaver Lake.

On the trail: Head northeast down a rocky slope, past a TRAIL sign and into a forest of spindly lodgepoles, where Dinkey Creek splashes past gray limestone cliffs on your right. Use trails may be confusing here; your route dips almost immediately down to the creek, fords it, and goes right (east-northeast) at a junction with a use

---

* The topo (1982) predates the creation of the wilderness (1984) and doesn't show the wilderness or the trailhead as such.

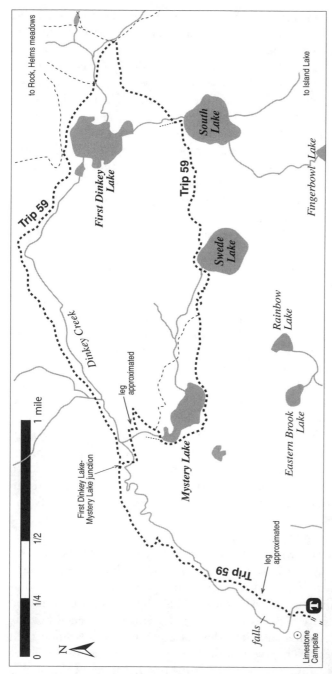

trail. Climb moderately away from the creek, cross an intermittent watercourse, and ascend moderately into dense, mature forest. The sandy trail's grade soon eases, and you enjoy an easy stroll, presently coming alongside Dinkey Creek. A little before ½ mile, you dip to cross the creek again and shortly enter Dinkey Lakes Wilderness. Now you traverse through snow-bent trees, past a meadow, and between steep slopes of light and dark granites. You wind moderately up a rocky slope, through glacier-polished slabs, before veering off to the northwest side of a widening valley to avoid the valley's soggy, meadowy floor. Through breaks in the dense forest you can see beautiful granite walls soaring on your left.

The pleasant, sandy trail rolls on and on through forest and meadow, where patches of dwarf bilberry in the understory make a brilliant show in fall. At a little over 1 mile you reach a junction that I'll call the First Dinkey Lake-Mystery Lake junction: left (east-northeast) to the First Dinkey Lake, right (southeast) to Mystery Lake ("Mastery Lake" on the topo). Those going only to pretty Mystery Lake on an out-and-back go right here, reversing the last leg of the loop part of this trip (see the paragraph below beginning

"You come alongside Mystery's outlet... ."). Those going to the First Dinkey Lake, perhaps the loveliest on this trip, either as an out-and-back only or as the first leg of the loop part of this trip, go left here.

Going left to the First Dinkey Lake, you soon meet Dinkey Creek again in a "garden" of erratics, ascending very gradually. At a little over 1⅔ miles you cross a tributary, beyond which the ascent becomes more noticeable. The beautiful valley widens as you go, and you presently curve right (east) into its boulder-strewn middle to cross an unmapped creeklet below the steep cliffs of Peak 9777. Continuing eastward, you climb gradually to moderately to a bench and follow the trail up a long meadow past a pond. You shortly reach an overlook of breathtaking **First Dinkey Lake at just over 2½ miles and 9239 feet**, splendidly set in a deep meadow and backed by the toothy ridge called Three Sisters. Numerous use trails lead to the pond and to the lake on your right, while other use trails lead to campsites on your left. A lakeside stop here is almost mandatory, so pick a use trail and picnic on the shore.

Back on the main trail, just past an obvious camping area, you reach a junction: right (southeast) toward this lake and Second Dinkey Lake, left (east) to other destinations. (The sign that marks this junction is on a tree some 35 yards farther on, on the left fork, and is hard to spot.) You go right to skirt the forested edge of First Dinkey Lake's meadow. At an unmarked junction near 3 miles, just before the lake's eastern inlet, you go right, stepping across the inlet and making a lazy curve across an open area. You reach another junction at just over 3 miles: leftmost (east) to Rock Meadow, ahead (middle, south) to Second Dinkey Lake, and right (west) to South Lake. Go right in moderate forest on rocky terrain, curving around First Dinkey Lake and then climbing away from it. The trail grows faint in the deep duff; ducks and blazes may help you keep to it. You step across a use trail paralleling a runoff channel, then cross the stream connecting First Dinkey and South lakes. At a **T**-junction just across the stream, the left branch is the main trail south to South Lake, while the right branch is a use trail. You turn left to reach **South Lake at just over 3½ miles and 9294 feet**. The lake, backed by tall cliffs and fringed by mountain hemlocks, is perfectly charming.

Leaving South Lake, you gradually ascend a moraine, passing immense erratics and topping out at 9380 feet at a little over 3¾ miles. As you descend the moraine moderately to steeply, lovely Swede Lake comes into view. Cliffs at its southeast end help to create a dramatic setting. You squish through a marsh along the outlet of **Swede Lake at a little over 4 miles and 9224** feet, then ford the outlet. From there, you soon begin a steep, switchbacking descent to the bench holding Mystery Lake. You level out in a small meadow at a junction at 4½ miles: right (northwest) and left (west). The right fork leads to grotty campsites above Mystery's north shore; the left fork spends more time beside Mystery Lake, so you go left on a nearly level trail that becomes muddy and rutted as you pass a small pond. Soon you see the lake ahead, and presently you trace the south shore of pretty **Mystery Lake at 4¾ miles and 8963 feet**. Near the west end of Mystery Lake, a use trail bears right to a knoll. You go left on the main trail, swinging north-

northwest through the flowery meadow west of the knoll, then skirting the west tip of the lake.

You come alongside Mystery's outlet and reach a junction at a little over 5 miles: left (north) on a use trail, right (northeast) to ford the outlet. (This junction is a little short of 1½ miles if you are hiking only the out-and-back to Mystery Lake.) Go right to cross the outlet and almost immediately reach another junction, where the right fork passes through filthy campsites near Mystery's north shore (a depressing sight) and the left branch goes north on a well-beaten track, curving north-northeast, then west, on a gradual descent. You cross Mystery Lake's outlet again, on big granite slabs, and find yourself once more down in the lovely valley below the lakes. You cross Dinkey Creek and curve north across the valley floor to the First Dinkey Lake-Mystery Lake junction at 4¾ miles. Turn left and retrace your steps to the trailhead, which you reach at a little over 6½ miles.

Swede Lake

60. Rancheria Falls 🌸

Place	Total distance	Elevation	Level	Type
Start	0	7560	–	–
Rancheria Falls viewpoint	1⅓	7530	E U	O&B

Permit required: None

Topo(s): Huntington Lake, Kaiser Peak 7½'*

Where to stay:
   Mountain: Lakeshore Resort, Huntington Lake Condo. Rentals, Tamarack Lodge
   Of Interest: None
   Other: None

*Neither the trail nor the falls is on the topos.

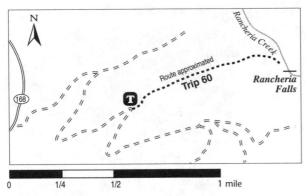

Highlights: An easy hike leads to a small canyon down whose headwall dash the seasonally high, showy cascades called Rancheria Falls.

How to get to the trailhead: The marked turnoff to Rancheria Falls is 0.5 mile south of the end of State Route 168, where the left fork heads west to Huntington Lake and the community of Lakeshore and the right fork, Kaiser Pass Road, heads northeast to Kaiser Pass At the Rancheria Falls turnoff, turn east on a road that almost immediately turns to dirt, and follow it to a junction at 0.5 more mile. Turn right to find the marked trailhead at a hairpin turn in 0.8 more mile, 1.8 miles from the end of State Route 168. Park along the shoulder as best you can.

At the trailhead: Non-hikers will prefer to be at the tiny community of Lakeshore, enjoying Huntington Lake and savoring a meal at the restaurant.

On the trail: The trail is narrow in places and traverses very steep terrain; parents should keep a tight rein on children. You immediately cross a tiny footbridge over a roadside runoff channel, then head northeast on a broad, dusty trail that almost certainly is a former logging road. There's a good flower display along this trail. Climbing moderately to steeply, you soon cross another footbridge and then curve east, high above Rancheria Creek. Big old stumps dot the steep hillside, evidence of former logging. By ⅓ mile the grade has eased considerably, and you can hear the noise of traffic on Kaiser Pass Road across the canyon of Rancheria Creek.

A little before ⅔ mile you abruptly begin a rocky, moderate-to-steep descent toward the noise of falling water, curving right (southeast) into a steep-walled, rocky little canyon where ahead you see the long, beautiful cascades of Rancheria Falls. The terrain is very steep here, so watch your step as the grade eases to gradual. The trail peters out at a **viewpoint for Rancheria Falls at a little over ⅔ mile and 7530 feet**, in clumps of creambush. The upper cascades leap over a succession of thin, rocky shelves, while the lower cascades crash through boulders, finally roaring away down the stony creekbed far below. The loose rock around you, which fills much of this handsome amphitheater, makes scrambling any closer to the falls a dicey proposition.

Retrace your steps.

61. Twin Lakes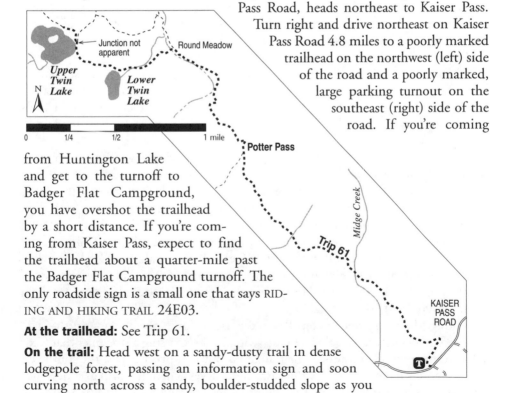

Place	Total distance	Elevation	Level	Type
Start	0	8300	—	—
Potter Pass	4	8980	M	O&B
Lower Twin Lake	5¾	8603*	S U	O&B
Upper Twin Lake	6¼	8601*	S U	O&B

Permit required: None

Topo(s): Mt. Givens, Kaiser Peak 7½'; USDA/USFS Kaiser Wilderness

Where to stay:
Mountain: Lakeshore Resort, Huntington Lake Condo. Rentals, Tamarack Lodge
Of Interest: None
Other: None

Highlights: An attractive, well-graded trail leads past flower-filled meadows to wonderful views at Potter Pass and to two pretty lakes in Kaiser Wilderness.

How to get to the trailhead: At the end of State Route 168, the left fork heads west to Huntington Lake and the community of Lakeshore, and the right fork, Kaiser Pass Road, heads northeast to Kaiser Pass. Turn right and drive northeast on Kaiser Pass Road 4.8 miles to a poorly marked trailhead on the northwest (left) side of the road and a poorly marked, large parking turnout on the southeast (right) side of the road. If you're coming from Huntington Lake and get to the turnoff to Badger Flat Campground, you have overshot the trailhead by a short distance. If you're coming from Kaiser Pass, expect to find the trailhead about a quarter-mile past the Badger Flat Campground turnoff. The only roadside sign is a small one that says RIDING AND HIKING TRAIL 24E03.

At the trailhead: See Trip 61.

On the trail: Head west on a sandy-dusty trail in dense lodgepole forest, passing an information sign and soon curving north across a sandy, boulder-studded slope as you

* You're not seeing things: Upper Twin Lake is officially a whisker lower than Lower Twin Lake.

Upper Twin Lake

climb moderately. Patches of forest and chaparral alternate as you switchback upward to top a small rise, beyond which a very gradual descent carries you around a little meadow and across a couple of streamlets that feed it. You resume a gradual to moderate ascent, passing a heap of huge boulders, and at ⅔ mile cross a footbridge over a trickling stream and its narrow, wildflower-filled hillside meadow. At ¾ mile you cross another streamlet and soon ford Midge Creek, which supports a fine, flowery meadow. The trail then climbs away from Midge Creek, and, nearing 1¼ mile, you cross a saddle and contour northwest through meadows and streams before breaking out into the open, where you have a view of rocky, unnamed peaks ahead to the west.

Near 1½ miles you begin climbing again, crossing a tributary of Potter Creek on a footbridge in a willow-choked meadow. In a few more steps, you'll find an opening in the forest that permits fine views of Huntington Lake to the southwest, as well as of ski-run-scarred Chinese Peak and of Highway 168. You make a last, hot, sandy haul up a moderate grade to a junction with a trail coming up from Huntington Lake from the left (south) just before you enter Kaiser Wilderness at **Potter Pass at nearly 2 miles and 8980 feet.** There's a sublime view northward over a small meadow below, toward nearby mountain ridges and a distant row of snowy peaks; views back over Huntington Lake to Chinese Peak (home to Sierra Summit Ski Area) are breathtaking.

Taking the trail over Potter Pass—the right fork, ahead and north—you descend moderately to steeply on sandy switchbacks, crossing a streamlet that feeds a blossoming hillside meadow. The trail levels out as it brushes past the southwest end of the small meadow below the pass, then curves generally north as it descends gradually to moderately into dense forest. After crossing an intermittent stream, you climb a little as you traverse a dry meadow from which you enjoy a good view of Kaiser Peak to the west. Soon you're back in forest, skirting a meadow and then making a short, steep descent to a junction: left (west-southwest) to Twin Lakes, right (northwest) to Sample Meadow. Go left to cross a stream and pass below a striking outcrop of white rock. An open traverse above Round Meadow offers more of those wonderful views of distant peaks, and stands of aspen in this area offer good fall color.

Beyond a wooded stretch, you find pleasant **Lower Twin Lake at a little over 2¾ miles and 8603 feet**, tucked below a peak of white rock and offering several picnic sites along its grassy edges. Leaving Lower Twin Lake, you make an easy ascent of a low saddle, passing a pond, and shortly spot lower Upper Twin Lake. You make a short, steep descent toward the lake to discover that the main trail skirts above the lake while use trails lead down to its edge. Pick a use trail and reach the east shore of **Upper Twin Lake at a little over 3 miles and 8601 feet**. Most of the lake is bound by low, rocky cliffs that, together with Kaiser Peak, which looms directly across the water, give this beautiful lake an especially picturesque setting. You won't be able to resist a long rest and a leisurely picnic here.

Retrace your steps to your car.

62. Dutch Lake ☼ ❦

Place	Total distance	Elevation	Level	Type
Start	0	7380	—	—
Dutch Lake	6¼	9100	S	O&B

Permit required: None

Topo(s): Florence Lake 7½'

Where to stay:
    Mountain: Mono Hot Springs Resort, Vermilion Valley Resort
    Of Interest: None
    Other: None

Highlights: An often-steep hike will have you giving it rave reviews when it deposits you at lovely Dutch Lake.

How to get to the trailhead: Don't even *think* about trying to daytrip from Huntington Lake to this trailhead or to those of Trips 63 and 64. It's not the miles but the road, the Kaiser Pass Road, which grows so narrow and tortuous that it makes the drive long and exhausting. This may be the worst drive to get to a resort in this book—and it's worth it. *There is no reliable source of gasoline beyond Lakeshore village at Huntington Lake!* (Sometimes there's gas at Mono Hot Springs Resort, but don't count on it.) The Kaiser Pass Road snakes from Huntington Lake up past the Potter Pass Trailhead (Trip 61) before turning into a twisting, often-steep, one-lane road. The road crawls painfully over Kaiser Pass and then winds down exposed cliffsides and through breathtaking scenery you can hardly appreciate when you're

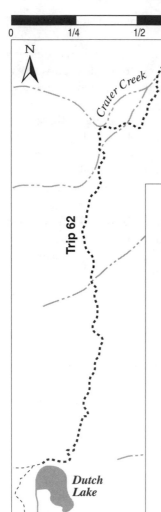

driving because you dare not take your eyes off the road. The farther you go, the worse the road's surface gets; in spite of this, people return year after year. Pulling off at seasonal High Sierra Ranger Station partway down lets you collect information, stretch your muscles, and enjoy some stupendous views. Farther on you reach a junction I'll call the Mono-Florence junction: left to Mono Hot Springs Resort, Lake Edison, and Vermilion Valley Resort; right to Florence Lake.

From the Mono-Florence junction, turn east for Florence Lake and follow this twisting, potholed, sometimes-unpaved road for 6 miles to a large, two-tiered parking area for Florence Lake. The first, upper tier is for overnight and overflow parking; the next, lower tier is for day-use parking, including picnicking at the adjacent picnic area. If the area's scenery hasn't already set your heart going pitty-pat, the view over Florence Lake to Mt. Shinn and Ward Mountain certainly will. Toilet; seasonal store nearby.

At the trailhead: Lovers of mountain scenery will revel in Florence Lake's beauty. A picnic here is sure to please. The nearby, seasonal Florence Lake Store operates a ferry service (seasonal; fee) across the lake in the summer. Taking the ferry for a scenic ride across the lake and back could be just the ticket!

On the trail: Your trailhead is at the right side of the lower parking tier, just beyond the gate that bars the public's vehicles from the road to Florence Lake's dam, and high above the lake's surface. It's signed DUTCH AND HIDDEN LAKE TRAIL. Pick up the rocky-dusty trail, which makes a switchback before reaching an information sign and trail-register box; sign in. In ⅙ mile you enter John Muir Wilderness as the trail winds generally northwest, ascending moderately through an interesting mix of chaparral, sparse forest, and granite slabs. You have excellent views over Florence Lake as the trail grows steeper. Nearing ½ mile, you climb while paralleling a seasonally-dry creekbed and lose the views when the trail angles across the creekbed. Up you go, steeply, taking a breather when the trail levels briefly at the next creek crossing. Climbing again, you follow lines of rocks and the occasional duck where the trail crosses huge granite slabs. Heavy stock use leaves the trail in mediocre-to-poor condition, full of loose rocks and deep dust, by late season.

Nearing 1 mile, the grade eases to moderate as you wind through handsome, rounded, granite outcrops. Beyond a stand of white fir and lodgepole, the climb grows very steep again. A little beyond 1¼ miles, the grade eases once in a while as you begin traversing through patches of while fir. Nearing 1¾ miles you pause at a somewhat-tree-obscured viewpoint from which you can pick out features like The Tombstone, with Florence Lake far below it; the peaks of the Mono Divide; Ward Mountain; and Mt. Shinn. At 2 miles you cross a meadowy area, pleasantly cool and flowery, and step over multiple, seasonal streamlets. Now you curve across an open, slabby, sandy area into a

Viewpoint above Florence Lake

stand of lodgepole and soon cross another stream. Beyond the stream, you make your way generally south across a broad area of water-stained slabs—slippery going in early season. The track fades out on the rock, but ducks, plus occasional piles of horse poop, help you navigate the slabs, which are interlaced with meadowy strips fed by seeps and supporting a wonderful array of flowers. There are fine views from this sparsely-wooded area.

Beyond the slabs, the trail returns to forest, then thrashes through muddy thickets of alder before curving west-southwest to climb steeply to moderately up the rocky lip of a moraine to the shallow bowl that holds forest- and meadow-ringed Dutch Lake. Scamper down to the shore of pretty **Dutch Lake at a little over 3 miles and 9100 feet** and find a picnic spot. Cliffs to the west are outliers of Mt. Ian Campbell (itself out of sight). In late season, you may have the lake all to yourself except for the big dragonflies that skim over its fringing meadow grasses and its masses of water lilies. Fall brings glowing patches of color—from subdued to vibrant reds—to the lake's shores.

Return the way you came, being sure to sign out.

63. Doris and Tule Lakes 🐾 ☼ 🍁

Place	Total distance	Elevation	Level	Type
Start	0	6540	—	—
Doris Lake *only*	1½	6823	E	O&B
Both lakes	3+	6780	M U	O&B

Permit required: None

Topo(s): Mt. Givens 7½'; USDA/USFS Ansel Adams Wilderness

Where to stay:
    Mountain: Mono Hot Springs Resort, Vermilion Valley Resort
    Of Interest: None
    Other: None

Highlights: Mostly easy hiking on uninteresting trails leads to two very pretty little lakes.

How to get to the trailhead: See Trip 62 for directions to the Mono-Florence junction on the Kaiser Pass Road. Go north for Mono Hot Springs and descend very steeply to cross the South Fork San Joaquin River on a one-lane bridge. Just over the bridge, at 1.7 miles, there's a spur road marked for Mono Hot Springs Resort. Take this spur road 0.25 mile more to parking in a marked day-use area in the midst of the resort's cabins, store, and café. If you are staying at Mono Hot Springs Resort, start from your cabin door. This hike starts just beyond the westernmost cabin and just before the westernmost loop of Mono Hot Springs Campground, where dirt Forest Road 7S10 angles right (northwest) past a huge, dark, lichen-spotted boulder. The official trailhead is near the end of Forest Road 7S10, but the road is truly dreadful and the walk from the resort is short. At the resort, toilets, water, store, café, outdoor hot tub (fee), and bathhouse offering private mineral baths and showers (fee).

At the trailhead: Non-hikers will enjoy relaxing at the resort. In addition to the resort-managed, hot-springs-fed mineral baths and showers for a fee, you can find a free soak in the once-developed, now-ruined tubs at the hot springs proper, which are on the other side of the river from the resort—a dangerous crossing when the water is high. Fishing is reportedly excellent along the river here.

On the trail: Follow dusty, rutted Forest Road 7S10 northwest, past marked, fenced Mono Tourist Pasture. Stay on the road as it passes a marked spur trail left to the campground's amphitheater, visible to the left. You shortly pass a capped but leaking spring, ascend moderately, and reach an unmapped fork where either branch will do, as they shortly rejoin. At ¼ mile, where the road widens to form a turnaround and parking area, you veer left (north) and soon pick up a foot trail in granite outcrops, by an information sign. The open, sandy-rocky trail begins a moderate-to-gradual ascent in a sparse, dry forest of Jeffrey pines. A little beyond ⅓ mile you meet a trail (not on the book's map) coming up a sandy slope on your

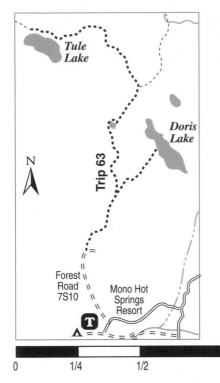

Tule
Lake

Doris
Lake

N

Trip 63

Forest
Road
7S10

Mono Hot
Springs
Resort

T

0   1/4   1/2   1 mile

right and joining your trail. You continue ahead (left) on the main trail, shortly entering Ansel Adams Wilderness. Continue your rocky ascent generally north over a parched landscape that seems more like the scorched foothills below Shaver Lake than the Sierra. Damp spots along the trail support occasional wildflowers.

At a little over ½ mile you reach the Doris-Tule junction: right (northeast) to Doris Lake, left (west) to Tule Lake and (eventually) Lake Edison. Arbitrarily, you go right to Doris Lake for now. After a short level stretch, you climb steeply through boulders to top out on a tiny saddle before descending steeply to curve north over the tops of boulders—watch the footing here. Next you gradually ascend a seasonally-damp draw, passing a stand of reeds, and reach the shore of beautiful little **Doris Lake at ¾ mile and 6823 feet**. A use trail (not on the book's map) leads around and then up the large outcrop just to your left; a brief climb to the top brings you to a marvelous picnic spot and viewpoint, featuring not only the wonderfully cliff-lined lake but handsome peaks to the east and southeast. You'll wish you could pitch a tent here and stay.

But you can't, so retrace your steps to the Doris-Tule junction where, with nearly a mile now on your boots, you turn right to continue to Tule Lake. You immediately begin a steep, loose, rocky climb that presently eases to a sandy trail with a moderate to gradual grade, topping out among boulders at 6920 feet. Now you descend moderately, leveling out as you pass some seasonal ponds. At 1½ miles all told, you reach a junction we'll call the Tule-Edison junction: right (northeast) to Mono Meadow and Lake Edison, left (north-northwest) to Tule Lake. You go left, following the trail as it wanders up and down through forlorn, dry, Jeffrey pine forest until you pass a huge stand of tules on your left and then cross a low saddle to see a sparkling, reed-rimmed Tule Lake ahead. Dark cliffs across the lake help frame the lily-pad-spangled sheet of water. Rocks near the northwest end of **Tule Lake at just over 1⅔ miles and 6780 feet** make nice, albeit exposed, picnic spots where black lizards join you to sunbathe.

Retrace your steps past the Tule-Edison junction and the Doris-Tule junction to the south end of Forest Road 7S10, to end your hike at a little over 3 miles. Your car is a few steps away at Mono Hot Springs Resort.

64. Along Lake Edison ☼ 🍁

Place	Total distance	Elevation	Level	Type
Start	0	7660	—	—
Slabs nr head of Lk Edison	9*	7650	S	O&B

Permit required: None

Topo(s): Sharktooth Peak, Graveyard Peak 7½'

Where to stay:
  Mountain: Mono Hot Springs Resort, Vermilion Valley Resort
  Of Interest: None
  Other: None

Highlights: A pleasant trail leads through forest to excellent views over the big, beautiful reservoir called Lake Edison and beyond it, eastward, into the High Sierra. Dense aspen groves near the lake's east end provide dramatic fall color.

How to get to the trailhead: See Trip 62 for directions to the Mono-Florence junction on the Kaiser Pass Road. Take the left fork and continue as in Trip 63, but don't turn off to Mono Hot Springs Resort. Instead, follow the winding, partly paved road to Lake Edison, eventually curving below the lake's hulking dam before ascending to the turnoff to Vermilion Valley Resort, which is just off the road. The trailhead is farther on, but a stop to visit the resort's store and café is a treat. In season, as long as the lake's level permits, you can cut your hike nearly in half by taking the resort-operated ferry (seasonal; fee) to or from the head of Lake Edison. But for completeness' sake, we'll assume you're doing the whole hike, so continue past the resort and toward the campground. Pass the first campground turnoff and instead head toward the pack station, then pass the pack

continued on facing page

N

to Graveyard Meadow

Trip 64

Cold Creek

Lake Thomas A Edison

Vermilion Valley Resort

s t a t i o n turnoff and follow the road through the camp- ground to the farthest end of the far- thest-east campground loop, to a parking area bounded by huge logs and to a trailhead that isn't on the 1982 topo. Park and start your hike here, 0.8 mile past the turnoff to Vermilion Valley Resort and 8.8 miles from the Mono-Florence junction.

* Optional one-way ferry ride (seasonal; fee) would cut hike nearly in half and make it moderate.

If you're staying at Vermilion Valley Resort, you can follow use trails tracing the lakeshore into the campground on foot and pick up this hike at the far end of the farthest-east campground loop.

At the trailhead: Non-hikers will probably prefer to relax at Vermilion Valley Resort. As for Florence Lake, a scenic ride on the ferry (seasonal; fee) across the lake and back is sure to please.

On the trail: An opening in a huge fallen log gives you access to the trail, which heads east towards an information sign and a trail sign directing you toward Goodale Pass, the Pacific Crest Trail/John Muir Trail (PCT/JMT), and Mono Creek. You follow the sandy trail through a moderate Jeffrey pine forest, enjoying the flowers scattered through the understory. The trail winds gradually through viewless forest, passing a junction just shy of ½ mile where a stock-worn trail comes in on the left to

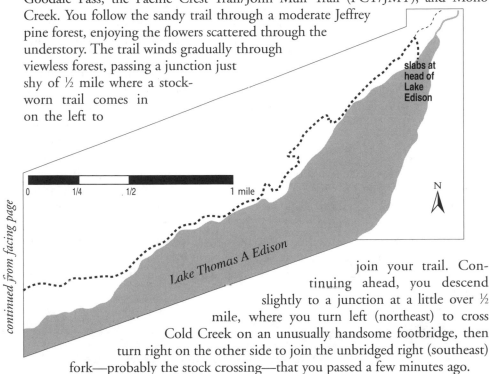

continued from facing page

slabs at head of Lake Edison

Lake Thomas A Edison

0   1/4   1/2   1 mile

N

join your trail. Continuing ahead, you descend slightly to a junction at a little over ½ mile, where you turn left (northeast) to cross Cold Creek on an unusually handsome footbridge, then turn right on the other side to join the unbridged right (southeast) fork—probably the stock crossing—that you passed a few minutes ago.

Turning left (east) on the reunited trail, you reach another junction at a little over ¾ mile: left (east-northeast) to Goodale Pass, right (east-southeast, lakeward) to Quail Meadow and the PCT/JMT. You go right, where you briefly have lake views around 1 mile as the trail veers near the water. The forest closes in again, but its dreariness is soon relieved by a flower-lined, seasonal creek that you hop across. By now you're wondering when you'll reach the wilderness boundary. You won't: on this hike, you skirt but don't enter the adjacent Ansel Adams and John Muir wildernesses. Leaving the creek, you climb a low, rocky ridge from which you enjoy some lake views, though the lake is now far below the trail. Climbing some more, moderately, you pass a treeless knob on your right from which, if you scramble out there, you have a nice view southwest across Lake Edison to its dam and beach and beyond it into the Kaiser Pass country. More viewpoints follow as you climb gradually, till you top out at a rocky point with a view of Bear Ridge across the lake and of the shapely white summits of Sierra peaks due east.

The views become obscured as you descend moderately through patchy forest to the lake's shore where, depending on the water level, tiny beaches between granite slabs beckon at a little over 2½ miles. The shoreline is steep and rocky, and the trail rolls up and down as it negotiates one shoreline obstacle after another. At a little over 2¾ miles you pass through a stand of aspens, possibly noting a dilapidated pit toilet uphill to the left. Beyond, you zigzag steeply up an outcrop dotted with deciduous oaks, beginning a rocky but view-filled ascent that's partly blasted out of the granite. Topping out at the hike's high point at 3⅓ miles and 7920 feet, you see glacier-polished granite surfaces on Bear Ridge opposite, the head of the lake and the rust-tinted Vermilion Cliffs to the east-northeast, and beyond them a line of huge gray cliffs.

Now you descend over high "steps" in the trail, cross a couple of granite slabs, and enter the shade of a grove of large aspens whose round, fluttering leaves are fresh green in summer, clear yellow to orange and red in fall. You cross a tiny, seasonal channel and climb a little over some big boulders before reaching a junction at a little over 4⅓ miles with the seasonal trail to the ferry landing near the lake's east end (right, southeast). The junction is unmarked when the ferry isn't running, but the heap of rocks that would prop up the sign is still pretty obvious. Turn right onto this spur trail and follow it down past boulders to **slabs near the head of Lake Edison at 4½ miles and 7650 feet**. In addition to being the ferry landing, these slabs provide wonderful camping and picnic spots with great views west across the lake, whose true head is normally farther east—how far depends on the lake's level and, late in a dry year, may actually be *west* of these slabs!

After enjoying your lunch here, retrace your steps, enjoying fine views westward as you go.

65. Mariposa Grove 🌸 ☼ 🍁

Place	Total distance	Elevation	Level	Type
Start	0	5600	—	
California Tree *only*	1⅓	5900	E	O&B
Museum semiloop *only*	3½+	6461	M	Semi
Entire semiloop	5⅓	6810	M	Semi

Permit required: None

Topo(s): Mariposa Grove 7½'; Rufus Graphics in cooperation with the Yosemite Association "Map and Guide to Wawona and the Mariposa Grove of Big Trees"

Where to stay:

    Mountain: Yosemite Peregrine, Yosemite's Four Seasons, Yosemite West Lodgings, Yosemite West Condominiums

    Of Interest: Wawona Hotel, The Redwoods

    Other: Town of Fish Camp, Town of Oakhurst

Highlights: This is the best, most-accessible grove of giant sequoias in Yosemite National Park.* At the hike's high point, you enjoy a magnificent vista from Wawona Point.

How to get to the trailhead: If you're staying in the Wawona area in the summer, take the free shuttle bus to the grove. Out of season or from elsewhere, take State Route 41 to Yosemite's South Entrance, between Fish Camp and Wawona. At the South Entrance, take the Mariposa Grove Road east—ahead if you've come from Wawona, right if you've come from Fish Camp—to a large parking area under giant sequoias at the Mariposa Grove, 2.1 miles from the South Entrance Station. Get an early start; even in off-season, this lot may be jammed by midday. Toilets, water, ranger station, gift shop.

Close-up of upper-grove roads and trails

At the trailhead: There are a couple of giant sequoias to stare at right in the parking lot. But non-hikers will enjoy purchasing a ticket for and taking one of the grove's tram tours. The open tram cars wind up paved roads through many of the best parts of the grove. (The roads are closed to the public's vehicles.)

On the trail: The whole grove consists of lower and upper groves, the lower grove being the easier to see and the upper grove sporting the finer trees. Numerous footpaths crisscross through the groves; beware: some trails marked on the maps may not still exist; the ones in this trip do. From the far (northeast) end of the parking lot, follow a broad duff-and-sand trail northeast past interpretive displays and into the lower grove. A sequoia grove is far from consisting purely of giant sequoias; you'll pass plenty of ponderosa pines, white firs, cedars, black oaks, and sugar pines. Giant sequoias, the largest living things on Earth, dominate by virtue of their size and longevity; they can live to be 3200 years old, maybe older, and never stop growing while they live.

In just a few steps you pass a toppled giant sequoia, "The Fallen Monarch," and cross the tram road. At ¼ mile you find fallen giant sequoias sawed through, with signs

*By far the finest giant sequoia groves in national parks are to the south in Kings Canyon and Sequoia national parks; see Trips 44, 49, and 53. Still, the Mariposa Grove is well worth your time, especially if you're *not* going to Kings Canyon or Sequoia.

explaining their annual rings. You shortly ascend a broad, low-stepped "staircase" to cross the tram road and meet a very handsome group of sequoias called "The Bachelor and the Three Graces." Between ⅓ and ½ mile a series of interpretive signs explains the many specialized requirements sequoias have for natural reproduction, leading you to the thought that overspecialization is one sure road to extinction. Around here, some sequoias have bark that's smooth on the side facing the trail, due to years of people stroking their shaggy red sides. You cross a stringer on a footbridge and enter a burned-over area, the result of a prescribed burn to reduce debris and the number of unnaturally competing species and to help giant sequoias reproduce. A little beyond ½ mile you reach the "Grizzly Giant Tree." Walk around it on either side and about halfway around, pick up the marked trail north to the "California Tree" and to the upper grove. The **"California Tree" at ⅔ mile and 5900 feet** is a walkthrough tree, its pedestrian tunnel carved out for tourists in 1895. Those wanting to hike only the lower grove should retrace their steps from the California Tree.

To continue with the entire hike, wind uphill, roughly paralleling the tram road, on a footpath that's less developed than the one you just left behind in the lower grove. You're leaving the giant sequoias behind for now. A little beyond ¾ mile you cross the tram road and head toward the upper grove's museum. At a junction a little farther on, you curve left (northeast) where the right fork heads south-southeast to Fish Camp. You climb past a particularly large tree on your left

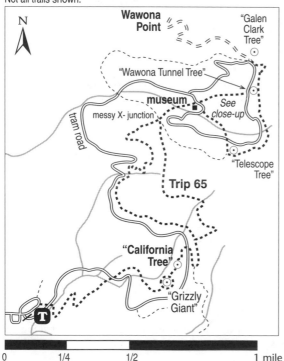

Route approximated based on field notes and several other sources. Not all trails shown.

to another junction at almost 1 mile: both branches go to the museum. Arbitrarily, to begin the first (lower) loop part of this hike, you take the right branch here, pass above a spring, cross an area dotted with patches of cedar seedlings, and enter the oppressive silence of a white fir forest. Now contouring across a hillside, you dip through a small gully and resume climbing, reaching the upper grove at 1⅔ miles at a sort of messy **X**-junction: ahead to the museum; right on the upper-loop trail; left toward the "Galen Clark Tree"; hard left to return to the lower grove and the parking lot via the Clothespin Tree and the Faithful Couple. The tram road, which makes a hairpin turn past this junction, makes an asymmetrical loop through the upper grove, and you'll cross, even briefly follow, the upper and lower sides of the tram-road loop as you hike the upper grove.

Take the branch that leads ahead to the museum, following the faint path through many immense, beautiful giant sequoias over ground thickly strewn with their hen's-egg-sized cones. The area is full of confusing trails, but you avoid confusion by heading for the museum, not the "Mariposa Tree." At the next junction, go right to skirt the meadow below the museum and pass some restrooms. In a few more steps, you reach another junction; turn left on a walkway across the meadow and toward the museum, now visible ahead. You reach the seasonally-open **museum in the upper grove a little short of 2 miles and at 6461 feet** and, if it's open, drop in for a visit. Tram tours stop here, too; you'll find books for sale as well as exhibits. To cut your hike short now, jump to "Retrace your steps past the museum… ," below.

To continue the full hike, as you leave the museum, follow the walkway *behind* it to pick up the lower side of the tram-road loop briefly; bear right for now. It's easier to follow this part of the hike on the "Close-up of upper-grove roads and trails" map in this book; the small arrows on the map show you which way this trip goes in the upper grove. At nearly 2 miles you spot a signed junction with the trail to the "Telescope Tree" and turn left (east) to pick up that trail.

On this trail, you soon pass the fallen "Stable Tree," in whose side rangers once put mangers for their horses. Winding upward, you pass one giant after another, and meet the road again. Turn left on the road and walk about 30 paces to the "Telescope Tree," a still-living giant whose heartwood has been gutted by fire from top to bottom. Turn right onto the trail that passes the tree, where you'll find an opening that lets you stick your head in and look up at the sky through the hollowed trunk. A tree's heartwood provides supporting structure; the living tissue is in an outer layer, nearer the bark, so this tree continues to thrive. Continuing up this same trail, at nearly 2¼ miles, you meet the Outer Loop Trail. Turn left (east) on the Outer Loop Trail, just shy of a rightward-leaning giant. Near 2½ miles you pass above two giant sequoias fused together at the base and nearly fused with a third tree. Just downhill and soon visible is the shattered corpse of the "Wawona Tunnel Tree," a former drive-through tree that toppled during the winter of 1968–69. The trail switchbacks down to meet the tram road at nearly 2⅔ miles, passing by the "Galen Clark Tree,"* at a junction. The left fork here is the tram road; the right fork, also a road, is now the "trail" to Wawona Point, accessible only on foot; and the middle fork is a foot trail that may be hard to spot—but you won't be taking it, anyway. Beginning an out-and-back segment, you follow the right fork up to a former parking lot at **Wawona Point at 3 miles and 6810 feet**, from which you have magnificent views over the South Fork Merced River.

* Yosemite pioneer Galen Clark (1814-1910) came west for his health in the 1850s. He expected to die soon but instead lived 43 more years, serving at various times as Yosemite's guardian. He "discovered" the Mariposa Grove, and many Yosemite features are named for him. One story about Clark says that when he was in his nineties, a visitor asked him how he got around Yosemite nowadays. He thought a bit and then said, "Slowly!"

Retrace your steps to the junction near the "Galen Clark Tree" and take the tram road left, toward the "Wawona Tunnel Tree," with a little over 3⅓ miles on your boots. Follow the road to the "Wawona Tunnel Tree's" root end, a little short of 3½ miles. This is perhaps the best vantage point from which to appreciate the "Wawona Tunnel Tree's" size. Nearby, on your right, you'll spot some wooden steps leading downhill toward the museum; take the steps downhill to meet a trail and follow it toward the museum. Cross the lower side of the tram-road loop to pick up the museum walkway again.

Continuing, retrace your steps past the museum and down and across the meadow, passing the tallest tree in the grove, the 290-foot "Columbia Tree," on your left. In this trail-confused area, you simplify things by following the signs that point you toward the parking lot via the "Clothespin Tree," not the "Mariposa Tree." Head uphill of the restrooms, following signs for the "Grizzly Giant Tree" and the parking lot. Meeting the tram road, you turn right on it for about 100 paces, to the point where the road makes a hairpin turn. Leave the road bearing right and downhill to return to the messy **X**-junction (see above, "Now contouring across a hillside…") a little short of 4 miles, where you take the westbound branch toward the "Clothespin Tree" and the "Faithful Couple."

Stay on this trail by veering left at a junction where another trail/road comes in on your right. Descend the hillside in long, lazy switchbacks. Stay on the trail when it approaches the road just downhill of the "Clothespin Tree" (turn around to enjoy an excellent view of this tree) by going left where a spur forks right leading to the road. On the trail, you continue your winding descent and meet the tram road again just opposite the "Faithful Couple Tree," a pair of giant sequoias fused together. Turn *left* (east) and walk a few steps down the road to pick up the marked trail to the "Grizzly Giant Tree" and the parking lot on (surprise!) the *left* side of the road. On this next trail segment, you wander up and down, generally northeastward, dodging deadfalls in a spectral, burnt forest and roughly paralleling the tram road, to close the loop part of this hike at the *second* junction you encountered on your way to the upper grove (see above, "You climb past a particularly large tree on your left to another junction at almost 1 mile…"), now with nearly 4⅔ miles on your boots.

Reverse your steps from here, past the "California Tree" and the "Grizzly Giant Tree," to reach the parking lot after nearly 5⅓ rewarding miles.

66. Chilnualna Falls 🌼

Place	Total distance	Elevation	Level	Type
Start	0	4200	—	—
Upper Chilnualna Falls	8–8⅓	6240–6400	S	O&B
Viewpoints above falls	8½	6440	S	O&B

Permit required: None

Topo(s): Wawona, Mariposa Grove 7½'

Where to stay:

   Mountain: Yosemite Peregrine, Yosemite's Four Seasons, Yosemite West Lodgings,
      Yosemite West Condominiums
   Of Interest: Wawona Hotel, The Redwoods
   Other: Town of Fish Camp, Town of Oakhurst

Highlights: Don't let the fact that you can't pronounce "Chilnualna" keep you away from these spectacular cascades and the lovely trail to them. (Tom Winnett, Wilderness Press' publisher emeritus, tells me it's "chill-NWALL-nah.")

How to get to the trailhead: From the junction of Highway 41 and the spur road to the Wawona Hotel, drive a little over 0.3 mile northwest up Highway 41 toward Wawona Campground and Yosemite Valley, passing the Wawona gas station and store. Turn right (east) on Chilnualna Falls Road and follow this road past a turnoff to the Wawona Ranger Station; you may want to take the short detour to pick up information at the station. Continuing up Chilnualna Falls Road, you stay on that road, passing a number of turnoffs to private cabins and resorts. At the road's end, you'll find a large dirt parking area on one side of the road and the marked trailhead, with an information sign, at the extreme east end of the road. Park here, 2 miles.

At the trailhead: Non-hikers will prefer to stay at their lodgings or to explore Wawona's Pioneer History Center, visit the charming old Wawona Hotel (in use since the 1870s), shop at the nearby Wawona Store, or play golf on the 9-hole course at the hotel.

On the trail: From the trailhead the trail angles northward up through moderate forest cover; stark Wawona Dome is visible to the right. In quick succession you cross a paved road, go left at an unmapped fork, climb some more, and go right at the next fork (also unmapped) onto a dirt road high above rushing Chilnualna Creek. The spring flower display along this road/trail can be amazing; beware of poison oak along the trail, too. You climb moderately to steeply as the forest thickens, and just ahead you spot dramatic cascades roaring down a steep, rocky streambed. Those daunted by the thought of the steep ascent ahead may want to stop right here and enjoy *these* cascades.

   For those continuing, the climb along the creek is beautiful and exciting but so steep that at times there are stone stairs to help you!

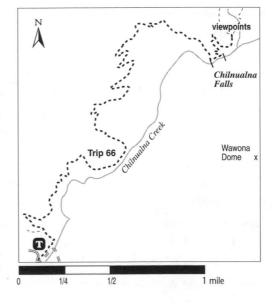

At ¼ mile you turn away from the creek to continue your steep climb through live oak and kit-kit-dizze to a junction near ⅓ mile with a horse trail coming in on the left (the spectacular, creekside section of trail you just ascended is too steep and exposed for equestrians). Now in Yosemite Wilderness, the grade eases as the leaf-littered trail contours a slope clad in manzanita, incense cedar, and live and deciduous oaks. Views southwest reveal the Chowchilla Mountains from some switchback legs; on others, you seem almost nose-to-nose with Wawona Dome. Flower displays continue to brighten your route, which is sometimes near the creek and sometimes far, occasionally obliging you to hop over seasonal seeps and tributary streams.

Near 2½ miles the trail winds past a view of a striking torrent of water crashing down a sheer rock wall. It's an inspiring sight, and by now you may need some inspiration to keep going. A little beyond 3 miles you cross a stream on mossy rocks between its small cascades, gaining more inspiring views of the falls ahead. Alas, these lower cascades, so showy from below, will turn out to be inaccessible from the trail—but the upper cascades will make up for that. You traverse a gully full of wild azalea and blue ceanothus before beginning a leg that's been blasted out of the cliff whose face you're crossing. You swing into Chilnualna Creek's steep channel at last and see that here, at upper **Chilnualna Falls at 4–4⅙+ miles and 6240–6400 feet**, the falls are a series of beautiful cascades separated by charming stretches where the creek pools or glides over slabs. Arbitrarily, this hike continues up to the next trail junction, but you may want to stop at any appealing place around here—there are some sublime spots—and enjoy your lunch from a creekside perch with a close-up view of the falls.

Optionally continuing a little farther, you reach a junction: left to Glacier Point, right to Chilnualna Lakes. You take neither fork but instead wander around here to take in the outstanding views over the South Fork Merced River from several nearby **viewpoints above the falls at 4¼ miles and 6440 feet**.

When you're ready, retrace your steps.

67. Sentinel Dome and Taft Point ☼ 🍁

Place	Total distance	Elevation	Level	Type
Start	0	7740	—	—
Sentinel Dome *only*	2	8122	E*	O&B
Taft Point *only*	2+	7503	E	O&B
Entire loop	4½	8122	M	Loop

Permit required: None

Topo(s): Half Dome 7½'; Rufus Graphics in cooperation with the Yosemite Association "Map & Guide to Yosemite Valley"

* Some hikers will judge the ascent of Sentinel Dome to be moderate rather than easy.

Where to stay:
> **Mountain:** Yosemite Peregrine, Yosemite West Condominiums, Yosemite West Lodgings, Yosemite's Four Seasons
>
> **Of Interest:** Wawona Hotel, The Redwoods, Ahwahnee Hotel, Yosemite Lodge, Curry Village
>
> **Other:** Town of Fish Camp, Town of El Portal

Highlights: This hike is a gem in every way: a beautiful trail offering wonderful contrasts and spectacular views, the best to be obtained by an exciting but surprisingly easy scramble to the top of one of Yosemite's famous granite domes. It's one of Yosemite's must-see trips.

How to get to the trailhead: Yosemite's Glacier Point Road winds generally northeast from its junction with State Route 41 at Chinquapin, which is between and about 2000 feet higher than Yosemite Valley and Wawona, and less than a mile from the turnoff for Yosemite West. Arbitrarily, start your mileage at Chinquapin. Turn north onto the Glacier Point Road, pass Badger Pass Ski Area and Bridalveil Campground, and at 13.6 miles turn into a large parking area on the left (west) side of the road. If you get to Glacier Point, you have gone too far. Get an early start; this parking lot may be jammed by midday. Toilet.

At the trailhead: Non-hikers will prefer a visit to Glacier Point, where they can enjoy incredible views over Yosemite Valley, including the major waterfalls, and far out across Yosemite's backcountry, all with a minimum of effort. People *in*

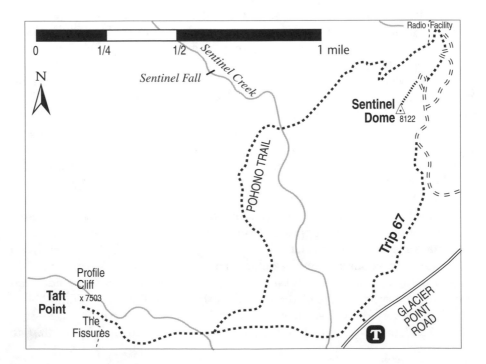

Yosemite Valley don't get this good a view of the falls by a long shot! There are toilets, water, telephone, and a snack/gift shop at Glacier Point, too.

On the trail: From the trailhead sign, head for the junction visible just ahead to the northwest. At the junction, it's left (south-southwest) for Taft Point, right (northeast) for Sentinel Dome. Looking at Sentinel Dome's steep, bald head from here, you may think, *No way!* It's better to climb Sentinel Dome early in the hike, while you have more energy, so turn right here in an open red-fir forest floored with coarse, light, decomposed-granite sand. You cross an unnamed, unmapped creeklet on a footbridge and climb a little over granite slabs. After a brief dip into forest, you contour along a mostly-open slope on the rocky-sandy trail, gaining a little altitude. Forest alternates with granite slabs, and rusty TRAIL signs help keep you on track. Far-reaching views open down Yosemite Valley, west to El Capitan, as you continue, while Sentinel Dome looms ahead. At ⅔ mile you pick up an old road and turn left (north) toward the dome, enjoying glimpses of Half Dome to the right as you wind through the forest behind Sentinel Dome.

The road climbs moderately to steeply to a loop from whose west side, at a little over ¾ mile, you begin your trailless but obvious ascent of Sentinel Dome. Imagine you're climbing a flight of stairs whose steps vary in height, and pick the route with the "step height" that suits you best; let yourself instinctively work back and forth across the slope, picking the most congenial route. Views get better and better the higher you go—pause to savor them—and if you decide that going all the way to the top is not for you, you'll still enjoy going partway. Depending on your route, you'll find yourself atop **Sentinel Dome at about 1 mile and 8122 feet**. The summit, though airy, is much more gentle and broad than you'd expect. Near a dead Jeffrey pine at the top is a compass rose inscribed to help you identify features in the magnificent scene around you.

Eventually you must retrace your steps to the road-loop's west side. Walk across the loop—now so worn and overgrown it may be hard to distinguish it as a road—and pick up a signed spur trail to the Pohono Trail (which starts at Glacier Point) on the loop's east side. Turn left (northeast) onto the spur trail and follow it downslope rather steeply toward a radio facility, enjoying a terrific view of Half Dome and crossing the road a couple of times. You veer left, pass below the radio facility/cell-phone site and find yourself on the northwest side of the ridge on which Sentinel Dome sits. You soon reach a junction with the Pohono Trail at 1½ miles: right (north) to Glacier Point, left (southwest) to Taft Point. Go left to begin a one-switchback, descending traverse from which you enjoy wonderful views of Yosemite Valley when the vegetation permits. At 2¼ miles you ford Sentinel Creek; not far below you, unseen, the creek plunges over Yosemite Valley's wall as Sentinel Falls; a use trail (not shown on the book's map) along the creek's east side leads north to an airy viewpoint of the top of the falls as well as of Yosemite Valley. Climbing out of the creekbed, you stroll briefly along the valley's edge—such views!—and then veer into forest again. You presently emerge from forest to ascend a ridge above Sentinel Creek and catch over-the-shoulder views of Sentinel Dome. Still climbing, you reach a junction at a little over 3 miles: left (east) to return to the parking area, right (west) to Taft Point.

Turn right for Taft Point and step across a trickle in a narrow, wet meadow. Head generally west to emerge from the forest onto a broad stone apron that's the edge of a large, rocky, chaparral-splattered bench. Use trails seem to splay every which way toward a cliff edge that's Yosemite Valley's south rim. The area is so open you don't really need a trail, so you explore here and there to see The Fissures, deep vertical slashes in an even deeper gash in the Valley's rim, and to stand on rail-ing-guarded **Taft Point at 3⅓ miles and 7503 feet** (just over 1 mile if you're hik-ing out-and-back to Taft Point only). The views over Yosemite Valley are breath-taking as well as vertiginous. While you don't need a trail to explore the Taft Point area, you'll need to find the trail you came in on in order to return. Look for it at the extreme left side of the broad stone apron just at the forest edge. Retrace your steps to the Taft-parking lot junction at nearly 4 miles (depending on your wan-derings around Taft Point) and go ahead (right) to Glacier Point Road. You bob over a pair of low, open ridges with views to the left of Sentinel Dome and ford Sentinel Creek in a gully as you near the road.

At a little over 4⅓ miles you close the loop near the parking lot, turn right on the spur to the parking lot, and reach the lot at a little less than 4½ miles.

68. To Yosemite Valley via Falls 🌸 ☼

Place	Total distance	Elevation	Level	Type
Start	0	7214	—	—
Happy Isles shuttle stop	7¾	4020*	S	Shuttle

Permit required: None

Topo(s): Half Dome 7½'; Rufus Graphics in cooperation with Yosemite Association "Map & Guide to Yosemite Valley"

Where to stay:
   Mountain: Yosemite Peregrine, Yosemite West Condominiums, Yosemite West Lodgings, Yosemite's Four Seasons
   Of Interest: Ahwahnee Hotel, Yosemite Lodge, Curry Village
   Other: Town of El Portal

Highlights: Like Trip 67, this is another Yosemite must-see hike. Spectacular views attend nearly every step past three of Yosemite's most famous waterfalls—three you can't see from the Valley proper. Unless the day is extremely hot or the season is late, bring rain gear for the Mist Trail along Vernal Fall.

---

* On the way, you descend to Illiloutte Creek at 5900 feet, then climb to Panorama Cliff at 6660 feet before resuming your descent.

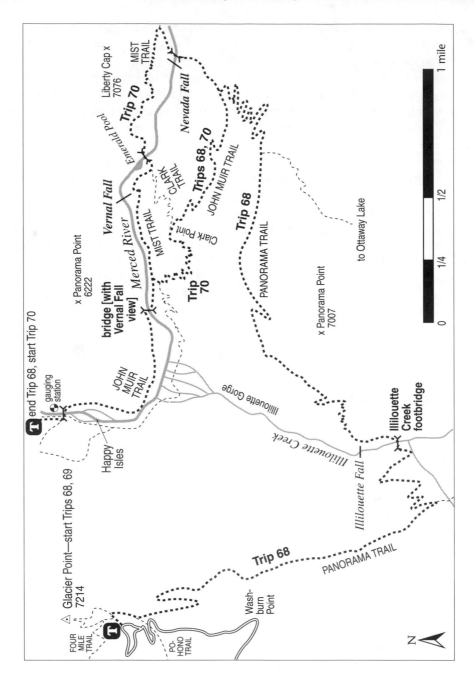

How to get to the trailhead: No matter where you're coming from, the best way to take this shuttle trip is to get to Yosemite Valley and take the hiker's shuttlebus to Glacier Point. Leave your car parked at your Yosemite Valley lodgings or at a day-use lot in the Valley, then buy your ticket and catch your shuttle at Curry Village, the Ahwahnee Hotel, or Yosemite Lodge. Take one of the earlier shuttlebuses; you'll want to allow plenty of time for this hike. The bus ride from the last pick-up point in the Valley to Glacier Point takes about an hour one way and is very beautiful. The driver educates and entertains the passengers by explaining Yosemite's geology and history and by telling Yosemite yarns. You'll end your hike at the Happy Isles shuttle stop in Yosemite Valley, from which you can take Yosemite Valley's free shuttlebus back to your lodgings or your car. At Glacier Point you'll find toilets, water, a telephone, and a snack/gift shop, too.

At the trailhead: Non-hikers can buy a ticket for the round-trip tour to Glacier Point, where they may want to arrange to meet their hiking friends and together enjoy the spectacle there (see Trip 67's "At the trailhead" and the next paragraph).

On the trail: Be sure to walk all around Glacier Point before leaving, as these are the finest Yosemite Valley views anywhere. You'll get a bird's-eye view of some of the scenic wonders you'll be visiting up close on this hike. In early season, your ears are not deceiving you: you *can* hear those huge waterfalls from Glacier Point! Your trail, the Panorama Trail, begins behind—southeast from the bare edge of—the Glacier Point area and appears to head off in a completely wrong direction, roughly paralleling the parking area and climbing above the toilets. Almost immediately, the trail swings into the forest and reaches a **Y**-junction: left (southeast) to Illilouette Fall on the Panorama Trail, right (south-southwest) on the Pohono Trail.

Go left on the Panorama Trail to begin a gradual descent through a forest of mostly-burnt trees on chaparral-clad slopes. From these leisurely switchbacks you'll see famous features such as Half Dome, Mt. Broderick, and Liberty Cap; see the John Muir Trail switchbacking down a slot on the east side of the Panorama Cliffs; and hear the roar of the great falls. At a switchback turn at a little over 1⅓ miles, you reach a junction: left on the next switchback leg of the Panorama Trail to continue this hike, right (southeast) to Mono Meadow. You go left, around the switchback turn, enjoying superb views of Half Dome, Panorama Point, and Mt. Starr King. At a little over 1¾ miles you cross a seasonal stream whose gully is filled with currant bushes, make a switchback turn, and near 2 miles reach a use trail that bears off left a few yards to the best, albeit vertiginous, viewpoint overlooking the top of 370-foot Illilouette Fall. These cascades, very impressive in early season, are tucked into the side of a deep slot called Illilouette Gorge and are invisible from most of the typical tourist viewpoints. There's no railing at this viewpoint, the drop is very steep, and the footing may be poor because of decomposed granite, so be careful.

Back on the main trail, the forest grows denser and cooler as you cross the currant-filled streambed a couple more times on your way down to the banks of Illilouette Creek, which makes a wonderfully picturesque dash over granite slabs here. A trestle footbridge over **Illilouette Creek at 2⅓ miles and 5900 feet** conducts you safely over the creek. Swimming is dangerous here because of the water's swiftness and iciness and the area's proximity to Illilouette Fall. But you'll find plenty of wonderful picnic spots around the bridge where you can safely relax and enjoy the scenery.

Sorry to inject a dark note into your sunny day, but take the no-swimming signs at Yosemite's waterfalls seriously. Every year, several people are killed when they ignore the signs, are caught in strong currents of numbingly cold water—remember, this is all snowmelt straight off Sierra peaks!—and are swept over one of the falls. Drowning is the most common cause of death in our national parks and monuments. Okay, back to the fun stuff.

When you can tear yourself away from lovely Illilouette Creek, bear left (north) on the far (east) side of the footbridge and begin climbing through sparse forest and chaparral relieved by occasional dense patches of oaks. You zigzag up moderately some 760 feet, at times staring straight across Illilouette Gorge to your starting point at Glacier Point—if you have trouble picking it out, look for sunlight glinting on the windshields of cars on the Glacier Point Road. At last, having risen high enough and gone far enough east, you can see beyond Glacier Point and into Yosemite Valley. Excellent views of North Dome, Basket Dome, Royal Arches, the Ahwahnee Hotel, and Washington Column enliven this leg of the ascent. Near 3⅔ miles the now-shadier trail levels out atop Panorama Cliff, where you pause to take in the wonderful view. Nevada Fall suddenly comes into heart-stopping view and hearing as you begin a gradual descent to a junction: left (ahead, east) to Nevada Fall, right (south) to Ottaway Lake.

You go left for Nevada Fall, switchbacking down a more-pronounced grade. You cross and recross an unnamed, unmapped streamlet, then play tag with another one as you now brush up to it, now veer away. There's a confusion of junctions as you approach 5 miles and the south side of Nevada Fall; most are just use-trail

Half Dome, Nevada Fall, and Vernal Fall as seen from the Panorama Trail

shortcuts between the area's major trails, the Mist Trail and the John Muir Trail. The major junction here is a **T**-junction where the Panorama Trail ends at the John Muir Trail: left on the John Muir Trail to Yosemite Valley; right on the John Muir Trail to Nevada Fall, to a junction with the Mist Trail, and, eventually, to Mt. Whitney. Whether you choose to take the Mist Trail or the John Muir Trail back to the Valley,* for now you turn right to see Nevada Fall.

Any questions about which way to go at other junctions as you head for Nevada Fall are resolved by the fall's roar, louder than a freight train here. You emerge from forest onto huge granite slabs—note this spot—on the south side of the Merced River at the top of 594-foot **Nevada Fall at 5 miles and 5940 feet**, opposite Liberty Cap. You'll spot a bridge that crosses the river a little upstream of the fall. The trail vanishes on the open, sand-dusted slabs, and you don't really need it to find the bridge or any of a number excellent picnic spots on both sides of the river. Enjoy your lunch but guard your chow; the ground squirrels here are determined beggars and skilled thieves. Exercise extreme care in approaching the sheer lip of this dangerous fall. Cross the bridge to the fall's north side and look around the north rim for a steep staircase leading down to a railing-protected overlook of the canyon below and of the fall's white plumes. On the north side of Nevada Fall you'll find a day-use area and restrooms as well as the upper junction of the John Muir and Mist trails. You'll need to decide whether the next leg of your hike will be on the Muir Trail or the Mist Trail. This description will follow the Muir Trail for now, switching to the Mist Trail later on.

After taking in the pleasures of Nevada Fall, retrace your steps to the south side and back to the junction of the John Muir and Panorama Trails: left on the Panorama Trail, right (west, ahead) on the Muir Trail. You take the Muir Trail west through forest, hopping over springs, avoiding use trails, and crossing slabs.

---

*Should you take the John Muir Trail or the Mist Trail when hiking down from Glacier Point? The John Muir Trail and the Mist Trail meet here at the top of Nevada Fall and will meet again below Vernal Fall. Between Nevada and Vernal falls, the John Muir and Mist trails are connected by the Clark Trail.

The excruciatingly steep Mist Trail descends far closer to Nevada and Vernal falls than the John Muir Trail does. The upper Mist Trail has a few good close-up views of Nevada Fall, but they are hard for *downhill* hikers to find and appreciate. This is because the upper Mist Trail twists steeply up/down on stones that are worn slippery-smooth by decades of use and that are dusted with sand. Little traction is available, and you'll be looking to avoid a fall, not to catch a view. But the lower Mist Trail has spectacular views of Vernal Fall and is in better shape than the upper part beside Nevada Fall.

The John Muir Trail is more moderately graded, long, and in better (safer) shape than the Mist Trail. The upper part of the John Muir Trail has excellent views of Nevada Fall.

The short, steep, rocky Clark Trail has good views of both falls.

Here's my recommendation for hiking down from Glacier Point. From Nevada Fall, take the upper John Muir Trail down to its junction with the Clark Trail to enjoy superior views of Nevada Fall. Then take the Clark Trail down to meet the Mist Trail, enjoying fine views of both falls. Then take the lower Mist Trail down past Vernal Fall, a leg that provides a complete visual, aural, and tactile experience of Vernal Fall. The Mist Trail ends a little below Vernal Fall, so take the John Muir Trail for your final leg to Happy Isles. If you want to experience Nevada Fall while climbing *up* the Mist Trail, see Trip 70.

Leaving the forest behind, the partly-paved trail traverses a dripping cliff face where it is partly protected on the steep downhill side by a stone wall. Over-the-shoulder views of Nevada Fall are amazing from this stretch. Beyond the damp traverse, long, sandy switchbacks carry you generally west on a moderate grade down toward the Valley, and there are stunning views of Nevada Fall and Liberty Cap either ahead or over your shoulder at nearly every point.

One of the best views is at Clark Point, by the junction with the Clark Trail at a little over 5¾ miles: left to continue on the John Muir Trail, right to descend the Clark Trail. Turn right onto the Clark Trail to begin descending steep, rocky, exposed switchbacks. The upper switchbacks afford excellent views of Nevada and Vernal falls, while an overlook about ⅔ of the way down, at a little over 6 miles, offers a breathtaking view of Vernal Fall. At nearly 6⅓ miles you reach a **T**-junction with the Mist Trail: right to Nevada Fall, left to Emerald Pool and Vernal Fall. Go left, shortly passing deep and dangerous Emerald Pool and a spur trail left to a pit toilet. Soon you stand on the railing-ed slabs at the top of 317-foot **Vernal Fall at a little over 6½ miles and 5000 feet**, exhilarated by the noise and mist in spite of the crowds normally found here. Now you veer left to make a steep friction walk up slabs on the south side of Vernal Fall. Topping out, you pause to catch your breath and to take a look at the descent the Mist Trail makes from here. If you don't want to get soaked on the next leg, now's the time put on your rain gear.

Between this point and the base of Vernal Fall, the Mist Trail is an extraordinarily steep series of high stone stairs, damp to soaking wet, rarely protected on the downhill side by railings. The trail clings to the side of the canyon next to the fall, often so close that you not only hear and see the fall but are practically *in* it. This segment has recently been reworked with new stones and with grooves in the stairsteps to help with traction and to carry away excess water. Watch your step and take your time, pausing often to look back at the fall—you will have to stop often for the crowds working their way upward. The grade eases at the base of Vernal Fall, and at just under 7 miles you pass huge boulders that provide viewpoints of the fall just before the Mist Trail blends back into the John Muir Trail.

Continue ahead (right, west, downhill) onto the John Muir Trail, shortly passing a spur trail to restrooms on your left and then a drinking fountain on your right as you veer right to cross the river on a footbridge. Pause on the **bridge at 7 miles and 4400 feet** to enjoy a wonderful view upstream to Vernal Fall, framed by sheer stone walls and nearby branches. Across the bridge, on the north side of the river, the trail curves west again to descend steeply past the mouth of Illilouette Gorge; when Illilouette Fall's volume is high, you may be able to spot it one last time. Beyond Illilouette Gorge, the trail curves northward as it continues its steep descent.

As you approach Happy Isles, a trail branches left down stone steps toward the isles. The Happy Isles are a pair of lovely, rocky, forested islets separated by picturesque branches of the Merced River, and many hikers enjoy a stop here on their way to or from the falls. Happy Isles' big-leaf maples and dogwoods provide welcome summer shade and glorious fall color. A wheelchair-accessible trail (not shown on the book's map) traverses the islets; non-hikers may enjoy the easy walk around Happy Isles as well as a visit to the Happy Isles Nature Center, which is on the west side of the river here.

But you continue ahead (right) to a large bridge by a gauging station at the Yosemite end of the John Muir Trail at 7⅔ miles, where you turn left over the bridge to meet the nature-trail system to and through Happy Isles. Turn away from Happy Isles—that is, turn right—at the second junction beyond the bridge and follow signs generally north, past restrooms on your left, to the Happy Isles stop for the free Yosemite Valley shuttlebus at 7¾ miles and 4020 feet, the end of this hike, where you catch a bus to your lodgings or your car.

69. Four Mile Trail 🌸 ☼ 🍁

Place	Total distance	Elevation	Level	Type
Start	0	7214	—	—
Yosemite Lodge shuttle stop	5⅓+	3980	M	Shuttle

Permit required: None

Topo(s): Half Dome 7½'; Rufus Graphics in cooperation with the Yosemite Association "Map & Guide to Yosemite Valley"

Where to stay:
   Mountain: Yosemite Peregrine, Yosemite West Condominiums, Yosemite West Lodgings, Yosemite's Four Seasons
   Of Interest: Ahwahnee Hotel, Yosemite Lodge, Curry Village
   Other: Town of El Portal

Highlights: Amazing views over Yosemite Valley attend your descent of the Four Mile Trail from scenic Glacier Point to the Valley floor. A stroll across the floor of Yosemite Valley to a shuttle stop completes your trip.

How to get to the trailhead: See Trip 68.

At the trailhead: See Trip 68.

On the trail: As for Trip 68, be sure to spend plenty of time enjoying Glacier Point before you hit the trail. When you're ready to hike, you'll find the trailhead behind the snack/souvenir stand. Forks to the right lead to Glacier Point, which you've already seen, so you bear left to descend through a moderate to dense forest on the duff Four Mile Trail, now longer than 4 miles thanks to reworking. You shortly pass a large boulder with a TRAIL RULES sign, which you pause to study, and then cross a seasonal stringer. Curving through a gully, you glimpse the north wall of Yosemite Valley ahead. A little past ¼ mile you reach a point where you have a view toward North Dome and Basket Dome, with Mt. Hoffman behind them; toward Mt. Watkins, with Tenaya (ten-EYE-ah) Peak behind it; toward Tenaya Canyon and Clouds Rest; and toward Half Dome. Farther on, the remnant of Mirror Lake—now becoming Mirror Meadow—is visible. Next, Yosemite Point and

Upper Yosemite Fall come into view—a truly breathtaking sight. Your gradual descent briefly shifts to a slight climb, and soon you spot Lower Yosemite Fall and the Middle Cascades between the falls.

Resuming your descent, you traverse exposed rock faces where the downhill side of the trail is a sheer drop to the Valley floor. At ⅔ mile you reach your first switchback turn at a fine view of Sentinel Rock as well as a view westward down the Valley to El Capitan. The descent becomes steeper and more switchbacking. You make another rock-face traverse at 1½ miles, then negotiate a gully whose loose rock demands that the downhill side of the trail be propped up in places. You swing out of the gully to excellent views of Yosemite Falls, then zigzag down through another gully. Handsome Douglas big-cone spruce trees (*Pseudotsuga macrocarpa*) shade the trail here and there. The trail surface becomes looser—rocks and coarse sand—and the grade becomes steeper, while the exposure on the downhill side continues to be nerve-racking. But the views more than compensate for the steep, exposed going, although you should pause before taking your eyes off the trail.

At nearly 3½ miles you cross a pretty but unnamed stream, enter a viewless forest of live oak, and make a long traverse downward. Like most live-oak woods at this altitude, this one is apt to be full of tiny flying insects whose goal, it seems, is to commit suicide by flying into your eyes, up your nose, or down your throat. To foil most of them, keep your sunglasses on and tie a bandana bandit-style over your nose and mouth, or pick up a fallen brush of twigs and leaves with which to fan the critters away. Nearing 4 miles, road noise tells you you're close to the Valley floor. At a little over 4¼ miles you pass a trailhead sign as your trail becomes paved and veers left Follow the paved path across the intersecting Valley floor footpath

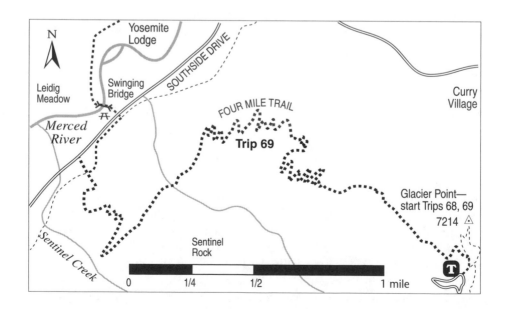

that roughly parallels the road to reach the road at just over 4⅓ miles and 3980 feet, the end of the Four Mile Trail.

But you need to pick up a shuttlebus to get back to your car or your lodgings, so go back a few steps to that last intersection and pick up the Valley floor footpath, turning northeast on it (left if you're coming back from the main road, right if you turn onto it directly from your descent of the Four Mile Trail). It's roughly 1 mile more to the nearest shuttlebus stop, at Yosemite Lodge. Follow the Valley floor footpath till you're roughly opposite Swinging Bridge, near a picnic area with restrooms. Cross the road, traverse the picnic area, cross Swinging Bridge over the Merced River, and follow the footpath across Leidig Meadow to the cabins of Yosemite Lodge. Pick up the road system through the cabins and find your way to the shuttlebus stop at Yosemite Lodge, to end this hike at about 5⅓ miles (the exact distance depends on your route to Yosemite Lodge).

Cathedral Rocks (left) and El Capitan as seen from Four Mile Trail

70. Vernal and Nevada Falls 🌸 ☼

Place	Total distance	Elevation	Level	Type
Start	0	4020	—	—
Bridge *only*	1½	4400	M	O&B
Top of Vernal Fall *only*	2½	5000	S	O&B
Entire semiloop	6	5940	S	Semi

Permit required: None

Topo(s): Half Dome 7½'; Rufus Graphics in cooperation with the Yosemite Association "Map & Guide to Yosemite Valley"

Where to stay:

　　Mountain: Yosemite Peregrine, Yosemite West Condominiums, Yosemite West Lodgings, Yosemite's Four Seasons

　　Of Interest: Ahwahnee Hotel, Yosemite Lodge, Curry Village

　　Other: Town of El Portal

Highlights: On this steep, spectacular trip you visit two beautiful and famous Yosemite waterfalls, Vernal and Nevada falls, from the Valley floor (see Trip 68). As noted in Trip 68, you may want to take rain gear for the Mist Trail leg beside Vernal Fall.

How to get to the trailhead: From your lodgings in the Valley or from a day-use parking lot that you drive to, take the Valley floor's free shuttlebus to the Happy Isles stop. (You can't drive your own car to that stop.) Toilets, water, snack stand; nearby Happy Isles Nature Center.

At the trailhead: As described near the end of Trip 68 ("As you approach Happy Isles... ."), Happy Isles is a delightful spot in which to linger—but see page 199's footnote. Thanks to the shuttlebus system, non-hikers can also explore many of the Valley's other sights and amenities while their hiking buddies collect blisters.

Fall foliage on the Merced River

On the trail: See Trip 68's map. From Happy Isles, reverse the steps of Trip 68 to ascend the steep John Muir Trail to the wonderful view of Vernal Fall from **the bridge at ¾ mile and 4400 feet**. For those going to Vernal Fall, continue reversing Trip 68's steps to go across the bridge and up the trail as far as the lower junction with the Mist Trail. Take the left fork, the Mist Trail, here, beginning the loop part of this trip by reversing the steps described in Trip 68 to the **top of Vernal Fall at 1¼ miles and 5000 feet**. Because the trail is extremely steep and often very narrow, it's best to put on your rain gear before you begin ascending the stairs.

Still reversing the steps of Trip 68, those continuing to Nevada Fall descend the slabs at the top of Vernal Fall before heading east past Emerald Pool and past the junction with the spur trail to the toilet. For this trip, you now stop reversing Trip 68's steps and pass the junction with the Clark Trail; instead, stay on the Mist Trail, which is easier to ascend than descend. You soon begin traversing slabs while following a line of boulders. Near 1⅔ miles you cross the Merced River on a footbridge, beyond which the trail angles northeast toward Mt. Broderick and Liberty Cap, climbing gradually in a buggy thicket of live oak. You veer away from, then back toward, the river and through a day-use area in a cool grove of incense cedars.

As you resume a moderate climb, the roar of Nevada Fall makes your ears perk up, and at 2 miles you find yourself abreast of the base of Nevada Fall. Trees interfere with your view from the trail, so you pick your way over to the water's edge to take in this heart-stopping spectacle. Now you zigzag steeply up too-smooth, sand-dusted rock "steps" through a jumble of boulders, enjoying occasional excellent views of the fall. The climb becomes steeper and steeper, and the switchbacks tighter and tighter, as the trail veers into a rocky chute between the canyon's north wall and an outcrop on Nevada Fall's north side, where you lose your views of the fall. At the top of this exhausting climb, you reach another day-use area, this one with toilets, and a **T**-junction (the upper junction) with the John Muir Trail: left to Little Yosemite Valley, right to Nevada Fall and to return to Yosemite Valley on the John Muir Trail.

Take the right fork and curve west on a gradual, sandy-rocky tread to reach the footbridge over the Merced River just upstream of **Nevada Fall at 2¾ miles and 5940 feet**. Explore both sides of the fall, being careful to stay out of the water. As mentioned in Trip 68, there's a steep access to a railinged-in area on the extreme north side of the fall. From that overlook you have a vertiginous view of the fall and the canyon below. There are terrific picnic spots here as well as some of the begging-est, thieving-est ground squirrels anywhere.

When you're ready to leave Nevada Fall, make your way across the slabs on its south side to the junction of the John Muir and Panorama Trails as described in Trip 68 ("After taking in the pleasures of Nevada Fall... ."). The junction isn't obvious and there are lots of use trails in the area, but keep your eyes peeled for the Muir Trail headed back down toward Yosemite Valley. Follow it generally westward on the view-rich leg described in Trip 68 to the junction with the Clark Trail at Clark Point at 4 miles. After enjoying the fabulous views at Clark Point, you depart from Trip 68's steps and turn left to continue to the Valley on the Muir Trail, often in the shade of big-leaf maple trees. If this stretch is buggy, see the suggestions in Trip 69 ("Like most live-oak woods at this altitude..."). There's wonderful fall color on this leg in season. Zigzag down, down, down along the east side of Panorama Cliff until you pass a marked horse trail on your left just before you close the loop part of this trip at the lower junction with the Mist Trail at 5¼ miles. Don't take the horse trail: not only is it exclusively for equestrians, but it's ankle-deep in dust and dung.

From this lower John Muir Trail-Mist Trail junction, retrace your steps to Happy Isles at 6 miles to complete your eye-popping hike.

71. Lookout Point 🌸

Place	Total distance	Elevation	Level	Type
Start	0	4680	—	—
Lookout	2⅔	5309	E	O&B

Permit required: None

Topo(s): Lake Eleanor 7½'

Where to stay:
  Mountain: None
  Of Interest: Evergreen Lodge
  Other: None

Highlights: An easy, wildflower-blessed trail leads to a knob commanding a view of Hetch Hetchy Valley with its lovely waterfalls and its notorious reservoir.*

How to get to the trailhead: The reference point for drives in the Hetch Hetchy district is its one lodging, Evergreen Lodge. To find Evergreen Lodge, drive State Route 120 toward Yosemite's Big Oak Flat entrance station, to 120's junction with Evergreen Road, just outside the Park and just north of the entrance station. You've overshot this junction if you get to Big Oak Flat entrance station while eastbound or go more than a mile west of the entrance station while westbound. Follow Evergreen Road east and then north about 6.6 miles to Evergreen Lodge.

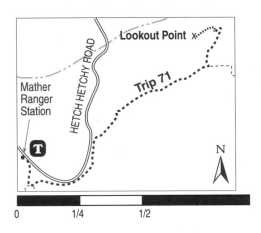

From Evergreen Lodge, follow Evergreen Road north to the junction with Hetch Hetchy Road by Camp Mather (private). Bear right on Hetch Hetchy Road to the boundary of Yosemite National Park and Mather Ranger Station, 1.9 miles. Park on the east side of the road, opposite the ranger station; the trailhead is across the road, next to the ranger station.

---

* John Muir regarded Hetch Hetchy Valley as another Yosemite Valley and was horrified when, in 1901, the city of San Francisco proposed to turn Hetch Hetchy into a reservoir. Old photos of Hetch Hetchy Valley tend to confirm Muir's judgement. He and the infant Sierra Club fought the dam for many years but finally lost in 1913. The reservoir you see now is the result of the project, completed in 1923, and of an increase in the dam's height in 1938. San Francisco still drinks the water.

Yosemite Valley has become the vacation goal of millions around the world and is badly shopworn. Hetch Hetchy Valley, largely inaccessible because flooded (boating is not permitted), has remained little-known and relatively little visited. Which valley has suffered the worse fate?

At the trailhead: Non-hikers will probably prefer to be at Evergreen Lodge or at Hetch Hetchy, enjoying the scenery (see Trip 72).

On the trail: Head south-southeast under moderate to dense forest cover, skirting a fenced meadow on your right. Veering away from the fence, you reach a marked junction; go left (northeast) toward Smith Meadows. Lupine carpets the forest openings here, including the eye-catching red-purple-yellow harlequin lupine as well as the more common blue lupine. Soon you find yourself above and paralleling Hetch Hetchy Road through an oak-and-incense cedar forest. Bobbing over a little rocky area, you enjoy a dazzling display of wildflowers in season.

After climbing through a rocky draw along a seasonal trickle, you cross several marshy spots spangled with wildflowers. A little beyond 1 mile you reach a fork: ahead (right) to Hetch Hetchy, left to Lookout Point. Go left, passing a seasonal pond which you may have to skirt, and pick up the trail on the other side of the pond. Beyond, the trail is occasionally faint as it winds up a sunny outcrop where flowers bloom in pockets of soil. The last few hundred yards are pathless, so pick your way up the open slope past some stunted Jeffrey pines to **Lookout Point at a little over 1⅓ miles and 5309 feet**, by a lone Jeffrey pine at the summit. The 270-degree view encompasses Hetch Hetchy Reservoir—let's face, it makes a very pretty lake—with wispy Tueeulala (twee-LAH-lah) Falls and huge Wapama (wah-PAH-mah) Falls pouring over its encompassing walls, and the peaks beyond Hetch Hetchy. This is a great spot for a snack.

Return the way you came.

72. Tueeulala and Wapama Falls 🌸

Place	Total distance	Elevation	Level	Type
Start	0	3813	—	—
Tueeulala Fall	3	4020	E	O&B
Wapama Fall	4	3880	M	O&B

Permit required: None

Topo(s): WP Hetch Hetchy 15'; Lake Eleanor 7½'

Where to stay:
Mountain: None
Of Interest: Evergreen Lodge
Other: None

Highlights: Flooded or not—see the footnote at the end of Trip 71—Hetch Hetchy Valley remains a beautiful place to visit. This trip to two of Hetch Hetchy's waterfalls, Tueeulala ("twee-LAH-lah") and Wapama, is also unforgettable because of its wildflowers.

How to get to the trailhead: Follow Trip 71 to Evergreen Lodge and continue north to the junction with Hetch Hetchy Road by Mather Camp (private). Bear right on

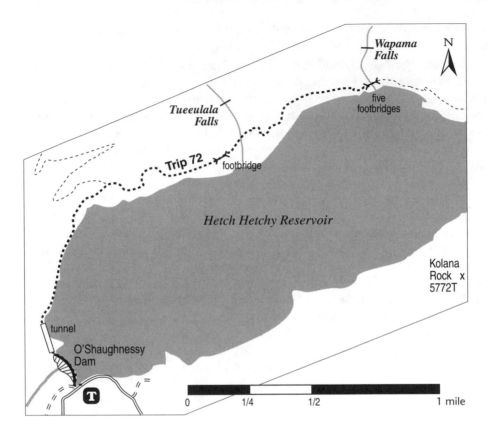

Hetch Hetchy Road past the boundary of Yosemite National Park and Mather Ranger Station. Continue on this winding, narrow road—the scenery can be distractingly lovely, especially the sight of Hetch Hetchy Reservoir—to a very large roadend loop with a parking area at its north end, by O'Shaughnessy Dam, 9.5 miles. Park here. Toilets, water.

At the trailhead: See Trip 71.

On the trail: Head north-northwest across the dam, pausing to enjoy the wonderful views over Hetch Hetchy Reservoir, especially eastward: Tueeulala and Wapama falls and Hetch Hetchy Dome to the left (north), Kolana Rock to the right (south). Soon you curve through a lighted tunnel and emerge on a broad trail along the reservoir's shore. In season, you can already hear the falls as well as see both of them ahead. At ⅓ mile you begin a gentle climb through big-leaf maple, then dip into a ferny nook where cottonwoods crowd a tiny stream and wild-grape vines drape the trees. At ½ mile you cross a stream on a footbridge as water cascades down the rock face on your left, and the wildflower display in season is exquisite.

At ⅔ mile you reach a junction: ahead (left) to Laurel Lake, right (lakeward) to Wapama Falls and Yosemite Valley (a mere 47.5 miles away, says the sign!). Go right, around a point, and soon begin descending through meadow, then oak woodland. You ford one streamlet and then, at a little over 1 mile, ford another stream that splashes down from the cliffs above you to glide over the granite slabs you're hiking on—a double line of rocks may help you keep to the trail here. Beyond the slabs you find the beaten path again, with Tueeulala Falls visible ahead. On this leg of the hike, the cascades of Rancheria Falls (beyond the range of this book) are visible in the distance, next to Le Conte Point. Continuing, you make an exposed, rocky climb into a bit of forest, top out at 4060 feet, and then make a stony descent to a bridged crossing of a rockfall. You pass below delicate, seasonal, 1000-foot **Tueeulala Falls at just over 1½ miles and 4020 feet**, shortly making a rocky ford of the fall's unnamed stream.

One final, long, rocky, steep, switchbacking descent leads to the base of two-tiered, 1400-foot **Wapama Falls at about 2 miles and 3880 feet**, in season a raging monster of snowy foam and bright rainbows that leaves you drenched in seconds. Looking up Wapama Falls to see its full drop is nearly impossible because you're blinded by spray. It takes five footbridges to span the boulder-choked stream, Falls Creek, that forms Wapama Falls. The creek can be so high in early season that you can't get across the bridges. If it's safe, walk over the footbridges and back to take in the full spectacle.

Retrace your steps, enjoying different but equally wonderful views over Hetch Hetchy Reservoir on your return.

Lukens Lake

Marsh marigolds above May Lake

CHAPTER 8

Northern Sierra:
State Route 120,
the Best of Yosemite

Yosemite National Park's most famous scenery may lie in Yosemite Valley (Chapter 7), but its grandest scenery is along State Route 120, the Tioga Road. The road crosses the Sierra Crest, topping out at 9945-foot Tioga Pass. Granite peaks, glacier-carved lake basins, mine ruins, fabulous Valley views from one of Yosemite's famed granite domes: they're all here along the Tioga Road. Not all of these hikes are in Yosemite; some of the best are just east of the park's boundary in an area that *should* have been part of the park but which was held out to satisfy mining interests.

Mining is what first brought people to the Tioga Pass region. Because the region is a contact zone (see Trip 16), prospectors expected to find precious ores way up here. On these next hikes, you'll visit the ruins of some of these ventures. Alas,

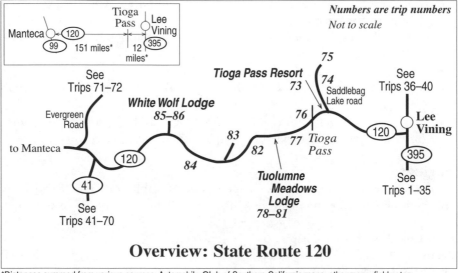

Overview: State Route 120

*Distances summed from various sources: Automobile Club of Southern California maps, other maps, field notes.

213

there are no precious ores along the Tioga Road. But you'll find riches aplenty in the satisfying hikes here, which are arranged east to west off the Tioga Road.

Recommended reading

Some of the sources recommended in previous chapters apply to this region, too, so to keep it short, I'll list those sources briefly and refer you back to the **Recommended reading** sections of those chapters.

▶ Krist, John, *50 Best Short Hikes in Yosemite and Sequoia/Kings Canyon.* Berkeley: Wilderness Press, 1993, revised 5th printing 2001. See Chapter 7.

▶ Schaffer, Jeffrey P. and Thomas Winnett, *Hiker's Guide to the High Sierra: Tuolumne Meadows: The Meadows and Surrounding Highlands of Yosemite National Park.* 4th ed. Berkeley, CA: Wilderness Press, 2002. Invaluable pocket hiking guide with detailed trail descriptions, plus information on geology, flora, and fauna.

▶ Schaffer, Jeffrey P., *Yosemite National Park: A Natural-History Guide to Yosemite and Its Trails.* 4th ed. Berkeley: Wilderness Press, 1999. See Chapter 7.

▶ Semb, George and Patricia, *Day Hikes on the Pacific Crest Trail.* 1st ed. Berkeley, CA: Wilderness Press, 2000. Hikes on the 2665-mile Pacific Crest Trail that you can do in a day, with accessible entry and exit points. The book covers all of the PCT in California.

▶ Smith, Genny, ed., *Mammoth Lakes Sierra: A handbook for roadside and trail.* 6th ed. Mammoth Lakes, CA: Genny Smith Books, 1993. See Chapter 6.

▶ White, Michael C., *Snowshoe Trails of Yosemite.* 1st ed. Berkeley, CA: Wilderness Press, 1999. For winter wanderings in the Yosemite area.

Recommended maps

▶ *Guide to Eastern Sierra.* Los Angeles: Automobile Club of Southern California. See Chapter 6.

▶ *Guide to Yosemite National Park.* Los Angeles: Automobile Club of Southern California. See Chapter 7.

▶ USDA/USFS *Inyo National Forest.* See Chapter 6.

▶ *Yosemite National Park and Vicinity, Calif.* Berkeley: Wilderness Press, 1999. See Chapter 7.

▶ *Yosemite National Park Recreation Map (2002)* and *Yosemite High Country Trail Map* (2002). Tom Harrison Maps. TomHarrisonmaps.com

Lodgings

Some of the lodgings listed in Chapter 6 are suitable for Tioga Road hikes. Alphabetically, the true mountain lodgings and lodgings of interest in the region are—

Lundy Lake Resort—See Chapter 6.

Silver Lake Resort—See Chapter 6.

Tioga Pass Resort—See Chapter 6.

Tuolumne Meadows Lodge—See Chapter 6.
Virginia Lakes Resort—See Chapter 6.

White Wolf Lodge
Yosemite Reservations, 5410 East Home Ave., Fresno, CA 93727   (209) 252-4848
7875 feet. Just off State Route 120 in Yosemite National Park west of Tioga Pass. *Mountain.* Sleeping cabins with bath, tent-cabins. Restaurant, camp store, stables. No pets. 2002 rates: cabin with bath $88/night, canvas tent-cabin $55/night.

Communities
Lee Vining—See Chapter 6.
June Lake—See Chapter 6.

Hikes
73. Bennettville Site and Lakes ☼ ❦

Place	Total distance	Elevation	Level	Type
Start	0	9520	—	—
Bennettville site *only*	1½	9800	E	O&B
Shell Lake *only*	2	9842	E	O&B
Fantail Lake	3⅓–3¾	9891	M	O&B

Permit required: None

Topo(s): WP Tuolumne Meadows 15′; Tioga Pass, Mount Dana 7½′

Where to stay:
   Mountain: Tuolumne Meadows Lodge, Lundy Lake Resort, Virginia Lakes Resort
   Of Interest: Silver Lake Resort, Tioga Pass Resort
   Other: Town of Lee Vining, Town of June Lake

Highlights: Near Tioga Pass, 19th-century mining town Bennettville's picturesque remains will have shutterbugs scrambling to record the mellow colors and striking terrain. Beyond, you follow a chain of pretty lakes into a magnificent cirque in Hall Research Natural Area between Yosemite and Hoover Wilderness. This magnificent area was left out of Yosemite National Park to placate commercial (in this case, mining) interests.

How to get to the trailhead: The driving directions for all trips off State Route 120 begin at Tioga Pass. Just 2.2 miles east of Tioga Pass and just past Tioga Pass Resort is a junction with a road going north to Saddlebag Lake. (You've overshot the turnoff if you get to Tioga Pass while westbound or Ellery Lake while eastbound.) Turn north here and almost immediately turn left into the parking area next to the entrance to Junction Campground, 2.3 miles from Tioga Pass. The trailhead is just inside the campground. Toilets in campground.

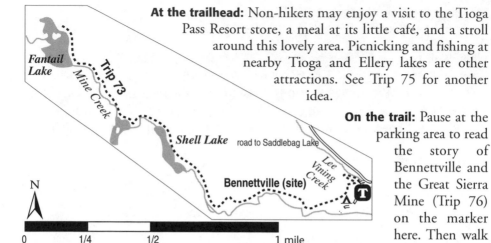

At the trailhead: Non-hikers may enjoy a visit to the Tioga Pass Resort store, a meal at its little café, and a stroll around this lovely area. Picnicking and fishing at nearby Tioga and Ellery lakes are other attractions. See Trip 75 for another idea.

On the trail: Pause at the parking area to read the story of Bennettville and the Great Sierra Mine (Trip 76) on the marker here. Then walk about 50 yards into Junction Campground, crossing Lee Vining Creek on a bridge and heading for an information sign on your right, near the streambank. The trail here is faint, but it's marked by a row of rocks. Sometimes there's a trailhead register; if it's there, sign in. Turn right onto the trail, briefly paralleling the creek to a **Y**-junction: right (ahead) on a use trail along the creek, left (northwest) to Bennettville. Go left, making a short, steep climb to traverse above the campground and enjoy a view of Mt. Dana's west face. You shortly climb again, this time moderately, before making a wide turn northwest above Mine Creek, then make a switchback turn as you descend to cross an unnamed tributary of Mine Creek.

Heading southwest now, you come out above Mine Creek's deep, rocky channel; where the creek makes a gooseneck and forms a handsome little waterfall. You trace the streambank, which is surprisingly flowery for such a rocky region, before skirting a small meadow, crossing a streamlet, and switchbacking up a little ridge overlooking Mine Creek. At a **Y**-junction, you can take either fork: they soon meet again. Curving around the base of a knob, you presently see a tailings heap on the slopes ahead and buildings upslope on your right. You make a short, steep climb to the buildings, which are the reconstructed remains of **Bennettville at ¾ mile and 9800 feet**. The two standing buildings are the barn/bunkhouse to the south and the assay office to the north, and their soft, weathered colors against the rust-colored rock and the deep blue sky are a photographer's delight. You can explore both, but watch out for soft floors and questionable stairways; look but don't damage or remove anything. Distinctive artifacts of the early days here are flat-sided, handwrought nails, a few rusty examples of which you may find strewn about.

From Bennettville the trail heads southwest past a sign concerning the wilderness and natural areas you'll enter if you continue. Now you curve up and over an outcrop to another **Y**-junction: tracks, neither seeming more than a use trail, diverge here, one descending to the banks of Mine Creek, the other staying higher on the outcrop. You'll find the higher trail to be easier going, but you can take

Bennettville

either; they converge and diverge several times. Just stay within sight of the creek and lakes. You reach the east side of lovely **Shell Lake at a little over 1 mile and 9842 feet**, where beautiful White Mountain rises to the west-northwest. As you trace Shell Lake's shore, the valley holding these little lakes begins to open before you, revealing views up the valley to majestic Mount Conness. The next lake, with a tiny grassy islet, is unnamed.

You enter Hall Research Natural Area at 1½ miles and touch the southeast shore of charming **Fantail Lake at 1⅔ miles and 9891 feet**, surely the prettiest lake in this chain, and in the prettiest setting: surrounded by a flower-spangled meadow, backgrounded by White Mountain and the Sierra Crest. At nearly 2 miles, a low, broad outcrop of light-colored rock on Fantail's northeast shore provides a wonderful picnic site from which you can see cascades from the crest glaciers and from higher Spuller Lake.

When you must, return the way you came.

74. Gardisky Lake ☼ ❦

Place	Total distance	Elevation	Level	Type
Start	0	9720	—	—
Gardisky Lake	2+	10,483	M	O&B

Permit required: None

Topo(s): WP Tuolumne Meadows 15'; Tioga Pass, Mount Dana 7½'; Rufus Graphics in cooperation with the Yosemite Association "Map & Guide to Tuolumne Meadows"

Where to stay:
   Mountain: Tuolumne Meadows Lodge, Lundy Lake Resort, Virginia Lakes Resort
   Of Interest: Silver Lake Resort, Tioga Pass Resort
   Other: Town of Lee Vining, Town of June Lake

Highlights: The short, steep climb to Gardisky Lake brings you to a gem of an alpine lake in a jewel of a meadow.

How to get to the trailhead: Just 2.2 miles east of Tioga Pass, turn north on the road to Saddlebag Lake as described in Trip 73's driving directions. Continue up the Saddlebag Lake road, which is largely unpaved and sometimes quite rough. At 3.4 miles you'll spot a small parking area on the left (west) side of the road; if you get to Saddlebag Lake, you've overshot this parking/trailhead area. The trailhead is on the right (east) side of the road.

At the trailhead: See Trip 75.

On the trail: You begin a deceptively moderate ascent northwest up a west-facing slope. The going soon becomes steeper, and you shortly cross a flower-lined creek (not on the book's map). As the trail becomes steeper yet, short switchbacks help tame the climb. The higher you rise, the better the views you enjoy over Lee Vining Creek to the Sierra Crest, including White Mountain and Mt. Conness. One last steep pull brings you to a bench with a flowery meadow flanked by white-bark pines. The grade eases to gentle, and soon you see the small ponds below Gardisky Lake. The trail fades out as you approach Gardisky. You get to the lake proper, as opposed to the ponds, by bearing slightly left to reach **Gardisky Lake at a little over 1 mile and 10,483 feet**. The lake's setting is treeless, but the broad meadow around the lake supports a wonderful flower garden. The ground is spongy with ground-squirrel burrows; bare, red-brown Tioga Peak towers over the lake's south shore; and the rusty rocks around the lakeshore are spattered with chartreuse and red lichens.

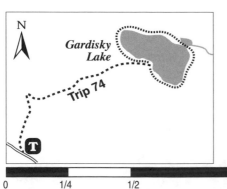

This trip ends here, but you may want to circle the lake. An angler's trail, faint in places, circles the lake, and you can follow it to the lake's east bay, which is cut off from the rest of the lake by a dense band of willows you'll have to bash your way around. Gardisky's outlet plunges down the steep cliffs that you stand atop here, and you can stare straight down the outlet to the Tioga Road, down Lee Vining Canyon, across Mono Basin to Mono Craters and the distant White Mountains—a spectacular view.

Retrace your steps to your car.

75. 20 Lakes Basin ☼ 🍁

Place	Total distance	Elevation	Level	Type
Start	0	10,080	—	—
Greenstone Lake *only*	2½	10,127	E	O&B
Steelhead Lake *only*	4⅔	10,270	M	O&B
Hummingbird Lake *only*	3¾+*	10,230	M	O&B
Single loop, ferry both ways	4½	10,360	M	Loop
Entire double loop, no ferry	7½	10,360	S	Loop

Permit required: None

Topo(s): WP Tuolumne Meadows 15'; Tioga Pass, Dunderberg Peak 7½'; Rufus Graphics in cooperation with the Yosemite Association "Map & Guide to Tuolumne Meadows"

Where to stay:
   Mountain: Tuolumne Meadows Lodge, Lundy Lake Resort, Virginia Lakes Resort
   Of Interest: Silver Lake Resort, Tioga Pass Resort
   Other: Town of Lee Vining, Town of June Lake

Highlights: Can you imagine a rugged, near-timberline basin set among majestic peaks and full of pretty lakes, yet so near a trailhead that you could visit nearly all those lakes on a dayhike? And what if, in spite of the rugged setting, the trail you'd follow stayed on gentle to moderate terrain? Does it sound too good to be true? Well, it *is* true—and this is it.

How to get to the trailhead: Just 2.2 miles east of Tioga Pass is the junction with the road to Saddlebag Lake as described in Trips 73 and 74. Follow the road to its end at 4.8 miles, where, on the edge of huge Saddlebag Lake, it suddenly turns into a parking lot. In season there's a summer ranger station just before the parking lot and on the left (northwest) side of the road; stop here to pick up information on 20 Lakes Basin. Café, store, and ferry service (fee) across Saddlebag Lake at adjacent Saddlebag Lake Resort. Toilets, water.

At the trailhead: At 10,080 feet, this is one of the highest trailheads in the Sierra. It's a wonderful trailhead for non-hikers: expansive alpine scenery, picnic spots, restrooms, water, and a resort with a store and cafe (but no lodgings). Non-hikers may also enjoy a scenic ferry ride (seasonal; fee) across the lake and back.

*Out-and-back on Saddlebag's *west*, not east, side.

Options: This trip is a double loop—a figure-8—one loop around Saddlebag Lake and the other within 20 Lakes Basin. Taking the ferry ride would change your hiking distances by eliminating one or more of these legs: west (left) side of Saddlebag Lake, 1¼ miles; east (right) side of Saddlebag Lake, a little less than 1¾ miles. Taking the ferry can therefore save you nearly 3 miles when compared to making a loop that includes both sides of Saddlebag Lake (short out-and-back from/to ferry not included). The best part of the hike is the loop within 20 Lakes Basin; you won't miss much by taking the ferry. To cover all the bases, however, I'll write up the trip *without* the ferry ride, from the *west* side of Saddlebag Lake—left side as you stand at the resort and look across the lake—near the summer ranger station's site, circling through 20 Lakes Basin from *west to east* (Greenstone Lake to Hummingbird Lake), and returning on the *east* side of Saddlebag Lake.

On the trail: You'll find the trailhead a few steps past the summer ranger station and south of the dam, where the trail begins as an old road (shown as a trail on the book's map)

that dips down below the face of the dam. Crossing on the dam isn't recommended. Climbing up on the other side, the road becomes a footpath north-northwest along SaddleSbag Lake's west side; occasional use trails doodle down to the water. The trail wanders over shattered rocks in rust, brown, gray, and cream colors, and through a surprising array of flowers. The splendid peaks around the head of 20 Lakes Basin come into view, with North Peak and Mt. Scowden particularly striking. The trail changes from rocky to dusty as you approach the lake's head, crossing a seasonal trickle, at a little over a mile, and fades out as you approach the stream that's the outlet of Greenstone Lake and an inlet of Saddlebag

Mimulus

Lake. Continue across the stream to pick up the trail coming from the ferry landing at Saddlebag's head. A spur trail (not on the map) curves a short distance around Greenstone's south shore. **Greenstone Lake at 1¼ miles and 10,120 feet** is very beautiful, and a stop here to rest on some of the greenish rocks for which it's named is sure to please.

Continuing, you meet a use trail coming up from the ferry landing and bear west on the main trail, entering Hoover Wilderness at just over 1⅓ miles. You skirt the east end of Greenstone Lake as you begin a gradual—to-moderate climb on this wide, dusty trail that was once a road to a now-defunct mine deep in the basin. You traverse above skinny, rock-rimmed Wasco Lake and an unnamed companion, crossing a divide: behind you, streams drain southeast through Saddlebag Lake and Lee Vining Creek; ahead, streams drain north into Mill Creek through Lundy Canyon. Now you descend a little, passing Wasco's head and the ponds on its outlet, to reach lovely **Steelhead Lake at a little over 2⅓ miles and 10,270 feet**. The stream from higher, unseen Cascade Lake spills noisily into Steelhead's southwest side. Picnic spots are few here but worth searching out. As the trail approaches Steelhead's north end, it swings east, descends a little, veers north past tarns and a pretty lakelet on the east, and crosses Steelhead's outlet to reach a signed trail junction at 2¾ miles: right (northeast) to Lake Helen and Lundy Canyon, left (north) to defunct Hess Mine.

Go right, climbing steeply but briefly up a knob north of the lakelet, on a trail that's well-beaten but not yet on the topo—probably a classic example of a trail's development from cross-country track to use trail to official trail. North of the lakelet now, you pass a seasonal tarn before descending through a flowery meadow past another charming lakelet. You reach islet-filled **Shamrock Lake at just over 3 miles and 10,250 feet**, perhaps the prettiest in the basin and another good lunch spot— try one of the little peninsulas on its shore. Back on the main trail, you climb up and over a talus slope on Shamrock's north side, then descend a little before climbing a knob east of Shamrock. Atop the knob, the trail may be indistinct—rows of rocks and ducks help—as it leads you to an overlook of beautiful Lake Helen, Lundy Canyon, and Great Basin peaks far to the east. The meadow south of Lake Helen is a gem, and on the east side of Lake Helen you can see your return trail.

Keep your eyes peeled here. The route to Lake Helen from this overlook curves right (northeast) and descends the knob's north face—look for more rows of rocks—rather than swinging left (east) onto the obvious slopes above Lake Helen. You descend short, rocky switchbacks to the knob's base, then continue down an obvious path past the lovely cascades and ponds southwest of Lake Helen. The stony trail bobs over a couple of rocky ridgelets—picnic perches here—to skirt the lake's northwest bay, touching down at last at **Lake Helen's outlet at 4 miles and 10,107 feet**. Ford the outlet to find a junction: left (northeast) to Lundy Canyon,* right (south) to Odell Lake and back to Saddlebag Lake. There are lovely views over Lundy Canyon and its waterfalls about five minutes down the lefthand fork. But your route for this hike lies on the righthand fork, which begins with a short, steep climb to circumvent a low cliff. You trace the east shore of Lake Helen on a rocky path before climbing moderately southeast up a rocky draw through which Odell Lake's outlet flows into Lake Helen. In season, there is a fine flower display along this little stream.

The climb tops out above handsome **Odell Lake at 4¾ miles and 10,267 feet**, and you stay above the lake as you climb gradually to high point just south of it: unmarked Lundy Pass at 10,320 feet, where there are fine views of the surrounding peaks. Now you begin your gradual descent to Saddlebag Lake, crossing the outlet of little **Hummingbird Lake at just over 5 miles and 10,230 feet**—veer left (east) up the tiny stream for a few steps to enjoy Hummingbird.

At nearly 5⅓ miles you leave Hoover Wilderness, and at almost 5¾ miles you reach a junction: right (west) on a spur that meets the main trail near Greenstone Lake; ahead (south) on a use trail to the ferry landing; and left (east) to begin traversing Saddlebag Lake's east side. For this trip, you turn left into forest cover and pass a cabin at 5⅔ miles—don't disturb the resident. On an old road above the lakeshore, you stroll through an open lodgepole forest, climbing a little on a gradual grade. The forest vanishes as you cross above the peninsula that juts south into the lake. Runoff on the steep slopes above the lake supports long, narrow, flowery meadows, and there are fine over-the-shoulder views back into 20 Lakes Basin.

Trees reappear as you near the south end of the lake, and signs warn you out of the meadow below the trail: WILDLIFE HABITAT AREA...CLOSED TO FOOT TRAFFIC. The old road curves around the meadow, rising slightly to a gate that separates trail from parking lot where, at nearly 7½ miles, you close your loop at the parking lot by the restrooms.

---

* It's possible to set up a shuttle trip between 20 Lakes Basin and Lundy Canyon (see Trip 37), but this trail, which connects them, is for the mist park knee-destroyingly, heart-stoppingly steep and loose, and may remain snow-covered all summer. It's a beautiful trip but so taxing that I can't recommend it.

76. Gaylor Lakes, Mine Ruins ☼ 🍁

Place	Total distance	Elevation	Level	Type
Start	0	9943	–	–
Middle Gaylor Lake *only*	2+	10,334	M U	O&B
Upper Gaylor Lake *only*	3⅓	10,510	M U	O&B
Great Sierra Mine ruins	4	10,760+	S U	O&B

Permit required: None

Topo(s): WP Tuolumne Meadows 15'; Tioga Pass 7½'; Rufus Graphics in cooperation with the Yosemite Association "Map & Guide to Tuolumne Meadows"

Where to stay:
   Mountain: Tuolumne Meadows Lodge, Lundy Lake Resort, Virginia Lakes Resort
   Of Interest: Silver Lake Resort, Tioga Pass Resort
   Other: Town of Lee Vining, Town of June Lake

Highlights: The steep initial climb leads to two lovely alpine lakes; the sight of Yosemite's Cathedral Range reflected in Middle Gaylor Lake on a peaceful morning is guaranteed to stop you in your tracks. Beyond Upper Gaylor Lake, the ruins of an old mine beckon, and views from the ruins are spectacular.

How to get to the trailhead: This trailhead is right at 9945-foot Tioga Pass on State Route 120 (Tioga Road). The parking lot is on the north side of the road immediately west of Yosemite National Park's entrance station and therefore just inside the park. Telephone.

At the trailhead: There is little for the non-hiker except for the spectacular scenery here. See Trips 73–75 for other ideas.

On the trail: Head steeply northwest up a multi-rutted trail through a mix of forest and meadow. A little beyond ⅓ mile you step across a seasonal trickle and traverse a sloping meadow. The rocky-dusty trail gradually inches north as it continues its steep climb, and at a little over ¾ mile you emerge on an open saddle at 10,540 feet with fabulous views: to the north, the gray rock of Gaylor Peak; to the east, Mts. Dana and Gibbs soar above blue ponds on the Dana Fork of the Tuolumne River in Dana Meadows; to the south and southeast, rounded Mammoth Peak and the jagged Kuna Crest claw at the sky. Just a few steps farther north, below the saddle, you spot big, blue middle Gaylor Lake—it seems as if you could take a running jump into it—and the Cathedral Range, with Cathedral Peak easily identifiable, to the south.

About 50 feet below the saddle on its north side, a use trail branches left and you bear right (north-northwest) to complete a steep, rocky, loose descent to the shore of **middle Gaylor Lake at a little over 1 mile and 10,334 feet.** At 1¼ miles you step across the stream linking middle and upper Gaylor lakes and reach a junction: left on a use trail around middle Gaylor Lake, right (north) to upper Gaylor Lake. You turn right to follow the linking stream gradually up a broad, flower-sprinkled

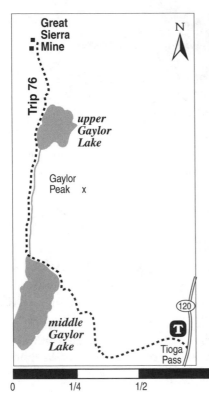

alpine meadow strewn with glacial erratics. Following this path and hopping over tributary streams in the meadow, you reach the shore of shimmering **upper Gaylor Lake at nearly 1⅔ miles and 10,510 feet**. The lake is flanked by narrow meadows and cupped in rocky knolls, graced by only a scattering of stunted trees. Graceful Gaylor Peak, with a permanent snowfield low on its north face, rises abruptly from the lake's south shore.

The stony trail continues along upper Gaylor Lake's west shore to an unmapped runoff stream from a permanent snowfield high in a steep draw north of the lake. Avoid a use trail that will tempt you to head up the draw on the draw's *west* (nearer) side but that soon peters out. Just over (east of) the runoff stream, you find an indistinct junction: right (north) up the draw to the ruins of the Great Sierra Mine, left on a use trail to continue circling the lake. While this hike turns right to the mine ruins, adventurous hikers may want to follow the use trail around to the low point on the northeast side of the lake, where they can work their way cross-country up a shallow draw and past a couple of seasonal tarns to an eye-popping overlook of Tioga and Ellery lakes, State Route 120, Tioga Peak on the Tioga Crest, Lee Vining Peak, and Mts. Dana and Gibbs.

Meanwhile, back on this hike's route, you turn north up the steep draw for ⅓ mile more of very steep climbing to a ruined stone building with yard-thick, unmortared walls and a still-standing chimney. This is one of several ruined structures left by the unsuccessful **Great Sierra Mine** (also called the Tioga Mine) **at 2 miles and 10,760 feet**, most of whose workers lived in Bennettville (unseen and far below; see Trip 73). There are more ruins scattered over the slopes above this first, most impressive ruin. Walk around to explore them all, but watch out for the vertical mineshafts. There may be no precious ores here, but it is an El Dorado of Sierra views: the view over upper Gaylor Lake, Gaylor Peak, and middle Gaylor Lake and of the Sierra peaks beyond is breathtaking.

When you must, tear yourself away from this wonderful scene and retrace your steps.

77. Summit and Spillway Lakes ☼ ❦

Place	Total distance	Elevation	Level	Type
Start	0	9689	—	—
Mono Pass, Summit Lake *only*	7	10,604	S	O&B
Spillway Lake *only*	7+	10,450	S	O&B
Entire trip	8½	10,640	S	O&B

Permit required: None

Topo(s): Tioga Pass, Mount Dana, Koip Peak 7½'

Where to stay:
    Mountain: Lundy Lake Resort, Tuolumne Meadows Lodge
    Of Interest: Silver Lake Resort, Tioga Pass Resort
    Other: Town of Lee Vining, Town of June Lake

Highlights: Walking along Parker Pass Creek between the peaks of the Sierra Crest and the Kuna Crest, you enjoy heart-filling mountain scenery on your way first to Mono Pass and Summit Lake and second up a flower-lined trail to lovely Spillway Lake. Abandoned cabins near Mono Pass make a worthwhile detour and a striking reminder of the hardships faced by Eastern Sierra miners in the late 1800s.

How to get to the trailhead: Just 1.5 miles west of Tioga Pass is a large turnout and parking area on the south side of the road, marked as the Mono Pass Trailhead. (You have overshot the trailhead if you get to Tioga Pass while eastbound or Tuolumne Meadows while westbound.) Toilet.

At the trailhead: See Trips 73–75.

On the trail: Pick up the trail from the parking lot and head south-southeast gradually downhill on an old road now closed to vehicles, soon leaving moderate-to-dense forest behind for a meadow in the shadows of Mts. Dana and Gibbs. Forest and meadow alternate as you approach the Dana Fork of the Tuolumne River. Just before the river, a footpath branches left and that's the track you take as you soon reach the river and cross two branches of it. You climb a low ridge, veering east, then descend to skirt another meadow before ascending the next ridge. A little beyond 1 mile as you are heading southeast, you have a beautiful view of Mt. Gibbs over the creek below to the southwest, Parker Pass Creek. A few more steps brings you to a ruined cabin left of the trail and then to a large clearing with a tremendous view south-southeast of the Kuna Crest. The trail begins a long, gradual climb, and a little beyond 1¾ miles fords a tributary of Parker Pass Creek just before reaching a junction: left (southeast) to Mono Pass, right (south) to Spillway Lake. If you must choose between these destinations, the visit to Mono Pass, Summit Lake (an uninteresting puddle), and the miners' cabins offers better views and a tangible slice of local history, while Spillway Lake is certainly the more beautiful spot.

Arbitrarily, go left to Mono Pass to find that the trail grows rockier as the climb turns to moderate to steep and the forest closes in. Patches of flowers brighten open

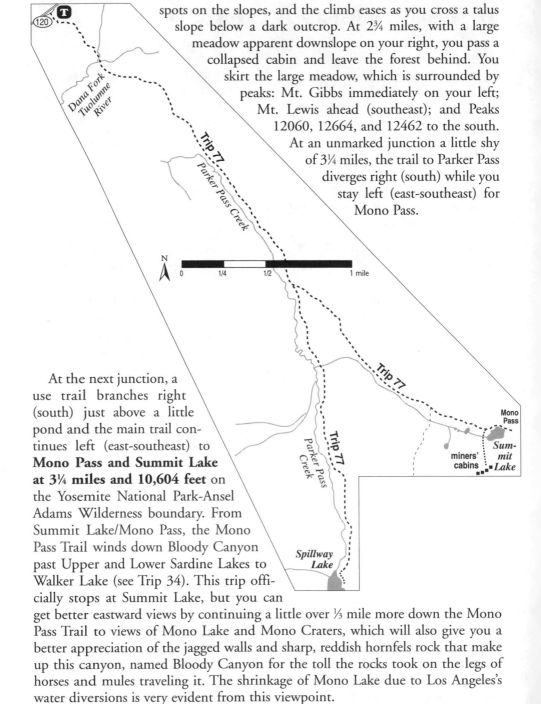

spots on the slopes, and the climb eases as you cross a talus slope below a dark outcrop. At 2¾ miles, with a large meadow apparent downslope on your right, you pass a collapsed cabin and leave the forest behind. You skirt the large meadow, which is surrounded by peaks: Mt. Gibbs immediately on your left; Mt. Lewis ahead (southeast); and Peaks 12060, 12664, and 12462 to the south. At an unmarked junction a little shy of 3¼ miles, the trail to Parker Pass diverges right (south) while you stay left (east-southeast) for Mono Pass.

At the next junction, a use trail branches right (south) just above a little pond and the main trail continues left (east-southeast) to **Mono Pass and Summit Lake at 3¼ miles and 10,604 feet** on the Yosemite National Park-Ansel Adams Wilderness boundary. From Summit Lake/Mono Pass, the Mono Pass Trail winds down Bloody Canyon past Upper and Lower Sardine Lakes to Walker Lake (see Trip 34). This trip officially stops at Summit Lake, but you can get better eastward views by continuing a little over ⅓ mile more down the Mono Pass Trail to views of Mono Lake and Mono Craters, which will also give you a better appreciation of the jagged walls and sharp, reddish hornfels rock that make up this canyon, named Bloody Canyon for the toll the rocks took on the legs of horses and mules traveling it. The shrinkage of Mono Lake due to Los Angeles's water diversions is very evident from this viewpoint.

Back at the junction west of Mono Pass, the one with the use trail just above a little pond, you take the use trail left (south) across the meadow and ascend a small

Parker Pass Creek

ridge to find a cluster of well-preserved but long-abandoned miners' cabins at 3½ miles and 10,640 feet, remains of the Ella Bloss Mine—one more Eastern Sierra non-bonanza, according to Genny Smith in *Mammoth Lakes Sierra*. Views of Mt. Gibbs from the cabins' doorways are thrilling sights for today's hikers who have cozy rooms to return to by car, but chilling reminders of how hard and lonely life must have been in this remote, barren, windswept landscape in the late 1870s and early 1880s.

Retrace your steps to the Mono Pass Trail from here and turn left, now with 3¾ miles on your boots, back to the junction with the trail to Spillway Lake at 4½ boot-miles. Turn left (south) to Spillway Lake and gradually ascend the long meadow Parker Pass Creek nourishes, occasionally fording seasonal tributaries. There are excellent views north to Gaylor Peak and the Sierra and Tioga crests, over-the-shoulder for now and straight ahead on your return. At 5½ miles the trail pulls alongside noisy cascades on Parker Pass Creek; there are superb over-the-shoulder views here. Soon, hemmed in by willows, the trail gets a bit steeper as it climbs toward a great open bowl below the three 12,000-foot peaks you noted earlier. You reach **Spillway Lake at nearly 6 miles and 10,450 feet**, splendidly set below the peaks and ringed with flower-spangled meadows. The trail soon peters out on the other side of a seasonal tributary, so find a rock, pull out your lunch, and soak in this wonderful scenery.

The scenery ahead to the north as you leave Spillway Lake almost makes up for having to retrace your steps to the trailhead, just over 3½ miles back for a total of 8½ wonderful miles for the whole trip.

78. Dog Lake and Dog Dome ☼ 🍁

Place	Total distance	Elevation	Level	Type
Start	0	8584	—	—
Dog Lake *only*	2½	9170	E	O&B
Entire semiloop*	3⅔	9300*	M	Semi

Permit required: None

Topo(s): WP Tuolumne Meadows 15′; Tioga Pass 7½′; Rufus Graphics in cooperation with the Yosemite Association "Map & Guide to Tuolumne Meadows"

Where to stay:
   Mountain: Lundy Lake Resort, Tuolumne Meadows Lodge, White Wolf Lodge
   Of Interest: Silver Lake Resort, Tioga Pass Resort
   Other: Town of Lee Vining, Town of June Lake

Highlights: From the east edge of exquisite Tuolumne Meadows, at the foot of awe-inspiring Lembert Dome, an easy trail leads to pretty Dog Lake and then to the back sides of Lembert Dome and its unnamed neighboring dome to the north, unofficially known as "Dog Dome." A scramble onto Dog Dome's summit offers panoramic views over Tuolumne Meadows; bouldering skills will be helpful.

How to get to the trailhead: Just 7 miles southwest of Tioga Pass is a turnoff signed for Lembert Dome and Soda Springs, just before the highway crosses the Tuolumne River. Turn northwest into a large parking area on the north side of the road. If the lot is full—it often is by midday—you may be able to find parking farther along the spur road. Toilets, picnic tables. A modest store, a snack shop, and a gas station, all seasonal, are a little farther west on the highway.

At the trailhead: In spite of the picnic tables, the busy, dusty parking lot is probably not interesting enough for non-hikers unless someone is trying to climb the face of Lembert Dome and the non-hikers enjoy watching that sport. Non-hikers will probably be happier a little farther west on the highway, at seasonal Tuolumne Meadows visitor center, where there are exhibits and a bookstore. The huge, lovely meadows are a short walk away from the visitor center, on the other side of the highway.

On the trail: From the toilets the spur road heads west-northwest while your trail heads north-northwest through spindly lodgepole, skirting the base of massive Lembert Dome. The trail is broad and sandy at first, then crosses granite slabs between parallel rows of rocks. A few steps beyond the slabs you reach a junction: right (east) to Lembert Dome—this is the trail on which you'll return, and it's not on the topo; left (northeast) to Dog Lake. You take the left fork, beginning a moderate climb and passing a spur trail on your left marked stable parkinG. You continue ahead (right) and in a few steps pass yet another spur (unmapped) to the stables on your left. Again you go ahead (right), under Lembert Dome's sheer west face and then below a low dome north of Lembert: this is Dog Dome.

* Not including the optional scramble to Dog Dome's 9400+-foot summit.

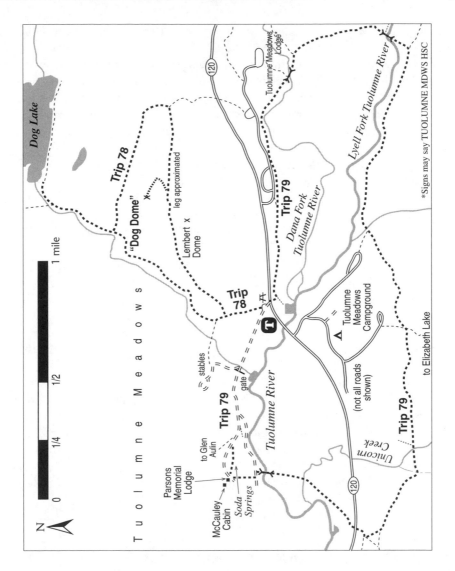

The trail becomes steeper as you ascend a forested draw to the bench on which Dog Lake sits, and Dog Lake's outlet stream splashes down the draw on your left. The grade eases around ¾ mile, just below the bench, and at nearly 1 mile you reach another junction: left (ahead, northeast) to Dog Lake, right (southeast) to Lembert Dome, Dog Lake parking, and Tuolumne Meadows Lodge. You go left to Dog Lake, leaving Lembert Dome behind. At 1 mile you reach a junction: left (north) to Young Lakes, right (northeast) to Dog Lake. You go right to gain your first view of big, blue **Dog Lake at just under 1¼ miles and 9170 feet**, where the trail curves right and down to the lakeshore. As lovely as the lake is, the sight of the Sierra Crest beyond the lake's east end is its most striking feature, and this is a great spot for a snack.

Reluctantly leaving Dog Lake, you retrace your steps to the next-to-last junction you passed on the way to Dog Lake, the one at nearly 1 mile. Pause to consider whether the ascent of Dog Dome's back (east) side and the subsequent steep descent between the domes, which may require a little bouldering, is for you. If not, retrace your steps to the Lembert Dome parking area from here. Otherwise, to continue, turn left to Lembert Dome, etc., with 1½ miles on your boots. You pass a seasonal pond tucked hard under Dog Dome's north face as you ascend gradually, presently swinging south to top out at nearly 2 miles on a forested ridge on the east side of both domes, which are all but invisible through the trees. From here the main trail begins descending and almost immediately passes a junction: right (west) on a trail not on the topo, to Lembert and Dog domes; ahead (left) to Dog Lake parking (your car is at Lembert Dome parking).

You turn right toward the domes and follow the track west nearly ½ mile to a saddle between Lembert and Dog domes at almost 3 miles. Lembert Dome's summit, massive and steep, is on your left; Dog Dome's flatter, easier summit is on your right. From here, it's a short cross-country stroll onto **Dog Dome's summit at 9400+ feet** following the route of your choice (mileage not included in distances given herein). From the summit you enjoy breathtaking views over Tuolumne Meadows to the west; into Yosemite's backcountry to the north; of the Sierra Crest to the east; and of the Cathedral Range to the south, with only Lembert Dome in the way.

Back on the saddle between the domes, you continue west and shortly begin a very steep descent on a beaten track between the domes, along which a low rock ledge may call for a little boulder-scrambling—nothing serious. This track is a return trail for those who have climbed the difficult Class-5 routes on the faces of Lembert and Dog domes. You cross an unmapped seasonal stream draining the area between the domes on your way down. At the bottom you close the loop part of this trip at 3½ miles at the junction just beyond the granite slabs. Turn left and retrace your steps to the parking lot to end this trip at 3⅔ miles.

79. Tuolumne Meadows Loop 🌿 ☼ 🍁

Place	Total distance	Elevation	Level	Type
Start	0	8584	—	—
Entire loop	4⅔	8740	M	Loop

Permit required: None

Topo(s): WP Tuolumne Meadows 15'; Tioga Pass, Vogelsang Peak 7½'; Rufus Graphics in cooperation with the Yosemite Association "Map & Guide to Tuolumne Meadows"

Where to stay:
   Mountain: Lundy Lake Resort, Tuolumne Meadows Lodge, White Wolf Lodge
   Of Interest: Silver Lake Resort, Tioga Pass Resort
   Other: Town of Lee Vining, Town of June Lake

Highlights: Maybe steep climbs to alpine lakes or airy scrambles onto granite domes just aren't your thing. But nearly everyone will find strolling through beautiful Tuolumne Meadows and along the tumbling, infant Tuolumne River to be richly rewarding.

How to get to the trailhead: Follow the driving directions of Trip 78.

At the trailhead: See Trip 78.

On the trail: See Trip 78's map. From the Lembert Dome parking lot, take the dusty spur road west-northwest, avoiding the turnoff right to the stables. Beyond the gate across the spur road at ⅕ mile, continue out into Tuolumne Meadows' east edge, where Lembert Dome is back on your right (northeast) and Unicorn and Cathedral peaks are to the southwest—not to mention the wonderful array of granite domes surrounding you. The road curves west with you on it, and interpretive signs along the way help you understand the area's history and ecology. There are lots of official and unofficial trails in this very popular area—maddening, but what can you do? In general, you're going to stroll west through Tuolumne Meadows on the north side of Highway 120; then curve south to cross the Tuolumne River and the highway; then work your way generally east through the meadow's forested edge on the south side of the highway, toward the Tuolumne River; and then northwest back to Lembert Dome. Pause to familiarize yourself with the local landmarks before setting out, and that will help you stay on course.

At a Y-junction at ½ mile, take the marked right fork (west-southwest) slightly uphill toward Parsons Lodge and go right again at the next junction. Continuing, go left at the signed junction with the trail to Glen Aulin and left at the next junction to pass some natural soda springs bubbling up through rust-colored earth, as well as a tumbledown cabin. Meeting an old road at nearly ⅔ mile, you turn left and continue toward the lodge, which once belonged to the Sierra Club and now is rarely open for Park functions. Pause to admire the lodge's stonework and the logwork of adjacent McCauley Cabin, but don't disturb either building unless they're open for visitors. There's a restroom near McCauley Cabin. From the front of Parsons Lodge, a marked trail (VISITOR CENTER) heads southeast toward the sparkling Tuolumne River. Take the trail downhill to meet another old road; turn left and follow it as it curves toward Lembert Dome to shortly meet a trail that goes right to cross the river on a footbridge as it heads for the visitor center. (Routes around the Parsons Lodge area are approximated on the book's map. If you find the tangle of roads, trails, and use trails in this area confusing, it's not a problem: from the junction with the trail to Glen Aulin, you can plainly see the lodge and the footbridge over the river. Head for the lodge and then for the footbridge on whichever route pleases you.)

Go right, cross the river, and follow this trail through the vast meadow. Heading toward the highway, you cross two streamlets that pass under the trail through culverts (the streamlets appear as one stream on the map) and then cross the highway at a little over 1 mile to pick up the trail on the other side of the asphalt. Here, the trail bears right (west) signed for Tuolumne Meadows Lodge—the signs actually say H S C, for "High Sierra Camp," instead of "Lodge"—seemingly in the wrong direction because, as you know, that lodge is farther east, toward Tioga Pass. However, you're just circumventing a little obstacle, and at almost 1¼ miles you reach a junction where you take the left fork southeast toward Tuolumne Meadows Campground and Elizabeth Lake. It's not long before you reach a junction where you take the left fork ahead (southeast) toward the campground. On this leg, south of the highway, the sandy-dusty trail rolls up and down through moderate-to-sparse lodgepole with a flower-speckled understory. At 1½ miles you dip across Unicorn Creek on a footbridge and reach a junction: left to the campground, right (ahead, east) for Elizabeth Lake. Go right (ahead), presently cross a pair of big runoff channels, and ramble along until, just past a third runoff channel, you step across the trail from Tuolumne Meadows Campground to Elizabeth Lake. Your trail continues ahead to a junction at a little over 2½ miles: left (northwest) to the campground, ahead (east) to Tuolumne Meadows Lodge.

Go ahead, toward the lodge, to cross a creek, enter Yosemite Wilderness, and cross yet another (unmapped) creek. Once in a while you glimpse the Lyell Fork Tuolumne River with its inviting slabs, pools, and low cascades as you continue east, roughly paralleling the river. Use trails lead to the river's charming banks, and you may want trot down there for a snack and a splash, if the water level and current permit. At a junction near 3¼ miles, it's left (northeast) over the river to Tuolumne Meadows Lodge, right (southeast) to Donohue Pass on the John Muir Trail. Go left and cross the river on a pair of footbridges—shown as a single bridge on the book's map. On the other side, curve left on the well-worn, sandy trail where a use trail leads right, farther along the riverbank. At the next junction, at a little over 3⅔ miles, beside the Dana Fork Tuolumne River, go left to parallel the smaller, prettily-forested Dana Fork on its south bank for a few yards. Turn right

Lyell Fork of the Tuolumne River

to cross the fork on a footbridge to another junction, where you turn left (west) to continue paralleling the Dana Fork on its north bank, rather than going to Tuolumne Meadows Lodge. You pass a couple of use trails back to the lodge and then a couple of spur trails to the Dog Lake parking area at nearly 4 miles. Paralleling a service road, you continue west past employee residences, the Tuolumne Meadows Ranger Station, and a parking area for people getting wilderness permits. Ignore any use trails branching left along this stretch.

The trail widens and the forest retreats as you begin to parallel the highway, and you can tell that Tuolumne Meadows is opening up ahead of you, to the west. At a fork at 4½ miles, you go right to cross the highway toward prominent Lembert Dome and reach the Lembert Dome parking lot at 4⅔ miles to close the loop.

80. Elizabeth Lake ☼ 🍁

Place	Total distance	Elevation	Level	Type
Start	0	8680	—	—
Elizabeth Lake	4	9487	M	O&B

Permit required: None

Topo(s): WP Tuolumne Meadows 15'; Vogelsang Peak 7½'; Rufus Graphics in cooperation with the Yosemite Association "Map & Guide to Tuolumne Meadows"

Where to stay:
   Mountain: Lundy Lake Resort, Tuolumne Meadows Lodge, White Wolf Lodge
   Of Interest: Silver Lake Resort, Tioga Pass Resort

   Other: Town of Lee Vining, Town of June Lake

Highlights: Elizabeth Lake's alpine setting under rugged granite peaks is a wonderful sight any time but gains added charm late in the year from dashes of fall color.

How to get to the trailhead: Just 7.2 miles southwest of Tioga Pass is the entrance to Tuolumne Meadows Campground. Turn south into the campground, stop at the entrance station to get permission to go to the Elizabeth Lake Trailhead, and then follow road signs toward the group-campground loop. The trailhead is off the spur road to the group-campground loop, the second paved turnoff left from the main campground road. Follow the spur to a gate just before the signed Horse Camp; the trailhead is here, another 0.4 mile from the highway. Park in the adjacent lot. There are toilets and water in the campground when it's open. If the campground is closed, park outside it near the entrance and walk through the campground.

At the trailhead: See Trip 78.

On the trail: Head generally south through moderate-to-dense lodgepole forest, climbing moderately up a moraine on a rocky-dusty trail, and soon reaching a junction: left (northeast) to Vogelsang High Sierra Camp, right (west) to

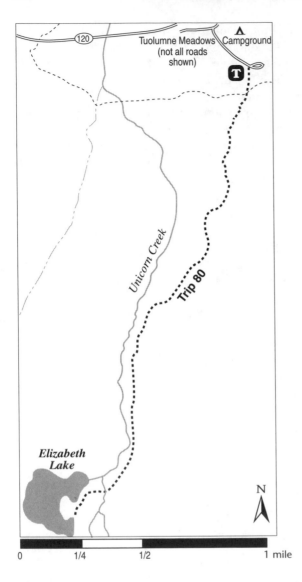

Cathedral Lake, and ahead (south) to Elizabeth Lake. Go ahead, continuing uphill. As the forest thins near ⅔ mile, you have over-the-shoulder glimpses of handsome peaks to the north and northwest. At a little over 1 mile you cross an unmapped seasonal trickle as you approach a bench on the moraine and swing a little southwest toward Unicorn Creek. You ford a seasonal tributary of the creek and notice the bare slopes of The Unicorn peeping through the thinning forest. Ahead you glimpse the lake but are obliged to keep your eyes on the trail, which is studded with rocks and criss-crossed by thick roots.

At an unmapped junction at a little over 1¾ miles, the right fork is a use trail branching toward the north end of the lake, while the official trail continues left along the lake's east side. At the next fork, also unmapped, you take the official trail, the right fork, toward the lake, crossing a tributary of Unicorn Creek (the left fork is another use trail). You shortly find yourself at pretty **Elizabeth Lake at 2 miles and 9487 feet**, in a dramatic cirque bounded by cliffs and by Unicorn Peak to the west and south and by Johnson Peak to the east. Use trails dart off to the lakeshore, so follow one to a welcoming log or rock and settle in to enjoy your lunch and the scenery.

Return the way you came.

81. Cathedral Lakes ☼ 🍁

Place	Total distance	Elevation	Level	Type
Start	0	8570	–	–
Lower Cathedral Lake *only*	6⅔	9288	S U	O&B
Upper Cathedral Lake *only*	7	9570	S	O&B

Permit required: None

Topo(s): WP Tuolumne Meadows 15'; Tenaya Lake 7½'; Rufus Graphics in cooperation with the Yosemite Association "Map & Guide to Tuolumne Meadows"

Where to stay:
   Mountain: Lundy Lake Resort, Tuolumne Meadows Lodge, White Wolf Lodge
   Of Interest: Silver Lake Resort, Tioga Pass Resort
   Other: Town of Lee Vining, Town of June Lake

Highlights: Lower Cathedral Lake, with its broad, stream-threaded meadow, is a joy to discover. Upper Cathedral Lake is a gem set among sculpted peaks, Sturdy hikers will have no trouble visiting both. They're especially lovely when their shared showpiece is on display: delicate Cathedral Peak reflected in the lakes' still surfaces.

How to get to the trailhead: Just 8.3 miles southwest of Tioga Pass on State Route 120, and just west of the turnoff to Tuolumne Meadows visitor center, is a small parking area on the south side of the highway, marked for Cathedral Lakes. (You have overshot the parking area if you get to the turnoff to the visitor center while eastbound or the west end of the huge meadow while westbound.) Toilets, water at nearby visitor center.

At the trailhead: See Trip 78.

On the trail: The rocky-sandy trail leads generally southwest away from the highway, almost immediately reaching a junction: ahead (southwest) on the John Muir Trail to Cathedral Lakes, Sunrise High Sierra Camp, and Yosemite Valley; right (west) to May Lake and Tenaya Lake; left (east) to Tuolumne Meadows Lodge. You continue ahead, climbing gradually to moderately through a mixed conifer forest. The trail's grade soon eases to the point where it feels almost level. Nearing 1 mile, the forest thins to reveal Cathedral Peak's outliers ahead and left and massive Medlicott Dome, barely glimpsed through the trees, ahead and right. The trail curves south through a meadowy area at a little over 1¼ miles, where the west face of an outlier of Cathedral Peak looms over you. You wind through some rocks, cross another meadow, and, coming abreast of a spring, begin a more-noticeable ascent. Up you go, topping out at a little over 2 miles and 9560 feet on a broad, sandy, lightly-forested saddle below Cathedral Peak. Medlicott and Mariuolumne domes are on your right, Echo Peaks ahead, and Cathedral Peak on your left. Leaving the saddle, you twine gradually down through forest to a **Y**-junction at 2¾ miles: left on the John Muir Trail to Sunrise High Sierra Camp and Yosemite Valley, right to lower Cathedral Lake.

To lower Cathedral Lake: You go right, curving downhill, swinging through a meadowy area and across a creek, and then descending steeply on a rocky track booby-trapped with tree roots. You level out on the east edge of the meadow that surrounds lower Cathedral Lake on two sides. Multiple tracks make ruts across the meadow between the granite slabs that dot it. You ford the streams threading the meadow several times, finally reaching the granite slabs that ring **lower Cathedral Lake at nearly 3⅓ miles and 9288 feet**. Talk about acres of glacial polish! This is a great place to enjoy your lunch. Optionally, you may want to pick your way around the north side of the lake to an overlook of Tenaya Lake, toward which lower Cathedral Lake's outlet flows down a very steep channel past Pywiack Dome.

To upper Cathedral Lake: From the junction with the trail to upper Cathedral Lake and Sunrise High Camp, go generally southeast (left if you've just come up the trail to this junction, right if you're coming from lower Cathedral Lake). You climb gradually on the sandy trail below the chiseled spire of Cathedral Peak, now through moderate forest, now in the open, before descending slightly toward a tarn east of upper Cathedral Lake. Just before the tarn, a use trail darts right over granite slabs to the lake proper, which sits in a beautiful, open, gently sloping bowl bounded by Cathedral, Tressider, and Echo peaks. Find a spot on the sides of the bowl where you can relax and enjoy your lunch in this wonderful setting. Retrace your steps when you must.

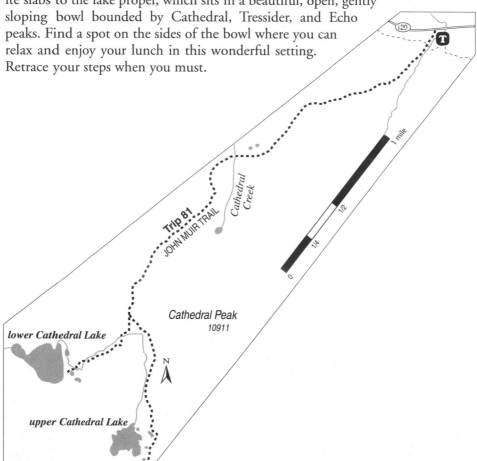

82. Lower Sunrise Lake ☼ 🍁

Place

Place	Total distance	Elevation	Level	Type
Start	0	8170	—	—
Lower Sunrise Lake	6½	9166	S	O&B

Permit required: None

Topo(s): WP Tuolumne Meadows 15'; Tenaya Lake 7½'; Rufus Graphics in cooperation with the Yosemite Association, "Map & Guide to Tuolumne Meadows"

Where to stay:
    Mountain: Tuolumne Meadows Lodge, White Wolf Lodge
    Of Interest: Tioga Pass Resort
    Other: None

Highlights: Views from the trail that climbs Sunrise Mountain help make up for the steep ascent, and pretty lower Sunrise Lake, the hike's destination, is a splendid place for your hard-earned picnic.

How to get to the trailhead: Just 15.8 miles west of Tioga Pass is a marked trailhead on the south (Tenaya Lake) side of the road at a turnout with a little parking. (You have overshot the trailhead if you get to Tenaya Lake while eastbound or Olmstead Point while westbound.) Toilet.

At the trailhead: This is a great area for non-hikers. Picnic tables dot the shore of lovely Tenaya Lake, the scenery around it is superb, and at its east end (this trailhead is at its west end) there is a fine beach.

On the trail: As you face the toilet, the trailhead is just to your left at a closed, gated road. Walk about 150 feet down the road to a marked trail on your right, turn right briefly to the edge of a flowery meadow, and find a trail junction:

right (southwest) to May Lake, left (east) to Sunrise Lakes. Go left, soon crossing Tenaya Lake's outlet and curving right (south) at a sign. You enter a lodgepole forest and reach a junction at ⅓ mile: left (east-northeast) to Tuolumne Meadows Lodge, right (south-southwest) to Sunrise High Sierra Camp.

Go right on the sandy trail, paralleling the outlet for about ⅓ mile before veering left into an area of slabs. Around ½ mile you begin a gradual-to-moderate, rocky climb that brings you out to a viewpoint of Sunrise Mountain, Clouds Rest, and granite domes. You descend again, crossing a boulder-strewn wash, top another low rise, and then cross the multi-stranded outlet of Mildred Lake at nearly 1¼ miles. Beyond this ford, you begin a moderate-to-steep ascent in forest, fording several more streams (not all on the book's map) before beginning the steepest part of the hike, a hot slog up Sunrise Mountain's slabby sides, through a sparse forest. The tough climb has its rewards: increasingly expansive views west and north, including landmarks like Tuolumne Peak and Mt. Hoffman. The going gets steeper, and eventually mountain hemlocks close in, restricting views but offering welcome shade. In places, the trail is "cobbled" with laid stones.

After nearly 2½ miles, you finally puff up to a junction on a saddle at 9270 feet in a mixed, dry forest: left (east-northeast) to Sunrise Lakes, right (south) to Yosemite Valley. A use trail near this junction leads southwest about 300 feet to a spectacular view of Clouds Rest, Half Dome, Mt. Watkins, and Glacier Point. From the main trail junction, you go left to Sunrise Lakes, contour along a slope, climb over a small saddle, and descend steeply to **lower Sunrise Lake at 3¼ miles and 9166 feet**. People throng to this pretty lake, which is set off by a beautifully exfoliating granite shoulder to the east. Your rest here is well-earned!

Retrace your steps to the trailhead.

83. May Lake ☼ ❦

Place	Total distance	Elevation	Level	Type
Start	0	8846	—	—
May Lake	2+	9329	E	O&B

Permit required: None

Topo(s): WP Tuolumne Meadows 15'; Tenaya Lake 7½'; Rufus Graphics in cooperation with the Yosemite Association "Map & Guide to Tuolumne Meadows"

Where to stay:
　　Mountain: Tuolumne Meadows Lodge, White Wolf Lodge
　　Of Interest: Tioga Pass Resort
　　Other: None

Highlights: A rather easy trail offers excellent views as it leads to a lovely lake, and next to the lake, a little granite dome offers the best views on the whole hike.

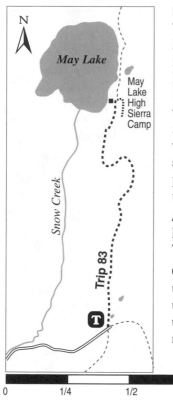

N

May Lake

May
Lake
High
Sierra
Camp

Snow Creek

Trip 83

T

0   1/4   1/2   1 mile

How to get to the trailhead: Just 19.5 miles west of Tioga Pass on State Route 120 is the turnoff to the May Lake trailhead. (You have overshot this turnoff if you get to Olmstead Point while eastbound or Porcupine Flat while westbound.) Turn right (north), through a small parking area, and drive 1.8 winding, sometimes steep miles up this one-lane road to a large parking area by a tarn. (In late season, when May Lake High Sierra Camp is closed, this spur road may also be closed and gated. In that case, park in the small lot where you turned off and hike up the road.)

At the trailhead: Non-hikers will prefer to be at their lodgings or at Tuolumne Meadows visitor center; see Trip 78.

On the trail: There are three trails leading away from this parking area: to the southeast, a trail leads back to Tenaya Lake and Sunrise High Sierra Camp; from the south end of the tarn, the May Lake Trail leads north to—you guessed it; and a third trail is a continuation of the road. You take the wide, sandy path that follows the west shore of the tarn through a mixed conifer forest. There's a view of Mt. Hoffman to the northwest. You presently climb a little through granite outcrops. After a bit, the grade eases as you traverse granite slabs, where the route is shown by the lines of rocks bordering it. As you ascend through boulders, spectacular views open up to the east, and you can plainly see the cascading outlet of lower Cathedral Lake (Trip 82) splashing between Pywiack Dome and Tenaya Peak on its way down to Tenaya Lake. Look for the Cathedral Range to the east, Mt. Lyell far away to the southeast, Half Dome and Liberty Cap to the south.

You switchback up the east side of a small dome, with the views getting better and better, till you curve around the dome's west side to a tiny saddle from which you see the white tents of May Lake High Sierra Camp a little below, by the lakeside. At a junction near a pit toilet, the right fork leads into the camp, while the left leads directly to the lake. Going left to the lakeshore, you find that some areas are roped off to permit them to restore themselves. You reach the shore of lovely **May Lake at a little over 1 mile and 9329 feet.** On the other side of the lake, the white cliffs of Mt. Hoffman soar into a deep blue sky. When the camp is in operation, noise from it may be distracting. A scramble up the low dome just east of the camp, perhaps requiring a little friction walking and maybe a handhold or two, is more a must than an option. The views from its top include not only those listed above but the Tioga Crest to the northeast, Tenaya Lake, many granite domes, and the Kuna Crest.

It's hard to leave, but when you must, retrace your steps.

May Lake

84. North Dome ☼ 🍁

Place	Total distance	Elevation	Level	Type
Start	0	8140	—	—
North Dome's summit	8*	7542	S U	O&B

Permit required: None

Topo(s): Yosemite Falls 7½'

Where to stay:
Mountain: Tuolumne Meadows Lodge, White Wolf Lodge
Of Interest: Tioga Pass Resort
Other: None

Highlights: North Dome, whose south face is alarmingly steep when seen from Glacier Point and Yosemite Valley, has an easy, broad, walk-up north slope that even the mildly acrophobic (like me) can ascend. At the dome's summit, views over Yosemite Valley are truly breathtaking. An optional out-and-back to Indian Rock gives you a close-up look at a natural arch, a feature that's extremely rare in the Sierra.

* Not including optional out-and-back to Indian Rock.

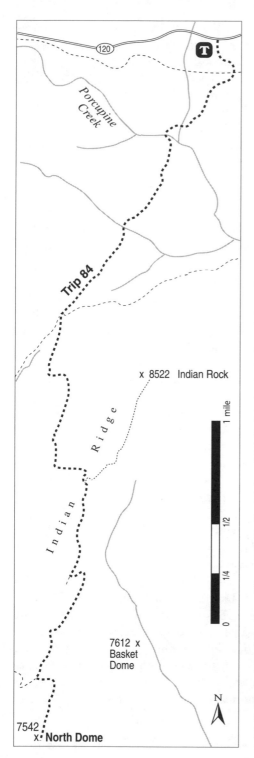

How to get to the trailhead: Just 22.1 miles west of Tioga Pass are a large turnout and parking area on the south side of the road, an area that's often filled by midday. The turnout is marked for the Porcupine Creek Trail. (You have overshot the trailhead if you get to Olmstead Point while eastbound or Yosemite Creek while westbound.)

At the trailhead: There is nothing here for non-hikers, who will probably prefer to be back at their lodgings.

On the trail: From the marked trailhead, go south through moderate to dense forest dominated by red fir. You descend rather steeply at first, soon meeting a paved road. Temporarily pick up the road to continue your descent, as advised by a rusty old sign, and follow it until it becomes blocked by fallen trees; then, take an obvious footpath to avoid the deadfalls, unless they've been cleared. Near ½ mile you ford a flower-lined stream, a tributary of Porcupine Creek, leaving the road behind once and for all. You shortly cross Porcupine Creek, then climb a little as you leave the creek behind. In season, there is a remarkable display of flowers scattered through this forest. You resume your descent a little past ⅔ mile, ford another creek at almost 1 mile, and presently traverse a small, grassy meadow fed by a little seep.

After a level stretch, you climb to a saddle where you find a junction at just over 1⅓ miles: left (northeast) to Yosemite Valley, right (southwest) for North Dome, Yosemite Falls, and (by another route) Yosemite Valley. Having gone right for North Dome, you find another junction almost immediately: left (southeast) for North Dome, etc., right (south-southwest) to Yosemite Falls and Yosemite Valley. Go left, soon curving south-southwest and climbing moderately through thinning forest. Near 1⅓ miles you emerge behind a ridge-nose. About 60 feet out onto this ridge-nose, you'll find a nice view over Yosemite Valley—invisible—to Sentinel Dome off the Glacier Point Road. Back on the main trail, you climb back into forest; openings in the canopy on the downhill side afford glimpses of the glacially-sculpted ridge across the canyons of Lehamite and Indian Canyon creeks.

At a little over 2 miles you ford an unnamed, unmapped stream just below a narrow, flower-filled meadow and then begin ascending a switchback moderately to steeply through an open-to-moderate forest. Near the top of this climb you meet a spur trail to Indian Rock: left to Indian Rock, right to North Dome.* The optional side trip is a steep scramble up a beaten track on a sparsely-timbered, sandy slope to Yosemite National Park's one and only natural arch, 8522-foot Indian Rock; it's an out-and-back detour of ⅔ miles and 402 feet, not included in the figures at the beginning of this write-up.

On the main trail, you continue toward North Dome and make an undulating traverse of the ridgeline of open, hot, sandy Indian Ridge. As the trail descends gradually toward the end of Indian Ridge, you reach a faint trail junction where you enjoy good views of Half Dome and Mt. Watkins, views that are even better if you walk a little farther out onto the ridge-nose following a spur trail, the right fork at the faint junction. North Dome is visible from here, below and to your left. The severely acrophobic may prefer to enjoy the view here and then retrace their steps. Continuing on the main trail—the left fork at the faint junction—you descend the east side of Indian Ridge very steeply at first. The grade eases as you re-enter forest and the trail crosses over Indian Ridge, growing faint (ducks may help). After a rocky, open descent, you reach a trail junction at 3⅓ miles: right to Yosemite Falls and Yosemite Valley; left to North Dome. Use trails lead to viewpoints, but you do your best to keep to the main route, heading for North Dome. You make an airy descent of the east side of the ridge, a descent that grows steep, rocky, and exposed.

You spot the forested saddle just below and north of North Dome, but before you can get there, you have to negotiate perhaps the worst few feet of this trail— no trail, just a steep friction walk across a section of granite slab. You reach the saddle at last and shortly find yourself on the sandy path that climbs moderately up the north side of North Dome. On **North Dome's top at 4 miles and 7542 feet**, you discover that the best views are a little beyond the summit, where there are some big potholes into which you can wedge yourself for a feeling of greater security. You have a hawk's-eye view of the floor of Yosemite Valley, some thirty-five hundred feet below your perch. Around the Valley you see Sentinel Dome, Glacier Point, Illilouette Fall, Half Dome, Mt. Broderick and Liberty Cap, and Clouds Rest. Half Dome seems so near you could reach out and touch it.

Enjoy—and then retrace your steps.

---

* High point with out-and-back to Indian Rock is 8140 feet at the junction with the spur trail to Indian Rock.

85. Lukens Lake 🌿 ☼ 🍁

Place	Total distance	Elevation	Level	Type
Start	0	7875	—	—
Lukens Lake	4–4⅔	8230	M	O&B

Permit required: None

Topo(s): WP Hetch Hetchy 15'; Tamarack Flat, Yosemite Falls 7½'

Where to stay:
   Mountain: Tuolumne Meadows Lodge, White Wolf Lodge
   Of Interest: None
   Other: None

Highlights: A pleasant forest stroll leads to quiet Lukens Lake where, pretty as the lake is, the big attraction is the magnificent, blooming meadow at its east end.

How to get to the trailhead: Just 32.3 miles west of Tioga Pass is the marked turnoff to White Wolf Lodge, on the north side of the road. You have overshot the turnoff if you get to Porcupine Flat while eastbound or Crane Flat while westbound. Follow the spur road to White Wolf 1.1 more miles to parking at White Wolf Lodge, just before the entrance to White Wolf Campground, for a total of 33.4 miles.* Toilets, water, store, lodging.

At the trailhead: Non-hikers will prefer to be at their lodgings.

On the trail: Head generally east from the marked trailhead on the east side of the parking lot, briefly skirting the campground and avoiding the

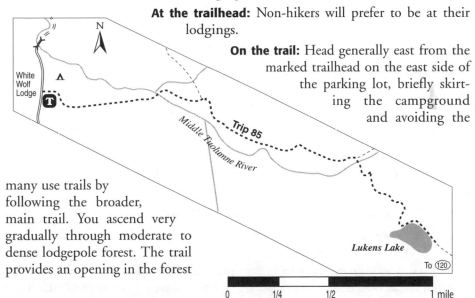

many use trails by following the broader, main trail. You ascend very gradually through moderate to dense lodgepole forest. The trail provides an opening in the forest

*There's a trailhead to Lukens Lake that's right on Highway 120, 2 miles east of the turnoff to White Wolf. To get to Highway 120 from the southeast end of the meadow east of the lake, you may have to brush your way through plants growing more than shoulder-high. You ascend through dense forest and, at a little under ¼ mile from the meadow, reach a saddle at 8340 feet. From there you begin descending, curving south, crossing and recrossing an unmapped seasonal trickle. You reach the highway at ⅔ mile from the meadow and at 8180 feet. Parking is in a turnout on the other side of the highway.

and is lined with flowers taking advantage of that little extra bit of sunshine. Boulders add variety to your route. At ½ mile you descend slightly and ford the Middle Tuolumne River—just a creek here. Resuming your gradual ascent, you soon traverse a series of meadows and at ⅔ mile reach a junction: sharp left (northwest) to Harden Lake, right (ahead, east) to Lukens Lake. The trail can be boggy and buggy here, but go ahead, pressing on to meet the Middle Tuolumne River again and parallel it for a while. The trail grade increases to moderate, and you leave the meadows behind.

Veering away from the river, the trail levels out and enters another meadowy, mucky section interrupted by a sandy rise that you bob over. You reach a junction at nearly 1½ miles: left (northeast) to Ten Lakes, right (southeast) to Lukens Lake. You go right to ford the Middle Fork again—may be dry by late season—and beyond it find that the trail abruptly becomes moderate to steep as well as rocky as it climbs into a mixed red fir/lodgepole forest. Soon you skirt a pretty hillside meadow above whose head you see a rocky, forested rim. In a few more minutes you top that rim to reach little **Lukens Lake at 2 miles and 8230 feet**. The peaceful lake is ringed by trees except for the meadow at its east end. What a meadow that is in season—flowers, flowers, flowers! Don't resist the temptation to follow the trail around the north side of the lake to walk through this wonderfully varied, natural garden, 2⅓ miles to the far end of the meadow. However, the better picnic spots are along the lake's north side.

Retrace your steps from here.

86. Harden Lake 🌸 ☼

Place	Total distance	Elevation	Level	Type
Start	0	7875	—	—
Harden Lake	4+	7484	M U	O&B

Permit required: None

Topo(s): WP Hetch Hetchy 15'; Tamarack Flat, Hetch Hetchy Reservoir 7½'

Where to stay:
   Mountain: Tuolumne Meadows Lodge, White Wolf Lodge
   Of Interest: None
   Other: None

Highlights: It's a pleasant, easy walk to surprisingly pretty Harden Lake, a shallow, blue pond that may dry up late in a dry year but is mighty nice when there's water in it.

How to get to the trailhead: Follow the driving directions of Trip 85 to White Wolf Lodge.

At the trailhead: See Trip 85.

On the trail: On foot now, continue north along the road you drove in on, passing the White Wolf Campground entrance and then employee residences, beyond which the road is closed to the public's cars. Just beyond a gate, which you circumvent, the road meets the Middle Fork Tuolumne River, creek-sized here. You cross the river on a bridge to continue you strolling along the sandy-rocky, gradually descending road, which now swings near, now swings away from the river. Keep one eye peeled for Park Service vehicles on the road, the other eye alert for flowers dotting the roadside. Nearing 1 mile a spur road veers left to a sewage pond; you stay on the main road. Beyond this fork, the road rises gradually to a junction at a little past 1 mile with a road on the right; you stay left, on the main road. There are fenceposts along the right side of your road on the next stretch, along with signs announcing do not drink water/sewage disposal area.

The road begins to descend again and the forest becomes quite dense. At the base of a huge red-fir tree at a little over 1¼ miles, a signed foot trail branches right (west), a shortcut as compared to staying on the road. You go right on the foot trail, climbing gradually to moderately on duff and sand, through a mixed forest with a bracken understory. At nearly 1½ miles a use trail comes in from the right; note this for your return, to avoid going off on the use trail. You continue west until the trail levels out and then swings north to begin a moderate descent through the forest and gradually curve west. Approaching 2 miles, you meet the road again and the foot trail ends. Turn right (northwest) on the road, soon passing a little meadow that offers a welcome break from the forest. At the next junction, at nearly 2 miles, the road continues left (northwest), while a footpath veers right (northeast) to Harden Lake. Go right to find

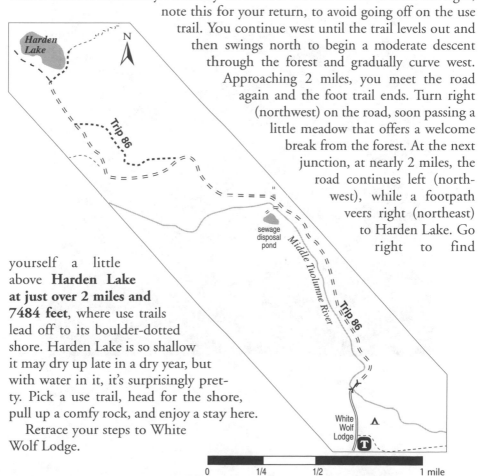

yourself a little above **Harden Lake at just over 2 miles and 7484 feet**, where use trails lead off to its boulder-dotted shore. Harden Lake is so shallow it may dry up late in a dry year, but with water in it, it's surprisingly pretty. Pick a use trail, head for the shore, pull up a comfy rock, and enjoy a stay here.

Retrace your steps to White Wolf Lodge.

0   1/4   1/2   1 mile

Above Relief Reservoir

CHAPTER 9

Northern Sierra:
State Route 108,
Sonora Pass Country

State Route 108, the Sonora Pass Road, topping out at 9628-foot Sonora Pass, is the next Sierra-crossing highway north of State Route 120, the Tioga Road (Chapter 8). South of State Route 108 lie Hoover and Emigrant wildernesses; north of it lies Carson-Iceberg Wilderness. For the dayhiker, it's a land where some of the granite grandeur of the southern Sierra begins to give way to the fantastic volcanic shapes more characteristic of the northern Sierra. From the east, after twisting very steeply over Sonora Pass, the road descends westward in the deep canyon of the Middle Fork Stanislaus River, hemmed in by the steep canyon walls. The region does not readily yield its secrets to the dayhiker; you must work a little for your reward. It's worth it!

Mountain men came here looking for furs; then miners came looking for gold. Now, visitors come looking for enjoyment in this tranquil region—tranquil as

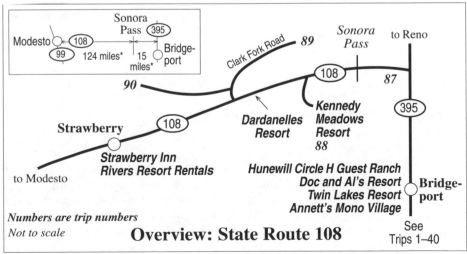

*Distances summed from various sources: Automobile Club of Southern California maps, other maps, field notes.

247

compared to bustling Sierra regions like Tioga Pass Road or Lake Tahoe. You'll come away with treasure aplenty in your cherished memories from these hikes.

Recommended reading

▶ Schaffer, Jeffrey P. *Carson-Iceberg Wilderness: A Guide to the High Sierra Between Yosemite and Tahoe*. 2nd ed. Berkeley: Wilderness Press, 1992. A concise description of the region's natural and human history is followed by an exhaustive inventory of its trails. Comes with a WP gray-scale topo.

▶ Schifrin, Ben, *Emigrant Wilderness and Northwestern Yosemite*. Berkeley: Wilderness Press, 1990. A brief overview of the region's natural and human history is followed by a detailed inventory of its trails. Comes with one of those terrific WP three-color topos.

▶ Semb, George and Patricia, *Day Hikes on the Pacific Crest Trail*. 1st ed. Berkeley, CA: Wilderness Press, 2000. Hikes on the 2665-mile Pacific Crest Trail that you can do in a day, with accessible entry and exit points. The book covers all of the PCT in California.

▶ White, Michael C., *Snowshoe Trails of Yosemite*. 1st ed. Berkeley, CA: Wilderness Press, 1999. For winter wanderings in the Yosemite area.

Recommended maps

▶ USDA/USFS *Stanislaus National Forest*. No topographic information, but invaluable road information.

Lodgings

Alphabetically, the true mountain lodgings and lodgings of interest in the region are—

Dardanelle Resort

State Route 108, Dardanelle, CA 95314   (209) 965-4355, fax (209) 965-4355

5800 feet. On State Route 108 west of Sonora Pass, near turnoff of Clark Fork Road. *Of interest*. Motel rooms and cabins. Store, restaurant (chuckwagon buffet), RV park, showers. Pets okay with $100 deposit. 2002 rates: motel room (2 persons), $99/night; cabin (2 persons), $119/night; cabin (4 persons), $149/night.

Kennedy Meadows Resort and Pack Station

P.O. Box 4010,
Sonora, CA 95370   (209) 965-3900

6320 feet. Off State Route 108 west of Sonora Pass, along Middle Fork Stanislaus River, at a major trailhead. *Mountain*. Housekeeping and sleeping cabins. Restaurant, store, pack station, gas, saloon. Pets okay. 2003 rates: $55-129/night, some cabins with 5-day minimum; $5/person/night for extra persons over stated cabin capacity; 1-week stay gets 1 day free; 2-week stay gets 10% discount. No credit cards.

Rivers Resort Rentals, The

P.O. Box 81, Strawberry, CA 95375   (800) 51-Go-RRR, (209) 965-3278

5400 feet. On State Route 108 west of Sonora Pass, on Stanislaus River. *Of interest.* Housekeeping cottages accommodate 4–8 people. Cable TV, centrally-located, heated swimming pool with sundeck, changing rooms. General store. Restaurant across highway. Some units non-smoking. Some units take pets; pet-damage deposit required, $150; may be extra daily/weekly charge for pets. Cleaning/security deposit required, $100. 2002 rates: $85–200/night/;$500–950/weekly. Extra person $5/night, maximum 2 extra persons.

Strawberry Inn   strawberryinn.com

P.O. Box 61, Strawberry, CA 95375   (209) 965-3662, (800) 965-3662

5400 feet. On State Route 108 west of Sonora Pass, along Stanislaus River. *Of interest.* Lodge rooms accommodating 1–4 persons. Strawberry Inn no longer has cabins. 2002 rates: $79/night. 10% senior discount. Rollaways for lodge rooms are $10.80/night.

Communities

Bridgeport—See Chapter 6.

HIkes

87. Leavitt Meadow Loop ☼ 🍁

Place	Total distance	Elevation	Level	Type
Start	0	7140	—	
Roosevelt, Lane lakes *only*	5⅓	7260	M	O&B
Entire semiloop	6+	7780	S	Semi

Permit required: None

Topo(s): WP Emigrant Wilderness; Pickel Meadow 7½'

Where to stay:
Mountain: Kennedy Meadows Resort, Dardanelle Resort
Of Interest: None
Other: Town of Bridgeport

Highlights: Broad Leavitt Meadow, ringed by impressive peaks and divided by the wide, meandering West Walker River, is one of the Sierra's prettiest meadows. The huge aspen grove on its west side puts on the region's best fall-color display. This hike begins along the meadow's east side and takes you to three very charming lakes; you return high on a ridge overlooking Leavitt Meadow and its magnificent setting.

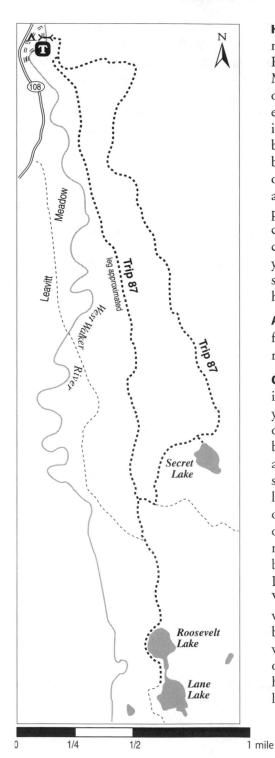

How to get to the trailhead: Just 7.8 miles east of Sonora Pass on State Route 108 is the turnoff into Leavitt Meadows Campground. (You have overshot the turnoff if you get to the entrance to the Marine Corpos facility at Pickel Meadow while eastbound or Sonora Pass while westbound.) Turn in here; the trailhead is on the lower campground road, just above the river at a small day-use parking area. Toilet, water when the campground is open. When the campground is closed, park as best you can off the highway and walk the short distance downhill to the trailhead.

At the trailhead: Non-hikers will prefer exploring quaint Bridgeport or relaxing back at their lodgings.

On the trail: From the day-use parking lot in the campground, make your way down to the footbridge over the West Walker River; there's beautiful fall color here thanks to the aspens along the river. On the other side of the river, you climb moderately to steeply to a lichen-splattered outcrop before descending slightly onto a wooded flat. You shortly (⅙ mile) reach a junction where you begin the loop: left (east) for Secret Lake, right (west) for the West Walker River Trail. Go right and find views of cliffs and peaks opening up before you. You descend to a junction with a mess of forks: use trails; once-official, now-closed footpaths; and horse trails. The fork you want is the leftmost one (southward), but before you take it, you may wish to follow a use trail down to the rocky riverbank for fall-color views.

Taking the leftmost fork puts you on the new West Walker River Trail, which isn't on the 7½′ topo but is on the Wilderness Press *Emigrant Wilderness* map. It makes an open, undulating traverse of the lower west side of the ridge east of Leavitt Meadow; you'll be returning along the ridge's top on a trail that *is* on the topo. Views across the meadow and of the surrounding mountains are more than enough to make up for the rough, dusty trail. Nearing 1 mile you cross a willow-lined seep and around 1½ miles enter a sparse forest. You ascend to a low saddle, then make a short, steep climb to traverse granite slabs. The grade eases as you work your way along a rocky slope, climbing gradually to moderately. Leavitt Meadow is occasionally visible below as you wind up through dry, rocky terrain.

At a little over 1¾ miles you reach a junction with the trail to Secret Lake on a little saddle: right (ahead, south-southeast) to Roosevelt and Lane lakes, left (north-northeast) to Secret and Poore lakes. Continue ahead to Roosevelt and Lane lakes to an unmarked junction where your main trail continues ahead (left, south-southeast) while another trail dives downhill to the right (northwest). Go ahead on the main trail and climb a little into a charming, narrow valley whose floor may be filled by seasonal ponds. You cross a low saddle and at a little over 2 miles find a historical marker explaining that your route was once part of the West Walker-Sonora Road, a wagon "road" of the early 1850s, so difficult it was soon abandoned. This is also the boundary of Hoover Wilderness, thanks to recent additions.

Continue, twining steeply down into a tiny valley full of evergreens and aspens. Your descent moderates as you approach lovely **Roosevelt Lake at nearly 2½ miles and 7260 feet**; the scenery southeastward over the lake is stunning. The trail winds along the west side of the little lake to reach the next gem, **Lane Lake at just over 2⅔ miles and 7260 feet**, where the setting is also an eye-popper. Be sure to take a rest stop at one of these pretty lakelets.

Next, retrace your steps to the junction with the trail to Secret and Poore lakes and, with a little over 3⅓ miles on your boots, go right (north-northeast). You climb quickly to a junction with the trail to Poore Lake: right (northeast) to Poore, left (north-northwest) to Secret. Go left, winding moderately up onto the ridge whose lower west slopes you traversed at the start of this trip. You pass a seasonal tarn and then descend into a pretty, forested swale with a pond or two.

Beyond the swale, you climb a low saddle and reach a junction at just over 3¾ miles: right (southeast) to Secret Lake, left (ahead, east-northeast) on the main trail. Go right a short distance to picturesque **Secret Lake at a little over 3¾ miles and 7500 feet**—another gem but, to judge from the trampled shoreline, no secret. Nevertheless, you'll want to stop to savor this lovely spot. When you're ready to leave, retrace your steps to the last junction and turn right onto the main trail, which undulates past Secret Lake's north end at 4 miles. Now you begin a moderate to steep climb on the open slope above large Poore Lake, marveling at the colorful slopes to the east. Views at the 7780-foot summit of this climb are spectacular: the Sweetwater Mountains to the east, Mt. Emma to the southeast over Poore Lake, the Sierra Crest beyond Leavitt Meadow to the west, and the meeting of the

Sierra Nevada and the Sweetwater Mountains to the north. A few more steps bring you to an overlook of the Marine Corps winter training facility at Pickel Meadow.

Continuing, the rocky trail undulates past more fine viewpoints and traverses a flat covered with sagebrush and mountain mahogany before dropping steeply through a wooded pocket, across a little meadow, down sagebrush slopes, and past a line of aspens. Beyond the aspens the trail hooks sharply west across a meadow at nearly 5⅔ miles. There's a faint, unmarked, messy junction in the middle of the meadow with use trails leading north toward Millie Lake—not worth the trouble—and south; avoid both. You probably won't even notice these tracks as you continue west across the iris-dotted meadow, bob over a low ridge, and reach another unmarked, unmapped, use-trail junction to your left. Avoid that one, too, and continue northwest to close the loop part of this trip at nearly 6 miles at the junction with the new West Walker River Trail.

Turn right to retrace your steps to the day-use parking lot at Leavitt Meadows Campground and end this wonderful trip at just over 6 miles.

88. Relief Reservoir Overlook ☼ 🌿

Place	Total distance	Elevation	Level	Type
Start	0	6320	—	—
Relief Reservoir viewpoint	6¼	7520	S	O&B

Permit required: None

Topo(s): WP Emigrant Wilderness; Sonora Pass 7½', USDA/USFS *Emigrant Wilderness*

Where to stay:
  Mountain: Kennedy Meadows Resort, Dardanelle Resort
  Of Interest: None
  Other: Town of Bridgeport

Highlights: A strikingly lovely hike leads to a big, beautiful backcountry reservoir in a splendid setting.

How to get to the trailhead: Just 9.1 miles west of Sonora Pass on State Route 108 is a marked turnoff for Kennedy Meadows on the south side of the road. (You have overshot the turnoff if you get to Sonora Pass while eastbound or Dardanelle Resort while west-bound.) Turn off here and follow the spur road 1 mile past campground turnoffs, to Kennedy Meadows Resort. There's additional parking 0.5 mile back up the road toward the highway, on the east side of the road, for overnighters. Dayhikers not staying at the resort may still park at the resort after getting the resort's permission. At the resort, toilet, water, store, café, saloon, lodgings.

At the trailhead: A day spent at Kennedy Meadows Resort relaxing, reading, fishing, enjoying meals at the café—whatever—on the banks of the infant Middle Fork Stanislaus River here is sure to please.

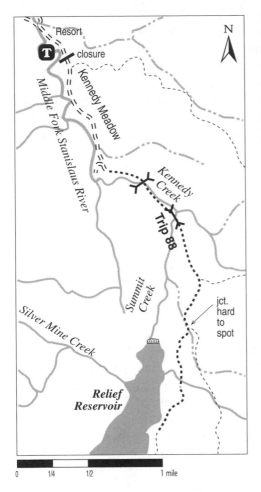

On the trail: Your route begins as an old road at the south end of the resort; the road is closed to the public's vehicles beyond here. Stroll away from the resort under incense cedar and white fir and between granite cliffs on your left and the river on your right. Soon you climb away from the river, uphill past a water tank and through a stock fence. You pass the signed NIGHT CAP trail on your left (a rough, unmapped route to aptly-named Night Cap Peak) and continue ahead (right, southeast) to top the rise, then descend to level out at Kennedy Meadow's south lobe, with a stunning view of Leavitt Peak. In season, the meadow is a grazing allotment, and you may find cattle here along with unpleasant quantities of dung in late season.

After skirting the meadow's far side and ignoring a spur road branching to the river, you head into forest to reach the signed HUCKLEBERRY TRAIL, your trail and a continuation of the old road you've been on, except that it's so rocky it's impassable to cars. Entering Emigrant Wilderness at a little over ¾ mile, you parallel tumbling Kennedy Creek to cross the creek at just over a mile on a stout footbridge. On the other side of the bridge, use trails branch right, while the main trail curves left. (Note that beyond here, the trails on the ground are considerably different from those shown on the 7½' topo; see one of the other maps.) A use trail merges on the right; you continue ahead here, noting this junction so that you won't get off-trail on your return. You soon begin climbing moderately to steeply on a wide, rocky-dusty trail blasted out of the local rock formations. The narrow walls of Kennedy Creek's canyon close in on you, adding drama to this scenic ascent. Near 1½ miles you cross another stout footbridge high above the creek, which roars down the rocky canyon here. At an apparent junction at 1½ miles, not on the book's map, the left fork appears to be a ruined, older track, while the right is more gradual, less rocky, and in better shape (they'll rejoin). You take the right fork; at 1⅔ miles the tracks rejoin, and you continue ahead (south-southeast) as Summit Creek comes rushing in from Relief Reservoir.

You veer left through a steep, dry, rocky slot, emerging into a sort of natural amphitheater cupped in handsome cliffs. At a little over 2 miles you reach a junction with the trail to Kennedy Lake: right (ahead) to Relief Reservoir, left (generally east) to Kennedy Lake. You go right, ford a seasonal rill, pass the signed PG&E RELIEF CABIN, and wind gradually to moderately uphill onto a rocky, open outcrop, where a pair of tracks diverge and soon converge by an old boiler. Beyond the boiler, you're on an open bench covered with sagebrush and rabbitbrush. An unsigned junction with an unmaintained, secondary trail in this area may be hard to spot; if you note it, take the right fork. You cross a couple of bouldery washes and, as you approach a granite outcrop on your right and a line of aspens near 3 miles, look down and to your right to see Relief Reservoir's dam. A noisy creek splashes down cliffs to the east, and you soon ford it in the shade of white firs. An optional, ½-mile, out-and-back detour to the outcrop offers excellent views over the reservoir and to the peaks around it.

You pass above the line of aspens—a gloriously colorful sight in the fall—and, as the trail begins a slight descent, take advantage of several opportunities to step off it at viewpoints overlooking the water below. Particularly from **a viewpoint above a little peninsula at a little over 3 miles and 7520 feet**, you'll find wide-ranging views over Relief Reservoir: south, deep into Emigrant Wilderness; north, beyond State Route 108 (invisible) and into Carson-Iceberg Wilderness.

Arbitrarily, this trip turns around here, so retrace your steps to Kennedy Meadows Resort from here.

Above Relief Reservoir

89. Boulder Creek and Lake ☼ ✿

Place	Total distance	Elevation	Level	Type
Start	0	6440	—	
Boulder Creek *only*	4⅔+	6920	M	O&B
Boulder Lake	8⅔+	8120	S	O&B

Permit required: None

Topo(s): WP Carson-Iceberg Wilderness; Disaster Peak 7½'; USDA/USFS Carson-Iceberg Wilderness

Where to stay:
Mountain: Kennedy Meadows Resort, Dardanelle Resort
Of Interest: Strawberry Inn, Rivers Resort Rentals
Other: None

Highlights: A generally easy stroll along the pretty Clark Fork Stanislaus River— good fall color—gives way near the river's confluence with Boulder Creek to a steep, interesting ascent to likeable little Boulder Lake.

How to get to the trailhead: Just 17.1 miles west of Sonora Pass on State Route 108 is the junction with the paved but ill-marked Clark Fork Road. The road sign is easier to spot if you're driving east. If you're driving west, the Clark Fork Road is the first paved road, other than campground roads, to the right after Sonora Pass. Also, there's a pay phone at this junction. (You have overshot the turnoff if you get to Dardanelle Resort while eastbound or Donnels Reservoir vista while west-bound.) Turn northeast onto the Clark Fork Road; stay on this narrow, paved road past campgrounds and junctions with dirt roads, to reach the abrupt roadend at Iceberg Meadow 9.2 miles from the highway. Park as best you can off the road.

At the trailhead: Non-hikers will be happier at their lodgings.

On the trail: The trailhead is on the right (south) side of the road as you face Iceberg Meadow (a grazing allotment); the Clark Fork flows nearby, and the stark peak called The Iceberg rises above it. The track is quite faint as you head across an unmapped trickle and enter Carson-Iceberg Wilderness on a duff trail. You curve between the meadow's fence and a creeklet, heading east-northeast to ford the creeklet and pass a trail sign just before you zigzag up into an area of large boul-ders. At the top, at a little past ⅓ mile, you're at a spot with a nice view of The Iceberg and of the surrounding hills and cliffs. You make a gradual descent to the Clark Fork's banks and enjoy a long, leisurely, near-streamside stroll through beau-tiful woods—good fall color. At a little over 2 miles you finally veer uphill, away from the stream, and at a little over 2⅓ miles you reach a junction: right (south) to Clark Fork Meadow; left (northeast) to Boulder Creek and Boulder Lake. Those wishing to stop at the creek should scamper down the right trail fork as far as the waterside a few steps below, at **Boulder Creek at a little over 2⅓ miles and about 6920 feet** and then retrace their steps from there.

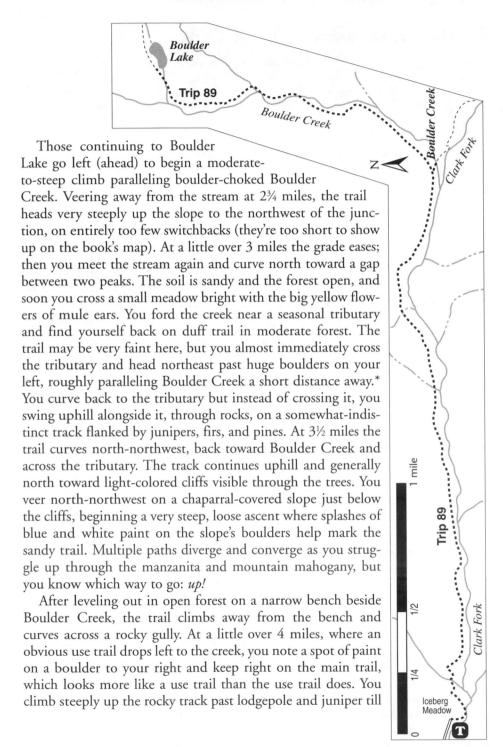

Those continuing to Boulder Lake go left (ahead) to begin a moderate-to-steep climb paralleling boulder-choked Boulder Creek. Veering away from the stream at 2¾ miles, the trail heads very steeply up the slope to the northwest of the junction, on entirely too few switchbacks (they're too short to show up on the book's map). At a little over 3 miles the grade eases; then you meet the stream again and curve north toward a gap between two peaks. The soil is sandy and the forest open, and soon you cross a small meadow bright with the big yellow flowers of mule ears. You ford the creek near a seasonal tributary and find yourself back on duff trail in moderate forest. The trail may be very faint here, but you almost immediately cross the tributary and head northeast past huge boulders on your left, roughly paralleling Boulder Creek a short distance away.* You curve back to the tributary but instead of crossing it, you swing uphill alongside it, through rocks, on a somewhat-indistinct track flanked by junipers, firs, and pines. At 3½ miles the trail curves north-northwest, back toward Boulder Creek and across the tributary. The track continues uphill and generally north toward light-colored cliffs visible through the trees. You veer north-northwest on a chaparral-covered slope just below the cliffs, beginning a very steep, loose ascent where splashes of blue and white paint on the slope's boulders help mark the sandy trail. Multiple paths diverge and converge as you struggle up through the manzanita and mountain mahogany, but you know which way to go: *up!*

After leveling out in open forest on a narrow bench beside Boulder Creek, the trail climbs away from the bench and curves across a rocky gully. At a little over 4 miles, where an obvious use trail drops left to the creek, you note a spot of paint on a boulder to your right and keep right on the main trail, which looks more like a use trail than the use trail does. You climb steeply up the rocky track past lodgepole and juniper till

*The scale of the map in this book is too coarse to show this muddling-along-the-tributary in detail.

Boulder Lake

you level out on a sandy shelf. In a few more steps you enter a wooded basin with Boulder Peak's impressive cliffs to the northeast. You shortly reach an unmarked junction where the main trail continues left (east) up the basin and a use trail drops right (south) to small, lodgepole-ringed **Boulder Lake at a little over 4⅓ miles and 8120 feet**. It's a charming spot, and you'll want to find a log against which to lean while you enjoy your lunch and watch the dragonflies skim over the shallow water.

Return the way you came.

90. Sword Lake ☼ 🍁

Place	Total distance	Elevation	Level	Type
Start	0	7180	—	—
Sword Lake	4¾	6859	M U	O&B

Permit required: None

Topo(s): WP Carson-Iceberg Wilderness; Spicer Meadow Res. 7½'; USDA/USFS Carson-Iceberg Wilderness

Where to stay:
 Mountain: Kennedy Meadows Resort, Dardanelle Resort
 Of Interest: Strawberry Inn, Rivers Resort Rentals
 Other: None

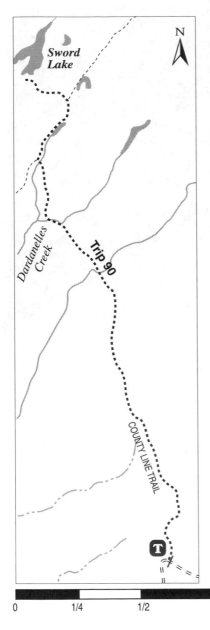

Highlights: Sword Lake and the little ponds near it, set in forested knolls and separated by glacially polished granite slabs, are simply beautiful—well worth the trip.

How to get to the trailhead: As for Trip 89, turn northeast on Clark Fork Road and go 0.4 more miles to a junction just past the second bridge; turn left onto this winding, sometimes extremely rocky and dusty dirt road. Follow it to its end at a large, dusty parking area 6.4 more miles. Get an early start; the trail is very popular, and the parking area is apt to be jam-packed with cars by midday on a weekend.

At the trailhead: Non-hikers will be happier at their lodgings.

On the trail: Head generally north into an open, mixed conifer forest with big patches of scrub. Almost immediately you reach a fork: left (north) on the County Line Trail, right (east) on an old road to McCormick Creek. You go left to begin a very steep climb on a very dusty trail. At ¼ mile the grade eases briefly before the trail makes a yet-steeper attack on the slope. Then you top out, gasping, at a little over ⅓ mile and 7540 feet, and enter Carson-Iceberg Wilderness. There's a nice view over Spicer Meadow Reservoir from a rocky knoll just left of the trail. Now you begin an undulating traverse of a forested slope, skirting a small, mule-ears-splashed meadow downslope to your left. Nearing ¾ mile you pass through a gate in a barbed-wire fence; be sure to close the gate behind you. At ¾ mile you reach a junction: left (north-northwest) to Sword Lake, right (north) to an unspecified destination.

You go left to find a view of a granite valley ahead, a valley dotted with small aspens and willows that give it fall color. You soon begin a moderate to steep descent next to a damp meadow, crossing its little stream as the grade eases. Near 1 mile a granite outcrop offers views northwest over huge Spicer Meadow Reservoir, while a glance up and to the right reveals the "pillars" of The

Dardanelles. The Dardanelles is a remnant of an ancient volcanic flow down a long-vanished canyon whose walls and surrounding terrain have eroded away, leaving The Dardanelles and similar features standing thousands of feet above the rest of the present landscape. You continue down steeply, crossing an alder-lined fork of Dardanelles Creek and then winding through rocky knolls. Near 2 miles you reach a junction: left (southwest) on the Dardanelles Creek Trail, right (north) to Sword Lake. Go right in dense forest, soon passing a tiny lake to your right. You find another junction at nearly 2¼ miles: left (northwest) to Sword Lake, right (north) to Gabbot Meadow—now under the waters of the huge reservoir.

Go left, ascending slightly, then descending to serene, rockbound, enchanting **Sword Lake at a little over 2⅓ miles and 6859 feet**. The fact that this charmer is very busy on weekends doesn't detract much from its beauty. There are lots of good rocky outcrops around the lake that offer picnic spots, so find one that appeals to you. Contrary to the topo, there is no maintained trail to Lost Lake (not on the book's map). If you want to find it, scramble west over granite slabs between Sword Lake and Lost Lake, passing a couple of attractive ponds; mileage not included in this trip's figures.

Return the way you came.

Duck Lake

CHAPTER 10

Northern Sierra:
State Route 4,
Ebbetts Pass Country

State Route 4, the Ebbetts Pass Road, topping out at 8732-foot Ebbetts Pass, is the next Sierra-crossing highway north of State Route 108, the Sonora Pass Road (Chapter 8). Carson-Iceberg Wilderness lies south of State Route 4, Mokelumne Wilderness lies north of it. The region is a fascinating mix of granitic and volcanic landscapes, continuing the scenic promise of the Sonora Pass region. Unlike much of State Route 108, State Route 4 isn't in a river canyon, and the scenery from the road is often breathtaking. Down in the western foothills, outside the geographical range of this book, you'll find a grove of giant sequoias at Calaveras Big Trees State Park, east of the little town of Arnold.

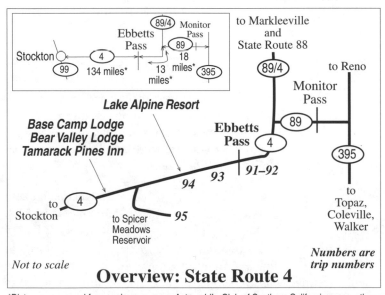

Overview: State Route 4

Not to scale

Numbers are trip numbers

*Distances summed from various sources: Automobile Club of Southern California maps, other maps, field notes.

I'll never forget my first trip over Ebbetts Pass. I was driving east on broad, well-graded State Route 4, having come from Spicer Meadow Reservoir. Suddenly, the line down the middle of the highway vanished and I found myself on a paved, one-lane road to Lake Alpine Lodge. Certain that I had somehow strayed off Highway 4 and onto the resort's driveway, I pulled into the resort to ask for directions. "I'm sorry to trouble you," I said, "but I seem to have missed the highway and ended up on your driveway." "That's no driveway," she said, "*that's* Highway 4." And it was: steep, one-lane, and twisting from a little west of Lake Alpine, 17 miles west of Ebbetts Pass, to about the 7000-foot marker some 11–12 miles east of Ebbetts Pass. But once I saw what the region had to offer, I came back as soon as I could. You will, too.

The eponymous Major Ebbetts apparently thought the pass would make the perfect emigrant route across the northern Sierra, but other routes received far greater use. Perhaps that explains why the most scenic part of State Route 4 remains largely undeveloped. That's great news for us hikers!

Recommended reading
▶ Schaffer, Jeffrey P. *Carson-Iceberg Wilderness: A Guide to the High Sierra Between Yosemite and Tahoe.* See recommended reading for Chapter 9.

Recommended maps
▶ USDA/USFS *Stanislaus National Forest.* No topographic information, but invaluable road information.

Lodgings
Alphabetically, the true mountain lodgings and lodgings of interest in the region are—

Base Camp Lodge
Mountain Adventure Seminars   (209) 753-2344
P.O. Box 5034, 148 Bear Valley Rd., Bear Valley, CA 95223   fax (209) 753-2440

7000 feet. Off State Route 4 on Bear Valley Road, west of Ebbetts Pass. *Of interest.* Lodge rooms share centrally located bathrooms. Very good restaurant. Saloon, sauna. In adjacent Bear Valley Village there are stores, restaurants, mountain-bike rentals. No stated pet policy. 2002 rates: $45–55 up to 4 people; $15/night/per additional person; bunks, $15/weeknights, $25/weekends.

Bear Valley Lodge
P.O. Box 5440,   bearvalleylodge.com
Bear Valley, CA 95223   (209) 753-BEAR (753-2325),
                                                         fax (209) 753-6218

7200 feet. Off State Route 4 west of Ebbetts Pass. *Of interest.* Hotel rooms and condominiums. Lounge, bar, dining room, outdoor hot tubs, heated outdoor pool, conference and meeting facilities, shops, restaurants, mountain-bike sales and rentals. No pets. No smoking. 2002 rates: $75–265/night.

Lake Alpine Lodge   lakealpinelodge.com
summer: P.O. Box 5300, Bear Valley, CA 95223   (209) 753-6358
winter: P.O. Box 579, Big Sur, CA 93920   (831) 667-2424

7400 feet. On State Route 4 west of Ebbetts Pass, next to Lake Alpine. *Of interest.* Housekeeping cabins, some with fireplaces; sleeping-only tent-cabins. Tent-cabins share centrally-located public bathroom. General store, restaurant, full bar, laundromat, boat rentals, mountain-bike rentals. Pets allowed in tent cabins. $110–120/night/peak season, $100–120/night/off-season; $720–1350/week/peak season, $670–1300/week/off-season; studio cabins, $95–105/night, $565–635/week; tent cabins, $35/night, $225/week.

Tamarack Pines Inn
18326 State Route 4, Tamarack, CA,   tamarackpinesinn.com
P.O. Box 5234, Bear Valley, CA 95223   (209) 753-2080

6960 feet. On State Route 4 west of Ebbetts Pass. *Of interest.* Lodge rooms/suites, some with kitchenettes. Horse boarding ($5/day, $30/week), massage by appointment. Store, restaurant in nearby Bear Valley. No pets. No smoking. 2002 rates: $50–100/night; room with kitchenette is $90–125/night; suite with kitchen is $100–160.

Communities

There are no eligible communities in the region (the drive west from Markleeville over Ebbetts Pass makes Markleeville ineligible in my judgment).

Hikes
91. Sherrold, Upper Kinney Lakes ☼ 🍁

Place	Total distance	Elevation	Level	Type
Start	0	8732	—	—
Sherrold Lake *only*	1	8740	E U	O&B
Upper Kinney Lake	3	8670	M U	O&B

Permit required: None

Topo(s): WP Carson-Iceberg Wilderness; Ebbetts Pass 7½ '; USDA/USFS Mokelumne Wilderness

Where to stay:
   Mountain: Base Camp Lodge, Bear Valley Lodge
   Of Interest: Lake Alpine Lodge, Tamarack Pines Inn
   Other: None

Highlights: This short, attractive hike to two good-looking lakes offers views and variety, too.

How to get to the trailhead: Parking is right at Ebbetts Pass, on the south side of the road, in a grassy pullout. Two trailheads are a couple minutes' walk *east* down the road; they're both for the Pacific Crest Trail, which crosses State Route 4 here. You want the trailhead on the *northwest* side of the road.

At the trailhead: Non-hikers will prefer to be back at their lodgings.

On the trail: From the pass, carefully walk downhill east on State Route 4's shoulder to the ill-marked trailheads on either side of the road; the beaten paths are obvious. Turn northwest on the Pacific Crest Trail on the northwest side of the road; the marker here is a low, dark-colored post. You shortly curve northeast across an intermittent creeklet just below Ebbetts Peak, where there's a nice scattering of flowers. Cross an old road and pick up the trail as it winds up a sparsely-forested, flower-dotted slope on sandy footing, shortly passing a use trail that goes sharply downhill on your right. Staying on the main trail, you continue ahead on a moderate grade, enjoying wonderful views east and west. At a little over ¼ mile you reach a signed spur that beckons you to go right (east) about 120 feet to a dizzying overlook to the east and south of Highland Peak, State Route 4, an outlier of Tryon Peak, and peaks in Carson-Iceberg Wilderness. On the main trail you shortly top out on a saddle at 8860 feet just east of Ebbetts Peak and west of a tarn. Now you curve northwest toward distant, striking Reynolds and Raymond peaks in Mokelumne Wilderness, and begin the descent to Sherrold Lake. Soon you pass another overlook, on your right, where you see Kinney Reservoir below.

Back on the main trail, you curve west below Ebbetts Peak, continue your moderate descent past a small tarn, and then stroll between bright little **Sherrold Lake at ½ mile and 8740 feet** on your left and a pond on your right. You dip across Sherrold's outlet to begin a gently-rolling traverse of moderately-forested slopes, curving gradually till you're heading west-southwest as you cross a small creek in a pretty meadow a little shy of 1 mile. After passing a tiny, meadowed lake, you begin a moderate-to-gradual descent over rolling, sandy terrain, through striking granite outcrops, crossing the tiny lake's outlet and a couple of runoff channels. At 1⅓ miles you reach a marked junction: the Pacific Crest Trail goes left (west), while the spur to Upper Kinney Lake goes right (northwest). You go right to an excellent overlook of **Upper Kinney Lake at nearly 1½ miles and 8670 feet**. Upper Kinney Lake has a small dam and

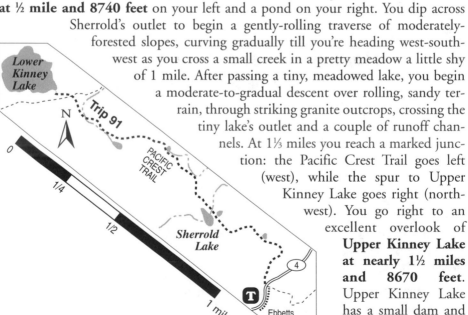

Lower Kinney Lake

Trip 91

N

PACIFIC CREST TRAIL

Sherrold Lake

0

1/4

1/2

1 mile

T

4

Ebbetts Pass

late in the year may boast an extensive beach. An outlier of Reynolds Peak towers dramatically in the north-northwest. I'll let you find your own way down to that beach, to which a couple of use trails lead. You're sure to enjoy a stay here.

Retrace your steps to Ebbetts Pass.

92. Noble Lake 🌸 ☼ 🍁

Place	Total distance	Elevation	Level	Type
Start	0	8732	–	–
Flower-gardens-in-gullies	3½–5	8400–8320	M U	O&B
Noble Lake	7⅔	8870	S U	O&B

Permit required: None

Topo(s): WP Carson-Iceberg Wilderness; Ebbetts Pass 7½'; USDA/USFS Carson-Iceberg Wilderness

Where to stay:
Mountain: Base Camp Lodge, Bear Valley Lodge
Of Interest: Lake Alpine Lodge, Tamarack Pines Inn
Other: None

Highlights: This hike is simply fabulous, with one beauty spot after another en route, while the destination that anchors the far end of the trip is no big deal. What's so wonderful about those beauty spots? In season, flowers, flowers, flowers, particularly in a series of lovely flower-gardens-in-gullies between 1¾ and 2½ miles on the way to Noble Lake.

How to get to the trailhead: See Trip 91. You want the trailhead on the *southeast* side of the road.

At the trailhead: See Trip 91.

On the trail: From the pass, carefully walk downhill east on State Route 4's shoulder to the ill-marked trailheads on either side of the road and pick up the Pacific Crest Trail on the *southeast* side of the road; the marker here is a bare post. You skirt between a knoll on your right and a tiny meadow on your left; the flower display here, while modest, is attractive. You curve around the meadow's head and begin a moderate-to-gradual ascent with over-the-shoulder glimpses of Ebbetts Peak. At a little over ¼ mile you meet a spur from a parking lot 0.4 mile farther east on State Route 4 coming in on the left (north). You go right (east), staying on the Pacific Crest Trail, soon passing the eroding edges of some ancient volcanic mudflows. At a little before ½ mile you top out on a knob at 8860 feet in an open spot dotted with cheery yellow mule ears and with a view of Highland Peak ahead. Now you descend moderately to gradually, curving around the head of an unnamed drainage and crossing several runoff channels full of stones from the ancient mudflow above you. For a while you have little to do except to enjoy a rolling traverse through patches rich with flowers; a sweetly fragrant lupine is espe-

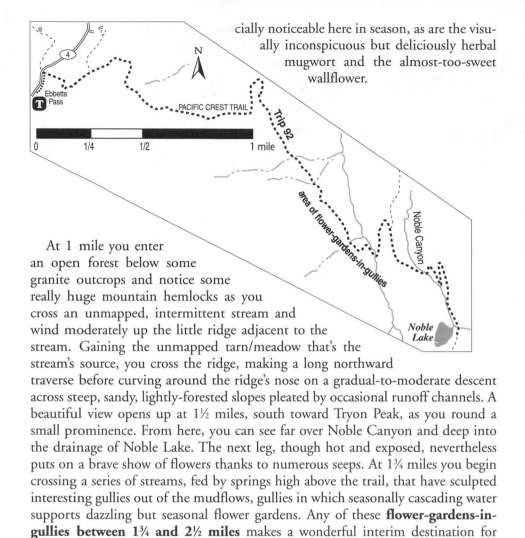

cially noticeable here in season, as are the visually inconspicuous but deliciously herbal mugwort and the almost-too-sweet wallflower.

At 1 mile you enter an open forest below some granite outcrops and notice some really huge mountain hemlocks as you cross an unmapped, intermittent stream and wind moderately up the little ridge adjacent to the stream. Gaining the unmapped tarn/meadow that's the stream's source, you cross the ridge, making a long northward traverse before curving around the ridge's nose on a gradual-to-moderate descent across steep, sandy, lightly-forested slopes pleated by occasional runoff channels. A beautiful view opens up at 1½ miles, south toward Tryon Peak, as you round a small prominence. From here, you can see far over Noble Canyon and deep into the drainage of Noble Lake. The next leg, though hot and exposed, nevertheless puts on a brave show of flowers thanks to numerous seeps. At 1¾ miles you begin crossing a series of streams, fed by springs high above the trail, that have sculpted interesting gullies out of the mudflows, gullies in which seasonally cascading water supports dazzling but seasonal flower gardens. Any of these **flower-gardens-in-gullies between 1¾ and 2½ miles** makes a wonderful interim destination for those who don't care to go all the way to Noble Lake. The last garden, the low point of this hike at 8320 feet, is tucked deep into a side canyon in the mudflow walls of Noble Canyon.

After fording its stream, you begin a moderate-to-steep climb up a loose, open slope, leveling off a little when you round a small ridge. You climb again, this time gradually to moderately, gaining over-the-shoulder views north down Noble Canyon. At 2⅔ miles you meet the trail that goes left (north) down into Noble Canyon; you go right (ahead, south-southeast), staying on the Pacific Crest Trail. In moderate forest now, you contour deep into the head of Noble Canyon until, at the canyon's head, the forest abruptly gives way to sunstruck, crumbling slopes. At nearly 3 miles you ford Noble Lake's outlet and begin a series of switchbacks that carry you gradually to moderately up the rough, rocky slope. The views get better the higher you go, especially those of Reynolds and Raymond peaks and the peaks around Blue Lakes to the northwest (off State Route 88). Watch your footing; these slopes erode quickly, and the trail tread may be very narrow and loose.

At a little over 3½ miles you cross an unmapped streamlet near the top of the last switchback before coming alongside the lake's meadowy outlet—what do you know, more flowers! After another loose, rocky stretch you squish upward through a marshy section, gain Noble Lake's bench and spy the lake to your right, cross the outlet of the lakelet above Noble Lake, and just beyond 3¾ miles find use trails down to Noble Lake's overused shore. Take a use trail down past dirty campsites to **Noble Lake at a little over 3¾ miles and 8870 feet.** The landscape all around you is volcanic, without a trace of the Sierra's granite grandeur, as if you'd strayed into a completely different mountain range. Noble Lake is nothing special except for its mitigating presence in this harsh, dry, forbidding landscape—and for that, you are thankful. Dead snags rising over the lake's southwest shore add to the sense of loneliness and desolation, and numerous use trails crisscross the southwest slope. *Being* here may not be so hot, but wasn't *getting* here great?!

Enjoy your lunch here and then retrace your steps to Ebbetts Pass.

93. Heiser and Bull Run Lakes ☼ 🍁

Place	Total distance	Elevation	Level	Type
Start	0	8060	—	—
Heiser Lake *only*	4	8340*	M U	O&B
Bull Run Lake	9**	8333**	S U	O&B

Permit required: None

Topo(s): WP Carson-Iceberg Wilderness; Pacific Valley, Spicer Meadow Res. 7½';
USDA/USFS Carson-Iceberg Wilderness

Where to stay:
Mountain: Base Camp Lodge, Bear Valley Lodge
Of Interest: Lake Alpine Lodge, Tamarack Pines Inn
Other: None

Highlights: A beautiful, undulating trail leads from Mosquito Lake on State Route 4 to two very lovely lakes, each of which is an ample reward for the significant ups and downs required to get to it.

How to get to the trailhead: Just 8.2 miles west of Ebbetts Pass on State Route 4 is little Mosquito Lake, one lake at high water and two at low, on the south side of the road. (You have overshot the trailhead if you get to Ebbetts Pass while eastbound or Lake Alpine while westbound.) There is a small parking lot just west of the lake(s) at the trailhead. Toilet in adjacent Mosquito Lake Campground.

*8160 feet for low point between Mosquito Lake and Heiser and Bull Run lakes; 8460 feet for shoulder above Heiser Lake.
**Distance includes 1-mile out-and-back to Heiser Lake. 7820 feet for low point between Mosquito Lake and Bull Run Lake.

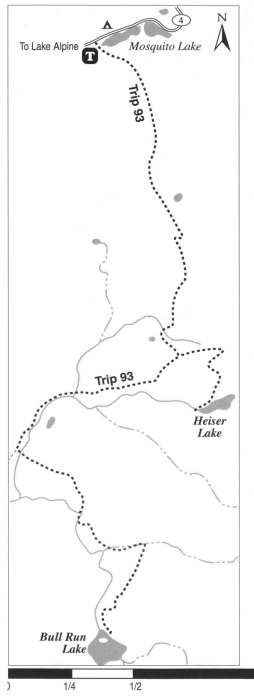

To Lake Alpine

Mosquito Lake

Trip 93

Trip 93

Heiser
Lake

Bull Run
Lake

N

| | 1/4 | 1/2 | | 1 mile |

At the trailhead: When it's bug-free, pretty Mosquito Lake is an attractive spot for picnickers, though there's no formal picnic area, and for anglers. Otherwise, non-hikers will prefer to relax at their lodgings.

On the trail: Head briefly south on the marked Heiser Lake Trail, almost immediately meeting a junction: right (west) to Lake Alpine on the Emigrant Trail (not on the topo), left (south) to Heiser Lake. You go left, curving around Mosquito Lake before veering south to begin a steep climb up the moraine south of the lake in moderate-to-sparse forest. Gaining the ridge at last, you veer a few steps to the left to the ridgetop, from which you enjoy fine views northeast to Raymond and Reynolds peaks. Back on the main trail, you begin a descent on a sandy trail and enter Carson-Iceberg Wilderness at nearly ½ mile. You continue, generally south-southeast, through forest relieved by a couple of small meadows and then, at a little over ¾ mile, climb up the next moraine. From the rocky summit at 1 mile and 8360 feet, you have views of Henry and Bull Run peaks. Now you make a sometimes-steep descent through a forest interrupted by beautiful granite formations—a nice change from the volcanic formations that dominate so much of this area.

You bottom out in a forested nook with a seasonal stream near 8160 feet but soon begin climbing again. At 1½ miles you reach a junction, the Heiser-Bull Run junction: left (east) to Heiser Lake, right (southwest) to Bull Run Lake. Go left, beginning a gradual-to-moderate ascent and topping out on another moraine, this time at 8460 feet above Heiser Lake, whose blue water you can just glimpse through the forest to the south. A moderate-to-steep descent brings you to a bench on which you find slim, sparkling **Heiser Lake at 2 miles and 8340 feet**. Granite outcrops at Heiser's west end provide excellent views over this little gem, which proves once more that good things come in small packages.

Retrace your steps to the Heiser-Bull Run junction and, to continue to Bull Run Lake, turn left with some 2½ miles on your boots. Heading southwest, you enjoy a short, level segment in the forest before plunging steeply down a loose, open, rocky slope to a series of forested benches. The grade eases and, continuing, you cross a couple of intermittent streams on a gradual-to-moderate descent through alternating patches of sandy meadow and dry forest. At nearly 3¼ miles, you reach a junction: right (west-southwest) back to State Route 4 by a different route and to a different trailhead some miles west of Mosquito Lake; left (east) to Bull Run Lake. Go left to cross the boulder-choked outlet of Heiser Lake and continue a gradual descent through moderate forest, bottoming out near 7820 feet. Having crossed an unnamed intermittent stream, you begin following a gradual to moderate, circuitous, rocky, sometimes-faint track through granite outcrops. Blazes and ducks help you stay on track, and the occasional level stretch helps you catch your breath.

You work your way up the narrowing, rockbound gully around Bull Run Lake's outlet, passing a lovely tarn on your right at a little over 4 miles. At a little over 4⅓ miles you meet Bull Run Lake's outlet and turn south-southeast along it. This path is so ill-maintained that it's little better than a use trail, and requires some very easy friction-walking up granite slabs. When you see water to your right, you simply make a beeline for **Bull Run Lake at 4½ miles and 8333 feet**. This is a gorgeous little lake, set in an amphitheater of granite cliffs, ringed by forest and meadow; its beauty is accentuated by a tiny, rocky islet. Logs around the shore make fine picnic seats; enjoy!

Retrace your steps to Mosquito Lake.

94. Duck Lake ☼ 🍁

Place	Total distance	Elevation	Level	Type
Start	0	7380	—	—
Entire semiloop	3⅓+	7540	M	Semi

Permit required: None

Topo(s): WP Carson-Iceberg Wilderness; Spicer Meadow Res. 7½'*; USDA/USFS Carson-Iceberg Wilderness

Where to stay:
  Mountain: Base Camp Lodge, Bear Valley Lodge
  Of Interest: Lake Alpine Lodge, Tamarack Pines Inn
  Other: None

Highlights: A hike that's so leisurely it's almost "easy" instead of "moderate" takes you past the shore of charming Duck Lake, which is a great picnic spot.

How to get to the trailhead: Just 16.4 miles west of Ebbetts Pass on State Route 4 is the East Shore Road turnoff. (You have overshot the turnoff if you get to Mosquito Lake while eastbound or Lake Alpine while westbound.) Turn south here and drive 0.4 mile more to the Silver Valley/Highland Creek Trailhead, where the East Shore Road elbows west, 16.8 miles. There's no lot; park on the shoulders as best you can.

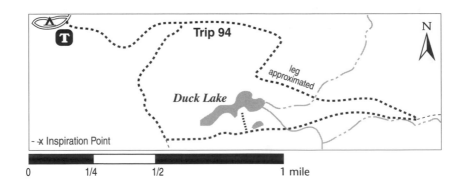

---

* Note that among its other shortcomings, the out-of-date Spicer Meadow Res. 7½' topo does not show all the trails necessary to hike this loop. You'll be better off with one of the Carson-Iceberg Wilderness maps.

At the trailhead: Non-hikers will prefer a leisurely lunch at the picnic area over-looking Lake Alpine, back at the junction of the East Shore Road and State Route 4.

On the trail: From the trailhead, hike southeast past an information sign on the Highland Creek Trail through a moderate forest whose understory is dotted with wildflowers. You begin a gradual-to-moderate ascent, passing an unmarked trail on your right, then another on your left. In *Carson-Iceberg Wilderness*, Jeffrey P. Schaffer says this is the Emigrant Trail, which you can also meet at the Heiser Lake Trailhead by Mosquito Lake (Trip 93). Ignoring the Emigrant Trail, you continue ahead (east-southeast) on the broad, dusty track, passing another information sign and entering Carson-Iceberg Wilderness. The trail veers east-northeast along a pleasant ridgetop, soon using a hiker's pass-through to negotiate a wire fence. You top out at a little over ⅓ mile at 7340 after a gradual climb, then begin a gradual-to-moderate descent to a junction at a little under ½ mile: left (east) to Rock Lake, right (south) to Duck Lake. This is the start of the loop part of this hike, and, arbi-trarily, you go left for now, on the leg that's not on the 7½′ topo.

You descend across a dry slope where Jeffrey pines provide sparse shade for a chaparral understory. The trail surface changes to duff as it pursues its leisurely downhill course through the fragrant forest. Nearing ¾ mile you turn south past a huge, four-trunked juniper and presently veer generally southeast to east where patches of duff-floored forest alternate with areas of sandy-footed granite slabs and outcrops. At a little over 1¼ miles you skirt a seasonal tarn and a meadow on your right while passing some very handsome outcrops on your left. Just beyond 1½ miles you cross an intermittent stream and reach a junction: left (east-northeast) to Rock Lake, right (southwest) to Duck Lake. You go right, along an unmapped streambed and then *in* it—fortunately, the streambed is usually dry. At 1⅔ mile you exit the streambed on its left side, following blazes on the trees because the trail is extremely faint and ill-maintained through here. As you pass a meadow on your right a little beyond 1¾ miles, the trail begins to curve northwest, becoming more distinct as you enter a patch of damp forest. You cross an intermittent stream at nearly 2 miles, then emerge at a tiny, seasonal pond (unmapped) and its little meadow. You first skirt the meadow and then, where the trail fades out, swing left to cross the meadow, ford the stream, and pick up the tread on the other side in the forest edge. Look for blazes on the trees to help you.

Now heading west on the south side of the meadow, you pass a shallow, seasonal pond, wind through some granite outcrops, spot a sheet of water to your right (north), and take any of several use trails down to the shore of meadow-ringed **Duck Lake at 2¼ miles and 7180 feet**. It may not be spectacular but it's mighty pretty, set off by a handsome granite dome to the northeast (Point 7766) and by an intriguing mudflow monument to the west, Inspiration Point. This is graze-land, so you may see cattle here and hear cowbells. And fittingly, there are some picturesquely derelict cabins just west of the lake. Leaving Duck Lake, you return to the trail, continue west, and reach a junction at nearly 2½ miles: right (north-northwest) to Lake Alpine, left (east-southeast) to Elephant Rock Lake.

Go right, enjoying the view east over Duck Lake as you head for the ridge north of the lake. You spot Bull Run Peak over Duck Lake, then reach the forest edge and begin climbing moderately to steeply on a wide, dusty-sandy trail, angling east-northeast on a big switchback. The grade soon eases, and at almost 3 miles you reach a junction—the one where you began the loop part of this trip. Turn left to return to the trailhead at a little over 3⅓ miles.

95. Three Lakes Loop 🌸 ☼ 🍁

Place	Total distance	Elevation	Level	Type
Start	0	6940	—	—
Elephant Rock Lake	Negligible	6922	E	O&B
Entire loop	4⅔	7315	M	Loop

Permit required: None

Topo(s): WP Carson-Iceberg Wilderness; Spicer Meadow Res. 7½'*; USDA/USFS Carson-Iceberg Wilderness

Where to stay:
   Mountain: Base Camp Lodge, Bear Valley Lodge
   Of Interest: Lake Alpine Lodge, Tamarack Pines Inn
   Other: None

Highlights: A leisurely loop carries you past three pretty lakes, two of which are real stunners, with the help of a stretch of dirt road.

How to get to the trailhead: Just 22.6 miles west of Ebbetts Pass on State Route 4 is the turnoff for Spicer Meadow Reservoir. You have overshot the turnoff if you get to the Bear Valley turnoff while eastbound or the community of Dorrington while westbound. Turn south and go 8.1 more miles (30.7 miles) to a turnoff east onto dirt Forest Road 7N01 (if you get to the reservoir, you have overshot this turnoff). Follow it 4.1 more miles to dusty roadend parking for Elephant Rock Lake, passing the turnout/trailhead for Summit Lake 0.5 mile before the roadend and avoiding a side road that hooks left and uphill 0.25 mile before the roadend.

At the trailhead: Non-hikers may enjoy picnicking at Elephant Rock Lake or may prefer to be at their lodgings.

On the trail: At least two very obvious paths—the right one not shown on the book's map—lead northeast from the parking lot; the left one should be signed for Rock Lake and Duck Lake, but isn't. Take it anyway, in dense forest, shortly crossing a marked mountain-bike trail (not on the book's map). By a sign that says

---

*Note that among its other shortcomings, the out-of-date Spicer Meadow Res. 7½' topo does not show all the trails necessary to hike this loop. You'll be better off with one of the Carson-Iceberg Wilderness maps.

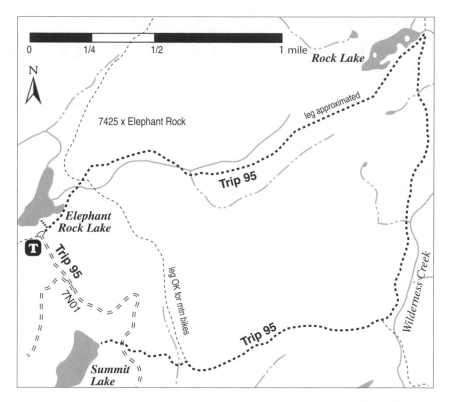

LAKESIDE ZONE, you reach a junction with a use trail: left (north) to the shore of **Elephant Rock Lake at a negligible distance from the trailhead and 6922 feet**, right (northeast) on the main trail. Scoot down the left fork to see Elephant Rock over beautiful Elephant Rock Lake (day-use only). I'd suggest you linger here, but you are barely a minute into your hike, so head back for the main trail and turn left (northeast) on it.

You cross a runoff channel, skirt the meadowed east bay of Elephant Rock Lake, and pass a low granite dome on your right. As you cross Elephant Rock Lake's inlet you may smell cowpies and hear cowbells: a small herd of cattle grazes here in season. You shortly reach a junction by the boundary of Carson-Iceberg Wilderness: left (northwest) to Duck Lake, middle (ahead, north) to Rock Lake, and right (northeast) on a mountain-bike trail leading away from the wilderness and to Summit Lake. Go ahead for Rock Lake, entering the wilderness and curving around Elephant Rock. At ½ mile you dip across a runoff channel and come abreast of Elephant Rock Lake's east tributary. After paralleling the tributary for a while, you cross it and make a brief climb over a little rocky ridge. Around ¾ mile you hop over another stream and, heading generally east-northeast-ward, begin winding gradually up another rocky ridge, this one with an unmapped streamlet creasing its ridgeline. The trail crosses the stream in order to continue ascending the ridge on its easier northwest side. You twine through a maze of rocks and chaparral that threatens to choke off the trail at any moment—but a well-trod track does exist. Nevertheless, the occasional duck or blaze is helpful as you head gradually to moderately up to cross the streambed once more at nearly 1¼ miles.

Leaving the stream behind, you continue ascending on a gentle, sandy, forested slope. You cross a secondary ridgeline almost imperceptibly at nearly 1½ miles before descending to the shore of **Rock Lake at nearly 1⅔ miles and 7315 feet**. The lake's opposite shore is rocky indeed, but there are sublime picnic spots on this side of this beautiful lake, and you'll be reluctant to leave. At an apparent junction at 1¾ miles you go either way because the forks rejoin shortly, and you reach a real junction in a few more steps: left (north) to Lake Alpine, right (south) to Highland Lakes. Go right to Highland Lakes on a sandy trail through moderate-to-open forest, level at first and then descending, curving southwest. At a junction at a little over 2¾ miles, the forks go ahead (left, south) to Highland Lakes, right (west) to Summit Lake. Go right and begin a moderate-to-steep climb up a ridge; once up the ridge, the trail's grade eases as you curve west-northwest on a duff trail. You exit Carson-Iceberg Wilderness at a little over 3⅓ miles. Veering northwest, you ascend a little to a junction at 3⅔ miles: left (west) to Summit Lake, right (north) to Elephant Rock Lake on that mountain bike trail you passed earlier.

Go left for Summit Lake, meeting Forest Road 7N01 a little short of 4 miles at the signed Summit Lake Trailhead, where there's a small parking area. Cross the road and pick up the trail to Summit Lake; in a few steps you spot the lake, then reach its shore. **Summit Lake at nearly 4 miles and 7068 feet** is good-sized, attractive, and has densely forested shores (day-use only). Back at the road you turn left (north) to follow the road to the Elephant Rock Lake Trailhead, descending very gradually. You close the loop at nearly 4⅔ miles at the roadend parking lot for Elephant Rock Lake.

CHAPTER 11

Northern Sierra:
State Routes 89 and 88,
Wildflower Country

South of Lake Tahoe, State Route 89 swoops west from U.S. Highway 395 over Monitor Pass in the Pine Nut Mountains to meet State Route 4 near Markleeville and then State Route 88 from Nevada, near Woodfords, where State Route 4 ends. State Routes 89 and 88 briefly roll west together before parting company, State Route 89 going north over Luther Pass to Lake Tahoe and State Route 88 continuing west over Carson Pass to the Central Valley. South of 88 lies Mokelumne Wilderness, a wonderland of rolling volcanic terrain. North of 88 and around 89 lies a similar region that's not official wilderness; it's often called the Dardanelles Roadless Area. The Carson Pass region is famed for its flower displays,

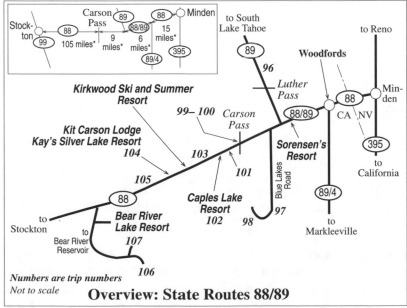

Numbers are trip numbers
Not to scale

Overview: State Routes 88/89

*Distances summed from various sources: Automobile Club of Southern California maps, other maps, field notes.

in season grander in variety and sheer abundance than those in any other region of the Sierra. This justly popular area is sure to become one of your favorites, too.

In the 1840s, famed explorers John C. Frémont and the eponymous Christopher (Kit) Carson roamed the Sierra near Carson Pass. From 1856 to 1876, John A. (Snow-shoe) Thomson (Americanized "Thompson") carried mail between California and Nevada in the winter, using Carson Pass. He traveled on heavy, homemade, ten-foot wooden skis crafted from his memories of his boyhood in Norway. He carried 50–80 pounds of mail but almost no special clothing for himself, relying on his exertions for warmth. His heroic feats have never been equalled, much less excelled, by European-Americans in the Sierra. Luther Pass is named for Ira Luther, who settled near here in the 1850s.

Recommended reading

▶ Schaffer, Jeffrey P. *The Tahoe Sierra: A Natural History Guide to 106 Hikes in the Northern Sierra*. 4th ed. Berkeley: Wilderness Press, 1998. In this highly regarded guide, Schaffer provides a concise natural history of the region followed by a thorough inventory of the region's trails. Detailed, gray-scale, topographic maps accompany the hikes.

▶ Hauserman, Tim, *The Tahoe Rim Trail: A Complete Guide for Hikers, Mountain Bikers, and Equestrians*. 1st ed. Berkeley, CA: Wilderness Press, 2002. An engaging guide to the 150-mile trail that circles the lake.

▶ Semb, George and Patricia, *Day Hikes on the Pacific Crest Trail*. 1st ed. Berkeley, CA: Wilderness Press, 2000. Hikes on the 2665-mile Pacific Crest Trail that you can do in a day, with accessible entry and exit points. The book covers all of the PCT in California.

▶ White, Michael C., *Snowshoe Trails of Tahoe*. 1st ed. Berkeley, CA: Wilderness Press, 1998. For winter wanderings in the Tahoe area.

▶ Winnett, Thomas, et al. *Sierra North*. 8th ed. Berkeley: Wilderness Press, 2002.

Recommended maps

▶ USDA/USFS *El Dorado National Forest*. No topographic information, but invaluable road information.

▶ USDA/USFS *Toiyabe National Forest, Carson Ranger District*. No topographic information, but invaluable road information.

Lodgings

Alphabetically, the true mountain lodgings and lodgings of interest in the region are—

Bear River Lake Resort   bearriverlake.com
40800 State Route 88, Pioneer, CA 95666   (209) 295-4868, fax (209) 295-4585

5820 feet. On Lower Bear River Reservoir off State Route 88, west of Carson Pass. *Of interest.* Housekeeping units. Small country store (groceries, novelties), café, boat/canoe rentals, campground. Damage deposit, $100. No pets. 1996 rates (4 persons, 1 vehicle): $93.50 single night, $82.50/night for 2 or more nights, $495/week. Extra person $5/night.

Caples Lake Resort   capleslakeresort.com
P.O. Box 88, Kirkwood, CA 95646   (209) 258-8888

7800 feet. On State Route 88 at Caples Lake, west of Carson Pass. *Of interest.* Lodge rooms accommodating 1–2 persons; housekeeping cabins accommodating 1–6 persons. Lodge rooms share centrally-located bathrooms. Outstanding restaurant, sauna, store, launch ramp, boat/canoe rentals. No smoking. No pets. $10 cleaning fee for less-than-minimum stay. 2002 rates: lodge rooms, $80/2 people/midweek, $100/weekend, $120/holiday; cabins with kitchen, linens and fireplaces, sleep 4–6 people, $80–130/midweek, $110–180/weekend, $150–200. Winter rates are $20–30 higher.

Kay's Silver Lake Resort
48400 Kay's Road, Pioneer, CA 95666   (209) 258-8598 (9 a.m. to 5 p.m.)

7209 feet. On State Route 88 west of Carson Pass, next to Silver Lake. *Of interest.* Housekeeping cabins accommodating 1–6 persons depending on cabin. Store, gas, boat rentals. No pets. No tents, RVs, or visitors from local campgrounds allowed in cabin area. 2002 rates: $70–150/night Sunday–Thursday; $80–170/night Friday, Saturday, and holidays; $405–870/week (7 nights arriving any day but Saturday).

Kirkwood Ski and Summer Resort (agency)   kirkwoodskiresort.com
P.O. Box 1, Kirkwood Meadows Drive,   reservations (800) 967-7500,
Kirkwood, CA 95646   information (209) 258-6000, fax (209) 258-8899

7600 feet. Off State Route 88 on Kirkwood Meadows Drive, west of Carson Pass. *Of interest.* Condominiums of various sizes, all with fully-equipped kitchens, fireplaces, TVs, VCRs. Area includes 2 restaurants, general store, post office, service station, stables, tennis courts. No pets. 2002 summer rates: $99/night/1 bed studio, $119/night/2 queen-size beds, $109–129/night/deluxe studio units with kitchens; $129–199/1 bedroom condominiums (up to 4 people); $189–269/2 bedroom condos (up to 6 people).

Kit Carson Lodge   kitcarsonlodge.com
Kit Carson, CA 95644   (209) 258-8500

7209 feet. On Silver Lake, off State Route 88, west of Carson Pass. *Mountain.* Bed-and-breakfast rooms (1–3 persons depending on room; no children under 12; includes continental breakfast); housekeeping cottages accommodating 1–6 persons with fireplaces and barbecues. Very good restaurant, store, post office, laundromat, campfire area (nightly campfire), art gallery, dock, boat rentals, beach, protected swimming area, fly-fishing workshops. Housekeeping units do not provide kitchen linens or bath towels, or toiletries. No pets. 2003 rates: B&B rooms $85–135/night; housekeeping cottages $90–225/night, $645–1550/week.

Sorensen's Resort

14255 State Route 88   sorensensresort.com
Hope Valley, CA 96120   (530) 694-2203, (800) 423-9949

7120 feet. On State Route 88 east of Carson Pass. *Of interest.* Bed-and-breakfast rooms and cabin; housekeeping cabins and homes; accommodating 1–6 persons depending on unit. Very good restaurant, bookstore, gift shop, fishing supplies, fly-fishing school. No smoking. Pets okay in some units; inquire when you book. 2002 rates: $80–295/night depending on unit. Extra person $25/night. Cribs and rollaways $10 fee. Wedding/honeymoon and other special packages available.

Communities

Alphabetically, the eligible communities and their Chambers of Commerce and Visitors Bureaus are—

Alpine County Chamber of Commerce   alpinecounty.com
P.O. Box 265, Markleeville, CA 96120   (916) 694-2475, fax (916) 694-2478

Lake Tahoe Visitors Authority   virtualtahoe.com/LTVA
P.O. Box 16299, 1156 Ski Run Blvd.,   (800) AT-TAHOE,
South Lake Tahoe, CA 96151   fax (916) 544-2386

Markleeville
See Alpine County Chamber of Commerce

Markleeville straddles State Routes 89 and 4 west of Monitor Pass, near Grover Hot Springs State Park.

South Lake Tahoe Chamber of Commerce   tahoeinfo.com
13066 Lake Tahoe Blvd., South Lake Tahoe, CA 96150   (530) 541-5255

Towns of South Lake Tahoe
See Lake Tahoe Visitors Authority, South Lake Tahoe Chamber of Commerce

Numerous vacation communities around California side of south end of Lake Tahoe, most on State Route 89. The town of South Lake Tahoe is probably the largest town in the area covered by this book.

Hikes

96. Dardanelles and Round Lakes ☼ ❦

Place	Total distance	Elevation	Level	Type
Start	0	7260	—	—
Big Meadow *only*	1	7500	E	O&B
Round Lake *only*	5+	8037	M	O&B
Dardanelles Lake *only*	6¼	7740	S	O&B
Both lakes	7½	8037	S	O&B

Permit required: None

Topo(s): Freel Peak, Echo Lake 7½'

Where to stay:
  Mountain: Kit Carson Lodge
  Of Interest: Sorensen's Resort, Caples Lake Resort, Kirkwood Ski & Summer Resort, Kay's Silver Lake Resort
  Other: Towns of S. Lk. Tahoe, Town of Woodfords, Town of Markleeville

Highlights: The Dardanelles Roadless Area, in which both of these lakes lie, offers wonderful scenery and a number of lakes. Dardanelles Lake is one of the prettiest and Round Lake one of the most interesting. As a bonus, you get to try out a leg of the new, multiple-use (foot, horse, bike) Tahoe Rim Trail on your way. See Trip 100 for another route to Round Lake.

How to get to the trailhead: Just 3.4 miles northwest of Luther Pass on State Route 89 is the Big Meadow Trailhead turnoff on the northeast side of the road. (You have overshot the turnoff if you get to Luther Pass while southbound or the junction with U.S. Highway 50 while northbound.) Turn here onto a short spur road that leads to a **T**-junction: right into an undeveloped campground; left a little over 0.1 more mile to a trailhead parking loop, 3.5 miles total. Toilets, water, in season. The trailhead here may be very poorly marked; the trail leaves from the far end of the parking loop and looks very unpromising, but it gets better.

At the trailhead: Non-hikers will prefer to be at their lodgings, soaking at Grover Hot Springs State Park, shopping in South Lake Tahoe, or trying their luck at the casinos just over the border in Stateline, Nevada.

On the trail: From the far end of the parking lot, head south on a sandy trail marked TAHOE RIM TRAIL. In ⅒ mile you reach State Route 89 and cross the highway carefully to pick up the trail again; it's well-signed here. You curve south-southwest as you leave the highway, climbing moderately to steeply on a dusty duff trail into dense conifer forest. At a little over ⅓ mile the grade eases, and shortly thereafter you negotiate a hiker's pass-through. At nearly ½ mile you reach a junction: left (southeast) to Scotts Lake, right (south-southeast) to Meiss Meadow. Go right to find the forest giving way to splendid **Big Meadow at ½ mile and 7500 feet**, where you soon cross its stream on a footbridge. The meadow, cradled by handsome peaks, sports a wonderful variety of flowers in season.

The trail continues south-southeast across the meadow toward a ridge, and you re-enter forest at ¾ mile near the meadow's south end. You resume a gradual to moderate climb broken by a few short, steep hauls, and patches of dense forest alternate with bright, flowery openings. Beginning at a little over 1½ miles you come abreast of a small stream that nourishes a long, narrow, flower-rich meadow. At a little over 1⅔ miles, you find another hiker's pass-through in a wood-and-barbed-wire fence and, as the trail angles up the east side of a ridge, head toward blue sky seen through the red firs atop the ridge. The trail tops out in a few more steps and then begins a gentle descent on the west side of the ridge. You soon have views of volcanic mudflow formations and of a granite basin to the west. Unusual boulders full of smaller rocks, looking like some strange kind of conglomerate rock, dot the landscape as you near the bottom of this descent; the rocks have eroded from those ancient mudflows. At 2 miles and the bottom of the descent, you reach another junction: ahead (south) for Round Lake and the mudflow formations on the Tahoe Rim Trail; sharp right (northwest) for Dardanelles Lake and Christmas Valley. Decide here if you want to go to both lakes and if so, which lake you want to see first.

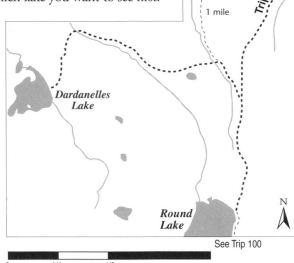

To go to Dardanelles Lake, turn right here, soon tracing a stream on your left (west). At an unmarked **Y**-junction, the trail ahead (right) goes to Christmas Valley, while the spur trail that heads left across the stream (southwest) goes to Dardanelles Lake. Go left, ford the stream, cross a wet meadow, and pass north of a lily-pad-covered lakelet. The trail descends gradually to moderately to meet and parallel another stream. You stroll northwest until, at a little over 2¾ miles, the trail turns southwest to cross the stream. Now you climb south gradually to moderately before abruptly swinging west to the trail's end on the shores of beautiful, popular **Dardanelles Lake at a little over 3 miles and 7740 feet**. The lake is ringed by slabs offering many pleasant picnic sites as well as by handsome cliffs on its south side. Enjoy your stay here, then retrace your steps to the junction with the Tahoe Rim Trail.

To go to Round Lake, go ahead, staying on the Tahoe Rim Trail if you're coming from Big Meadow, or turn right onto the Tahoe Rim Trail if you're coming from Dardanelles Lake. You begin a series of steep but very short ascents and descents. At an apparent but unmarked junction at nearly 2⅓ miles, take the left fork through a red fir forest full of those bizarre conglomerate rocks. One more steep, dusty ascent and then a level stretch take you to a point slightly above the dusty north shore of **Round Lake at a little over 2½ miles and 8037 feet** (a little over 4¾ miles on your boots if you went to Dardanelles Lake first). A web of use trails spreads out from here, leading around the lake. The formation on the lake's east shore is a volcanic mudflow formation like the Dardanelles (see Trip 90) and looks rather like an Assyrian ziggurat. The better picnic spots are on the east and west sides, and the main trail, your Tahoe Rim Trail, continues south along the east side of the lake from here, toward the junction in Meiss Meadow in Trip 100. Have lunch at this pleasant lake, then return to the junction with the trail to Dardanelles Lake.

Retrace your steps to your car, a little less than 7¼ miles if you went to both lakes.

97. Lily Pad, Upper Sunset Lakes 🌸 ☼ 🍁

Place	Total distance	Elevation	Level	Type
Start	0	7960	—	—
Lily Pad Lake *only*	3¾+	7830	M U	O&B
Upper Sunset Lake	4½	7830	M U	O&B

Permit required: None

Topo(s): Pacific Valley 7½'; USDA/USFS Mokelumne Wilderness

Where to stay:
Mountain: None
Of Interest: Caples Lake Resort, Sorensen's Resort
Other: Town of Woodfords, Town of Markleeville

Highlights: A great viewpoint, fine flowers, and two pretty lakes—one with a knockout flower display of its own in season—await you on this leg of the famed Pacific Crest Trail.

How to get to the trailhead: Just 6.3 miles east of Carson Pass on State Route 88 is the junction with the Blue Lakes Road. (You have overshot this junction if you get to the junction of State Routes 88 and 89 while eastbound or Carson Pass while westbound.) Turn left (south) onto the Blue Lakes Road and follow it up toward Blue Lakes as it grows rougher and the pavement ends, for 10.6 more miles (16.9 miles total) to Forest Road 097 on your left. Turn left onto Forest Road 097 and almost immediately turn left again onto a very short spur road to a large parking area reached in less than 0.1 more mile (call it 17 miles total). The parking area is marked for the Blue Lakes Trailhead of the Pacific Crest Trail. Toilet.

Granite Lake

To stay on track, follow the lakelet's east shore to its outlet, perhaps scrambling over some boulders, then cross the outlet going northwest, and climb steeply up a sparsely-shaded slope. The grade eases as you gain a shoulder, and you continue west through small meadows and past tarns. Climbing again, you top a small ridge and then descend a little to follow a trail that curves west-southwest along Granite Lake's outlet, fording the outlet twice. You reach beautiful **Granite Lake at a little over 1¾ miles and 8700 feet**, where a lakeside rest stop is a real treat. An optional ascent of a draw about halfway around the lake brings you to an overlook of Meadow, Rice, and Evergreen lakes and of the peaks surrounding the area. You'll want to stay a while.

Return the way you came.

99. Frog and Winnemucca Lakes ☼ 🍂

Place	Total distance	Elevation	Level	Type
Start	0	8573	—	—
Frog Lake *only*	2	8860	E	O&B
Winnemucca Lake	4	8980	M	O&B

Permit required: None

Topo(s): Carson Pass, CA 7½'; USDA/USFS Mokelumne Wilderness

Where to stay:
   Mountain: Kit Carson Lodge
   Of Interest: Sorensen's Resort, Caples Lake Resort, Kirkwood Ski & Summer Resort, Kay's Silver Lake Resort
   Other: Town of Markleeville, Town of Woodfords

Highlights: The Carson Pass region is justly famed for its wildflower displays, and in season these are not just little gardens here and there or flowery strips along creeks but great carpets of blossoms. On this hike and the next two, you'll revel in these carpets while visiting some wonderful lakes.

How to get to the trailhead: This trailhead is right at Carson Pass, next to a visitor center, where you'll find good advice for free and relevant maps and books for sale. There's a good-sized parking lot that's often full by midday. Toilets, ranger station.

Note that there are two parking lots at Carson Pass. The one at the Carson Pass visitor center, on the southwest side of the road, serves southbound trailheads. The other lot is 0.3 mile west of the pass proper, on the north side of the road, and serves northbound trailheads; you'll use it for the next hike.

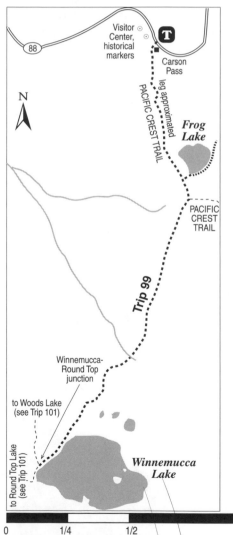

At the trailhead: Non-hikers may enjoy a stop at the visitor center at Carson Pass, but otherwise they'll prefer relaxing at their lodgings or picnicking and fishing at nearby Red Lake or Woods Lake.

On the trail: This trailhead is incorrectly shown on the Carson Pass 7½′ topo; it starts near the southeast side of the parking lot that's on the south side of State Route 88, between the visitor center and the toilets. Head south-southwest on a dusty duff trail, descending gradually into a moderate conifer forest and passing an unmapped tarn and some granite outcrops. You curve around a meadow and cross a stream as you near ⅓ mile, then enter Mokelumne Wilderness at a little over ⅓ mile. Now you begin a moderate to gradual climb through a mix of tall grass and dryland flowers. The grade eases as you cross a shoulder, and you spot the odd peak named Elephant's Back ahead (southeast). Round Top towers to the right (south) as the trail heads southeast. You make a lazy contour of an open, flowery slope, and nearing 1 mile you reach an unsigned junction with the spur trail to Frog Lake: left (northeast) to Frog Lake, right (ahead) on the main trail. You go left to pretty **Frog Lake at a little**

under 1 mile and 8860 feet. The lake sits on a little bench above the valleys to the east. You'll find excellent views eastward on the far side of the lake—follow a use trail around the lake and then across the meadow on the lake's east side to slabs overlooking Red Lake Peak, State Route 88 and Carson Pass, Red Lake, Hawkins Peak, Hope Valley, and Reynolds and Raymond peaks. What a perch!

Back on the main trail with a mile on your boots, you turn left to continue your hike and climb moderately toward Round Top to an overlook of Caples Lake. There's a junction at a little over 1 mile: left (southeast) on the Pacific Crest Trail to Ebbetts Pass, right (south) to Winnemucca Lake. Go right, passing Elephants Back and drifting in season into an eye-popping dry and then very wet meadow: hawkweed, popcorn flower, lupine, catchfly, pearly everlasting, mountain pride, threadstem phlox, knotweed, wild carrot, columbine, lungwort, Queen Anne's lace, onion, green gentian, elephant heads, bistort, valerian, green orchids, white violets, marsh marigolds, meadow rue... . At nearly 1⅔ miles you cross a stream lined by plants that love very wet environments. Shortly before 2 miles you top out and begin a brief descent to dramatically set **Winnemucca Lake at 2 miles and 8980 feet**. If the flowers haven't impressed you, the cliff-backed lake, right under Round Top peak, will. From the rise above the lake you have excellent views of Elephants Back and Round Top and across unseen Carson Pass to Red Lake Peak. And if the flowers *did* impress you, you should know that there's another, equally impressive but different meadow, below the lake and traversed by the trail from Woods Lake (see Trip 101); you can pick it up at the west end of Winnemucca Lake at the "Winnemucca-Round Top junction" on the book's map.

But that's not part of this trip, so after having enjoyed a picnic in this spectacular setting, you head back to your car by way of that dazzling flower display.

100. Meiss and Round Lakes 🌱 ☼ 🍁

Place	Total distance	Elevation	Level	Type
Start	0	8560	—	—
Lakelet on saddle *only*	2+	8780	E	O&B
Meiss Lake *only*	6⅓	8314	S U	O&B
Round Lake *only*	8+	8037	S U	O&B
Entire hike	9¾+	8790	S U	O&B

Permit required: None

Topo(s): Caples Lake, Carson Pass 7½'; USDA/USFS Mokelumne Wilderness

Where to stay:
   Mountain: Kit Carson Lodge
   Of Interest: Sorensen's Resort, Caples Lake Resort, Kirkwood Ski & Summer Resort, Kay's Silver Lake Resort
   Other: Town of Markleeville, Town of Woodfords

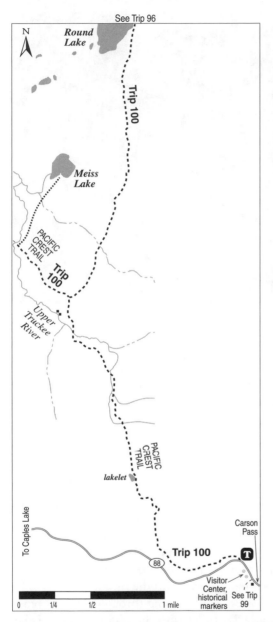

Highlights: The seasonal display of flowers along the first leg of this hike is breathtaking. Beyond, you climb to a lovely, unnamed lakelet and descend through more flowers to the infant Upper Truckee River, beautifully marshy Meiss Lake, and interesting Round Lake.

How to get to the trailhead: See Trip 99. This trip starts from the parking lot 0.3 mile west of Carson Pass, on the north side of the road. Toilets, water, visitor center 0.3 miles east at the south-side parking lot.

At the trailhead: See Trip 99.

On the trail: Pick up the trail at the northwest corner of the lot. Amid dryland flowers, you head west over a seasonal trickle and past an information sign. The trail traverses between the highway to your left, below, and juniper-crowned gray granite cliffs on your right. The sandy trail reaches a junction at a little over ¼ mile: right (north) on a use trail that shortly peters out, left (southwest) on the Pacific Crest Trail. You go left, still traversing above the highway, aiming at the stark buttes beyond Caples Lake. You descend slightly as you veer northwest to excellent views of Caples Lake from a trail bracketed by a fine display of blossoms and a small stand of conifers. At ⅔ mile you curve through a patchy lodgepole forest and emerge to a seasonally amazing—stupendous!—magnificent!—flower display: a steep hillside thickly carpeted with bright yellow, daisy-like mule ears and sky-blue lupine.

Dazzled, you continue, crossing a pair of unmapped, seasonal streams, and begin switchbacking up a slope, heading for an obvious low point just west of Red Lake Peak. The grade eases as you reach a saddle with a lovely, unnamed **lakelet at a little over 1 mile and 8780 feet** to the west of a fence with a hiker's pass-through.

Meiss Lake

Double ruts lead away into a high meadow spangled with blue iris, and spectacular views open up as you continue north, rising very gradually to a broad saddle: Lake Tahoe in the distance, peaks in Desolation Wilderness, granite slopes in Dardanelles Roadless Area, and the strange volcanic formation that towers over Round Lake. The paired ruts depart your main trail, heading up to the right, while your Pacific Crest Trail swings left, downhill. Numerous runoff channels crease these rocky, windswept slopes you're descending, and at nearly 1½ miles you cross a stream bright with blossoms. You make a steep, rocky descent to the broad meadows visible below, and the grade eases as you come alongside, then ford, a fork of the Upper Truckee River at 1⅔ miles.

The trail rolls across broad, flower-strewn Meiss Meadow, crossing the river again, before reaching an unmapped **Y**-junction at almost 2¼ miles: left (west) to the picturesque cabins of a cow camp, right (north) on the Pacific Crest Trail. The meadow was formerly a grazing allotment and reportedly was a dusty ruin by summer; now, the cattle have been banished temporarily, and the meadow seems to be recovering. You go right on the Pacific Crest Trail, passing through a ruined fence and shortly reaching a junction at nearly 2⅓ miles with the trail to Round Lake: left (northwest) on the Pacific Crest Trail to Showers and Meiss lakes; right (northeast) to Round Lake on the Tahoe Rim Trail.

To go to Meiss Lake, turn left on the Pacific Crest Trail for Showers and Meiss lakes and cross a low, forested ridge before approaching the Upper Truckee River again at 2⅔ miles. You can plainly see Meiss Lake shimmering a short distance away, north-ish down a branch of the meadow, and you'll spy a use trail trekking north toward the lake here. Make your way toward Meiss Lake, picking your way through the meadow when the use trail peters out. Early in the season, much of the meadow around the lake is an extension of the lake, ankle- to calf-deep in water. You make for a prominent, rocky "islet" on the lake's south edge, where you find dry ground, views over **Meiss Lake at a little over 3 miles and 8314 feet**, and picnic spots.

To go to Round Lake, turn right on the dusty Tahoe Rim Trail to cross broad, forested knolls before making an abrupt descent to cross a stream at 3 miles at the south edge of another, smaller, flowery meadow. You skirt an old log fence as you cross this boggy meadow to ascend the next knoll, atop which you find more meadows. After topping out, you begin a long, gradual descent to the east edge of the meadow south of Round Lake, crossing the unmapped intermittent streams feeding the meadow. You reach **Round Lake at a little over 4 miles and 8037 feet**—also a destination for Trip 96. There's a wonderful mudflow formation towering over Round Lake, the ziggurat-like one that you saw plainly from the saddle at 8790. Use trails branch to picnic spots around the lake.

101. Woods Lake Loop 🌸 ☼ 🍁

Place	Total distance	Elevation	Level	Type
Start	0	8220	—	—
Winnemucca Lake *only*	2⅔	8980	M	O&B
Entire loop	4+	9420	M	O&B

Permit required: None

Topo(s): Caples Lake, Carson Pass 7½'; USDA/USFS Mokelumne Wilderness

Where to stay:
   Mountain: Kit Carson Lodge
   Of Interest: Sorensen's Resort, Caples Lake Resort, Kirkwood Ski & Summer Resort, Kay's Silver Lake Resort
   Other: Town of Woodfords

Highlights: Exceptional flower displays line your looping route to two beautiful lakes in dramatic settings under Round Top Peak.

How to get to the trailhead: Just 1.9 miles west from Carson Pass on State Route 88 is the turnoff south for Woods Lake Recreation Area. (You have overshot the turnoff if you get to Carson Pass while eastbound or Caples Lake while westbound.) Follow narrow, paved Woods Lake Road all the way to its end, past the turnoff into the Woods Lake Campground, to day-use parking at Woods Lake, 1.4 miles more. Toilets, water, picnic area. The trailhead is just before the picnic area and slightly past the campground entrance, on the opposite side of the road from that entrance, at a footbridge over Woods Lake's outlet. This is a very pretty, very popular area. If the day-use parking area is full, go back up the road and over the bridge to find day-use-only parking at a big dirt turnout next to the stream. There

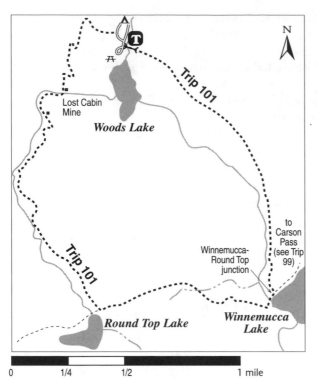

is a small day-use parking area right across from the campground entrance, but there's a fee to park there.

At the trailhead: Non-hikers will enjoy a chance to relax at the picnic area at Woods Lake and to soak in the beautiful scenery here.

On the trail: The trailhead is poorly marked on the Woods Lake Road, but the footbridge is obvious, so off you go, eastward over the footbridge, and almost immediately begin winding gradually to moderately up a rocky outcrop in open forest. Round Top Peak soon comes into view, and the scattering of flowers along this first leg is a delight—but it will turn out to be barely an appetizer compared to the floral feast to come. A little beyond ½ mile you pass the marked ruins of one of the many old mining operations around here and pause to read about them. Continuing, the flower display grows more impressive until, starting about ⅔ mile, you emerge into an immense, gently-sloping meadow below Winnemucca Lake, where flowers cover the slope like a carpet. Indian paintbrush in blazing hues dominates but is far from the whole story.

The trail traverses the meadow, ascending gradually, and near 1 mile you enter Mokelumne Wilderness. You cross multiple runoff channels, one of which is likely to be the trail early in the season. Near the south end of the meadow, you begin a steep climb toward Round Top, enjoying over-the-shoulder views of Red Lake Peak. At 1⅓ miles you reach a junction I'll call the Winnemucca-Round Top junction: ahead a few steps on use trails to the shore of beautiful Winnemucca Lake; hard left (east-northeast) to Carson Pass (see Trip 100); and right (southwest) to Round Top Lake. After a rest at **Winnemucca Lake at 1⅓ miles and 8980 feet**, you backtrack to the Winnemucca-Round Top junction and head southwest for Round Top Lake to continue the loop. You ford Winnemucca's flower-blessed outlet and begin climbing through alpine meadows, curving westward high on the side of this cirque. You're heading for a windy saddle dotted with whitebark pines, and you reach the saddle at a little over 2 miles and 9420 feet. Views include Hawkins Peak to the east as well as nearby, towering Round Top.

Views open to the west as you descend gradually to stark, lovely **Round Top Lake at a little over 2¼ miles and 9340 feet**, just under rugged Round Top and a jagged ridge called The Sisters. Here you reach another junction: left (southwest) to Fourth of July Lake, right (northwest) back to Woods Lake. The topo shows a trail southeast to Round Top, but that's a use trail/scramble at best. You'll want to stop here to take in the scenery and have a snack. To continue looping back to Woods Lake, take the northwest fork, descending toward a view of Caples Lake on a rocky, moderate to steep trail paralleling Round Top Lake's outlet. You exit Mokelumne Wilderness at almost 3 miles and continue your descent on open, rocky slopes past a Land Survey Monument, leveling out briefly on benches. You cross a stream, pass the ruins of a stone cabin at almost 3⅓ miles, brush the lake's outlet stream, and almost immediately veer right (north-northeast) past mine ruins on both sides of the stream. Lost Cabin Mine is still an active claim, and signs warn you not to trespass onto the claim.

The trail heads over a low saddle before resuming its steep descent past more mine signs. Curving east-northeast, it offers views of the mine ruins and of Woods Lake below. You cross the outlet stream on a marked new trail, just below more mine ruins, at nearly 3½ miles. You meet a jeep road in a few more steps and continue your descent on it, being careful to stay out of the mining claim area. You circumvent a gate and meet the road through Woods Lake Campground near Site 12 at a little under 4 miles. Turn right, toward Woods Lake, on the campground road, and continue descending to meet the Woods Lake road near the trailhead and the day-use parking lot to close this loop at just over 4 miles.

102. Emigrant Lake ☼ 🍁

Place	Total distance	Elevation	Level	Type
Start	0	7780	—	—
Emigrant Lake	7¾+	8580	S	O&B

Permit required: None

Topo(s): Caples Lake 7½'; USDA/USFS Mokelumne Wilderness

Where to stay:
Mountain: Kit Carson Lodge
Of Interest: Sorensen's Resort, Caples Lake Resort, Bear River Lake Resort, Kirkwood Ski & Summer Resort, Kay's Silver Lake Resort
Other: None

Highlights: Beginning with a leisurely stroll along the west shore of big, blue Caples Lake, this trip then makes an interesting ascent to lovely Emigrant Lake, which has an impressively alpine setting.

How to get to the trailhead: Just 4.9 miles west of Carson Pass on State Route 88, past the turnoff for Caples Lake Resort, is a parking lot just beyond the dam at the western tip of Caples Lake. (You have overshot the parking lot if you get to the turnoff to Caples Lake Resort while eastbound or Kirkwood Inn while westbound.) Your trailhead is near the restrooms, just below the dam. Toilets, water.

At the trailhead: For non-hikers, nearby Caples Lake Resort offers boat rentals, a tiny store, a fine restaurant, and a chance to enjoy relaxing around pretty Caples Lake.

On the trail: Head southeast through willows on the marked trail and climb up to the lake's level to begin a leisurely traverse of its scenic, forested shore on a well-worn, dusty, duff trail. You enter Mokelumne Wilderness almost immediately, and on your way between here and where you begin ascending to Emigrant Lake, you'll cross a number of seasonal streams. The changing views of Red Lake Peak, Elephants Back, and Round Top across the lake, and of the lake itself, are the principal attractions on this stretch. At a little over 1 mile you veer away from the lakeshore on a dry, gravelly slope with a scattering of lodgepoles—this is the short, wide peninsula that pooches northeast into the lake about halfway along its western-southwestern shore. You cross a trace of the old Emigrant Road, as marked on a dead tree. Where a sign indicates that you could turn right onto the old Emigrant Road, you say, "No, thanks," and continue on the left fork, going south-southeast. (The old Emigrant Road isn't on the 7½' topo but is on the wilderness map.) You soon dip to the lakeshore again and then, nearing the southeast end of Caples Lake at a little over 1⅓ miles, begin climbing. At an apparent **Y**-junction, either fork will do; they soon rejoin.

At nearly 1⅔ miles, heading almost south now, you top a rocky shoulder and descend to cross an unmapped creeklet. With the south arm of the lake still visible below, you pursue your way now over rocky outcrops, now in forest, now across a meadow. At a little over 2¼ miles, you begin climbing, sometimes steeply, beside a strand of multi-channeled Emigrant Creek. Nearing 3 miles, you pass an ill-marked junction with an ill-maintained trail that goes right (west) to Kirkwood Meadows. You continue ahead (left, south) and soon cross that strand just beyond some handsome cascades. You continue

Caples Lake

old Emigrant Road (approx.)

Trip 102

N

Emigrant Lake

climbing gradually to moderately southward, working your way over to the next strand of Emigrant Creek to the east. You cross that next strand at nearly 3¼ miles, just below a beautiful little waterfall. Now you zigzag up, glimpsing more pretty cascades, until a final level stretch brings you alongside Emigrant Lake's outlet and then to the lake itself. Chilly but lovely **Emigrant Lake at nearly 4 miles and 8580 feet** sits in a very stark cirque under Covered Wagon Peak. The lake's shores are softened by meadow grasses and dotted with flowers. Pull up a log or rock and enjoy your picnic in this dramatic setting.

Retrace your steps to your car.

103. Lake Margaret ☼ ❦

Place	Total distance	Elevation	Level	Type
Start	0	7660	—	—
Lake Margaret	4⅔	7540	M U	O&B

Permit required: None

Topo(s): Caples Lake 7½'; USDA/USFS Mokelumne Wilderness

Where to stay:
  Mountain: Kit Carson Lodge
  Of Interest: Sorensen's Resort, Caples Lake Resort, Bear River Lake Resort, Kirkwood Ski
    & Summer Resort, Kay's Silver Lake Resort
  Other: None

Highlights: A stroll through the beautiful meadows along Caples Creek precedes your scramble to pretty Lake Margaret. Near the end, you have to friction-walk steepish slabs; bouldering skills will be helpful.

How to get to the trailhead: Just 5.2 miles west of Carson Pass on State Route 88, past the turnoff for Caples Lake Resort and past Caples Lake's west dam, is a turnoff onto a spur road to the north about 0.3 mile west of the west dam. Sometimes the turnoff is marked, at others it's not. (If you get to the Kirkwood Inn as you drive west, or to Caples Lake as you drive east, you have overshot this turnoff.) Follow the rough spur road 0.1 more mile to a small, rough parking area and a trailhead on the edge of a cliff.

At the trailhead: See Trip 102.

On the trail: Head generally north, at first on sparsely-timbered slopes, descending into moderate forest and scattered flowers. At a little over ⅓ mile, you reach a branch of Caples Creek and ford it as best you can; it may be difficult in early season and dry by late season. Get back on the main trail on the far side of the creek and follow it northeast along the forested margin of the beautiful meadows that spread along Caples Creek here. The trail strikes out across a meadow near ⅔ mile to cross another branch of Caples Creek on a footbridge that's in pretty sad shape—but you don't have a choice. Beyond, you wind over a rocky ridgelet,

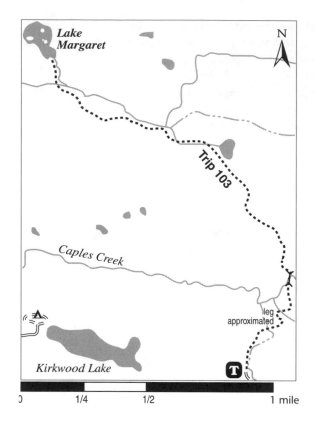

heading generally west. Nearing the top of the ridgelet, you curve past an unmapped, lily-pad-dotted tarn on your left and head north again. At a little over 1 mile you top the ridgelet and enter an area of granite slabs where the descending trail is a bit hard to follow; carefully note your surroundings at the top of these slabs in order to be sure of keeping to the main trail on your return. Continue north, looking for ducks and blazes on trees and paralleling a runoff channel. The trail soon becomes distinct again as it re-enters forest and curves northeast.

At a little over 1⅓ miles, you pass a large pond on your right, ringed by rocks and alders. You trace its outlet—may be dry—along a long, narrow meadow before crossing it at 1½ miles, then recrossing it. Nearing 2 miles you negotiate a boggy section along the sluggish creek. The route becomes hemmed in by high, wonderful flowers—look for giant larkspur here. At 2 miles you ford the creek, a ford made somewhat difficult by the sheer density of the blooming plants here. You soon veer into a more open, drier area below a handsome, rocky outcrop. You begin winding up into the rocks, friction-walking on the slabs at times. You abruptly curve north onto a forested trail through the rocks and shortly reach the rocky shores of lovely **Lake Margaret at 2⅓ miles and 7540 feet**. Picturesque rocky islets dot Lake Margaret, and rocky knolls around it add to the sense of seclusion you find here. Pick a boulder or log from which to enjoy this tranquil spot.

Retrace your steps to your car when you're ready to leave.

104. Silver Lake to Granite, Hidden Lakes

Place	Total distance	Elevation	Level	Type
Start	0	7300	—	—
Granite Lake *only*	2	7580	E	O&B
Hidden Lake	6	7700	M	O&B

Permit required: None

Topo(s): Caples Lake 7½'; USDA/USFS Mokelumne Wilderness

Where to stay:
   Mountain: Kit Carson Lodge
   Of Interest: Sorensen's Resort, Caples Lake Resort, Bear River Lake Resort, Kirkwood Ski
      & Summer Resort, Kay's Silver Lake Resort
   Other: None

Highlights: Two surprisingly pretty lakes invite you to explore beyond beautiful Silver Lake. From granite slabs around the first lake you visit, you have wonderful views over Silver Lake. There's no alpine grandeur at these lakes; what you'll find is the quiet charm of the mid-elevation Sierra.

How to get to the trailhead: Just 11.1 miles west of Carson Pass on State Route 88 is the turnoff south to Kit Carson Lodge. (You have overshot this turnoff if you get to Kirkwood Inn while eastbound or the shore of Silver Lake while westbound.) Follow signs through dense forest dotted by summer cabins toward Camp Minkalo; the road is very narrow and its surface poor past Kit Carson Lodge. Drive 0.5 more mile past the lodge's turnoff to a fork where you go left. In 0.2 more mile there's another fork; go right here. In 0.6 more mile you reach a dusty parking area just beyond the trailhead and just outside the gate for Camp Minkalo.

At the trailhead: Non-hikers will prefer to be at one of the resorts around big, beautiful Silver Lake or at their lodgings.

On the trail: Find the trailhead where the road you drove in on meets the parking area; it's on the right as you face back down the road. Head east-southeast between forest and granite slabs on a dusty trail with a sparse flower display. You briefly parallel a stream on your left, then veer right (south-southeast) away from the stream and onto the slabs. Follow the dusty track between the slabs, nearing ½ mile you cross an unnamed, intermittent creek on a footbridge just upstream of a very pretty little waterfall. A little beyond the bridge, at ½ mile, you reach a junction: right (west) to Plasse's Resort (no lodging), left (south) to Granite Lake. Go left, temporarily leaving the forest behind as you ascend sunstruck slabs on a footpath worn between them. Occasional patches of forest offer needed shade, and a little before 1 mile you cross a small patch of forest to reach the north shore of stunning **Granite Lake at nearly 1 mile and 7580 feet**. Sky-mirroring waters fill a nearly-rectangular hollow sculpted in handsome, light-colored granite. You're high on a ridge overlooking Silver Lake, and there are excellent lake views from the slabs west of Granite Lake. What a wonderful place for a picnic!

Unfortunately, this is an extremely popular stop for equestrians, and, particularly at a junction at the southwest end of the lake, the dust is deep and the poop is ripe. The fact that its shores are mostly granite rather than more-easily displaced dirt or sand probably helps keep Granite Lake from become a mud puddle. A smaller lake northwest of and below Granite, visible from the red-stained slabs on Granite's west shore, may appeal to hikers who don't mind doing a little bushwhacking. You round Granite Lake on its west side and reach an unmapped junction at the lake's southwest corner: left (east, then south) for Hidden Lake, right on a well-horse-traveled use trail that drops off this ridge. You turn left around Granite's south end, then curve south to pass a pretty tarn on your left. You'll have plenty of equine company from here on. Regardless of what you think of equestrians, stand quietly off the trail to let them pass.*

You stroll into patchy lodgepole forest, cross a seasonal stream, and skirt a long meadow full of corn lilies. At a little over 1¾ miles, you reach a signed but unmapped junction: left (south) to Hidden Lake, right (west) to who knows what. Go left through an open, dry forest on a dusty trail to reach an apparent three-way, unsigned junction at a little over 2 miles: left (east-southeast) and uphill; ahead (south) and slightly down; and right (west) downhill, then north. Only the middle fork is blazed, so take the middle fork and stay on the blazed route, ignoring the many dusty use trails threading the area. At 2⅔ miles the trail begins to curve around the pretty valley of a nameless stream. You cross the stream a little past 2¾ miles and find yourself just above **Hidden Lake at 3 miles and 7700 feet**. There's an unmapped junction near the lakeshore: left to round the lake on a use trail, right (south-southeast) to Plasse's Resort. With all the horse traffic, you probably expected Hidden Lake to be a trampled, poop-filled disappointment. Wrong. Hidden Lake, backed by granite

Silver Lake

Camp Minkalo

Granite Lake

Trip 104

Hidden Lake

0   1/4   1/2   1 mile

* Equestrians have the right of way because horses are very easily spooked, and shying horses could injure or kill their riders.

cliffs and shaded by lodgepoles, is very pretty, especially if the equestrians are somewhere else. A picnic stop at Hidden Lake can be a real pleaser.

Retrace your steps past Granite Lake from here.

105. Shealor Lake ☼ 🍁

Place	Total distance	Elevation	Level	Type
Start	0	7440	–	–
Shealor Lake	2½	7180	M U	O&B

Permit required: None

Topo(s): Tragedy Spring 7½'*; USDA/USFS Mokelumne Wilderness

Where to stay:
   Mountain: Kit Carson Lodge
   Of Interest: Sorensen's Resort, Caples Lake Resort, Bear River Lake Resort, Kirkwood Ski
      & Summer Resort, Kay's Silver Lake Resort
   Other: None

Highlights: Shealor (SHAY-ler) Lake is one of the prettiest of the dozens of small lakes caught in the hollows the glaciers left behind in the low, rolling, lightly forested country north of State Route 88 (Trip 103's Lake Margaret is another such lake). You'll enjoy your ascent of the viewful granite dome separating Shealor Lake from the highway as much as you'll enjoy relaxing at the lake.

How to get to the trailhead: Just 17.9 miles southwest of Carson Pass on State Route 88 is a tiny parking lot just off the highway to the west, in an area where the highway makes a pronounced curve between a couple of granite domes. (This turnoff is ill-marked; if you get to Silver Lake while eastbound or the turnoff for Plasse's Resort while westbound, you have overshot the trailhead.)

At the trailhead: Non-hikers will prefer to be back at their lodgings or to take in the pleasures of nearby Silver Lake from one of the resorts or picnic areas beside that lake.

On the trail: Find the trail at the upper end of the parking lot and bear right (north) away from the lot. At first the duff trail is in moderate forest, but it soon enters boulder-studded, patchy forest. You ascend gradually to moderately now, enjoying over-the-shoulder views of Thunder Mountain, to reach an area of granite slabs. You head northwest up the slabs without veering off into the dirt below the slabs; ducks are helpful here. You shortly pick up the dusty trail again

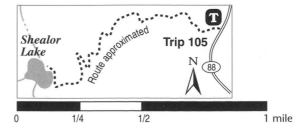

Shealor Lake

Trip 105

Route approximated

N

88

0   1/4   1/2   1 mile

* Trail not shown on topo.

and climb gradually to moderately, mostly curving along the forest edge between slabs and meadow. Presently you make a switchback turn and begin climbing southwest up another, larger area of slabs—up a small granite dome, in fact. Ducks are again helpful as you switchback up to the ridgeline of this long, sloping dome.

At the ridgeline at almost ½ mile, you're on a saddle between knobs at 7720+ feet near the red number 6 printed on the 7½′ topo. You have beautiful views east toward Silver Lake (the lake itself is mostly obscured by the foreground forest) and of the peaks around it. Now you head west down the other side of the dome, to a rolling, once-glaciated landscape where other bare domes beckon. Far ahead and below to your left, a pretty cliff-, forest-, and meadow-bound lake sits on a step-like bench amid the domes. It's one of the Shealor Lakes, and the sight is inspiring. The other lakes come into view as you begin to descend. You descend moderately on an open, rocky, very loose trail; the footing is poor, so be careful. The trail is sometimes indistinct, too, so keep your eyes peeled and use your own best judgment. Perhaps because the area is so open and it seems as if you could almost take any route you like, there are a confusing number of use trails, too. Your goal is to keep working your way down to that lake.

Continue down, steeply at times, friction-walking a few slabs and noticing bits of glacial polish glinting in the sun that strikes the granite cliffs around the lake. At the bottom of the descent, you level out briefly by a patch of forest south of the lake, then veer right (north) through chaparral and onto the open slabs on the lake's east shore. Pick your way down to the shore of this little gem, **Shealor Lake at 1¼ miles and 7180 feet**, which is picturesquely rockbound on most sides. There are great picnic sites on these slabs.

Return the way you came.

106. Shriner Lake 🌿 ☼ 🍁

Place	Total distance	Elevation	Level	Type
Start	0	6560	—	—
Shriner Lake	3⅓	6860	M	O&B

Permit required: None

Topo(s): Bear River Reservoir 7½′; USDA/USFS Mokelumne Wilderness

Where to stay:
   Mountain: None
   Of Interest: Bear River Lake Resort
   Other: None

Highlights: A circuitous drive on a confusion of Forest Service roads leads to the Tanglefoot Trailhead, from which you make a leisurely hike through an attractive landscape to very pretty little Shriner Lake.

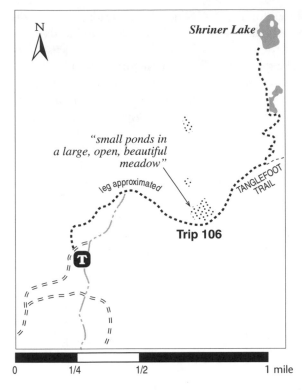

N

Shriner Lake

"small ponds in a large, open, beautiful meadow"

leg approximated

TANGLEFOOT TRAIL

Trip 106

T

| 0 | 1/4 | 1/2 | 1 mile |

How to get to the trailhead:
Look on this drive as an adventure; allow plenty of time, and be prepared to get lost once or twice. A sturdy, high-clearance vehicle is necessary for this drive. Just 31 miles southwest of Carson Pass on State Route 88 is a signed turnoff for Bear River Reservoir (it actually goes to Lower Bear River Reservoir) and Bear River Lake Resort on the south side of the highway. You have overshot this turnoff if you get to Silver Lake while eastbound or Cooks Station while westbound. It is a total of 13.8 circuitous, sometimes-rough miles from this turnoff to the trailhead for this hike. These roads can be extremely rough early in the year before the Forest Service does its springtime road maintenance. You are headed for Tanglefoot Trailhead/Shriner Lake, so adjust these directions accordingly if the road signs differ from them.* Zero your odometer here.

Turn south to Bear River Reservoir on the paved road and follow it 1.9 more miles (1.9 miles cumulative) to a **Y**-junction: left to Bear River Lake Resort, right to the reservoir, dam, campgrounds, and trailheads. Go right to cross the reservoir's dam on a narrow road, curve around the reservoir's south shore, pass the entrance to South Shore Campground, then veer south, away from the reservoir, to a flattened **Y**-, almost a **T**-, junction in 2.4 more miles (4.3 miles). Here, you go hard left to Cole Creek and Bear River Group Campground, arcing northeast on Forest Road 8N14/National Forest Road 81. The road's pavement deteriorates as you pass the Bear River Group Campground turnoff and the Deer Valley turnoff.

You reach a three-way junction in another 2.5 miles (6.8 miles). I think of this junction as *The Big Junction* because it's where you decide between going to the

---

*The area on the south side of Lower Bear River Reservoir is threaded by logging and other dirt roads that probably change from year to year, growing like parasitic dodder over a meadow. Some of the land around here is private, and the Forest Service told me the owners have the right to bulldoze a road and to log pretty much when and where they please. Don't expect the roads to be accurately reflected on any map.

trailhead for this trip or the trailhead for Trip 107. The left fork leads to the Devils Lake trailhead (see Trip 107), the middle fork is Forest Road 8N14 and leads eventually to the start of this trip, and the right fork is a dirt road that hooks sharply up and away. For this trip, you take the middle fork, Forest Road 8N14, and head northeast, then south to the next junction in 0.8 more mile (7.6 miles), where you go right (southwest). In 0.8 more mile (8.4 miles) you reach another three-way junction; take the middle fork (south); the going is very slow as you dodge potholes. At the next junction, in another 1.6 miles (10 miles), you turn left (east) to Tanglefoot Trailhead/Shriner Lake on what is still Forest Road 8N14 but seems by this time like The Road to Nowhere. You soon cross two bridges and stay on the main dirt road, avoiding all turnoffs and heading south and then roughly east, for 3.4 more miles (13.4 miles) to a **Y**-junction. Take the *rougher* left fork here to a rocky parking lot at the Tanglefoot Trailhead in 0.4 more mile (13.8 miles from the junction of State Route 88 and the road to Lower Bear River Reservoir).

At the trailhead: Non-hikers will prefer to be back at their lodgings or to take in the pleasures of nearby Bear River Reservoir—strictly speaking, *Lower* Bear River Reservoir.

On the trail: From the signed TANGLEFOOT TRAIL trailhead on the north side of the parking area, follow the dusty trail north through a forest dominated by incense cedar, Jeffrey pine, and aspen. The trail soon curves east along the side of a ridge to enter Mokelumne Wilderness at ⅓ mile. The gradually ascending trail curves southeast as it traverses a forest where scrub oak now intrudes. Entering a marshy area, you curve through aspens as the trail veers east-north-east to skirt a small meadow with a good flower display. At just over ¾ mile you come abreast of small ponds in a large, open, beautiful mea-dow, probably the remains of the lake shown just north and west of the trail at about 6820 feet— not south as shown on the USDA/USFS Mokelumne Wilderness map— between the words PACK and TRAIL on the 7½′ topo. Leaving this pretty spot behind, you wind through an open area of boulders as you cross a moraine, noting pyramidal Mokelumne Peak to the east.

You descend a little through a forested patch to an unsigned junction preceded by three stone "steps" a little shy of 1¼ miles: left (northeast) to Shriner Lake, right (east) to Tanglefoot Canyon on the Tanglefoot Trail. Go left, resuming a gradual climb, passing a meadow to your right, and then winding up a duff trail into moderate forest. Now you descend a little to head north and traverse the west shore of a small lake that's meadowing in quickly—it's mostly meadow with small ponds now. You top out to see a sheet of blue ahead to the north: **Shriner Lake at 1⅔ miles and 6860 feet**, very picturesque in its setting of lightly-forested, low granite domes. A short descent brings you to the lakeside at a spot marked "Campground" on the 7½′ topo; the ruins of a picnic table here may hearken back to times when you were allowed to camp this close to the water. Pull up a log, get out your lunch, and enjoy.

When you're ready, return the way you came.

107. Devils Lake 🌿 ☼ 🍁

Place	Total distance	Elevation	Level	Type
Start	0	7120	–	–
Devils Lake	2+	7141	M U	O&B

Permit required: None

Topo(s): Bear River Reservoir 7½'; USDA/USFS Mokelumne Wilderness*

Where to stay:

Mountain: None

Of Interest: Bear River Lake Resort

Other: None

Highlights: Beautiful Devils Lake is a destination worthy of a far longer hike, but this one is quite short, and the drive to the trailhead isn't nearly as circuitous as the one to Shriner Lake (Trip 106).

How to get to the trailhead: A sturdy, high-clearance vehicle is necessary for this drive; 4WD is a welcome option. Follow the driving directions of Trip 106 to *The Big Junction* at 6.8 miles from the Bear River Reservoir turnoff from State Route 88, and take the left fork north here. At a **Y**-junction in 0.3 more mile (7.1 miles), go left again. Continue 2 more miles up a road that grows increasingly steep and rough, to a wide spot on the downhill side of the road (left) with a sign that says TRAIL (9.1 miles from the turnoff). Park in the wide spot. The last half-mile or so before the wide spot/trailhead is quite steep and may be so rough and loose that you'll prefer to walk it.

At the trailhead: See Trip 106.

On the trail: The duff track takes off near the TRAIL sign and contours northeast above a steep gully in moderate to dense forest with a

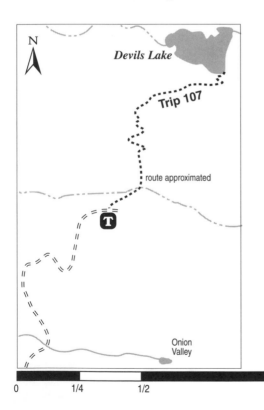

N

Devils Lake

Trip 107

route approximated

T

Onion Valley

0   1/4   1/2   1 mile

* The trail is shown incorrectly on these maps.

pretty sprinkling of flowers in its understory. There's little elevation change at first, and you shortly ford a broad, seasonal stream. The trail grows rocky as you wind up through granite slabs that may once have sported glacial polish. Nearing ⅓ mile you climb briefly over trailless slabs, with the help of ducks, a line of smaller rocks, splashes of paint, and orange plastic ribbon. The next leg is damp and woodsy, the trail a deep groove in the woods, sometimes multiple grooves. Nearing ½ mile you begin a steep to moderate, switchbacking climb up a ridge on a rocky trail. The terrain is open enough to reveal the curve of steep granite cliffs to the east.

Near the ridgetop, you find huge erratics as well as over-the-shoulder views through the trees to Lower Bear River Reservoir. The trail aims you briefly at Peak 7925, and you presently catch a glimpse of fair-sized Devils Lake below. At a little over ¾ mile the climb tops out at 7270 feet before you begin a moderate to steep descent into increasingly lush vegetation. The trail peters out by the southeast end of **Devils Lake at a little over 1 mile and 7141 feet**. Devils Lake is simply beautiful; it should be "Angels Lake." Hunt around for a picnic spot and enjoy yourself here.

When you must, retrace your steps.

CHAPTER 12

Northern Sierra: U.S. Highway 50, South of Tahoe

From its junction with State Route 89 in South Lake Tahoe, U.S. Highway 50 twists east to Nevada and west to Echo Summit. On the way west, it passes below the seasonally-showy cascade that's the outlet of Echo Lakes (see Trip 108). Crossing the summit, 50 begins descending the steep, forested canyon of the American River, passing fine viewpoints and long, striking Horsetail Falls. *Great scenery,* you'll think, *but no hiking unless you're a human fly.* The explanation is simple: marvelous hiking lies just off the roads that branch north from 50 to Desolation Wilderness trailheads. If you think the scenery on 50 is great, just wait till you see what lies along these trails!

Desolation Wilderness. Small, lake-filled Desolation Wilderness is the gem of the Tahoe Sierra. Desolation Wilderness's proximity to the San Francisco-Sacramento area and to crowded Lake Tahoe means the wilderness is very heavily used. Bring your very best trail manners to minimize your impact on the area, and expect plenty of company no matter where you go within the wilderness. Dayhikers are required to have permits; all Desolation Wilderness trailheads in this book have self-issue stations.

Recommended reading

▶ Schaffer, Jeffrey P. *The Tahoe Sierra: A Natural History Guide to 106 Hikes in the Northern Sierra.* See recommended reading for Chapter 11.

▶ —, *Desolation Wilderness.* 3rd ed. Berkeley: Wilderness Press, 1996. Schaffer illuminates Desolation Wilderness with his usual thoroughness and clarity. Book includes as a pocket map the 4-color WP *Desolation Wilderness* 15' topo with insets that make its coverage of the wilderness complete.

▶ Hauserman, Tim, *The Tahoe Rim Trail: A Complete Guide for Hikers, Mountain Bikers, and Equestrians.* 1st ed. Berkeley, CA: Wilderness Press, 2002. An engaging guide to the 165-mile trail that circles the lake.

▶ Semb, George and Patricia, *Day Hikes on the Pacific Crest Trail.* 1st ed. Berkeley, CA: Wilderness Press, 2000. Hikes on the 2665-mile Pacific Crest Trail that

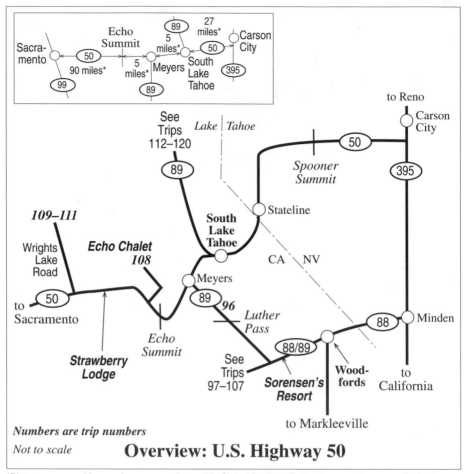

Numbers are trip numbers

Not to scale   **Overview: U.S. Highway 50**

*Distances summed from various sources: Automobile Club of Southern California maps, other maps, field notes.

you can do in a day, with accessible entry and exit points. The book covers all of the PCT in California.

▶ White, Michael C., *Snowshoe Trails of Tahoe*. 1st ed. Berkeley, CA: Wilderness Press, 1998. For winter wanderings in the Tahoe area.

▶ Winnett, Thomas, et. al., *Sierra North*. 8th ed. Berkeley, CA: Wilderness Press, 2002. See recommended reading for Chapter 7.

Recommended maps

▶ USDA/USFS El Dorado National Forest. No topographic information, but invaluable road information.

▶ USDA/USFS Lake Tahoe Basin Management Unit. No topographic information, but invaluable road information. Covers the entire lake and vicinity.

▶ *Desolation Wilderness*. Berkeley, CA: Wilderness Press, 1996. A useful 15′ topographic map of the area.

Lodgings

Alphabetically, the true mountain lodgings and lodgings of interest in the region are—

Echo Chalet
echochalet.com
9900 Echo Lakes Road, Echo Lake, CA 95721   (530) 659-7207, fax (530) 659-7035

7400 feet. At Echo Lakes off U.S. Highway 50. *Mountain*. Nine rustic cabins. Operates from Memorial Day through Labor Day weekend. Limited services in fall. Store, deli counter, picnic area, gas station, boating service, water-taxi service, seasonal post office, some office services. Pets okay. 2002 rates: 2-person cabin, $80–215/night depending on cabin; 4-person cabin, $100–140/night. Two night minimum.

Sorensen's Resort
See Chapter 11

Strawberry Lodge
strawberrylodge.com
Highway 50, Kyburz, CA 95720
(530) 659-7200

5800 feet. On U.S. Highway 50 west of Lake Tahoe. *Of interest*. Lodge rooms and one sleeping cabin; some rooms share bath down the hall. Restaurant. No smoking. No pets. 2002 rates: lodge rooms $55–125/night, sleeping cabin $125/night.

Communities

Alphabetically the eligible communities and their Chambers of Commerce/Visitors Bureaus are—

Lake Tahoe Visitors Authority—See Chapter 11
South Lake Tahoe Chamber of Commerce—See Chapter 11
Towns of South Lake Tahoe—See Chapter 11

Hikes
108. Tamarack and Triangle Lakes ☼ ❦

Place	Total distance	Elevation	Level	Type
Start	0	7414	–	–
Tamarack Lake *only*	7+	7740	S	O&B
Entire semiloop	9⅓	8360	S U	Semi

Permit required: Yes; self-issue station for day-use permits *only* at trailhead.

Topo(s): WP Fallen Leaf Lake 15′; Echo Lake 7½′; USDA/USFS Desolation Wilderness

Where to stay:
Mountain: Echo Chalet
Of Interest: Sorensen's Resort, Strawberry Lodge
Other: Towns of S. Lk. Tahoe

Highlights: This is a wonderfully scenic hike, and the pleasure starts right at the trailhead by Echo Chalet, beginning with the breathtaking view over Echo Lakes.

How to get to the trailhead: The turnoff from U.S. Highway 50 is perhaps the worst-marked *major* junction for hikers that I have ever not-found several times. Start from Echo Summit, which is the high point and on a hairpin turn between South Lake Tahoe and Strawberry. Head north-northwest on U.S. Highway 50 around the densely-forested hairpin, as if toward Strawberry and the Central Valley. You pass the ruins of a defunct resort called Little Norway on your right before reaching a junction with obscurely-signed Johnson Pass Road on your right, 1 mile from *signed* Echo Summit. (You have overshot this turnoff if you get to Echo Summit while eastbound or Strawberry while westbound.)

Turn east (right) onto Johnson Pass Road and follow it 0.6 more mile (1.6 miles total) to a messy **Y**-junction with Echo Lakes Road. Turn north (left) here and follow Echo Lakes Road another mile to a couple of large parking areas at 2.6 miles total, a little before the road elbows down to Echo Lakes. Ignore turnoffs to summer camps and cabins on the way. There's a paved lot on the left, right off the road, and a dirt lot visible off a spur to the right, where the Pacific Crest/Tahoe-Yosemite Trail passes through this area. Unless you are staying at Echo Chalet, you cannot park in the cabin-renters' parking spaces farther down the road or in the small lot at the roadend in front of the Chalet's lodge building. Rather, you will have to park up here and then walk steeply down the last part of the road to the trailhead or the water-taxi dock, about 0.2 mile depending on where you park. Remember this for your return; the hiking mileages given below are from the trailhead only. Toilets, water, telephone, water-taxi service near trailhead; small store at Echo Chalet if it's open.

N

Triangle Lake

to Lily, Fallen Leaf lakes

Triangle-Echo junction

Trip 108

Triangle-Tamarack junction

Tamarack-Aloha junction

Tamarack Lake

water-taxi landing

Upper Echo Lake

continued on facing page

At the trailhead: Non-hikers will enjoy relaxing in this beautiful area. A scenic ride on the water-taxi would be a wonderful addition to a non-hiker's day.

On the trail: Taking the water-taxi one or both ways can save you a lot of walking—over 2⅓ miles if you take the water-taxi one way, 4⅔ miles if both ways—by eliminating one or both legs along the Echo Lakes' north shores. You won't miss much by taking the water-taxi. For completeness' sake, I'll write this trip as if you did *not* take the water taxi; all mileages will reflect that extra 4⅔ miles.

The trailhead is at Lower Echo Lake's dam, next to Echo Chalet; you'll be hiking the combined Pacific Crest Trail and Tahoe-Yosemite Trail for now. Near the trailhead you find a self-issue station for day-use permits only; fill one out as directed. You walk across the dam and then wind up a knoll north of the dam where you find nice views over South Lake Tahoe. The trail angles west-northwest along the slopes north of Lower Echo Lake, soon crossing angled slabs on an airy path that's been blasted right out of them. Views across Lower Echo Lake and of the lake itself lend interest to this leg, which can be very hot as the forest is sparse. The downhill slopes can be very steep, so watch your step. Beyond the slabs, you avoid any turnoffs to the charming lakeside cabins below as you make an up-and-down traverse, pass beneath some low cliffs, and presently round the ridge that pinches Lower Echo Lake off from Upper Echo Lake except for a narrow channel. Now the forest cover is fuller and the going much cooler; paths dart off here and there to dolls'-house cabins, but you stay ahead on the main trail. At 2⅓ miles you reach a junction: right (south) on a spur ⅒ mile downhill to the water-taxi landing at Upper Echo Lake, where there's a shack with a phone for calling for a return water-taxi; left (ahead, west) on a duff trail for Desolation Wilderness, Tamarack Lake, and Lake Aloha.

Those taking the water-taxi pick up the trip here and, together with those who walked from the dam, go ahead toward the wilderness, still on the combined

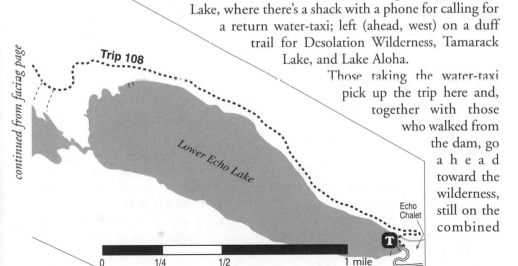

continued from facing page

Trip 108

Lower Echo Lake

Echo Chalet

0   1/4   1/2   1 mile

Pacific Crest/Tahoe-Yosemite Trail. You cross a stream at 2½ miles and are soon climbing in open country on another rocky trail segment blasted through the granite—great over-the-shoulder views along this leg. You reach the boundary of Desolation Wilderness at a little over 3 miles and then almost immediately reach a junction: right (north) to Triangle Lake, left (ahead, west-northwest) on the Pacific Crest/Tahoe-Yosemite Trail to Tamarack Lake and Lake Aloha. I'll call this the *Triangle-Tamarack junction*; if you go to Triangle Lake, your return leg from Triangle will bring you back here. For now, you go ahead, enjoying a surprising wildflower display considering the sandy, dry terrain. At 3⅓ miles you reach another junction: left (southwest) to Tamarack Lake, right (ahead, west) to Lake Aloha; I'll call this the *Tamarack-Aloha junction*. You scamper off to the left, descending a little toward Tamarack Lake, under sparsely-wooded slopes of gray granite. The trail grows faint as it swings easily through this lightly-wooded basin, but very soon you curve southeast beside lovely **Tamarack Lake at nearly 3½ miles and 7740 feet**, looking for a picnic spot, perhaps fording its multistranded outlet stream in your search. Tamarack is by far the prettiest of the lakes in this small basin. Contrary to what's on the topo, there's no real trail looping from Tamarack to Ralston and Cagwin lakes—just confusing fragments of use trails. So unless you're up for some cross-country scrambling, you settle down at Tamarack for a delightful rest stop.

Continuing to Triangle Lake, you retrace your steps to the Tamarack-Aloha junction, now with a little over 3½ miles on your boots, and turn left (west) toward Lake Aloha. With good views over Tamarack Lake to your left, you avoid a use trail that shortly comes in on the right. The trail, though hot and exposed, is flowery in season, and you ascend to a junction with the next trail to Triangle Lake at 4⅓ miles: left (west) on a very well-trod trail to Lake Aloha, right (east-southeast) on a less-used trail to Triangle Lake. (You won't be coming back here, so I won't bother to name this junction.) You go right, climbing gradually to moderately on the hot, open south slope of Keiths Dome, finding a few flowers and a wealth of fabulous views, especially as you round the dome's southeast-trending ridge and gain its high point: to Echo Lakes; to Tamarack and Ralston lakes; to crags and peaks in Desolation Wilderness; and, to the east, a glimpse of Lake Tahoe. Saying goodbye to these spectacular views, you round the northeast side of the ridge and begin descending into a forest of lodgepole and red fir.

At a little over 5 miles you reach a junction on a saddle: left (north) to Triangle Lake; ahead (east) to Lily Lake near Glen Alpine and Fallen Leaf Lake; and right (south-southeast) to Echo Lakes. I'll call this the *Triangle-Echo junction*. From here, you make an out-and-back leg to Triangle Lake, so turn left to follow a somewhat-faint trail downhill and generally north through a damp, mixed conifer forest, along meadows, over knobs, and then steeply down a little swale to an unmapped pond near Triangle Lake. From here, cross slabs to come out a little above the southwest shore of charming, secluded **Triangle Lake at 5½ miles and 8020 feet**. There are fine picnic spots in the rocks along its pretty shore.

Saying farewell to Triangle Lake, you retrace your steps to the *Triangle-Echo junction* on the saddle: right to the *Triangle-Aloha junction* (no), middle (ahead) to the *Triangle-Tamarack junction* (yes), left to Lily and Fallen Leaf lakes (no). With nearly 6 miles on your boots now, you take the middle fork back to Echo Lakes, descending a rocky duff trail moderately to steeply, through red fir and lodgepole.

The trail becomes very rocky as you emerge on an open slope and then reach the Triangle-Tamarack junction with the Pacific Crest/Tahoe-Yosemite Trail at 6½ miles.

Turn left (east) here and retrace your steps to exit Desolation Wilderness and traverse above the north shores of the Echo Lakes to the trailhead, ending your semiloop at the trailhead at a little over 9⅓ miles if you didn't use the water-taxi.

109. Bloodsucker Lake 🌸 ☼ 🍁

Place	Total distance	Elevation	Level	Type
Start	0	7040	—	—
Bloodsucker Lake	4	7420	M	O&B

Permit required: None

Topo(s): WP Fallen Leaf Lake 15'; Pyramid Peak 7½'; USDA/USFS Desolation Wilderness

Where to stay:
    Mountain: Echo Chalet
    Of Interest: Strawberry Lodge
    Other: Towns of S. Lk. Tahoe

Highlights: Bloodsucker Lake is mighty pretty, and its resident population of leeches (bloodsuckers) makes it unusual and interesting.

How to get to the trailhead: The lower part of Wrights Lake Road, the former route to this trailhead, is permanently closed after having suffered severe rain damage in 1997. The "new" route is via Ice House Road. Just about 27 miles west of Echo Summit on U.S. Highway 50, turn north at the Crystal Basin Recreation Area turnoff (Forest Route 3 and Ice House Road). (You have overshot this junction if you get to White Hall while eastbound, Pacific House while westbound.) Follow this road 9 miles to Ice House Resort, then continue 1½ miles farther to Forest Route 32. Turn right and take this road 9 more miles, past Ice House Reservoir, to a junction with Forest Road 4 (Wrights Lake Road). Turn left and drive 1.8 miles to a spur road on your right, and turn right here into a large, dusty parking lot that also doubles as the entrance to Wrights Lake Horse Camp. Follow either branch of the road loop through the camp to its far (south) end at a small parking lot and the trailhead, 0.2 mile more; the official trailhead is here. Alternatively, park back in the large, dusty parking lot; an unofficial trailhead near here may be a better choice when Silver Creek is high.

At the trailhead: Non-hikers may enjoy relaxing at beautiful Wrights Lake. Or they may prefer to be at their lodgings, shopping in South Lake Tahoe, or emptying their wallets at the casinos in Stateline, Nevada.

On the trail: Early in the year, when Silver Creek is running high, there may be good reason to consider starting from the large, dusty parking lot rather than from the official trailhead. Here's the situation: from the official trailhead, the broad,

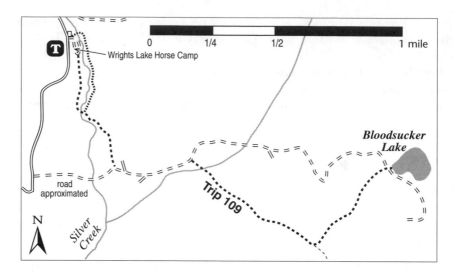

sandy, well-trod Bloodsucker Lake trail heads south along the west bank of Silver Creek, shortly dipping to an equestrian crossing of the creek and then climbing back up the other side to meet a use trail coming in on the left while the main trail curves right, along the creek. When the water is high and swift, there may be no place for a hiker to ford safely near the equestrian crossing. However, from the east side of the large, dusty parking lot, you'll find a well-worn use trail that leads down to a relatively narrow part of Silver Creek and to a big log wedged into a clump of living trees on the west bank and securely settled on the east bank—not the worst log you ever teetered on. From the east bank, one use trail leads along the creek proper while another use trail climbs up the bank to meet yet another use trail on which you can turn right (south) to meet the Bloodsucker Lake Trail coming up from the equestrian crossing. To judge by the condition of the use trails and of the tree, this is a well-used alternative. They're about equidistant.

One way or the other, you find yourself on Silver Creek's east bank at the junction of the use trail and of the Bloodsucker Lake trail. Follow this trail southeast into moderate lodgepole forest. At ⅓ mile you cross an unmapped tributary; horses have made the trail crossing very broad and muddy. You shortly veer southeast away from Silver Creek and climb a moraine to meet a dirt road at a little over ½ mile. Note this spot for your return. Turn left (east) onto the road and note that another road very shortly comes in from the left (northwest)—avoid it. You continue east toward the Crystal Range, visible in the distance. The going is sunstruck and dusty, and you shortly pass another road junction where a road comes in from the right (south)—avoid it, too. Continue east; red firs and alders lining the road here give a little shade. At a trail sign at nearly ⅔ mile, as the road curves northeast, you turn right (east) off the road and onto a footpath.*

*Although the road eventually goes to Bloodsucker Lake, it's very hot and dusty and in places very steep. I don't recommend taking it.

You soon reach a very swampy part that may be wonderfully flowery but difficult in early season, and a little over ¾ mile cross a multistranded tributary of Silver Creek. The trail, growing dusty again because it's badly chewed up by horses, heaves itself up a moraine. Multiple tracks diverge and converge, and the going is increasingly unpleasant, dusty, and sunblasted as you near the top of the moraine. At the moraine's top at nearly 1½ miles, you reach a junction: left (northeast) to Bloodsucker Lake, right (ahead, southeast) to Lyons Creek. Go left and find that, after a level stretch, the trail climbs as the going becomes muddy and the trail surface poor—but the flowers around it are a sight to behold. At nearly 2 miles you reach a road—it's actually another segment of the road you walked on earlier—and see the lake a few steps ahead.

Step across the road and down to the cool shore of lovely **Bloodsucker Lake at 2 miles and 7420 feet**. Find a lakeside spot where you can relax and enjoy the scenery here. Blue Peak rises to the northeast and other Crystal Range peaks are visible from here. You may see a leech or two swim by; if not, try stirring the water a little with a stick. They're about 2–3 inches long, about ¼ inch wide, yellowish to grayish, flattened, and slightly tapered at either end; they swim in an undulating fashion. They're not native; no one knows how they got here.

When you're ready, return the way you came.

110. Grouse and Hemlock Lakes ☼ ❀

Place	Total distance	Elevation	Level	Type
Start	0	6940	–	–
Grouse Lake only	4⅔	8140	M	O&B
Hemlock Lake	6	8380	S	O&B

Permit required: Yes; self-issue station for day-use permits only at trailhead

Topo(s): WP Fallen Leaf Lake 15′; Pyramid Peak 7½′; USDA/USFS Desolation Wilderness

Where to stay:
   Mountain: Echo Chalet
   Of Interest: Strawberry Lodge
   Other: Towns of S. Lk. Tahoe

Highlights: From beautiful Wrights Lake you ascend through a dramatic landscape to a chain of lovely little lakes. Each has its own beauty and character.

How to get to the trailhead: Follow the driving directions of Trip 109 to Wrights Lake but continue past the large, dusty parking lot/equestrian campground entrance 0.2 more mile to the car campground entrance. Turn right into the campground and follow the main campground road a mile more all the way to its end at a small parking loop at the north-northeast corner of Wrights Lake. If the lot is full, don't park along the road or in the parking spaces for the adjacent cabins; rather, you'll find an overflow parking lot 0.6 mile back down the road the way you came.

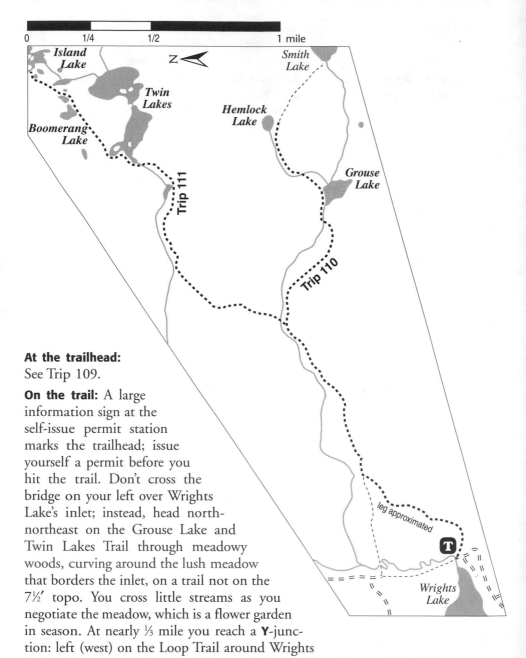

At the trailhead:
See Trip 109.

On the trail: A large
information sign at the
self-issue permit station
marks the trailhead; issue
yourself a permit before you
hit the trail. Don't cross the
bridge on your left over Wrights
Lake's inlet; instead, head north-
northeast on the Grouse Lake and
Twin Lakes Trail through meadowy
woods, curving around the lush meadow
that borders the inlet, on a trail not on the
7½' topo. You cross little streams as you
negotiate the meadow, which is a flower garden
in season. At nearly ⅓ mile you reach a **Y**-junc-
tion: left (west) on the Loop Trail around Wrights
Lake, right (east-northeast) to Twin and Grouse lakes. You go right to skirt granite slabs and begin climbing, ignoring a use trail on your left. At a little over ½
mile, the trail levels out atop a small dry ridge. Now you dip into forest, then begin
climbing again, noticing a stream to your left. You climb up a rocky ridge on loose
zigzags, fording an unmapped stream at ¾ mile. You continue up slabs, following
ducks and coming abreast of Grouse Lake's outlet stream (on your left).

At a little under 1¼ miles you enter Desolation Wilderness, and at 1⅓ miles you reach a junction: right (east) to Grouse Lake, left (north) to Twin Lakes. Turn right for Grouse Lake, following more ducks up slabs full of potholes, keeping generally to the right side of the lovely granite bowl here, down which the outlet spills in picturesque cascades. You soon veer right, out of the bowl and into forest, and presently curve east-southeast in an open, slabby valley on a sandy trail. At a little over 2 miles, at the head of the slabby valley, you veer left (northeast) to climb steeply, briefly enjoy expansive views north and west, and then come alongside the noisy outlet. At 2¼ miles you ford the broad, multistranded outlet between cascades; there's a fine display of flowers here in season. You reach beautiful **Grouse Lake at just over 2⅓ miles and 8140 feet.** The trail traces Grouse's north shore over slabs that make nice picnic spots, then veers away from the wonderland of meadows and streams around the lake's inlet to begin climbing the ridge separating Grouse and Hemlock lakes. The trail climbs steeply northeast on a rocky, often faint track before leveling out in open forest to ford the stream between Grouse and Hemlock lakes, then veer northeast to little **Hemlock Lake at 3 miles and 8380 feet.** The lake is set in handsome cliffs on the north and east; its south shore, where you stand, is shaded by mountain hemlocks. Sandy picnic sites beckon along this pretty shore.

To continue to Smith Lake, see the footnote (*) below. Otherwise, retrace your steps to your car.

*To see the highest lake in the drainage, Smith Lake, at about 3½ miles (one-way) and 8700 feet, follow Jeffrey P. Schaffer's directions from *The Tahoe Sierra* (quoted by permission):

Hiking southeast [from Hemlock Lake], we make a final ducked climb and reach nearly treeless Smith Lake, which at 8700 feet elevation is almost at timberline. Its steep, confining slopes, most having snowfields that last well into summer, are also detrimental to growth. Nevertheless, a small stand of lodgepole and western white pines does thrive above the lake's northwest shore. From a rocky, emergency bivouac spot near the lake's outlet we can look out over the Wrights and Crystal Basin recreation areas and identify Wrights Lake and Dark Lake below us and Union Valley Reservoir in the distance. This is the only lake [on this trail] from which you can get such expansive views of these two areas.

111. Twin and Island Lakes 🌿 ☼ 🍁

Place	Total distance	Elevation	Level	Type
Start	0	6940	—	—
Lower Twin Lake only	5½	7880	M	O&B
Island Lake	7	8140	S	O&B

Permit required: Yes; self-issue station for day-use permits *only* at trailhead

Topo(s): WP Fallen Leaf Lake 15'; Pyramid Peak 7½'; USDA/USFS Desolation Wilderness

Where to stay:
    Mountain: Echo Chalet
    Of Interest: Strawberry Lodge
    Other: Towns of S. Lk. Tahoe

Highlights: Starting at Wrights Lake at the same trailhead as for Trip 110, you climb through a spectacular landscape to two splendid lakes.

How to get to the trailhead: Follow the driving directions of Trip 109 from Echo Summit to Wrights Lake and then of Trip 110 to the trailhead.

At the trailhead: See Trip 110.

On the trail: See Trip 110's map. Follow Trip 110 from Wrights Lake into Desolation Wilderness and then to the junction at 1⅓ miles, where you must choose between Grouse Lake and Twin Lakes: right (east) to Grouse Lake, left (north) to Twin Lakes. Go left to Twin Lakes, fording Grouse Lake's outlet stream almost immediately. You begin a gradual ascent of slabs through a shallow bowl of mostly-bare granite, picking your way northeast and soon crossing other strands of Grouse Lake's outlet in season. The trail can be hard to follow, but in general it takes you well to the west of the bowl, west of three slabby peaklets at the east end of the ridge at the head of the bowl. Nearing 2 miles you top that ridge at its lower, east end, about ¼ mile east of a low knoll. Now you descend north-northeast into

Eriogonum Lobbii near Island Lake

forest and toward the showy, cascading outlet of Twin Lakes. Just before you reach the outlet, you veer east-southeast on more slabs, making you way into the next cirque and beginning a long, climbing curve to the north. Blast marks in the slabs show how the route was built.

At last the trail, such as it is, levels out below those slabby peaklets at the east end of the ridge you topped earlier, and you curve into a peak-ringed cirque, passing a pond to your left (north). At a little over 2⅓ miles you ford Twin Lakes' outlet on built-up stones before continuing deeper

Island Lake

into the cirque. You reach dramatic **lower Twin Lake at 2¾ miles and 7880 feet**. Across the lake, the cascading outlet of higher lakes makes a springtime spectacle. The lake's sparsely-shaded, rocky shore offers some delightful picnic spots, so pull up a boulder and enjoy your stay. Continuing, you ford lower Twin Lake's outlet on a ruined dam that's more hindrance than help. You veer northeast on a very rocky trail along the north side of lower Twin Lake, making your way over a ridgelet above tiny Boomerang Lake.

The trail passes over the "strait" between Boomerang and a little pond and then follows a rocky track as it rolls up and down, presently skirting the north end of a long, narrow pond below Island Lake. After you ascend to the ponds below Island Lake, it's just a few steps to the shore of high, barren **Island Lake at nearly 3½ miles and 8140 feet**. The trail peters out a little before the lakeshore, so pick your way to the stony shore and get an eyeful. There are few picnic sites around here, so you'll probably want to retrace your steps to lower Twin Lake for a lunch stop.

Return the way you came.

Mt. Tallac

CHAPTER 13

Northern Sierra:
State Route 89
Around Lake Tahoe

From its junction with U.S. Highway 50 in South Lake Tahoe, State Route 89 curves west and then north around the California side of Lake Tahoe, past Tallac Historic Site and the Lake Tahoe Visitor Center. The highway soon begins swooping along cliffs overlooking Emerald Bay, past breathtaking viewpoints, and through woodsy hamlets. Unfortunately, Lake Tahoe is like Yosemite Valley in one respect: tranquil and sublimely beautiful early in the morning and in the evening, at midday it is hot, dusty, noisy, crowded, and choked with cars. You creep along State Route 89 in bumper-to-bumper traffic, all sense of mountain peace shattered. The solution? Simple: like Yosemite Valley, the best way to enjoy Lake Tahoe at midday is to be somewhere else, such as on the wonderful trails high above the lake. You'll find the best of them here, mostly in Desolation Wilderness (see the note in the introduction to the previous chapter).

But all is not lost at lakeside. Real treats are a stop at the Lake Tahoe Visitor Center just past the turnoff onto Fallen Leaf Road but on the opposite side of the road, and another stop at Tallac Historic Site, between Richardson's Resort and the visitor center. At the visitor center, short, easy nature walks prove both entertaining and educational. A visit to the wonderful Stream Profile Chamber is a must. It allows you to walk through through a tunnel one side of which is a window on a natural stream—the streambed is a little below the window, the water's surface is a couple of feet higher, near eye level. At Tallac Historic Site, interpretive signs explain the fascinating remains of lakeside resorts and of homes of the very wealthy, from the 1890s through the 1920s; an easy path connects the sites and remains.

Recommended reading
► Schaffer, Jeffrey P., *The Tahoe Sierra: A Natural History Guide to 106 Hikes in the Northern Sierra*. See recommended reading for Chapter 11.
► —, *Desolation Wilderness*. See Chapter 12.

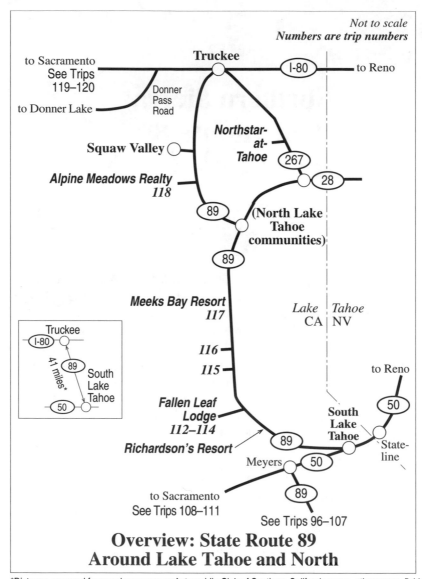

Not to scale
Numbers are trip numbers

Overview: State Route 89
Around Lake Tahoe and North

*Distance summed from various sources: Automobile Club of Southern California maps, other maps, field notes.

▶ Hauserman, Tim, *The Tahoe Rim Trail: A Complete Guide for Hikers, Mountain Bikers, and Equestrians.* 1st ed. Berkeley, CA: Wilderness Press, 2002. An engaging guide to the 165-mile trail that circles the lake.

▶ Semb, George and Patricia, *Day Hikes on the Pacific Crest Trail.* 1st ed. Berkeley, CA: Wilderness Press, 2000. Hikes on the 2665-mile Pacific Crest Trail that you can do in a day, with accessible entry and exit points. The book covers all of the PCT in California.

▶ White, Michael C., *Snowshoe Trails of Tahoe.* 1st ed. Berkeley, CA: Wilderness Press, 1998. For winter wanderings in the Tahoe area.

▶ Winnett, Thomas, et. al., *Sierra North*. 8th ed. Berkeley, CA: Wilderness Press, 2002. See recommended reading for Chapter 7.

Recommended maps

▶ USDA/USFS El Dorado National Forest. See Chapter 12.
▶ USDA/USFS Lake Tahoe Basin Management Unit. See Chapter 12.

Special Note
Area codes in the Tahoe area have changed from 916 to 530.

Lodgings
Alphabetically, the true mountain lodgings and lodgings of interest in the region are—

Alpine Meadows Realty (agency)   alpinerentalgroup.com
P.O. Box 1176, Tahoe City, CA 96145   (530) 583-1545

About 6560 feet. On Alpine Meadows Road, off State Route 89 north of Lake Tahoe. *Of interest.* Condominiums and private homes available. Amenities depend on the condo or home you rent. No pets except by special arrangement that may result in higher security deposit. 2002 rates vary by condo or home; $185–810/night.

Always Inn Bed and Breakfast [formerly Traverse Inn Bed and Breakfast]
10108 Soda Springs Road, P.O. Box 861   alwaysinn.com
Soda Springs, CA 95728-1012   (530) 426-3010
(See map on page 341)   (877) 56-TAHOE fax (530) 426-1100

6880 feet. On Soda Springs Road off Interstate 80 west of Donner Summit. *Mountain.* Pets are okay. No smoking. Four rooms have private baths, television, VCR, CD and spas. Rates include full breakfast and range from $100–175/night.

Clair Tappaan Lodge
P.O. Box 36, Norden, CA 95724   (530) 426-3632
(See map on page 341)

7000 feet. On Donner Pass Road south of I-80. *Of interest.* Lodge with rooms varying from 2-person cubicles to family bunk rooms and single-sex dormitories. Very Spartan. Common rooms: living room, library, dining area, social room, hot tub (bathing suit required). Weekend seminars in the summer. Guest must provide own sleeping bag or comparable bedding and towels. Nightly rate includes one night and 3 meals the following day. A guest performs a house chore each day s/he eats at the lodge. No pets except seeing-eye dogs. 2002 rates for adult Sierra Club members: $39–43/1 night, $175–200/5 nights, and $240–275/7 nights. 2002 rates for adult non-members: $43–50/night; $195–230/5 nights; $280–315/7 nights. Children's rates lower.

Donner Summit Lodge—closed for renovation in 2002. Call for current information.
P.O. Box 696, Soda Springs, CA 95728   (530) 426-3638
7000 feet. On Donner Pass Road (old State Route 40) off Interstate 80 near Donner Pass. *Of interest.* Hotel rooms. Restaurant. Nearby gas station.

Fallen Leaf Lodge (agency)   (800) 335-1716
6380 feet. Off Fallen Leaf Road at Fallen Leaf Lake, off State Route 89 west of Lake Tahoe. *Mountain.* The Lodge, in former years a true lodge with cabins, lodge build-ing, and campground, was closed for several years. Now, all but one of the old lodge's buildings have been demolished, and the site has been under reconstruction for several more years as a development of private vacation homes called Fallen Leaf Lodge. 4 homes presently available; more expected to be available in the future. Call the number above to get a packet of information on the homes currently available for rent. After you get the information, you then must call the listed owner(s) of the home(s) to make arrangements. The homes available are full housekeeping units. Stores, restaurants in South Lake Tahoe. All: no smoking. No pets. 2002 rates: $600–900/weeknight depending on the number of people and particular home; $1100–1400/weekend night; $3300–4200/weekly. Cleaning fee from $150–175. Deposit $1000–2000.

Ice Lakes Lodge [formerly Serene Lakes Lodge and RV Park]   icelakeslodge.com
1100 Soda Springs Rd., Soda Springs, CA 95728   (530) 426-7660
6880 feet (the lakes are called the Ice Lakes on the Soda Spring 7½′ topo). On Soda Springs Road off Interstate 80 west of Donner Summit. *Mountain.* Restaurant, bar, volleyball net, games room, kayaks, water activities on lake (no motors). Special events welcome, by arrangement. No pets. 2002 rates: $90–160/night.

Meeks Bay Resort   meeksbayresort.com
Box 787, Tahoma, CA 96142   (877) 326-3357
6230 feet. Off State Route 89 at Lake Tahoe's Meeks Bay. *Mountain.* Housekeeping "mansion" (7 bedrooms, 3 baths), cabins, and condos accommo-dating 1–12 persons depending on unit. Marina (slips reserved), launch ramp, campground, sales of snack foods and ice cream. Nearby store. Stays limited to 14 days; most rentals on a weekly basis only. No pets. 2002 rates: $375/cabins/per night with a 2 night minimum; $240/night for off-season; $200/lodge rooms/per night with a 2 night minimum; $90/night for off-season. Most rooms (both cab-ins and lodge rooms) sleep up to 6. Cost per week is $1825.

Northstar at Tahoe northstar.com

P.O. Box 129, (800) GO-NORTH, (530) 562-1010,

Truckee, CA 96160 fax (530) 562-2215

6300 feet. Off State Route 267 north of Lake Tahoe. *Of interest.* Resort complex. Sleeping-only lodge rooms; housekeeping lofts, condominiums (studio to 4 bedroom), homes (3–5 bedrooms), all with fireplaces. In-room color TV, VCR, telephone; housekeeping units have microwave ovens, dishwashers. Rentals, facilities, and lessons for golf, mountain biking (mountain-bike park), tennis. Also adventure park, horseback riding, swimming pool, recreation center, special kids' activities, licensed child-care and children's day camp. 2 restaurants, shops, deli counter, groceries. No pets. 2002 rates: lodge room (1–4 persons) $149–255; loft (2 persons) $169–349; condos (1–8 persons) $149–625; homes $379–1055.

Rainbow Lodge Bed and Breakfast (530) 426-3871, (800) 500-3871

P.O. Box 1100, Soda Springs, CA 95728 fax (530) 426-9221

5800 feet. Off I-80 on Rainbow Road west of Donner Summit. *Of interest.* Bedrooms with private bath, with shower and sink, with sink only; bridal suite; family suite. Includes full breakfast. Restaurant. No pets. 2002 rates: Summer rates range from $89–139/night; winter rates, $99–159/night. Additional persons may share a room at the rate of $15 per night. No charge for children 6 years and younger, although their breakfasts are not complimentary.

Richardson's Resort camprich.com

P.O. Box 9028, South Lake Tahoe, CA 96158 (800) 544-1801, (530) 541-1801

6230 feet. On State Route 89 on Lake Tahoe, north of South Lake Tahoe. *Of interest.* Hotel rooms (lodge and "beach inn") for 1–4 persons; duplexes with woodstove or fireplace for 1–6 persons; cabins, some with woodstove or fireplace for 1–8 persons. Very good restaurant, marina, RV campground, tent campground, meeting room, ice-cream parlor, deli, playground, country store, gas station, bike rentals and tours, horseback riding/pack station, tennis, volleyball, beach, special events (e.g., rock concert). No pets. 1994 rates: lodge room $59–69/weekday (Sunday–Thursday) night, $69–79/weekend night; "beach inn" room $79/weekday night, $89/weekend night; duplex $180/night, $1260/week; cabins $68–137/night, $480–960/week. Cribs $5/night, rollaways $10/night.

Summit House at Donner Ski Ranch summithouse.com

P.O. Box 66, Norden, CA 95724 (See map on page 331) (530) 426-3622 ext. 0-4111

7000 feet. On Donner Pass Road (old State Route 40) off Interstate 80 near Donner Pass, at Donner Ski Ranch. *Of interest.* Sleeping-only and housekeeping condominiums for 1–10 persons. Restaurant, cafeteria, bar at ski area; meeting and conference facilities. No smoking. No stated pet policy. 2002 rates: $100–220/weeknight; $120–250/weekend night or holiday. An additional cleaning fee of $15–70 is also charged, depending upon unit.

Communities

Alphabetically, eligible communities and the Chambers of Commerce and Visitors Bureaus are—

Donner Lake

See Truckee-Donner Chamber of Commerce

Vacation community around Donner Lake, east of Donner Summit, off I-80.

Squaw Valley

Squaw Valley Central Reservations   (800) 545-4350, information (530) 583-6955

Resort community next to Squaw Valley Ski Area/Mountain Bike Park on Squaw Valley Road off State Route 89 north of Lake Tahoe, south of Truckee.

Tahoe North Visitors Bureau and Convention Bureau

P.O. Box 5578, Suite #3, 950 N. Lake Blvd.,   (800) TAHOE 4-U, (530) 583-3494,
Tahoe City, CA 96145   fax (530) 581-4081

Serves towns of north Lake Tahoe.

Towns of North Lake Tahoe

See Tahoe North Visitors Bureau and Convention Bureau

Numerous vacation communities around north end of California side of Lake Tahoe.

Towns of South Lake Tahoe

See Chapter 12.

Truckee

See Truckee-Donner Chamber of Commerce

Town straddling Interstate Highway 80 north of Lake Tahoe, east of Donner Summit.

Truckee-Donner Chamber of Commerce

12036 Donner Pass Rd., P.O. Box 2757, Truckee, CA 96160   (530) 587-2757

Handles Truckee and Donner Lake.

Hikes

112. Angora Lakes ☼ 🍁

Place	Total distance	Elevation	Level	Type
Start	0	6400	—	—
Angora Lookout only	2½	7290	M	O&B
Entire loop	4⅓	7480	S	Loop

Permit required: None

Topo(s): WP Fallen Leaf Lake 15'; Emerald Bay, Echo Lake 7½'; USDA/USFS Desolation Wilderness

Where to stay:
Mountain: Fallen Leaf Lodge, Meeks Bay Resort
Of Interest: Richardson's Resort
Other: Towns of S. Lake Tahoe

Highlights: Pretty upper Angora Lake, with a day-use* resort, offers boating, picnicking, sunning, and swimming in a lovely mountain setting free of cars. While the hike is steep and requires some time on a road, it's well worth it for the sweeping views from the trail as well as for the charming Angora Lakes (there are officially three of them). Non-hikers have a mostly-driving alternative explained below at the second footnote (**).

How to get to the trailhead: Near the south end of Lake Tahoe, northbound State Route 89 meets U.S. Highway 50 in Meyers at a **T**-junction: left on U.S. Highway 50 to Echo Summit and Echo and Wrights lakes; right on combined U.S. Highway 50/State State Route 89 to destinations around Lake Tahoe. Turn right and drive into the bustling, noisy town of South Lake Tahoe, where State Route 89 and U.S. Highway 50 part company at a **Y**-junction: left on 89 around Lake Tahoe's west side, right on 50 to Lake Tahoe's east side and Nevada. We'll call this

---

* While the lodge does in fact rent cabins to overnight visitors, I am told by a reliable source that it is fully booked years in advance. So for most of us, it's a day-use resort. On the other hand, it can't hurt to ask while you're there... .
** Non-hikers up for a short walk should note that it is possible to drive most of the way to Angora Lakes. Hiking and non-hiking friends might consider meeting at the upper trailhead and walking to the lakes together if the road is open.
On the way around Fallen Leaf Lake, you pass a badly marked turnoff left (east) for Tahoe Mountain Road, about ⅓ of the way around the lake. A short distance up Tahoe Mountain Road, there's a badly-marked Y-junction with Angora Ridge Road. You can drive Angora Ridge Road (the right fork at the Y-junction) to the parking lot described in
   On the trail, beginning at "Nearing 2 miles from your start, ..." This lot is ½ mile from Angora Lakes Resort. However, Angora Ridge Road may be closed at times, such as when there's snow on it. Check out the road's condition and availability before making plans to meet your hiking friends up near the closure below Angora Lakes.
   See **On the trail** at "Follow that dirt road..." for walking directions; the out-and-back distance is 1 mile total on a dirt road, the elevation gain 280 feet (moderate to steep).

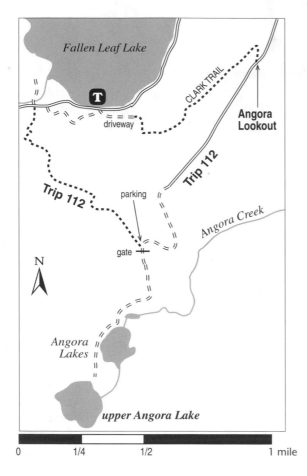

the Tahoe **Y**. There's a visitor center at the **Y**; it's a great place to stop and pick up reams of useful Tahoe information.

Turn left at the Tahoe **Y** and drive 3.7 miles past Richardson's Resort (also called Camp Richardson) to the junction with Fallen Leaf Road on the south (left) side of the road. (You have overshot this junction if you get to Inspiration Point while northbound or Richardson's Resort while southbound.) Turn left onto Fallen Leaf Road and drive nearly all the way around beautiful Fallen Leaf Lake on an increasingly narrow, potholed road. Just by lakeside Fallen Leaf Lodge at the south end of Fallen Leaf Lake, there's a driveway that hooks sharply left, *away* from the lake and Fallen Leaf Lodge, and past some cabins, at about 4.6 miles from the State Route 89-Fallen Leaf Road junction. The driveway, marked NO DRIVING! NO PARKING!—no kidding!—leads to your starting trailhead. You'll return by way of a trailhead by a church about 0.25 mile farther up Fallen Leaf Road and close your loop by walking to your car. Park off Fallen Leaf Road near one of these trailheads as best you can; there may not be a formal parking lot. Walk back to the driveway by Fallen Leaf Lodge from there.

At the trailhead: There is little for the non-hiker at this trailhead, but there are numerous recreational opportunities—picnicking, fishing, boating, just plain relaxing, shopping, gambling—around Lake Tahoe, as well as visits to the Lake Tahoe Visitor Center and Tallac Historic Site (see the beginning of this chapter). And there's a mostly-driving alternative for visiting upper Angora Lake (see the second footnote (**) on the previous page).

On the trail: From Fallen Leaf Road, walk up the driveway past some cabins. Where the driveway forks, take the dirt left fork to an obscure trailhead, marked CLARK TRAIL, at the roadend. This hike's mileage starts here. You begin climbing very steeply south-southeast, zigzagging through white fir. After ⅓ mile, the grade eases, and the rocky-dusty trail offers occasional excellent views of Fallen Leaf Lake and of Lake Tahoe beyond. Mt. Tallac (tah-LACK) and Cathedral Peak rise across Fallen Leaf Lake, and you can see far south into the glacial valley of Glen Alpine Creek. It's apparent from here that Fallen Leaf Lake is impounded by a low moraine at its north end; a low dam at its north end artificially raises its level a little more. Were the moraine to wash away or to be flooded by rising lakewater, Fallen Leaf Lake would become Fallen Leaf Bay, like Emerald Bay: Emerald Bay would be Emerald Lake if its moraine weren't under water. Speaking of moraines, what you're ascending is Fallen Leaf's huge east-lateral moraine.

Pressing on through scrub oak and manzanita, you enter El Dorado National Forest as the views continue to improve. After a long northward traverse across the moraine's steep west slope, **Angora Lookout at nearly 1¼ miles and 7290 feet**. There's a welcome bench under Jeffrey pine and white fir here, and the views, outstanding before, are stupendous from here. The Clark Trail ends here at Angora Lookout, and you continue your hike by turning south (right) on Angora Ridge Road. Descending slightly and now walking on a paved road, you walk the ridgeline of this moraine toward Angora Peak until the pavement ends, enjoying the tremendous panorama. Continue on the now-dirt road as it swings left through forest, then right around a knob.

Nearing 2 miles from your start, the road swings left into a paved parking lot where you'll meet your friends who drove up from Fallen Leaf Lake. The parking lot has two levels connected by a short road. Follow the road through the parking lot to its upper end at just over 2 miles, where a dirt road, closed to the public's vehicles but not the resort's, begins. Follow that dirt road as it curves moderately to steeply uphill toward Angora Lakes Resort. At just over 2¼ miles several use trails branch left (south-southeast) toward the lowest Angora Lake. You stay on the road, continuing past handsome middle Angora Lake, to upper Angora Lake and **Angora Lake Resort at 2½ miles and 7480 feet**. Here you'll find a beach, boat rentals, restrooms, snacks, and cold drinks in a delightful setting right under Echo and Angora peaks. You eventually retrace your steps to the parking lot and bid your non-hiking friends farewell.

Pick up a poorly marked trail on the northwest side of the road connecting the two levels of the parking lot, and turn left onto it. You shortly cross a forested saddle, then begin a steep descent. The trail winds down through a lavish, seasonal display of wildflowers and frequently crosses areas of shattered rock where hundreds of sharp fragments in the trail's tread make for slippery footing. You presently emerge behind a little church at a poorly signed trailhead, cross a tiny footbridge, and reach Fallen Leaf Road at a little over 4 miles, almost exactly opposite a bridge that branches over Glen Alpine Creek to private Stanford High Sierra Camp. You turn onto Fallen Leaf Road, toward your car (right if it's back up near Fallen Leaf Lodge), to close your hike at about 4⅓ miles, depending on where you parked your car.

113. Grass Lake 🌸 ☼ 🍁

Place	Total distance	Elevation	Level	Type
Start	0	6560	–	–
Grass Lake	4½+	7420	M	O&B

Permit required: Yes; self-issue station for day-use permits *only* at trailhead

Topo(s): WP Fallen Leaf Lake 15'; Emerald Bay, Echo Lake 7½'; USDA/USFS Desolation Wilderness

Where to stay:
   Mountain: Fallen Leaf Lodge, Meeks Bay Resort
   Of Interest: Richardson's Resort
   Other: Towns of S. Lake Tahoe

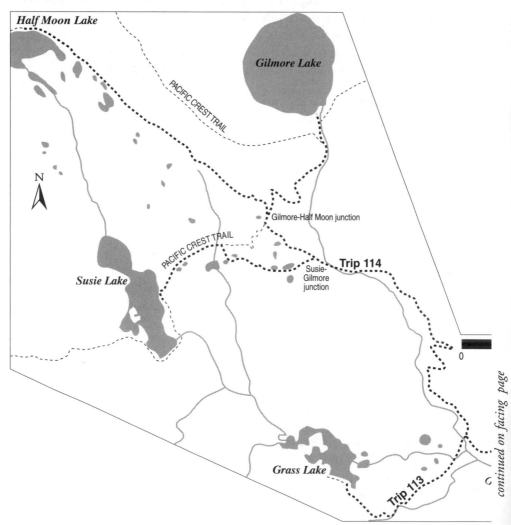

continued on facing page

Highlights: A peaceful hike leads to lovely Grass Lake, whose delightful setting will make you want to linger for a leisurely picnic.

How to get to the trailhead: As described in the driving directions of Trip 112, from the Tahoe **Y**, follow State Route 89 to Fallen Leaf Road; turn south and take Fallen Leaf Road past the turnoff to private Stanford High Sierra Camp (go left where a spur road goes right over tumbling Glen Alpine Creek to the camp). The road, its condition growing worse by the yard, then climbs past attractive Glen Alpine Falls to the Glen Alpine Trailhead, where you find parking at 5.6 miles next to Lily Lake. Toilets; self-issue station for day-use permits only.

At the trailhead: Non-hikers may prefer the numerous recreational opportunities—picnicking, fishing, boating, just plain relaxing, shopping, gambling—around Lake Tahoe. See also the beginning of this chapter.

On the trail: Your unmarked trailhead is just beyond the restrooms at a locked gate across a very rocky old road. You head generally west on that road, where the first leg is a public right-of-way through private land; please stay on the road. Side roads dodge in and out; you can stay on the main road by taking the right fork if the junction is unsigned and by following signs when they're present. At a little over ⅓ mile you reach a viewpoint for a very handsome cascade on Glen Alpine Creek. Continuing, you find that the road now rises, now is level, now is sunstruck, now is shady as it continues generally west past cabins, ponds, meadows, patches of forest, and patches of wildflowers. Nearing 1 mile you reach the road's end and pick up the trail to Susie, Gilmore, and Grass lakes, from which you wind gradually up rocky knolls. Now you dip into forest, pass the boundary of Desolation Wilderness, and reach a junction at a little over 1⅓ miles: left (southwest) to Grass Lake, right (north) to Dicks Pass and Gilmore, Half Moon, and Susie lakes. Note that the government maps show that the true wilderness boundary is a little beyond, not before, this junction.

Take the left fork, soon fording Gilmore Lake's and then Grass Lake's outlets. You come alongside a grassy pond and multiple, unmapped streamlets, making two more fords in short order. At an unmapped but apparent **T**-junction at just over 1⅔ miles you go left, climbing moderately through chaparral and more rocky knolls, to reach multi-lobed, meadow-fringed **Grass Lake at just over 2¼ miles and 7420 feet**. You'll want to continue beyond Grass Lake's first bay in order to get an across-the-lake view of the wonderful cascades on one of its inlets, which happens to be higher Susie Lake's outlet (see Trip 114). Beyond the lake rise Jacks and Dicks peaks, and impressive cliffs bound the lake on its far side. This is a beautiful spot, and you'll want to spend some time here.

When you must, retrace your steps to your car.

114. Gilmore, Half Moon, or Susie Lake ☼ ❦

Place	Total distance	Elevation	Level	Type
Start	0	6560	—	—
Gilmore Lake *only*	8²⁄₃	8300	S	O&B
Half Moon Lake *only*	10	8040	S	O&B
Susie Lake *only*	8½+	7800	S	O&B

Permit required: Yes; self-issue station for day-use permits *only* at trailhead

Topo(s): WP Fallen Leaf Lake 15'; Emerald Bay, Echo Lake, Rockbound Valley 7½'; USDA/USFS Desolation Wilderness

Where to stay:
    Mountain: Fallen Leaf Lodge, Meeks Bay Resort
    Of Interest: Richardson's Resort
    Other: Towns of S. Lake Tahoe

Highlights: Long-vanished glaciers carved the drainage of Glen Alpine Creek and scattered many beautiful lakes throughout it. Trip 113 visited one of the lower lakes, Grass Lake. This trip takes you to one of three beauties higher in the drainage.

How to get to the trailhead: See Trip 113.

At the trailhead: See Trip 113.

On the trail: See Trip 113's map. Follow Trip 113 up the Glen Alpine Trail into Desolation Wilderness, and to the junction at a little over 1⅓ miles: left (southwest) for Grass Lake, right (north) for Dicks Pass and Gilmore, Half Moon, and Susie lakes. You go right, winding now through forest, now over granite slabs, now up and around rocky outcrops, beneath a row of rust, gray, and brown peaks to the south and with an unmapped creek often nearby for company. At a little over 2½ miles, you ford the creek in forest, then ford two seasonal trickles in the next half mile, as you work your way up a lightly forested gully. Continuing, the trail is at first exposed, traversing over rusty rock above the cheery creek; then it enters a lodgepole-red fir forest, fords another creek, and shortly reaches a junction at 3⅓ miles: left (west) for Susie Lake and Lake Aloha, right (west-northwest) for Gilmore and Half Moon lakes and Dicks Pass. We'll call this the Susie-Gilmore junction—but note that later on, on the way to Gilmore and Half Moon lakes, you'll meet the Pacific Crest Trail and have another opportunity to go to Susie Lake. Just follow the signs, remembering that going to Glen Alpine is returning to your car. Going to two or three lakes is beyond the mileage limits of this book; you'll need to decide which lake to visit.*

To go to Gilmore Lake or Half Moon Lake. Go right on a rocky-dusty trail through open forest, ascending as you pass a talus slope on your right. Reddish Dicks Peak looms ahead. Soon, the gully to your left sprouts a lily-pad-dotted pond, while the Sierra Crest appears in the distance on your left. Near 3⅔ miles you meet the Pacific Crest Trail: left (southwest) to Susie Lake, right (northeast) to Half Moon and Gilmore lakes. Go right.

To go to Gilmore Lake. Almost immediately you reach another junction, and this one may be unsigned: left (north) to Half Moon Lake, right (north-northeast) to Gilmore Lake. We'll call this *the Gilmore-Half Moon junction.* Go right and switchback up a hot, open slope with occasional shade from big old junipers; your effort is rewarded with expansive views that include Susie Lake. Topping the ridge you've been climbing, you trade the views for a lodgepole forest, some pocket meadows, and, soon, the cascading outlet of Gilmore Lake. At a little under 4¼ miles you reach another junction: left (west) on the Pacific Crest Trail to Dicks Pass, right (north) to Gilmore Lake and Mt. Tallac. You go right for **Gilmore Lake at 4⅓ miles and 8300 feet**. An apparent fork signals the edge of this big, beautiful lake, where use trails scoot off to the lakeshore. There are many nice picnic sites here and across the outlet, so settle down for a relaxing stay. When you're ready, retrace your steps to the trailhead.

To go to Half Moon Lake. At the Gilmore-Half Moon junction, turn north for Half Moon Lake, soon veering west-northwest toward Jacks and Dicks peaks on chaparral slopes. The trail to Half Moon Lake may be faint at times. You climb gradually, and from a rubbly shoulder you have a good view of dramatic Cracked Crag. Now you descend into a damp forest of mountain hemlock, red fir, and lodgepole, meeting a tiny, unmapped creek that feeds pocket meadows and little tarns. You continue this ridge-and-forest pattern, gradually gaining elevation. Near 4½ miles you pass a large tarn on your left; it's one of Half Moon's outlying ponds. The trail, sometimes very faint, threads among pretty ponds to emerge on a grassy slope above a long, narrow lake that extends deep into a wonderfully rugged cirque bounded by Dicks and Jacks peaks. In season, the inlets bounding down this cirque form showy cascades. Make your way down to the shoreline of **Half Moon Lake at nearly 5 miles and 8040 feet** and find yourself a perch where you can picnic and enjoy the view. Return the way you came.

---

* It's not necessarily beyond the range of sturdy hikers who get an early start. Which should you visit? Gilmore is the highest of these three lakes. It's a large, very pretty, lightly-forested lake tucked under an outlier of Mt. Tallac; for my money, Gilmore has the most peaceful "feel" of the three lakes. Half Moon Lake, lower, is probably the least-classically-pretty lake and sees fewer visitors than Gilmore and Susie lakes, which are on or very near the Pacific Crest Trail. But Half Moon's relative remoteness and fewer visitors lend it a charm the others may lack. Susie Lake, the lowest, has the most dramatic setting and most alpine "feel": an irregular sheet of blue amid bare reddish knolls, almost right under the Sierra Crest.

To go to Susie Lake. At the Susie-Gilmore junction, not the junction with the Pacific Crest Trail, go left for Susie Lake and Lake Aloha, soon dipping through forest to pass several handsome ponds. You cross a seasonal stream feeding a meadow and pond on your left as you climb through moderate-to-dense lodgepole-red fir forest to reach a junction with the Pacific Crest Trail at a little over 3¾ miles: left (west) to Susie Lake and Lake Aloha; right (east) to Half Moon and Gilmore lakes. Go left, through meadow and forest, then up a chaparral slope. You wind through an open forest, passing more ponds, then pop over a tiny shoulder to a splendid sight: big, dramatic **Susie Lake at a little over 4¼ miles and 7800 feet**, ringed by shattered, rusty rock and set under the Sierra Crest. Make your way to the lakeshore and pull up a rock on which to relax, have lunch, and enjoy the scenery. Retrace your steps to the trailhead from here.

115. Granite, Velma, or Dicks Lake 🌸 ☼ 🍁

Place	Total distance	Elevation	Level	Type
Start	0	6880	—	—
Tahoe viewpoint *only*	1+	7270	E	O&B
Granite Lake *only*	2½	7660	M	O&B
Upper Velma Lake *only*	10	7940	S U	O&B
Middle Velma Lake *only*	10	7900	S U	O&B
Dicks Lake *only*	10	8420	S U	O&B
Cascade Falls *only*	1⅓	6800	E	O&B

Permit required: Yes; self-issue station for day-use permits *only* at trailhead

Topo(s): WP Fallen Leaf Lake 15′; Emerald Bay, Rockbound Valley 7½′; USDA/USFS Desolation Wilderness

Where to stay:
   Mountain: Fallen Leaf Lodge, Meeks Bay Resort
   Of Interest: Richardson's Resort
   Other: Towns of S. Lake Tahoe

Highlights: A dull first leg cleverly conceals the pleasures that await you farther on: a fabulous Emerald Bay-Tahoe viewpoint, then lovely Granite Lake, and then a chance to visit one of two higher lakes: alpine charmer Dicks Lake or islet-dotted Middle Velma Lake. An optional excursion to Cascade Falls rounds out the list of treats you can hike to from Bayview; see the last paragraph of this trip.

How to get to the trailhead: From the Tahoe **Y**, drive 7.7 miles northwest to Bayview Campground; turn south into the campground and drive through it to trailhead parking near its south end, about 0.2 mile more depending on where you park. (You have overshot the turnoff if you get to Meeks Bay while northbound or Richardson's Resort while southbound.) Toilets.

At the trailhead: See Trip 112.

On the trail: From the trailhead at the south end of the campground, walk about 45 feet south past the trailhead to a junction: left (south) to Cascade Falls (see the last paragraph of this trip), right (southwest) to Granite Lake. You go right for Granite Lake, zigzagging steeply up a dusty duff trail through a monotonous, claustrophobic forest of spindly white firs. At ½ mile you enter Desolation Wilderness near an intermittent stream and soon reach a rocky **viewpoint at just over ½ mile and about 7270 feet**. Use trails lead here and there to slightly different views, or you can scramble up on the surrounding boulders. Whatever you do, the scene here is simply magnificent, especially early in the morning before the midday haze settles in. The view is primarily east across Emerald Bay to Lake Tahoe and the Carson Range; no view of Emerald Bay from the highway is nearly as spectacular as this one is. The next switchback up reveals another superb view, this one including the head of Emerald Bay and a bit of highway.

The grade eases as you follow the alder-lined channel (not on the map) that is Granite Lake's seasonally-flowing outlet, through a mixed conifer forest with a flowery understory. As you near the lake, you veer away from the outlet and into a bouldery chaparral area. The trail soon levels out above pretty, lodgepole-shaded **Granite Lake at nearly 1¼ miles and 7660 feet**, nestled in the cleavage of Maggies Peaks. This is a charming area, well worth a picnic stop.

To continue, resume climbing steeply as you leave Granite Lake. Don't be misled onto use trails, particularly a large one leading south from the first big switchback above Granite Lake. The trail winds its way up the lightly wooded slope west of Granite Lake—the ridge between Maggies Peaks—on a series of rocky-sandy switchbacks. Views make the climb worth the trouble—increasingly excellent views over the South Lake Tahoe area, eventually including Lake Tahoe, Emerald Bay, Granite Lake, Cascade Lake, and Fallen Leaf Lake. The forest becomes thicker and the grade eases near the top of the climb, and the views you've been enjoying are at their most expansive just before you round the ridgetop near 2¼ miles. The other side of the ridge offers fine views west over Desolation Wilderness toward the Velma Lakes, and you top out at 8440 feet. You stroll through moderate-to-open forest, descending gradually to moderately, rounding some prominent knobs and ignoring a use trail that descends left to Azure Lake. Sometimes it seems as if you're pointed at Mt. Tallac, other times at Peak 9190.

* Visiting all is not necessarily beyond the range of sturdy hikers who get an early start. To stay within the limits, you can go to either the Velma Lakes or to Dicks Lake. If you choose the Velmas, you can go to either Upper Velma Lake or Middle Velma Lake but, strictly speaking, not to both—on the other hand, Upper and Middle Velma lakes are so close together that you may want to stretch the limits. Which lake to go to? Higher Dicks Lake has the more alpine feel to it; the Velma Lakes have a mellower, mid-Sierra feeling. I think Upper Velma is prettier, but Middle Velma is reportedly the better lake for swimming.

Finally, I can't resist adding that while it's beyond the mileage limits of this book, Fontanillis Lake is my favorite lake in this area. From either Trip 115's or Trip 116's trailhead, sturdy hikers who get an early start can make an outstanding semiloop that picks up the Velma Lakes, Fontanillis Lake, and Dicks Lake. Or, if you can set up a shuttle between the trailheads—it's too dangerous to walk between them—you can make a dynamite shuttle/semiloop trip.

You re-enter moderate forest and, at just over 3 miles, on a small, viewless saddle, meet the trail coming up from Eagle Lake at what we'll call the *Bayview-Velma-Eagle junction*: left (west-southwest) to the Velma Lakes and to Dicks Lake, right (northeast) to Eagle Lake. Go left and work your way up and down over a broad, sparsely-wooded saddle from which you have rare glimpses of Azure Lake far below and even some over-the-shoulder views of Lake Tahoe.

At 3⅔ miles and 8220 feet, you reach another junction, one I'll call the *Velma-Dicks junction*: left (southwest) to Dicks Lake, right (west-northwest) to the Velma Lakes. Going to all the lakes is beyond the mileage limits of this book, so you'll have to pick one.

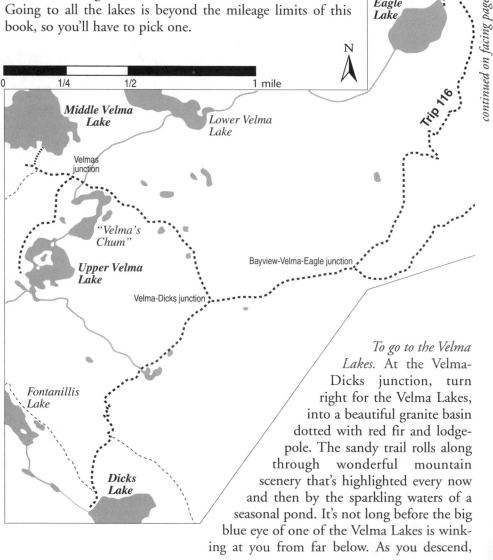

To go to the Velma Lakes. At the Velma-Dicks junction, turn right for the Velma Lakes, into a beautiful granite basin dotted with red fir and lodge-pole. The sandy trail rolls along through wonderful mountain scenery that's highlighted every now and then by the sparkling waters of a seasonal pond. It's not long before the big blue eye of one of the Velma Lakes is winking at you from far below. As you descend,

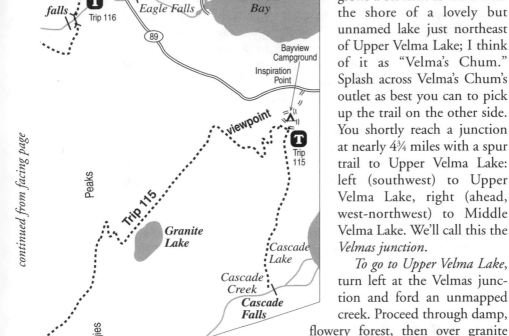

continued from facing page

twining down through lodge-pole and granite, the trail grows a bit faint as it traverses the shore of a lovely but unnamed lake just northeast of Upper Velma Lake; I think of it as "Velma's Chum." Splash across Velma's Chum's outlet as best you can to pick up the trail on the other side. You shortly reach a junction at nearly 4¾ miles with a spur trail to Upper Velma Lake: left (southwest) to Upper Velma Lake, right (ahead, west-northwest) to Middle Velma Lake. We'll call this the *Velmas junction.*

To go to Upper Velma Lake, turn left at the Velmas junction and ford an unmapped creek. Proceed through damp, flowery forest, then over granite slabs, till you're near the lake. Use trails radiate lakeward from here to charming **Upper Velma Lake at 5 miles and 7940 feet**. The outlet of higher Fontanillis Lake makes a handsome, noisy cascade down the open slopes to the south-southwest. By the way, some maps show a spur trail between Upper Velma Lake and the trail to Dicks Lake; it no longer exists as a maintained trail. Retrace your steps to your car from here.

To go to Middle Velma Lake, go ahead (right) at the Velmas junction and shortly meet the junction with a trail to Fontanillis and Dicks lakes (incorrectly shown on most maps or not shown at all): left (south) to Fontanillis and Dicks lakes, right (ahead, west) to Middle Velma Lake and Phipps Pass. Go ahead (right) about 300 feet to a great overlook of **Middle Velma Lake at nearly 5 miles and 7860 feet**, but about 50 feet below your trail here. You'll want to use up the rest of your 5 miles by picking your way down to Middle Velma Lake's shore for a picnic on one of the many granite slabs ringing this big lake. Retrace your steps to your car from here.

To go to Dicks Lake. At the Velma-Dicks junction, turn left and follow the sometimes-faint trail through a wonderful, sparsely forested granite basin. Keep a sharp eye out for the track on this hard-rock terrain, keeping in mind that you're heading generally for prominent Dicks Peak to the south-southwest. You pass several pretty tarns and then an unnamed lakelet whose multistranded outlet you presently ford at a low point on this leg. You cross a seasonal stream and begin ascending, presently switchbacking moderately up the rocky slopes below Dicks Lake and enjoying over-the-shoulder views of the Velma Lakes sparkling far below. Near the top you find a junction: left (southeast) for Dicks Pass, right (southwest) for Dicks and Fontanillis lakes. Go right for Dicks and Fontanillis lakes, pausing on the ridgetop at 8500 feet to take in a marvelous view over Desolation Wilderness, then descending a little to another junction at just under 5 miles: left (south) on a spur for Dicks Lake, right (northwest) for Fontanillis Lake. You go left, toddling downhill a little to lovely **Dicks Lake at 5 miles and 8420 feet**, cradled closely under Dicks Pass in half-wooded, half-talus slopes. Enjoy a lunch stop here before retracing your steps to your car.

Optional excursion to Cascade Falls. Some publications call Cascade Falls "White Cloud Falls" for the clouds of white mist it throws up in season. At the junction some 45 feet from trailhead parking at Bayview, the left fork leads south through open forest and then across chaparral slopes to excellent viewpoints of Cascade Falls above mostly-private Cascade Lake, and then to Cascade Creek as it slithers over granite slabs just above seasonally showy **Cascade Falls at ⅔ miles and 6800 feet**—the exact distance depends on how far you go out on the slabs around the head of the falls (watch your footing!). Return the way you came.

116. Fall; Eagle, Velma, or Dicks Lake 🌸 ☼ 🍁

Place	Total distance	Elevation	Level	Type
Start	0	6580	—	—
Waterfall *only*	⅕	6660	E	O&B
Slabs with views *only*	⅔	6800	E	O&B
Eagle Lake *only*	2	6880	E	O&B
Upper Velma Lake *only*	10+	7940	S	O&B
Middle Velma Lake *only*	10+	7900	S	O&B
Dicks Lake *only*	10+	8420	S	O&B

Permit required: None to go only to the waterfall; required for all other destinations; self-issue station for day-use permits *only* at trailhead

Topo(s): WP Fallen Leaf Lake 15'; Emerald Bay, Rockbound Valley 7½'; USDA/USFS Desolation Wilderness

Where to stay:
   Mountain: Fallen Leaf Lodge, Meeks Bay Resort
   Of Interest: Richardson's Resort
   Other: Towns of S. Lake Tahoe

Highlights: The handsome little waterfall below Eagle Lake is a very popular destination, and beyond it is a fine viewpoint. You can continue to attractive Eagle Lake and then high into Desolation Wilderness to visit one of the many beautiful lakes there—the same higher lakes visited by Trip 115. Note that you have to make some difficult choices; see the footnote to Trip 115.

How to get to the trailhead: From the Tahoe **Y**, drive northwest 8.7 miles to Eagle Falls Picnic Area/Trailhead; turn west into the picnic area/parking lot and park. (You have overshot this turnoff if you get to Meeks Bay while northbound or Inspiration Point while southbound.) The trailhead is on the west end of the lot, which gets *very* crowded by midday. Toilets.

At the trailhead: See Trip 112.

On the trail: See Trip 115's map. Go west from the trailhead on a broad, sandy trail that passes under a mixed conifer forest, then traverses chaparral. It presently begins to climb moderately to steeply on stone steps past junipers to a footbridge over a creek, overlooking a charming **waterfall at less than ⅓ mile and 6660 feet**. The officially-named Eagle Falls are below the highway, but to countless visitors, *this* waterfall is "Eagle Falls." The fall dashes down a small, narrow, rocky valley that enhances its beauty but limits over-the-shoulder views back toward Emerald Bay. To continue to Eagle Lake and beyond, you cross the footbridge and almost immediately enter Desolation Wilderness. Pause to admire the steep, rocky cliffs hemming in this little valley before taking the rocky-sandy trail steeply upward on the creek's south bank. The grade eases as you near ⅓ mile and cross an open area of juniper-dotted granite **slabs with excellent views at ⅓ mile and 6800 feet** east over Emerald Bay and Lake Tahoe. Leaving the sunny slabs, you turn back into forest and reach a junction at 1 mile with the spur trail down to Eagle Lake: right (southwest) to Eagle Lake, left (south-southeast) to the Velma Lakes and Dicks Lake. We'll call this the *Eagle-Velma* junction. Going to Eagle Lake and then on to either Velma Lakes or Dicks Lake will add ⅕ mile to your total trip.

*To go to Eagle Lake, go right at the Ea*gle-Velma junction and dash ¹⁄₁₀ mile down the trail to the east shore of little **Eagle Lake at a little over 1 mile and 6880 feet,** where you'll find some picnic rocks next to its outlet.

To go to the Velma Lakes or to Dicks Lake, go left at the Eagle-Velma junction (right if you're returning from a visit to Eagle Lake) to climb a chaparral slope on a rocky-sandy trail, very steeply at first, then moderately. You have views over Eagle Lake for a while as you climb; then you veer into forest, cross an unmapped stream, and zigzag moderately to steeply up a shady slope. You emerge briefly on sparsely wooded granite slabs and then continue switchbacking upward, now on a sandy-rocky trail over the slabs, now on a duff trail through forest. At a little over 2½ miles you swing around the nose of the ridge you've been climbing and into a beautiful granite basin. You descend a little, making a rolling, sandy traverse of the west side of the ridge, with views of a lily-pad-dotted lakelet deep down in a boggy pocket you'd need wings to get to. Next the trail winds uphill alongside an unmapped little stream, eventually crossing it. Beyond, the trail grows very faint, especially as you reach a long, granite slab. You could say the trail vanishes here, but there's nowhere else to go except south-southwest right up the slab, at the top of which you pick up the well-trod trail again. You pass to the south of a bouldery knoll to reach the Bayview-Velma-Eagle junction of Trip 115 at a little over 3¼ miles: right (west-northwest) for the Velma Lakes and Dicks Lake, left (south, then east) for the Bayview Trailhead (Trip 115). And even though they're slightly beyond the mileage limits of this book, you throw caution to the winds and pick one of the higher lakes of Trip 115 for your destination—lovely "Velma's Chum" is closest.

Retrace your steps from wherever.

117. Genevieve, Crag, Shadow Lakes 🌿 ☼ 🍁

Place	Total distance	Elevation	Level	Type
Start	0	6235	—	
Lake Genevieve *only*	8	7420	S	O&B
Crag Lake *only*	8½	7460	S	O&B
Shadow Lake	10	7660	S	O&B

Permit required: Yes; self-issue station for day-use permits *only* at trailhead

Topo(s): WP Fallen Leaf Lake 15'; Homewood, Rockbound Valley 7½'; USDA/USFS Desolation Wilderness

Where to stay:
Mountain: Fallen Leaf Lodge, Meeks Bay Resort
Of Interest: Richardson's Resort
Other: Towns of S. Lake Tahoe

Highlights: This has to be the easiest long hike in this book, on the "moderate" side of "strenuous." After a start on a dirt road by a seasonally flower-filled meadow, a well-graded trail leads you through forest to three charming lakes, each with its own ambience.

How to get to the trailhead: From the Tahoe **Y**, drive 16.2 miles north on State Route 89 to a very-hard-to-find trailhead on the west side of the highway at bare-ly-visibly-signed Log Cabin Road just north of a bridge over Meeks Creek. Parking is on the east side of the highway, opposite the trailhead. The trailhead is *north* of the resort-related road signs south of Meeks Bay Resort (e.g., HISTORIC RESORT AHEAD) but *south* of the resort's entrance. The trailhead is also opposite a large parking lot backed by a chain-link fence and on the east side of the highway; this is where you park. There is a trailhead display about 100 feet west of the trailhead proper—difficult but not impossible to spot from the highway. (You have overshot this trailhead if you get to Meeks Bay Resort while northbound or Inspiration Point while southbound.)

At the trailhead: See Trip 112.

On the trail: The "trail" begins as a dirt road at a locked gate across that road just off State Route 89. The gate bars the general public's vehicles from the road, but you may still meet vehicles on it. Beyond the gate, you pass a big stump and head generally west on marked Forest Road 14N13. You follow the dusty road between a meadow on your left and a forested slope rising on your right; there is a wealth of wildflowers on display here in season. Presently, the meadow on your left gives way to forest. The road climbs very gradually as it lazily swings south. Near 1 mile you glimpse another meadow off to your left, through the trees, and then, in a few more steps, reach a junction: left to stay on the road, right (west) on the Tahoe-Yosemite Trail (this is its northern terminus).

You go right on the dusty Tahoe-Yosemite Trail, climbing gradually to moderately, often through dense forest. Open areas offer few dramatic views except occasional over-the-shoulder views of Lake Tahoe. As you approach a ridgeline, the forest thins and you traverse rocky outcrops. Rounding the ridge, you brush against Meeks Creek's bracken- and alder-lined channel before re-entering forest. At nearly 2 miles you enter Desolation Wilderness; the trail, now duff, wanders levelly through moderate forest with a dense understory of bracken. Presently you swing through a sandy area dotted with sagebrush and mule ears, then climb moderately to steeply on the rocky, switchbacking track. The trail levels out in damp forest and then crosses the creek on a footbridge at nearly 3 miles.

On the other side of Meeks Creek, the trail traverses below a ridge in dry forest, then climbs moderately and veers east around the head of a steep, west-trending gully. You emerge on a hot, chaparral-covered ridge nose, high above the east fork of Meeks Creek, and soon meet the creek again—it's a refreshing sight. At nearly 4 miles you reach a junction: right (west) on the Lake Genevieve Trail, left (ahead, southeast) to Lake Genevieve, Crag Lake, and Shadow Lake. You go ahead to **Lake Genevieve at just under 4 miles and 7420 feet**, only a few steps away and prettier than any picture, especially as it's backed by the cliff-like east slopes of Peak 7820. Its shoreline offers numerous picnic spots. Back on the Tahoe-Yosemite Trail, you climb a little to discover beautiful **Crag Lake at nearly 4¼ miles and 7460 feet**, the loveliest of these three lakes. Picnic sites are numerous here, too, and a stop is sure to please if you don't mind company—the lake is very popular.

If you'd prefer more solitude, press on, making a nearly level traverse a little above Crag Lake before climbing moderately toward Shadow Lake, crossing its outlet and spying Hidden Lake below, to the right. Passing a use trail to the right and steeply down to Hidden Lake, you continue ahead to wind through jumbo boulders before reaching small **Shadow Lake at almost 5 miles and 7660 feet**. It's full of lily pads and surrounded by a forest of large, dead trees. Shadow Lake is a beaver pond; its rising waters have drowned the forest here. The beavers may be gone now—they are not native to the Sierra—but the pond remains. Shadow Lake is the most tranquil of the three lakes on this trip and a nice place to rest before you turn back.

Return the way you came.

118. Five Lakes Basin 🌿 ☼ 🍁

Place	Total distance	Elevation	Level	Type
Start	0	6560	—	
Largest, westernmost lake	4+	7500	M	O&B

Permit required: None

Topo(s): Tahoe City, Granite Chief 7½'

Where to stay:
   Mountain: Always Inn, Meeks Bay Resort
   Of Interest: Alpine Meadows Realty, Northstar at Tahoe, Clair Tappaan Lodge, Summit House at Donner Ski Ranch, Richardson's Resort, Rainbow Lodge, Donner Summit Lodge
   Other: Town of Truckee, Towns of N. Lake Tahoe, Squaw Valley, Donner Lake

Highlights: Immediately around Lake Tahoe, you can hardly find an easier hike to attractive lakes than this one to Granite Chief Wilderness's Five Lakes Basin. The maintained trail goes only to the largest, westernmost lake, but use trails dart off to the other, smaller lakes in the east part of the basin, inviting the adventurous to explore.

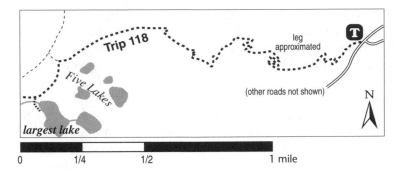

Trip 118

leg approximated

(other roads not shown)

Five Lakes

largest lake

N

0   1/4   1/2   1 mile

How to get to the trailhead: From the Tahoe **Y**, drive 30.9 miles north on State Route 89, past the junction with State Route 28, to the turnoff west for Alpine Meadows Road and Alpine Meadows Ski Area. (You have overshot this turnoff if you get to the turnoff for Squaw Valley while northbound or to the junction of State Routes 89 and 28 near Tahoe City while southbound.) The trailhead, which may be unmarked on the road, is 2.1 more miles up Alpine Meadows Road, on the right, just opposite the much more obvious turnoff left onto Deer Park Road. Park on the shoulder, 10.9 miles.

At the trailhead: Non-hikers will probably prefer to be at their lodgings or to explore the quaint and charming town of Truckee with its shops and good restaurants.

On the trail: At the trailhead you'll find an information sign and some warnings about Five Lakes Basin: it's day-use only (good), and you should look out for unexploded ammunition used for avalanche control at adjacent Alpine Meadows Ski Area (not good). With one eye peeled for ammo and the other fixed on any children in your party—kids may think an unexploded shell is a toy—you head westsouthwest, climbing on long, nearly shadeless, dusty switchbacks through chaparral and under the occasional Jeffrey pine or white fir. The trail, lined with a handsome sprinkling of flowers in season, has more switchbacks than are shown on the topo. As you rise, the wooded hills up and down the canyon of the Truckee River come into view, as well as the bare knobs on Ward Peak above the ski area.

The grade eases as you round a southwest-facing slope, and interesting pinnacle-like formations come into view uphill on your right. You cross a couple of runoff channels and negotiate another switchback or two on a gradual grade. Beyond, the trail swings briefly southwest toward some glaciated gray cliffs before crossing an outcrop of reddish rock. At 1 mile you dip across a southeast-trending gully, then bypass a blocked-off use trail to your right. Rounding an open ridge high above the gully now, you ignore another use trail descending to the left and continue gradually up the main trail. Ahead of you rise interesting knobs, spires, cliffs, and outcrops in subtle shades of rust, gray, and orange—some rocks so dark and jagged they look volcanic, others rounded and reminiscent of formations in Joshua Tree National Park in Southern California. A little past 1⅓ mile you pass a spring at the base of a dead tree before contouring around the head of the next gully, which is somewhat wetter and greener than the previous one. At somewhat over 1½ miles you enter Granite Chief Wilderness at a boundary not shown on the topo. The trail soon levels out on a bench in the welcome shade of an open-to-moderate red-fir forest, where the damper environment supports a lusher display of flowers than did the dry trail you've just ascended.

Approaching 2 miles you reach a junction: right to the Pacific Crest Trail, left (south-southwest) to Five Lakes Basin. After going left on the rocky-dusty trail, toward a forested hill and a bare, pyramidal little peak, you notice faint use trails darting off to the small lakes in the east part of this pretty little basin. You briefly trace the shore of the basin's westernmost, largest, and most trail-accessible lake, then reach a junction where a use trail branches left between huge firs, to cross the lake's alder-choked outlet and climb an outcrop. Taking this use trail, you scramble over the outcrop to find a view-filled picnic spot on the west shore of the **largest, westernmost lake in Five Lakes Basin, at just over 2 miles and 7500 feet**. To the west, you glimpse broad, brown Squaw Peak. But your attention is focused on enjoying the beautiful lakeside surroundings, which include fragrant red heather; shapely, droopy-topped mountain hemlocks; and sweetly-singing birds.

When you're ready, return the way you came, perhaps detouring to take some of those use trails to the smaller lakes.

CHAPTER 14

Northern Sierra: Interstate 80, Donner Summit Country

Beyond the Alpine Meadows turnoff for Trip 118, State Route 89 continues north to Truckee to meet Interstate 80. Interstate 80 roars in concrete, multi-laned, exhaust-fumed haste past Truckee and over Donner Summit between Reno and Sacramento. Donner—a name to send chills down the spine. The real Donner Pass and the site of the famous tragedy, Donner Lake, lie south of Interstate 80; see Robert Leonard Reid's *A Treasury of the Sierra Nevada* for eyewitness accounts. Those interested in more about the Donner Party may want to visit Donner Lake and Donner Memorial State Park. A stop at the park's museum to learn more about the tragedy may keep you from asking, as a history-challenged friend of

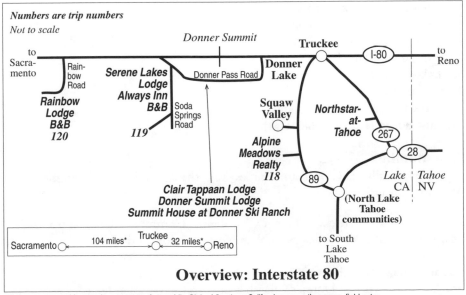

Overview: Interstate 80

*Distances summed from various sources: Automobile Club of Southern California maps, other maps, field notes.

mine did, "Why didn't those Donners hang out in Reno till the weather got better and then take I-80?"

For hikers, there's good reason to linger here: a couple of outstanding hikes are to be found just south of this incredibly busy road, which is the northern limit of this book.

Recommended reading

▶ Heid, Matt, *101 Hikes in Northern California*. 1st ed. Berkeley, CA: Wilderness Press, 2001.

▶ Schaffer, Jeffrey P. *The Tahoe Sierra: A Natural History Guide to 106 Hikes in the Northern Sierra*. See recommended reading for Chapter 11.

▶ Winnett, Thomas, et. al., *Sierra North*. 8th ed. Berkeley, CA: Wilderness Press, 2002. See recommended reading for Chapter 7.

Recommended maps

▶ USDA/USFS *Tahoe National Forest*. No topographic information, but invaluable road information.

▶ USDA/USFS *Lake Tahoe Basin Management Unit*. See Chapter 13.

Special Note

Area codes in the Tahoe area have changed from 916 to 530.

Lodgings

Alphabetically, the true mountain lodgings and lodgings of interest in the region are (see Chapter 13)—

Alpine Meadows Realty (agency)
Always Inn Bed and Breakfast
Clair Tappaan Lodge
Donner Summit Lodge
Ice Lakes Lodge
Northstar at Tahoe
Rainbow Lodge Bed and Breakfast
Summit House at Donner Ski Ranch

Communities

Alphabetically, eligible communities and the Chambers of Commerce and Visitors Bureaus are—

Donner Lake—See Truckee-Donner Chamber of Commerce, Chapter 13.
Towns of North Lake Tahoe—See Tahoe North Visitors and Convention Bureau, Chapter 13.
Squaw Valley—See Chapter 13.
Truckee—See Truckee-Donner Chamber of Commerce, Chapter 13.

Hikes

119. Long Lake 🌸 ☼ 🍁

Place	Total distance	Elevation	Level	Type
Start	0	6720	—	—
Long Lake	1⅓	6700	E U	O&B

Permit required: None

Topo(s): Soda Springs 7½'

Where to stay:
Mountain: Always Inn
Of Interest: Alpine Meadows Realty, Northstar at Tahoe, Clair Tappaan Lodge, Rainbow Lodge, Donner Summit Lodge, Summit House at Donner Ski Ranch
Other: Town of Truckee, Towns of N. Lake Tahoe, Squaw Valley, Donner Lake

Highlights: Delightful Long Lake offers fine picnic spots and great scenery in exchange for a rough drive and a short but briefly trying hike.

How to get to the trailhead: High-clearance vehicle desirable. Just 3.1 miles west of Donner Summit on I-80, get off at the Soda Springs exit and turn east on Donner Summit Road. Go 0.7 mile to Soda Springs Road; turn right and follow it 0.9 mile to Pahatsi Road. Turn right and follow it 3.9 miles to Devils Outlook Warming Hut; the road is unpaved, narrow, and rough beyond the buildings of Royal Gorge ski area. There is a large dirt parking area by Devils Outlook Warming Hut.

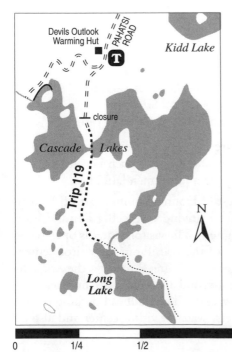

At the trailhead: Non-hikers may prefer a visit to Donner Lake with its woods and beaches and to the museum there.

On the trail: After taking in the scenery—Devils Peak to the south-southwest is exceptionally striking—you take off on foot south-southwest down a continuation of the road to a **Y**-junction in about 180 feet; take the left fork. The road is sparsely shaded and the going is sandy and rocky as you stroll along a ridge with glimpses of upper Cascade Lake to the left, lower Cascade Lake to the right. At ¼ mile you reach the marked Palisades Creek Trailhead and pause to enjoy the view of Cascade Lakes from here before heading very, very steeply down an old, blocked-off road toward the dam that separates upper and lower Cascade Lakes. You cross the dam to pick up a footpath in the shade of a patchy, moderate-to-dense lodgepole forest. In season, masses of red heather in bloom make the air incredibly sweet and fresh here. You pass between a low, rocky ridge to your left and seasonal tarns to your right, walking almost levelly, before making a very slight ascent between the ridge and a rocky outcrop. As you begin your descent, avoid a blocked-off use trail to your right.

Blue light sparkling ahead through the trees heralds your approach to **Long Lake at ⅔ mile and 6700 feet**. Numerous slabs along Long Lake's northeast shore offer excellent picnic sites overlooking this granite-cupped, bracken-fringed gem and its stern guardian, Devils Peak. You'll want to follow use trails along its shore and down to the water's edge to fully experience this lovely lake.

Your biggest problem here will be tearing yourself away, but retrace your steps when you must.

120. Loch Leven, Salmon Lakes 🌸 ☼ 🍂

Place	Total distance	Elevation	Level	Type
Start	0	5740	—	—
Lowest Loch Leven Lk. *only*	5½	6780	M	O&B
Middle Loch Leven Lk. *only*	6⅔	6780	S	O&B
High Loch Leven Lk. *only*	8¼	6860	S	O&B
Salmon Lake *only*	7⅓	6700	S	O&B
All four lakes	9½+	6860	S	O&B

Permit required: None

Topo(s): Cisco Grove, Soda Springs 7½′

Where to stay:
　　Mountain: Always Inn
　　Of Interest: Alpine Meadows Realty, Northstar at Tahoe, Clair Tappaan Lodge, Rainbow Lodge, Donner Summit Lodge, Summit House at Donner Ski Ranch
　　Other: Town of Truckee, Towns of N. Lake Tahoe, Squaw Valley, Donner Lake

Highlights: The beautiful Loch Leven Lakes are favorites of visitors to the Donner Summit area. Charming little Salmon Lake, just west of the Loch Leven Lakes, is nearly as pretty and sees far fewer visitors—quite a recommendation!

How to get to the trailhead: Just 9.1 miles west of Donner Summit, get off I-80 at the Rainbow Road exit and orient yourself by driving to the Big Bend Visitor Center on Rainbow Road* (the way is well-signed). The visitor center is open daily in midsummer, weekends only at other times of the year. From the visitor center, it is 0.1 mile northeast to the practical trailhead—at a gravel road on the *east* side of Rainbow Road—and 0.2 mile (0.1 mile beyond the trailhead) northeast to trailhead parking on the *west* side of Rainbow Road. The trailhead parking is also 0.4 mile west of Rainbow Lodge. Toilet; toilets, water at visitor center and also at

* Some sources call it "Hampshire Rocks Road."

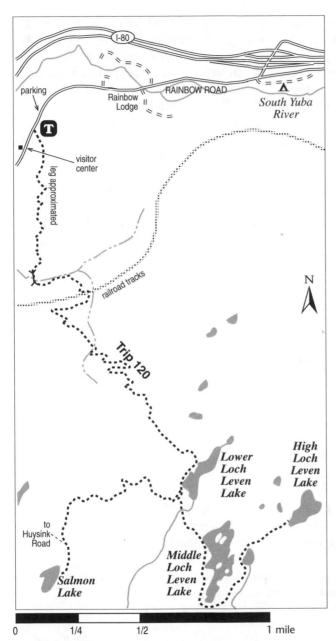

nearby Big Bend Campground.

At the trailhead: See Trip 119.

On the trail: From the practical trailhead, go southeast on that gravel road (shown as a trail on the book's map) to reach the official, signed trailhead shortly. You leave the old road here and begin ascending a rocky-dusty, up-and-down, switchbacking foot trail that's very different from the one shown on the 7½′ topo. The twisty trail is now in moderate forest, now on open slabs with patches of flowers between them. Around ⅔ mile, "steps" formed by slabs of rock lead steeply upward beside broad granite slabs that would otherwise demand friction-walking. At a little over ¾ mile you top out in forest on a duff trail and go south through terrain where birdsong is drowned out by the roar of nearby Interstate 80. Approaching 1 mile, you skirt an unmapped, lily-pad-speckled pond—probably seasonal—climbing a little through outcrops on the pond's shore. Beyond the pond, you descend an open slope and circle a pocket meadow bright with wildflowers. At a little over 1 mile you cross a tiny creek on a footbridge in an alder thicket, then climb away from the stream on a rocky trail that grows steeper as it nears some railroad tracks on the shelf above. At 1⅓ miles, you leave the forest and carefully cross the railroad tracks.

On the other of the tracks, to the right of a green shed, you re-enter forest and begin a gradual to moderate ascent on long switchbacks, trending westward. You squish across seasonal seeps as you approach the final set of rocky switchbacks. Finally, the grade eases on a forested bench as the trail curves generally southeast to emerge on a ridge from which you make a steep, rocky descent to the busiest lake, the **lowest Loch Leven Lake at 2¾ miles and 6780 feet.** You trace the lake's shore to its more open, south end, where you find not only lots of visitors as well as great picnic spots but a junction at nearly 3 miles: right (west) to Salmon Lake, left (south) to the upper Loch Leven Lakes. A use trail that makes a third fork confuses the issue here.

To go to the upper Loch Leven Lakes, you take the middle fork—the left fork if you ignore the use trail—south and down into into a little gully, then up over a low ridge to the **middle Loch Leven Lake at a little over 3⅓ miles and 6780 feet**. I find this lake far prettier and quieter than the first lake. Continuing, you follow the faint trail along the lake, with the help of painted blazes on trees and rocks. At the south end of the lake you find a junction: right (west) on the Cherry Point Trail, left to round the south end of the lake and go to High Loch Leven Lake. Go left and follow the faint, rocky trail past mostly-unmapped tarns and over outlet streams, ascending gradually except for a brief, very steep ascent up poor, rocky switchbacks atop which you level out again. A few more steps bring you to peaceful, beautiful **High Loch Leven Lake at just over 4 miles and 6860 feet**, the loveliest of these lakes. Its red-heather-fringed shores are the least visited of the three lakes, and you'll find wonderful picnic sites from which to enjoy the scenery.

To go to Salmon Lake, you take the right fork at the south end of the lowest Loch Leven Lake and wind gradually up and over a ridge in patchy forest. Then you dip briefly through a marshy spot and round the nose of the next ridge. You descend south-southwest moderately to steeply, winding through woods and open areas, crossing a couple of seasonal channels, and reach a signed junction at 3½ miles: ahead (south) to Salmon Lake, right (northwest) to Huysink Road. Go ahead to Salmon Lake, climbing a little over a low, rocky saddle. You descend moderately on a rocky track, level out in forest, and reach lodgepole- and granite-ringed little **Salmon Lake at 3⅔ miles and 6700 feet**. This pretty gem sees even fewer visitors than High Loch Leven Lake. Pick a spot, pull out your lunch, and enjoy!

Retrace your steps from your chosen destination(s) to your car.

Bibliography

Browning, Peter, *Place Names of the Sierra Nevada: From Abbot to Zumwalt.* 2nd ed. Berkeley: Wilderness Press, 1991.

Dilsaver, Lary M., and William Tweed, *Challenge of the Big Trees: A Resource History of Sequoia and Kings Canyon National Parks.* Three Rivers, California: Sequoia Natural History Association, 1990.

Farquhar, Francis P., *History of the Sierra Nevada.* Berkeley: University of California Press, 1965.

Felzer, Ron, *High Sierra Hiking Guide: Devils Postpile.* 5th ed. Berkeley, CA: Wilderness Press, 1990.

—, High Sierra Hiking Guide: *Hetch Hetchy.* 3rd ed. Berkeley: Wilderness Press, 1991.

—, *High Sierra Hiking Guide: Mineral King: Southern Sequoia Park & Part of Golden Trout Wilderness.* 3rd ed. Berkeley: Wilderness Press, 1992.

Hill, Mary, *Geological History of the Sierra Nevada.* (California Natural History Guide 37). Berkeley: University of California Press, 1975.

Krist, John, *50 Best Short Hikes in Yosemite and Sequoia/Kings Canyon.* Berkeley: Wilderness Press, 1993.

Putman, Jeff and Genny Smith, eds., *Deepest Valley: Guide to Owens Valley, Its roadsides and mountain trails.* 2nd ed. Mammoth Lakes, CA: Genny Smith Books, 1995.

Reid, Robert Leonard, ed., *A Treasury of the Sierra Nevada.* Berkeley: Wilderness Press, 1983.

Robinson, John W., and Andy Selters, *High Sierra Hiking Guide: Mt. Goddard.* 3rd ed. Berkeley, CA: Wilderness Press, 1986.

Schaffer, Jeffrey P., *Carson-Iceberg Wilderness: A Guide to the High Sierra Between Yosemite and Tahoe.* 2nd ed. Berkeley: Wilderness Press, 1992.

—, *Desolation Wilderness.* 3rd ed. Berkeley: Wilderness Press, 1996.

—, *Hiker's Guide to the High Sierra: Yosemite: The Valley and Surrounding Uplands.* 5th ed. Berkeley: Wilderness Press, 2002.

—, *The Tahoe Sierra: A Natural History Guide to 106 Hikes in the Northern Sierra.* 3rd ed. Berkeley: Wilderness Press, 1987 (1994 update).

—, *Yosemite National Park: A Natural-History Guide to Yosemite and Its Trails.* 4th ed. Berkeley: Wilderness Press, 1999.

Schaffer, Jeffrey P., and Thomas Winnett, *Hiker's Guide to the High Sierra: Tuolumne Meadows.* 3rd ed. Berkeley: Wilderness Press, 2002.

Schifrin, Ben, *Emigrant Wilderness and Northwestern Yosemite.* Berkeley: Wilderness Press, 1990.

Selters, Andrew, *High Sierra Hiking Guide #20: Triple Divide Peak: Kings River Canyon, Northern Sequoia.* 2nd ed. Berkeley: Wilderness Press, 1987.

Sequoia and Kings Canyon National Parks. Los Angeles: Automobile Club of Southern California, 1993.

Smith, Genny, ed., *Mammoth Lakes Sierra: A handbook for roadside and trail*. 6th ed. Mammoth Lakes, CA: Genny Smith Books, 1993.

Whitehill, Karen, and Terry Whitehill, *Best Short Hikes in California's Northern Sierra*. Seattle, WA: The Mountaineers, 1990.

—. *Best Short Hikes in California's Southern Sierra*. Seattle, WA: The Mountaineers, 1991.

Whitney, Stephen., *A Sierra Club Naturalist's Guide to the Sierra Nevada*. San Francisco: Sierra Club Books, 1979.

Winnett, Thomas, *Hiker's Guide to the High Sierra: Mt. Whitney*. 3rd ed. Berkeley, CA: Wilderness Press, 2001.

Winnett, Thomas, et al., *Sierra North: 100 Back-country Trips*. 8th ed. Berkeley, CA: Wilderness Press, 2002.

Winnett, Thomas, et al., *Sierra South: 100 Back-country Trips*. 7th ed. Berkeley, CA: Wilderness Press, 2001.

Hints for Staying in Lodgings

These hints are based on lessons I've learned the hard way and want to share with you in the hope of saving you from troubles I've encountered. If you have other hints or other experiences, I'd like to hear from you.

Remember: the experience of staying in true mountain lodgings and lodgings of interest isn't necessarily a House Beautiful experience. It's Mountains Beautiful, House Okay.

Be aware that lodgings are subject to the vicissitudes that affect any small business. They open, they close, they go broke, they burn down, they get rebuilt or renovated, they change ownership, and their quality may improve or decline. By the way, I can tell you only what I found on the day(s) I was at a particular lodging. I can make no other representation or guarantee regarding them or the kind of experience someone else might have there.

Confirm before you book that the place has the facilities you want. Call or write for the latest brochure and study it before booking.

Try to book well in advance. Self-explanatory. Note also that some lodgings have an established, loyal clientele; it may be difficult for "newcomers" to get a reservation, but it's always worth a try. Trying to book well in advance will probably enhance your chances of getting the reservation you want and will give you time to find another place if your first-choice place is booked solid.

Call a day or two before you leave home, in order to confirm your reservation and any other arrangements of interest. In particular, you'll want to know if things like the store and the restaurant are still open (see below).

Be patient. Leave your hurries as well as your worries at home. Time in the mountains—"mountain time"—moves more slowly than big-city time. For example, don't be upset if your meal doesn't arrive as promptly as it would at a big-city restaurant. Just say to yourself, *They're on mountain time.* Also, since many lodgings are shoestring operations, they're chronically short-handed, which slows things down.

Take your sense of humor. When your visit rubs up against a resort's rougher edges, you'll be ready to laugh about it.

If you are staying in accommodations where you can't cook and expect to take your meals at the resort's restaurant, double-check before you leave home to make sure that the restaurant will be open while you are there and for all the meals you'll want to take there. If it won't meet your meal needs, ask about other restaurants in the area.

If you are staying in housekeeping accommodations and plan to get groceries at the resort's store, double-check before you leave home to make sure that the store is open and well-stocked. If it will be closed, ask about other stores in the area or plan to bring your own groceries.

Rustic cabins in the forest are apt to have the occasional mouse. If you want to stay where you're close to the deer and the bears, you can't help but be close to the mice, too. Safeguard your food by keeping everything except the canned food in the refrigerator or in a hard-sided cooler. Dispose of your garbage properly.

Leakproof all liquids. Be sure all liquids you carry are sealed in containers that won't leak at 6000 feet or above. Most ordinary toiletry bottles, and most bottles sold for travel kits, will leak at higher altitudes. Be safe: use leakproof containers like Nalgene bottles or place containers in sturdy, self-sealing plastic bags.

Don't get impatient if the hot water doesn't run hot right away. Some places have to pipe the hot water quite a distance. Let it run for a while.

Take it easy on the electricity. Many remote lodgings have to generate their own power, so leave your electricity-hungry widgets like hair dryers at home. A few lodgings save on generation by turning off the generator after a certain hour, say, 10 o'clock at night, and not turning it back on until, say, 6 o'clock in the morning. Bring a flashlight!

Bring plenty of warm clothing. No matter how warm mountain days are, mountain nights can be very chilly. Don't forget the slippers!

Carry the following with you to ease your stay. As every experienced traveler knows, even the best-run places can sometimes fall short. Whether I'm headed for the Hilton or for the Bide-A-Wee Lodge, I carry a waterproof kit-bag containing:

- ▶ Assortment of sink stoppers (such as, basin, tub, and kitchen-sink sizes)
- ▶ Small sponge/scrubber pad
- ▶ Small bottle of dishwashing liquid
- ▶ Rubber gloves for dishwashing and washing clothes
- ▶ Travel clothesline
- ▶ Quarter-watt nightlights, one for each bedroom and another for the bathroom, to help stave off nighttime disorientation in a strange place
- ▶ Working flashlights to put by each person's bedside; extra bulbs and batteries for the flashlights
- ▶ Can opener (I carry a tiny Army can opener)
- ▶ Sewing kit
- ▶ First-aid kit

Hints for Getting Around in the Sierra

To see the Sierra, you'll take roads that spin south from Interstate 80, east from State Route 99, and west from U.S. Highway 395. No roads penetrate the Sierra (as defined in this book) from the south.

Travel in the Sierra is almost exclusively by car—more on that below—and is therefore determined by where the roads go. Highways link the west and east sides of the northern part of the range, crossing the crest at several points between Interstate 80 and the middle of Yosemite National Park. Those east-west highways thus determine where you'll find places to stay and trailheads to walk from in the northern Sierra. South of there, no road crosses the entire range, though several roads penetrate deep into the range from the west and one actually crosses the crest from the east. State Route 99 on the west and U.S. Highway 395 on the east, and the roads branching into the range from them, determine where you'll find places to stay and trailheads to walk from in the southern Sierra.

Driving from the west versus driving from the east. The range enjoys a long, slow rise from the Central Valley on the west and an extremely abrupt rise from valleys and plateaus on the east. Drives from the west side to lodgings and trailheads eligible for inclusion in this book are therefore long and slow. Drives to eligible lodgings and trailheads from the east side are short and sweet. A quick look at the California map shows that all the state's population centers are nearer the west side of the Sierra than the east. If you were coming from out of state and planned to rent a car to get to the Sierra, you might conclude that driving to west-side destinations would take you less time than driving to east-side destinations at equal altitudes—and that would be true from the San Francisco area. But from the Los Angeles area, the geography I've just described makes drives to east-side and west-side destinations roughly equivalent in terms of time.

Once in California, you need to drive a car. In a few places—Yosemite National Park, the Tahoe area—you may find public or private transportation that will let you go without a car while you visit that area. In the future, limited public transportation will probably be available in Sequoia National Park, too. Also, there's a combined rail-bus option for getting to Yosemite; ask Amtrak or your travel agent.

But for the overwhelming majority of visitors, only a car will offer the flexibility they need to enjoy their lodgings *and* their walks

Allow plenty of time for your drives. Driving distances in the Sierra may be greater than you think, and the roads may take much longer to drive than you can foresee. You can rarely maintain freeway speeds on Sierra highways. Always allow yourself plenty of driving time. Allow a full day to change your base of operations, even if it's just, for example, from lodgings on one highway to lodgings on the next highway south.

Never hitchhike. Never pick up a hitchhiker. Crimes involving hitchhikers do occur in the Sierra.

Join an auto club. In my peripatetic career I have found my membership in a national auto club to be one of the best investments I've ever made. If you set out to see the Sierra, particularly if you've never been to California or to the Sierra before, I strongly recommend you join a national auto club and sign up for their long-range emergency roadside service. You'll find their travel agency, maps, tour guides, emergency roadside service, and trip-planning advice invaluable.

Arm yourself with road maps and tour guides. Here's a case where a national-auto-club membership will repay you handsomely in just one visit: with a wide selection of free, accurate, up-to-date road maps of California and the Sierra and a comprehensive tour guide for California.

Get national-forest maps. You should also get the national-forest maps for the area you plan to visit. National-forest maps aren't good for hiking, but they're very good for driving. Each section in this book will tell you which national-forest maps apply to that area. If you can't find Forest Service maps at your travel store, order them from The Map Center, Wilderness Press's retail outlet. You'll find its addresses and phone numbers on page 5.

Be sure your car is trailhead-worthy. Under "trailhead-worthiness," I include a car's reliability, fuel economy, and attractiveness/vulnerability to thieves, vandals, and bears.

- ▶ Choose a reliable car.
- ▶ Choose a modest-looking car.
- ▶ Choose a high-clearance car. Some Sierra roads get very rough. However, if a road gets too bad but the data for the drive tell you the trailhead is only a short distance away (what *that* may be is up to you), you can park and walk the rest of the way to the trailhead.
- ▶ Keep your car in good shape. Whichever car you take, be sure it's in good, safe condition before you hit the road, and take good care of it. Check and replenish its vital fluids, including the air in the tires, often. Always make sure you have plenty of gas before you head out—gas may be unavailable in remote places.
- ▶ Store everything you must leave in the car out of sight—but not in the trunk. Car trunks are exceptionally easy to break into. Instead, carry everything of value with you in your daypack, and carry blankets or lightweight, inexpensive tarps to cover everything you must leave in the car, to avoid tempting bears and thieves. Bears recognize grocery bags and picnic coolers. No matter how hot it is, never leave the windows cracked open; you'd just be giving thieves and bears a head start. A cracked-open window also makes it easier for bears to smell any food in the car (below).
- ▶ *Never* leave food in a car. Period. A bear's sense of smell is about 300 times more sensitive than yours, and bears have been known to tear a car apart to get half a candy bar someone had left in the glove compartment. If you must

leave food in a car, wrap it well in odor-containing materials—and then cross your fingers.

▶ Never leave a pet in a car or tied up outside while you hike. The temperature inside a car can quickly rise to a lethal level. A tied-up pet is easy prey for bears, coyotes, and mountain lions.

▶ Consider carrying a cellular telephone—not just on the road but also on the trail. The help you can summon with your cell phone may save a life.

APPENDIX C
Top Picks

Best Overall Hikes
Superb combinations of scenery, views, lakes, flowers or fall color, and maybe even waterfalls

| 6–8 | 11 | 14 | 43 | 59 | 68 | 72 | 75 | 76 | 100 |
| 111 | 114 | 115 | | | | | | | |

Best Flower Hikes
Remember that flower displays are brief and seasonal and that the season's timing may vary from year to year. While most species peak in early season, some species, like gentians, may peak later

| 6 | 11 | 12* | 14 | 16 | 16 | 24** | 39–41 | 45 | 72 |
| 92 | 97 | 99 | 100 | 101 | | | | | |

* Meadow around Dorothy Lake
** Upper and lower Crater meadows

Best Waterfall Hikes
Like flower displays, waterfalls are usually seasonal and short-lived; timing is everything for the peak display. But hikes with asterisks (*) include cascades that put on a fair show throughout the hiking season except in dry years

| 4 | 29* | 37* | 47 | 58 | 66 | 68* | 70* | 72* |

Most-Lakes Hikes
All Sierra lakes are special; this category highlights hikes that visit lots of lakes—at least 4 beauties if you make the entire hike; maximum number of lakes shown parenthetically

3 (4) 7 (6) 8 (4–5) 9 (6)* 13 (4) 14 (6–7) 38 (5) 59 (4) 75 (6) 120 (4)

* Counting the Emerald Lakes

Best Streamside Hikes
For those who especially enjoy strolling along a stream, these hikes include lengthy streamside legs

| 5 | 7 | 8 | 11 | 14 | 32 | 33 | 37 | 38 | 59 |
| 68 | 70 | 73 | 76 | 77 | 88 | 89 | 100 | | |

Most Outstanding Views
Many hikes have fine views, but these hikes have one or more especially awe-inspiring, panoramic viewpoints

| 1 | 23–25 | 31 | 45 | 48 | 51 | 52 | 54 | 56 | 67 |
| 68 | 70 | 83 | 84 | 98 | 112 | 115 | | | |

Interesting Ruins Along the Way
Seeing the ruins of old cabins and mining operations, and evidence of current operations, is a special thrill for many hikers

19	31	36	37	38	73	76	77	100	101

Giant-Sequoia Hikes
Looking for giant sequoias? You'll find plenty on these hikes!

44	49	53	65

Best Fall-Color Hikes
Like flower displays, fall-color displays are seasonal and fleeting

10	11	16	32–37	40	59	64	70	73	87–89
117									

NOTE: for Trips 31–35, 38, and 39, the best fall-color display is along the drive to the trailhead

Best Meadow Hikes
Each of these hikes includes at least one big, beautiful, wet meadow. Like flower displays, the meadows you'll pass by or through on these hikes peak seasonally

12*	14	16	24	40	41	57	59	74	75
76	77	79	81	85	87	94	96	97	99
100	101	117							

* Dorothy Lake's meadow

Best Forest Hikes
For those who especially enjoy strolling among the trees, these hikes include lengthy forested legs

10	13	18	19–24	26	42	44	47–51	53	59
64	65	79–85	89	93	96	103	106	110	117

A Fine Destination with a Minimum of Effort
These hikes get you to a lovely destination, identified in parentheses, with little effort. Hikes with asterisks (*) have the added advantage of being very near one or more lodgings in this book (also named in the parentheses, following the slash):

4* (First Falls/Glacier Lodge)

14* (viewpoint at Mono Pass-Morgan Pass junction/Rock Creek Lakes Resort, Rock Creek Lodge)

17* (Two Jeffreys/Convict Lake Resort)

21* (Emerald Lake/Crystal Crag, Wildyrie, and Woods lodges, Tamarack Lodge Resort)

24* (McCloud Lake/Crystal Crag, Wildyrie, and Woods lodges, Tamarack Lodge Resort)

27* (Devils Postpile or footbridge over San Joaquin/Reds Meadow Resort)

37* (falls at ⅔ mile/Lundy Lake Resort)

38* (Blue Lake/Virginia Lakes Resort)

41* (Soda Spring/Silver City Mountain Resort)

52* (Buena Vista Peak/Montecito-Sequoia Lodge, Grant Grove Cabins)

54* (Panoramic Point/Grant Grove Cabins)
57* (Roaring River Falls/Cedar Grove Lodge)
60* (Rancheria Falls/Lakeshore Resort, Huntington Lake Condo. Rentals)
65* (California Tree/Wawona Hotel, The Redwoods)
75* (Greenstone Lake if you take the ferry/Tioga Pass Resort)
91 (Sherrold Lake)
95 (Elephant Rock Lake)
99* (Frog Lake/Caples Lake Resort)
108* (Tamarack Lake if you take the water-taxi/Echo Chalet)
112 (Angora Lakes if you drive to the parking lot below the lakes)
116* (waterfall at ⅕ mile/Richardson's Resort, Meeks Bay Resort)

Most Beautiful Sierra Drives

Not everyone in your party may be able to hike, so let's treat non-hikers to a beautiful drive! These are roughly in order of their scenic qualities according to my taste. Not all are actually in the Sierra, but all offer superb Sierra views:

▶ State Route 120 from its junction with U.S. Highway 395 to Crane Flat
▶ U.S. Highway 395 from Lone Pine through Walker Canyon to the town of Walker
▶ State Route 88 from Woodfords to the turnoff to Bear River Reservoir
▶ State Route 108 from its junction with U.S. Highway 395 to its junction with Clark Fork Road
▶ State Route 89 from its junction with U.S. Highway 395 to its junction with U.S. Highway 50 in Meyers (very airy in places)—recently scarred by fire (June 2002)
▶ State Route 4 from its junction with State Route 89 to the turnoff to Spicer Meadows Reservoir (difficult stretch from a little west of 89 junction to Lake Alpine)
▶ U.S. Highway 50 from its junction with State Route 89 in South Lake Tahoe combined with Nevada State Route 28 around Lake Tahoe's *east* shore
▶ Horseshoe Meadow Road from Lone Pine to Trip 1's trailhead (very airy)
▶ Whitney Portal Road from Lone Pine to Trip 2's trailhead (very airy)
▶ June Lakes Loop (State Route 158) between its north and south junctions with U.S. Highway 395
▶ State Route 168 (east) combined with South Lake Road, from Bishop to South Lake
▶ State Route 168 (west) combined with Kaiser Pass Road, from Shaver Lake to Florence Lake (difficult road from a little west of Kaiser Pass to its end at Florence Lake. Stop off to visit Lakeshore (Huntington Lake))
▶ Rock Creek Road from Toms Place to Mosquito Flat
▶ Blue Lakes Road from its junction with State Route 88 to its end at Upper Blue Lake (mostly unpaved)
▶ State Route 180 from its junction with the turnoff to Grant Grove Village to Roads End (Cedar Grove Roadend) in Kings Canyon
▶ Dinkey Creek Road
▶ Big Meadows Road from its junction with the Generals Highway to the end of the pavement (gets very narrow)

How I Got the Data

I estimated distances primarily by time, knowing that I hike 2 miles/hour. I compared the distances I got by time with distance values supplied by the agencies in charge of the trails. When those distances were close, I felt satisfied with the distance I'd estimated by time. I usually rounded the distances off to the nearest ¼ or ⅓ mile.

I got most driving distances from my car's odometer, which was consistent to within ±¹⁄₁₀ mile over routes I drove repeatedly. I found that in a some cases I did not get usable odometer data; in those cases, I used data from maps referred to in this book, principally the maps from the Automobile Club of Southern California.

I determined elevation from topos and with an altimeter. Where I had altimeter data, I looked for close correspondence between those values, topo values, and any values supplied by the agency in charge of the trail.

I made the trail maps by first scanning relevant pieces of the USGS or Wilderness Press topos into a computer. I put the resulting digitized topo information that applied to a trip or a set of trips into the bottom layer of a multiple-layer electronic drawing. I then traced selected topo information onto transparent electronic upper layers. I deleted the scanned data before I saved out the finished maps in a format compatible with the desktop publishing program I used to lay out this book. I left out the elevation contours because they would have taken me too long to draw and because they would have made these gray-scale maps too busy. I added, deleted, or modified topo information that I knew had changed. My choices of conventions for trails, roads, boundaries, etc., primarily reflect the software's capabilities.

A few trails do not appear at all on the topos or in usable form on any official agency map. For them, I approximated the route based on field notes and sketches and any other information I could find.

Trails change constantly. If, as you take these trips, you find significant differences between this book and what's on the ground, differences that you think are not just the result of two different people looking at the same things, please let me know in care of Wilderness Press, 1200 5th Street, Berkeley, CA 94710-1306.

As I reported earlier in this book, I did not stay at all of the true mountain lodgings and lodgings of interest in this book. Neither the time available nor my budget—principally the latter—permitted me to do so. I did visit all of them except for individual units run by agencies. When I was offered a tour of the premises, I took it; when offered literature, I accepted it.

The information on the individual lodgings is primarily from the lodgings' own literature; I noted nothing in that literature that was significantly different from what I'd found when visiting or staying at the lodging myself. Some of the literature made the lodgings portrayed look a little spiffier or more removed from real-world bustle than I had found them, but I think that that is to be expected. I did not attempt to rate the lodgings as, for example, my auto-club tour book does, because I have not stayed at all of them. I'm easy to please, anyway; a lodging's being in the Sierra is about all I ask for.

However, when I report a lodging's restaurant as "outstanding" or "very good," I have eaten there (usually more than once) and have formed that overall opinion of the food, atmosphere, and service myself.

Also, as I reported earlier, I visited all the communities listed under "Other" in this book and stayed in many of them.

I enjoyed every lodging in which I stayed and am eager to return to them, and I can hardly wait to stay at those I haven't stayed at yet. I look forward to hearing readers' opinions about and experiences at the lodgings and in the communities; please write to me at mail@wildernesspress.com, or to Wilderness Press (see address on previous page).

Index

About the Author

The backpacking bug hit Kathy Morey hard in the 1970s and has not let go yet. In 1990 she abandoned an aerospace career to write for Wilderness Press, authoring *Hot Showers, Soft Beds, and Dayhikes in the Sierra* and four guidebooks on Hawaii. She is a coauthor of *Sierra South*, *Sierra North*, and *Guide to the John Muir Trail*. Apart from the work (is that what it is?) she does to keep her books up-to-date, Kathy is a copy editor of her community's weekly newspaper. She is also a fine photographer and Wilderness Press has featured her pictures in many of her books and on the cover of its catalog.